A·Popovich

D0356784

FRANCE 18
POLITICS &

FRANCE 1848–1945
POLITICS & ANGER

By
THEODORE ZELDIN

OXFORD NEW YORK TORONTO MELBOURNE
OXFORD UNIVERSITY PRESS
1979

Oxford University Press, Walton Street, Oxford OX2 6DP

OXFORD LONDON GLASGOW
NEW YORK TORONTO MELBOURNE WELLINGTON
KUALA LUMPUR SINGAPORE JAKARTA HONG KONG TOKYO
DELHI BOMBAY CALCUTTA MADRAS KARACHI
IBADAN NAIROBI DAR ES SALAAM CAPE TOWN

© Theodore Zeldin 1973, 1979

First published as the third section of France 1848–1945, *volume 1,
by the Clarendon Press, 1974. First issued, with additional material,
as an Oxford University Press paperback, 1979*

*All rights reserved. No part of this publication may be reproduced,
stored in a retrieval system, or transmitted, in any form or by any means,
electronic, mechanical, photocopying, recording, or otherwise, without
the prior permission of Oxford University Press*

*This book is sold subject to the condition that it shall not, by way of
trade or otherwise, be lent, re-sold, hired out, or otherwise circulated
without the publisher's prior consent in any form of binding or cover
other than that in which it is published and without a similar condition
including this condition being imposed on the subsequent purchaser.*

British Library Cataloguing in Publication Data

Zeldin, Theodore
    France, politics and anger
      1. France – Politics and government
    I. Title
    320.9'44'07   JN2451   79-40249

    ISBN 0-19-285082-2

*Printed in Great Britain by
Lowe and Brydone Printers Limited
Thetford, Norfolk*

CONTENTS

LIST OF MAPS

LIST OF FIGURES

PREFACE

THIS is a book about passions and illusions. It tries to explain why Frenchmen have become what they are, to express the feelings that have lain behind their actions, to unravel their confusions and contradictions. It does not attempt to retell an old story that has been repeated often enough. It does not present history in the usual evolutionary or nationalist terms, as a movement of progress, or as one dominated by governments growing in power and self-confidence. It is concerned rather with the individual, resisting the political, economic, institutional and emotional pressures around him, coping with his own frailties and fears, finding ways of gratifying his ambitions and his tastes, solving problems only to find new ones created. It is a book about Frenchmen, but it seeks the universal man beneath the poses he adopts.

Politics and literature have traditionally been the two avenues used by foreigners to approach France. In these two domains France has indeed been so fertile, colourful and dramatic, that no one wishing to understand the working of modern democracy or the artistic imagination can afford to ignore its contribution. But I believe that the view of France that has been presented by politicians and men of letters is a misleading one. I have attempted to reconsider their interpretations and to place them in a wide perspective, by investigating as many different aspects of life as possible. I have tried, in so far as one person can achieve this, to write something approaching a total history, because it is impossible to appreciate the significance of any particular form of activity or behaviour until one sees it as part of a whole. My work analyses the hopes and ambitions of the different social classes, breaking them down into smaller groups, revealing them to be more preoccupied with their internal rivalries than with the class struggle. I question the traditional view of France as being dominated by the bourgeoisie: I perceive the country as a multitude of little worlds, a cellular society, each fighting battles and raising up defences against its enemies, every individual being a member of several cells, according to the nature of his work, hobbies, worries and tastes. I have not found that the family was the backbone of French society; from my investigation of the attitudes of parents to their children, of husbands to their wives, of women to their role in society, my conclusion is that the home was as much a source of tension as of a sense of security and that the close-knit family was held up as the ideal precisely because it existed so rarely in real life: in 1900 only 54 per cent of marriages lasted longer than fifteen years and 45 per cent of children were orphans in their teens. I am led to explore the weakness of the movement for women's suffrage, the vigour of pornography and prostitution, the skills the young used to foil the restraints society weighed upon them, the obstacles that stood in the way of friendship. When I examine the forces working for the creation of more uniformity and unity in the country, I find the growth of a sense of national identity to be superficial, despite the imposition or adoption of a common language, and of common ways of thinking and talking, which seem to distinguish Frenchmen from all other people. I show how the obsession with education opens up new horizons, but also stimulates the passion for examinations and competitiveness, supposedly in the name of egalitarianism. The creation of an intellectual elite devoted to culture leads one to overlook the hesitations of the masses in the face of values they did not share. I show how Frenchmen sought to differentiate themselves from foreigners and why they formed their stereotyped prejudices about the English, the Germans, the Americans. Despite this, however, a whole variety of provincialisms survived; I investigate what it meant to be a Breton or a Provençal, an Alsatian or an Auvergnat. Beneath the apparent uniformity there was a constant battle between individualism and conformity. I describe the rise of the artist, as the symbol of rebellion, the methods by which reputations were won in literature, the forces that determined fashions in clothes and developed new standards in food and wine. I try to explain why France won international pre-eminence in these fields just when it was losing its diplomatic and military supremacy. I show the ambivalent attitude people had towards scientific progress, the compromises they made with corruption and superstition, the attachment they preserved for conformity, the skill with which they used humour as an instrument to protect themselves against the tyranny of institutions they could not control. This brings me down to the private lives and emotions of individuals, to what they worried about, to the way they coped with their nervous troubles, while trying to cultivate individualism. I illustrate the place of violence and cruelty in their relationships, the influence military service had on them, the compensations they sought in the colonies, the frustrations they expressed in their religious disputes, the anxieties they experienced in their family planning.

More is known, more has been written, about politics than about the obscurer topics I have delved into: politics provides one with an opportunity of scrutinising behaviour in greater detail, and in a more comprehensive way, than is possible, say, with attitudes to friendship, or etiquette, or servants: the daily bickerings of domestic life have left far fewer records than those of public life. But I do not believe that it dominated people's conduct as much as political scientists have tended to assume. In many of the subjects I have written about, I have not found it necessary to bring in politics: each activity moved around its own axes, was absorbed by its own preoccupations and divided on lines peculiar to itself. For me, the importance of politics lies in the myths which it gave rise to and which confused Frenchmen as to what it was that they agreed and disagreed about. Instead of taking the traditional dichotomy of left and right as my guiding theme, I argue on the contary that this division was an obstacle to clear thought about current problems, that it perpetuated historical disagreements long after they had ceased to have significance, that it gave a false veneer of simplicity to the issues on which Frenchmen did have opinions, obscuring the multiplicity of their attitudes, and that as a result the real opitions before them were seldom clearly put to them. Democracy, therefore, remained rudimentary, infantile: people were not able to express, let alone achieve, their desires; they simply had the choice of voting red or blue. My thesis is that it was the intellectuals who were responsible for this simplification. It is generally assumed that intellectuals held a particularly influential place in French society. I try to show that their influence was not exactly what they believed or claimed it to be. They were, almost by definition, men ill at ease in their time, self-conscious of their individualism, sometimes to a pathological degree: they distinguished themselves by their inability to tolerate the contradicitions of life and the hypocrisy that made these tolerable; they sought to eliminate them, to reduce the complexity by simplification; they were, therefore, the great advocates of principles and formulae. They told the world what it was that divided it, their slogans were adopted by political parties and they provided interpretations of history. It does not follow that they were right in their interpretations or that historians should accept their categories.

The intellectuals propagated three illusions, which were highly influential. The first was that France was one and indivisible. They formed an ideal view of what a Frenchmen was; they castigated the provincial and the ignorant as almost sub-human. They had some success: Frenchmen did superficially grow more alike. But the regional diversities of France were not eliminated and are now reasserting themselves. The individualism the intellectuals encouraged, and of which they were the finest flowers, had the effect of accentuating differences between people, rather than producing a uniform type. Moreover there was much confusion in the intellectuals' view of what it meant to be French. In a hundred years' time, if Europe does unite, it may well appear that the nationalist phase was simply a hiatus in French history, a period when wishful thinking about national unity briefly acquired the status of an accepted myth. A recent thesis on mobilisation in 1914—when supposedly France forgot all doctrinal disputes to fight Germany with enthusiasm, to revenge itself for its defeat in 1870—has shown that there was very little enthusiasm and no strong nationalist feeling.[1] Another thesis, on the War Veterans between 1914 and 1939, reveals them not as chauvinist patriots, but as attached above all to their local communities, and profoundly disillusioned with the nationalist myths.[2]

The second illusion was that France was divided into two, left and right, or into bourgeoisie and proletariat. I have

---

[1] J. J. Becker, *1914: Comment les Français sont entrés dans la guerre* (1977).
[2] A. Prost, *Les Anciens Combattants, 1914–39* (1977, 3 vols.).

explained at some length, through my analysis of the political parties and social groups, why this dichotomy is too simplistic. In so far as people came to believe that they were inescapably members of one tendency, or one class, the intellectuals did exercise influence on thought, but in real life people behaved in a much more complicated way; their principles were not necessarily reflected in their actions. The peasant, for example, was simultaneously tormented by his landlord, his creditors, the usurers, the government tax collector, but also by his jealousies of his neighbours and his own search for respectability and prestige; his opinions have always had to be characterised by a series of paradoxes. The workers had long traditions of mutual hate in their guilds, so that, for example, the carpenters of the right bank in Paris even refused to work with those of the left bank. By 1966 less than half (44–47 per cent) of metal workers in large factories said that for them the capitalist was the enemy; in small firms only 12–15 per cent held that view. The trade unions have failed to recruit anything like a majority of the proletariat: in 1935 only 6 per cent of workers in private industry were unionists. I have suggested that social mobility, competitiveness and anxiety dominated personal behaviour more than the class struggle. Women and children, it should be added, had their own preoccupations and enemies. President Giscard d'Estaing has recently declared that France is divided not in two but in four: that seems to be one step nearer the truth: to me, France is a mosaic of tendencies and conflicts. The importance of the accepted dichotomy is that it prevents people who have views in common from co-operating, if they happen to consider themselves as belonging to opposed historical traditions. The intellectuals, who have sought change, have contributed more than anyone else to keeping France absorbed by its antiquated disputes, and firmly set in a rut.

The third illusion the intellectuals propagated was that most problems could be solved by education. Education had made the intellectuals what they were. Proudhon said Democracy is Mass Education. This was the medicine France drank most freely of for a whole century, transferring its major expenditure from the military to the schools. But education has not given the country what it has been seeking. Allied to this vain hope was the illusion that to bring about change one must change institutions by revolution or by legislation. In this they showed one of their own basic contradictions. They gave primacy to politics; but they believed also in the power of ideas; the truth was they were never sure how ideas could be changed. The effect of their stress on the need to modify the laws has been constant changes in laws and constitutions—which have always left them dissatisfied—but also the confirmation of the power of the bureaucrats and experts who ran the institutions. The nearest the intellectuals got to wielding power was by giving birth to a kind of bastard offspring, to whom they always felt ambivalent, the technocrats, but these in effect perpetuated the methods of the centralised benevolent despotism of the *ancien régime*.

My argument is that the French were mistaken as to what divided them. They were unable to express in their institutions what mattered most to them. The problem of democratic participation, which is what the revolution was supposed to have tackled, never even came within sight of solution. Governments, of every political colour, always maintained their rights against the people, and the traditions of the *ancien régime* state were continued, rather like those of the Tsars surviving into the Soviet system. The politicians insisted that, after the state, political parties had to be the instruments of change; and change was therefore always partisan, involving fighting the enemy rather than discovering what Frenchmen could agree on. Common ground was reached only as a result of deadlock in confrontation, of betrayals by extremists, who became more moderate when they won power, of laxness by the administration in enforcing the law, and of tax evasion and illegality by the masses. These practices, which were almost ritualised, became a substitute for the search for consensus. The political parties paid only lip service to the idea of consensus. The right wing from time to time declared war on party divisions and adopted slogans of national unity, but nearly always against its old enemies, like Jews, communists, freemasons, etc., whom it excluded from the national community; and its interpretation of the national cause was always partisan, drawn from a limited interpretation of the national heritage. The left hesitated between appeals for fraternity and belief in the rights of minorities, the need to expropriate the

rich, to destroy the church or to bring about the triumph of
one class over another. Putting aside the lofty principles they
proclaimed, politicians in real life were divided between
those who wished to force their ideas on the nation and
those who preferred gradual compromise. But a choice between these two methods was never offered to the people.
Institutions and ideology were obstacles in the way of any
genuine popular bargaining on the solution to problems, and
many problems, felt to be such by the masses, never even got
into the political arena. The quarrelling about regimes was
ultimately superficial.

In terms of political history, the major battle of the century
was between the priest and the schoolmaster. They did not
realise that they could have been on the same side. Yet both
believed in moral reforms, as opposed to materialism. Both
believed that self-discipline and altruism offered a surer
path to contentment than hedonism and the satisfaction of
greed; both were suspicious of the expanding world of commerce and sought to avoid its temptations. Against them
stood those whose faith was in increasing productivity and
material wealth as a first priority: the implication of the
materialist creed was urbanisation, industrialisation and
consumerism. These never became political issues. The anticlerical war prevented them from being seen as such by the
people. So what were clearly the most important changes of
modern times, the technological revolution and the transformation of ways of living, were carried out without any opinion
being expressed on them in the democratic process. The reason
was that disagreement on these fundamental questions cut
across the parties. Socialism was ultimately moral in its aims
(and in its early phase was very largely ethical in its approach),
but it increasingly made material prosperity, and the problem
of how material goods should be shared, its first priority. The
parties of the right for long supported Christianity, advocating resignation and humility, but they also justified the
accumulation of private wealth and property. The development of French civilisation therefore occurred in a way that
none of the parties envisaged.

The history of politics can too easily degenerate into the
history of a minority. France was ruled by a gerontocracy;

when that faltered, the old men shared their power with an
expanded technocracy. One needs to understand why the
majority of the nation, composed of women, children and
young people, tolerated this system. The answer is that those
in control of government controlled only relatively small
areas of life; there were several additional informal political
arenas in the home: the submissive wife and obedient son
were, quite often, the wishful dreams of male pride.

I do not see the parliamentary parties as the principal
protagonists in political life, drawing all discussion to them
like magnetic poles. I suggest that political thinkers, ministers,
party militants and the masses each interpreted politics
quite differently. What normally passes for political life is the
activity of the second and third of these. For the masses,
politics consisted largely of resistance to authority: the study of
democratic politics should revolve less around ideology,
elections and the framing of legislation than around the
subterfuges the individual devised to escape the pressures of
those who controlled the state. It was for this reason that
change percolated very slowly and inefficiently through
political institutions: the laws parliament passed, and what
actually happened, were quite separate matters. I suggest
that change, like new ideas, was often treated as an intruder,
or like a paying guest, confined to a separate room, so that he
seldom altered the whole of life. People were very skilled in
living inconsistently, maintaining different time scales for
different aspects of their lives. Part of them perpetuated the
middle ages; they read the horoscopes avidly; in 1963 53 per
cent of the French population did this regularly. Part of them
admired the ideals of the seventeenth and eighteenth centuries; they made classical literature their model; they taught
their children antique rhetoric. Part of them surreptitiously
resisted the tastes imposed on them, and feasted on pornography, popular romance and horror stories; the adventures of
Fantomas sold over five times as many copies as Proust. But
when Jean Renoir, cinéaste of the complexity of human
motivation, held up a mirror to them, they rejected the
pictures he showed them: they needed a generation to elapse
before they dared look at themselves.

Politics flowed in the same old traditional groove, not

because it expressed people's worries, but because it made it possible to argue impersonally, concealing the anxieties that were too sharp to discuss. There were all sorts of alternatives to political protest. The workers, for example, resisted oppression and monotony partly by changing jobs: in the 1950s, 42 per cent had changed their trade four or more times and 24 per cent had changed their place of work eleven times. Children resisted by developing their own culture; women by withdrawing into their own worlds. The man in the street, though faced by an apparently inexorable social hierarchy, never gave up trying to climb the ladder, defying the doctors' threats that ambition was a disease that brought terrifying symptoms; young people resisted the tyranny of the family by falling in love, by trying to be different from their fathers, by forming friendships which conflicted with the ties of clan and interest; and finally everybody resisted the heavy weight of the status quo through humour, through laughing at what they could not avoid, mocking and forgetting in the way the playwright Courteline captured so well. All these were political acts. Institutions survived only because they could thus be ignored. Much more oppressive, perhaps, were the loneliness and the neuroses that people found far greater difficulty in escaping.

Politics cannot therefore be understood apart from the anger, and from the other emotions, whose history I have tried to sketch. But I deliberately do not offer a new theory to displace those I criticise, and which would no doubt soon be displaced in its turn. To be a historian is to study the rise and fall of theories. I do not claim to have discovered a global explanation of human behaviour, nor even a formula to account for the peculiarities of the French. The demand for theories, ideologies and 'frameworks' is strong and insistent, precisely because they are always inadequate when they try to grapple with the complexity of human nature. Our knowledge of man is still far too rudimentary to allow wide generalisations: of the billions of cells in our brain, for example, we fully understand the working of only a few; we are only just beginning to penetrate some of the mysteries that surround the way our hormones influence our moods and our actions; the processes of ageing, which affect individuals so erratically, are still in large measure unexplained. To say that the ways of man are mysterious is to make a scientific, not a religious statement. I have therefore deliberately left my arguments and my suggestions in juxtaposition, rather than tying them all up in a specious causal web.

Instead of a theory, I offer an attitude. I believe that one's view of the world is inevitably coloured by one's personality (and I maintain that why we are what we are is still far from being capable of demonstration). History is a means of becoming aware of the subjectivity of one's outlook, of one's prejudices, of the sort of independence one is searching for, of one's fears. I have no wish to convert those who are attached to their own dogmas: they have their reasons for being dogmatic. The problem for each individual is to discover the attitude or explanation that suits his temperament. Difficulties arise less from disagreement than from people not knowing themselves, from their taking themselves too seriously and from their thinking they know the whole truth.

1. The Place of Politics in Life

THE history of French politics is usually presented as a record of failure. That is why French politics are confusing. But to present it as a failure is to misunderstand the significance of politics in French life.

France has the reputation of being a country tormented by repeated revolutions, ministerial crises and scandals. Political instability has long appeared to be its major problem. It has been unable to develop coherent parties and has seldom had anything but coalition governments, paralysed by internal dissensions. Success at the polls only occasionally leads to positive reform or real change, because laws take many years to get through the barrage of obstacles, first to their promulgation and then to their implementation. In any case, the country is said still to be in the grip of a powerful centralised bureaucracy. No escape is possible from this stalemate, because the nation is too divided. Disputes of the past accumulate, so that present issues are still debated in terms of historical precedents, and old allegiances produce permanent animosities. Religious, social, constitutional and regional divisions cut across politics in different ways, so that agreement is nearly always only partial. As though to compensate for the inevitable compromises, there is a constant appeal to principle. But this causes the compromises to be widely rejected. There seems little to show at the end of the strife.

To understand French politics, one must first get rid of the Anglo-Saxon model on which so much criticism of them is based, not least by Frenchmen. It is, often unconsciously, assumed that because France has adopted a form of constitutional government which has vaguely resembled, at different times, that of Britain or the U.S.A., that it has failed because it has not evolved the two-party system necessary to make it work on Anglo-Saxon lines. France has indeed borrowed ideas and labels from abroad but it has assimilated them very thoroughly into its own traditions, so that any resemblance to the original is largely nominal. Electoral practices and parliamentary usages in France have functions and a character which are substantially different from those in other countries. One must take into account, in assessing these practices and usages, the peculiar attitude towards power which surrounds their working. The legacy of France's troubled history, and of the rise of its monarchy to such heights among the nations was to discredit power, at least for internal consumption. The function of constitutions became to control and limit its exercise. Even Napoleon III, in resurrecting his uncle's dazzling empire, modified it to allow a large place to individual initiative; even General de Gaulle, while reviving France's prestige abroad, favoured mutual association, not state control, as the key to the country's renewal at home. All the more so, the Third Republic was devoted to preventing governments from becoming too powerful over their citizens. Nationalism was possibly the compensation for this. So though it was true that the political system which prevailed in France was not efficient in terms of passing laws and creating strong long-lasting ministries, that was not what it was intended to do. On the contrary, it was efficient in protecting the individual from excessive interference and allowing him to express his idiosyncracies with the minimum of constraint. The parliamentary constitutions check-mated the bureaucracy. Political and administrative power was on the whole used as a defensive mechanism. That is why the muddles into which it got were tolerated. Political skill revealed itself in *débrouillage*, more than in the manipulation of parties. Of course, there were reactions by minorities against this system, but it was the norm. To appreciate the role of politics, it is important to relate politics to the social conditions surrounding it. It is best to start not from a study of the central organs of the government but in the provinces, in the small towns and in the villages, to see what people wanted from the government, and how they adapted, as it were, the speech of Paris to their own dialects. Only then can one see the work of the politicians in its full context.

One of the most striking consistencies in France's political life has been the way certain regions have voted the same way over more than a hundred years. For example, very considerable areas of the west have been stalwart adherents of conservatism, from the days of the counter-revolution, through the long

years of hopeless monarchism, to the modern independent
right-wing parties. The extreme left by contrast has always
found support in certain areas of the south and centre. It was

Departments in which 'the Mountain' obtained over 40 per cent of the votes.

MAP 1. 'The Mountain' in the Election of 1849

persecuted there in the White Terror of 1815, it triumphed
there, as 'the Mountain', in 1849, and the communists still
draw much of their strength from these same regions. The
study of this phenomenon was pioneered by André Siegfried
(1875–1959), who invented 'electoral geography', later known
as electoral sociology. This has placed party divisions in a new

perspective. Siegfried had the great advantage of both knowing France very well and of standing somewhat aloof in it. He was a Protestant; he was the son of a self-made, American-style

MAP 2. The Right in 1885

millionaire; he had travelled round the world as a young man; he spoke in 'almost a foreign accent' and he wore check tweeds like a globe-trotting character out of Jules Verne. In four successive elections (1902–10) he tried to enter parliament; rejected, like Tocqueville, he turned to studying the mysteries of politics into which he could not fit.[1] His ingenious *Political Portrait of the West of France* (1913) made use of the detailed local knowledge he had acquired in his campaigns, to argue that

Map 3. The Right in 1936

political divisions could be closely related to regional 'temperaments'. 'Just as there are individual temperaments,' he wrote, 'so there are provincial temperaments and national temperaments.' In his book, he tried 'to translate into conscious terms

[1] F. Goguel, 'En mémoire d'André Siegfried', *Revue française de science politique* (June 1959), 333–9; *Hommage à André Siegfried* (1960). On Jules Siegfried see above, p. 68.

the profound unconscious of these psychologies'. He made, first, a geological study of his region, and classified it according to the type of soil and vegetation, distinguishing in particular between granite, woodlands, chalk plains, and quaternary marshlands. He made maps of the density and distribution of population, noting which areas had their population huddled in villages and which had them dispersed in isolated farms. He then compared these with maps of landed property, on which

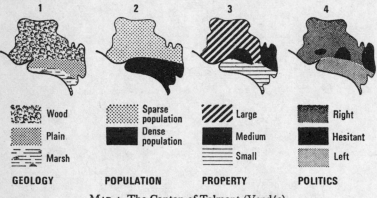

MAP 4. The Canton of Talmont (Vendée)

he had drawn the areas which had large, medium or small ownership. Finally he studied the political complexion of each commune, as revealed by their votes and the votes of the deputies they elected. He came up with a remarkable concordance. From this he concluded that it was possible to predict, more or less, how a particular village would vote by examining these factors. The decisive one was property. When the region was dominated by large resident landlords, when the peasants were dependent on them, directly for their tenancies and their livings, or indirectly on their goodwill, then they voted as the landlords did, that is to say right wing. Areas of small independent peasant proprietors, on the other hand, were the backbone of democracy. There was much more political life in regions of agglomerated population, which therefore tended to be more left wing, whereas scattered settlement reduced political discussion to a minimum and allowed the rural nobility to remain the principal influence.

An additional important factor was the power of the Church.

There were areas where the priest was all-powerful, even more so than the noble. The nobles had preserved their estates most successfully in Anjou, where they still lived in some splendour, but in Brittany they were often poor, at once pretentious and needy, frustrated and without initiative, their authority constantly challenged. In these latter areas, some priests enjoyed far higher incomes, like the curé of Folgoët, for example, who profited from a perpetual influx of pilgrims and whose living in 1913 was worth 50,000 francs a year. Such a man was king of his parish. His wealth, of course, was an exception: and it was not this wealth alone that made him influential. Much more important was that in areas like Léon, the clergy were the élite, of popular and local origin, and accepted as such. Though small property predominated here, the clergy were all-powerful. The Superior of the College of Lesneven, where the clergy were educated, was therefore the grand elector of the region and his orders were read from every pulpit.

In other regions, economically similar, the influence of the state was decisive. On the coast, the peculiar problems of naval conscription made the electorate keen to elect deputies who had the ear of the authorities. The large number of state jobs— in the customs, lighthouses and arsenals—made the government the dispenser of favours few men could ignore. More generally, many people considered it wise to be on the side of the government, since so many of the needs of daily life had to be approved or supported by it. When there were no strong religious convictions, the government, as in Normandy and Maine, could get its candidates elected without difficulty. In some regions, the power of the state was captured by a group, like the Catholics for example, and then these could offer a lot of local civil service jobs, in addition to posts in the world of insurance and railways which they controlled. But even when all these pressures were exerted, in other regions still the electorate seemed to be influenced by personal considerations, and an individual who knew how to please by his own personal charms, and by attuning his rhetoric and activities to those of his constituents, could succeed, with the vaguest of party affiliation. Finally there were regions which seemed to have no view of politics at all: to be totally indifferent doctrinally and to respond only to straightforward appeals to their material interest.

'According to a prevalent view,' concluded Siegfried, 'elections are the domain of nothing but incoherence and whim. By observing them at once closely and from afar, I have come to the opposite conclusion. If, as Goethe said, "hell itself has its laws", why should politics not have its own too?' His 'laws' were, at first sight, simple enough, that electoral results were the result of social relationships, modes of settlement, occupation, religious belief or finally mysterious ethnic characteristics. The great significance of this conclusion was that politics did not necessarily involve the expression of opinion, or a choice between different views of how the country should be run. Only in the towns, he thought, was there real political life. The majority of peasants followed leaders, noble, religious or governmental, who used their votes for their own purposes. What elections did therefore was to conceal the existence of a large variety of deep-seated 'temperaments' and to give France the appearance of unity, or at least of being divided into two basic parties, the left and the right.

The more carefully one reads Siegfried's work, the more one becomes conscious of his qualifications, reservations and subtle dependence on intuitive observation. He simplified French politics by showing the limitations of their ideological content. He showed that politics had a deeper psychological significance. Instead of preoccupying himself with the chaos of party labels and programmes he transferred attention to the problems of the attitude of the elector to his neighbours and to the world beyond. Siegfried made no claim to being a scientist and disclaimed the title of economist. He was proud to belong to the Moral section of the Academy of Moral and Political Sciences. 'It is perhaps as a moralist that I should be proudest to be regarded, on condition that a moralist is not one who makes morals, but one who discusses the conditions of conduct.' The value of his work, as he rightly realised, was in its suggestiveness. He abhorred simple explanations, which claimed to open all doors. 'I have a horror of standard questionnaires', wrote this father of psephology, 'of frameworks prepared in advance, of rigid structures which claim to organise the expressions of the human spirit but in doing so destroy it.' He believed in a constant renewal of the angle of approach in study, in intuition, in an understanding which based itself 'not on quantity but on curiosity and above all on affective curiosity, that is to say, a spontaneous sympathy for the varied forms of life.' He was the enemy of specialisation: he wrote books indiscriminately about the U.S.A., England, South America and New Zealand. He disliked over-elaborate techniques of research. But it was to his inspiration that a whole school of sophisticated electoral sociologists—a major branch of French political science after the war—proclaimed their allegiance. Their work, centred round the Fondation Nationale des Sciences Politiques, and published in numerous monographs, has moved the understanding of French politics on to a new plane.[1]

Siegfried's intuitions have remained fruitful, but it was quickly discovered that his generalisations were not based on really rigorous research. His statement, for example, that large property dominated in the Vendée was supported by figures for only three cantons out of twenty and he added vaguely that the same situation was found in the others. His assessment of the influence of the clergy is supported by maps of private girls' schools, with no statistics about religious practice. His electoral maps were too general, showing in the same way majorities of 51 and 90 per cent. Many problems are simply answered by new ones; right-wing voting is explained, for example, by religious conviction, but the reasons for this are only superficially examined. His rules were not capable of generalisation, and produced some strange anomalies. The new generation of electoral experts pushed his arguments to their extremes, and pointed out how, in simplified form, they did not work. Thus for example Lower Normandy—a region of small property, of few nobles, no religion, no royalist traditions—ought to have voted left wing, but it has on the contrary been stolidly conservative throughout the nineteenth and twentieth centuries. Likewise, Trégorrois in Brittany, a region of large property and a powerful nobility, suddenly in 1910 voted left. Why? Siegfried answered because they at last 'dared to'. But it was not clear why other people did not dare to vote against nobles and clergy who were supposed to be dominating

[1] Hommage à André Siegfried 1875–1959 (1960); F. Goguel, 'En mémoire d'André Siegfried', Revue française des sciences politiques (June 1959), 333–9; A. Siegfried, Tableau politique de la France de l'Ouest (1913), and Géographie électorale de l'Ardèche sous la Troisième République (1949).

them; or how strong a domination could be if it could be over-thrown simply by courage. Once Siegfried's subtle psychological nuances are omitted, his edifice collapses. The advantage of this is that it has stimulated some excellent work, some of it of almost equal imaginative brilliance.

Siegfried studied fourteen departments. Paul Bois took one of these, Sarthe, which was more manageable, for a detailed study. It is particularly suitable because its western half was royalist in the Revolution, voted right in 1848 and has continued to do so in all elections since then, while its eastern half was republican, voted for the Mountain in 1849 and then became strongly communist. The dividing line goes through the canton of Ecommoy, small enough for really thorough investigation. Now this canton contains one commune, Laigné, which is reactionary, but it is an area of small peasant proprietorship. Another commune in it, Saint-Mars, is very republican, but it has not got much small property. Siegfried's equations seemed to be disproved. A study of property ownership throughout the department showed that both the conservative and republican sides have large and small property in them. Siegfried did not always get his facts on property right. Bois therefore discards the view that the size of property ownership is a significant factor, particularly when, in investigating how noble landlords could influence their peasants, he found that the amount of land the nobles owned was, in total, really quite small—under 25 per cent, and much of it was forest. Only one in fourteen peasants were dependent on the nobles and in forest areas that dependence was as likely to produce hostility as subjection. Moreover, if the leases of the nobles' tenants are examined, it is found that the harsh controls in them do not seem to have affected political behaviour—for after the agricultural crisis of the 1880s, the severe clauses disappear from the leases, but the peasants continue to vote the same way.

Is prosperity or poverty the explanation of the contrasting politics of the two halves of the department? Certainly there were differences between them in this respect. The west was more prosperous than the east, but only up to the depression of 1880, after which it declined far more severely than the east. Yet the west continued to vote conservative throughout, whether it was prosperous or not.

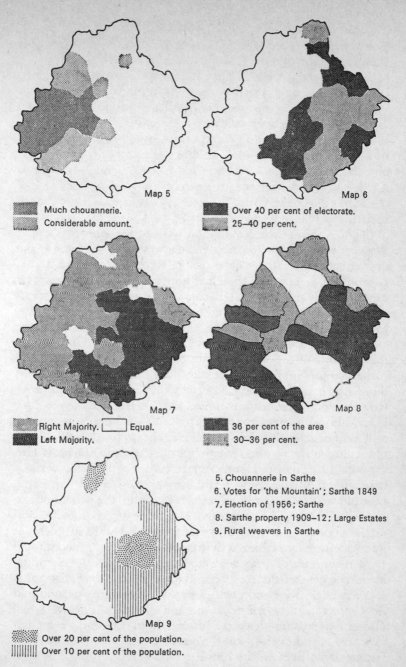

Map 5

Much chouannerie.
Considerable amount.

Map 6

Over 40 per cent of electorate.
25–40 per cent.

Map 7

Right Majority. ☐ Equal.
Left Majority.

Map 8

36 per cent of the area
30–36 per cent.

5. Chouannerie in Sarthe
6. Votes for 'the Mountain'; Sarthe 1849
7. Election of 1956; Sarthe
8. Sarthe property 1909–12; Large Estates
9. Rural weavers in Sarthe

Map 9

Over 20 per cent of the population.
Over 10 per cent of the population.

Maps 5–9. Paysans de l'Ouest

An alternative explanation could be that the division goes back to the Revolution and the *ancien régime* and that the east had been more subject to oppression by the privileged orders. If the *cahiers* of 1789 are examined, however, it emerges rather surprisingly that the people were hostile to the nobles and clergy in the conservative west but not in the east.

Bois suggests that what is important is not whether the land was owned in large or small holdings as Siegfried thought, but how the land was acquired and what social situation surrounded it. Thus in this department the peasants owned $12\frac{1}{2}$ per cent of the land. The bourgeoisie owned $51\frac{1}{2}$ per cent, that is, more than the privileged orders. It is a well-known fact that most of the land sold at the Revolution went to the bourgeoisie and this was very much the case here. However, in the west of the department of Sarthe, the peasants were, at the time of the Revolution, richer, and they had hopes of buying the land that came on the market. But because this western land was of better quality and more valuable, the bourgeoisie were anxious to buy it, while, on the whole, they neglected the land in the east. The result was that the Revolution set up tension between the peasants of the west and the bourgeoisie. The Revolution came to represent for these peasants the thwarting of their land hunger by intruders, and that is why they made common cause with the nobles against a common enemy. In the east, the poor land, sold off in smaller plots, attracted few bourgeois buyers, and no such hostility was created. The different attitude to the bourgeoisie by the two halves of the department is also explained by another factor. Agriculture was the basic activity throughout Sarthe, but it did not everywhere provide the peasants with enough to live on. Those in the west had an income a third higher than those in the east, because the soil was so very much better. The east therefore had to supplement its agriculture by artisan activities and accordingly it contained a great number of weavers, who often accounted for as much as 20 per cent of the rural population. There were also some weavers in the west and north, but they lived in towns, and had no contact with or influence on the peasants. The west had almost no peasant-weavers: instead it grew hemp, which it exported to the east. In the east, by contrast, there were weavers who lived in the hamlets with the peasants. The con-

clusion is not that the growing of hemp produces royalism and
that peasant-weavers are necessarily republican, but rather that
artisan activity produces a special kind of interaction between
town and country. The weaving areas have constant contact
with the towns, because merchants come to them to supply raw
materials and to collect the finished cloths, and they bring with
them the ideas of the towns. The weavers prove to be ready
recipients for revolutionary ideas, particularly because of their
jealousy of the richer peasants of the west. In years of bad
harvests, the rich peasants survive without difficulty, consuming
their own produce and profiting from rocketing prices, while
the weavers, who have to buy their food, cannot afford to.
The weavers, moreover, are hostile to the government which
hampers them with controls on their production and on quality,
controls which inevitably reduce their earnings. The westerners
know less of the towns, and to them the church serves the same
function as the town does to the easterners. It is to church that
they go to escape from their isolation; and it is to the church
that they rally when the emissaries of the towns attempt to
overthrow their priest. So, in this interpretation, the decisive
division in France is produced not by property and not by
landscape, but by the attitudes which different areas have
towards innovations and to capitalism. The principal factors
are therefore land hunger, and the strife of town and country,
with revolutionary ideas infiltrating from the former to the
latter through the artisans. It should not be forgotten that
until the end of the nineteenth century no towns ever voted conservative.[1]

Placed on a wider sociological canvas, this interpretation can
be developed to associate the progress of advanced ideas with
urbanisation. These ideas are to be found not only in towns,
but they also penetrate into rural areas affected by urbanisation, that is those which produce goods for the urban market,
which are linked to it by roads and the frequent exchange of
money. R. Arambourou, studying the *arrondissement* of La
Réole (Gironde) showed how the left-wing vote started at the
capital of the *arrondissement* at the beginning of the Third
Republic and gradually spread outwards to the countryside—

---

[1] Paul Bois, *Paysans de l'Ouest, Des structures économiques et sociales aux options
politiques depuis l'époque révolutionnaire dans la Sarthe* (Le Mans, 1960).

retracting, however, after 1914. In this way, electoral geography can escape from the accusation of presenting a static
view of politics.[1] Charles Tilly, studying the Vendée of 1793,
showed that the common opinion that economically backward
areas, with no urban contacts, are necessarily reactionary, is
too simple. In trying to explain why the counter-revolution was
so powerful here, he puts forward the explanation that counter-
revolution occurs not in totally backward areas, but in ones
in which a certain amount of penetration of urban forces had
occurred, but incompletely. The counter-revolution represents
a conflict of balanced forces. The effect of urbanisation on
a rural community is usually selective: only certain classes
and certain activities are affected at first. A conflict is set up
between those inhabitants who continue to be absorbed in local
affairs and those whose outlook and interests have become
bound up with outside, national concerns. Julian Pitt-Rivers,
the social anthropologist, has shown in a study of a French
village how there are two worlds of activity in it. Patois is used
when discussing animals, farming, the weather and family
matters. French is spoken when dealing with politics, fashion,
learning, commerce and national affairs. Today, most French
villagers have learnt to be bilingual and bicultural, but a
century ago their patois culture was being faced with French
culture as an intrusion and a challenge. If urban–rural conflict
is due to mutual ignorance or incompatibility, then one would
expect to find it strongest in areas where the two are most
insulated from each other. But two groups who do not meet
cannot fight. The conflict occurs as a result of the two cultures
meeting and setting up tensions. The representatives of the
towns introduce power into the village from new, outside
sources, as officials or as merchants. They challenge the old
ruling class and the established distribution of influence in the
village. They re-form local rivalries along new lines, linking
them with divisions having national significance. Thus the
most serious struggles of the counter-revolution occurred not
in the remotest woodlands of the Vendée, but near Cholet,
where in the eighteenth century the textile industry developed
rapidly, to create a sudden clash of new and old influences. The

[1] R. Arambourou, 'Réflexions sur la géographie électorale', *Revue française des
sciences politiques* (July 1952), 521–42.

new bourgeoisie celebrated the Revolution by expelling the nobles and peasants from village offices. There was no conflict where the bourgeoisie was already in unchallenged control of the town. The trouble occurred where they were still on their way to the acquisition of influence. This is partly a social explanation, but also a personal one. The counter-revolution was often begun by men seeking to settle personal scores and to redress entirely local grievances. They seldom had plans beyond rectifying the balance of power in their village. They got their support from young men, often hired hands, anxious to avoid conscription, which was one of the most serious forms of national intrusion into the village. The clash between the parties was therefore not on simple class lines (any more than it was in the English Civil War). Though the revolutionary forces were led by bourgeois, there were also some on the opposite side, and there were many artisans in the counter-revolutionary armies. The generalisations have to be made with many reservations.[1]

The sociologists are only one group among the electoral analysts. The geographers, who could claim to have started it all, continue to make important contributions. Siegfried's conclusions seemed to suggest that granite produced right-wing votes and chalk left-wing ones. He was never as simple minded as this, but he did have a strong belief in geographical determinism. In his *Electoral Geography of Ardèche* (1949) he related the different 'climates of opinion' to the geological map, which, he said, gave the 'veritable explanation'. The right was dominant in the mountains, the left in the plain. There was one psychology in the heights, another in the valleys and a third on the slopes. 'It is as though barometric pressure can generate opinions.' It is true that he goes on to modify this by adding that religious factors are overriding, but he seems to regard religion as a 'disturbing influence' rather than a fundamental one. The geographers, particularly of Grenoble University, have continued the study of these interrelationships. They have argued that geographical factors used to be decisive, but that they have ceased to be so as modern developments have brought in more powerful new influences.[2]

---

[1] C. Tilly, *The Vendée* (1964).
[2] André Siegfried, *Géographie électorale de l'Ardèche sous la Troisième République*

Historians who have contributed to this debate have been unable to produce any simple generalisations about the effects of modern changes. The increasing number of local histories based on a thorough investigation of all possible sources and factors have on the contrary tended to stress the diversity and originality of small regions, and to show how complicated the play of forces has been. Most disconcerting of all, perhaps, has been a brilliant study of the Hérault by Gérard Cholvy, which attempted, among other things, to isolate the influence of the political battles of the nineteenth century on opinion, by studying the effects of the introduction of a revolutionary and Catholic press and of lay and ecclesiastical schools. The political parties have attributed great importance to the propagation of their ideas in newspapers and they have often tried to repress those of their enemies, as dangerous and disruptive influences. But when one looks at the villages and towns where these newspapers were bought, it becomes clear that this influence has in fact been very limited. Newspapers seem to have given heart to the faithful, rather than converted opponents. In the commune of Roqueredonde, to take a small but precise example, in 1907 ten daily newspapers were regularly bought: three Catholic and seven republican. But this was a largely religious parish and the anticlerical newspapers did nothing to destroy its faith. The peasants did not read the newspapers, whose influence, if any, was on a small élite. In many places the republican papers were simply what republican civil servants bought. With the progress of time, newspapers won a wider audience, though at the same time they lost much of their political content. The effects of the press in the nineteenth and the twentieth centuries were by no means of the same kind. The formation of public opinion, in historical perspective, is still something of a mystery.

Likewise, it is usually assumed that the lay schools and the *instituteurs* were important agents in converting the new generations to the republic. But here again it emerges in detailed local study that this is by no means proved, and that their influence has almost certainly been exaggerated. Only a minority of *instituteurs* seem to have been really vigorous in

(1949), 113; G. Veyret-Verner and others in *Revue de géographie alpine* (Jan.–Mar. 1954).

the campaign of laicisation; there were great differences in their personalities and attitudes and their action varied over the century. The Church thought it could win back ground by establishing its own schools, but these probably halted a tide rather than changed a situation, and they were not successful in regions which had already become detached from Christianity. The growth of towns is another factor which has been linked with an increase of hostility or indifference to the Church. Here detailed investigation of opinion in the town before it grew shows that there was often no change as a result of growth. Immigrants, arriving with a feeling of inferiority towards the older residents, may be quick to assimilate the accepted attitudes: the resulting city's attitudes will depend on a combination of the immigrants' past and the way they are treated when they arrive. The Spaniards who flooded into southern France, for example, came from an ostensibly Catholic country, but their conformity there had usually been purely social, and their move to France was a liberation and escape from the old pressures. One is repeatedly brought back to more and more distant historical factors.[1]

Another crucial historical problem is that of the changing composition of the ruling class in politics. Philippe Vigier (whose penetrating thesis—one of the most important since the war—on the Alpine region from 1848 to 1852, contains insights and ideas of far wider significance than his title might suggest) has illuminated the varying fortunes of the old notable class in the face of universal suffrage. In contrast to Siegfried, who dealt with an area where the nobility's influence survived in a rather special way, he has investigated a region with far less large property and few nobles. Here the emancipation of the people from the rule of the notables occurred at different speeds in different areas. In some places, particularly where the ruling class of Louis-Philippe had wasted itself in petty internal quarrels and coterie jealousies, the advent of universal suffrage revealed that they were discredited, and already in July 1848 the peasants were using the municipal elections to start a 'république paysanne'. Whereas in the west of France the poor continued to leave politics to their traditional rulers or to the educated classes for over half a century, here their participation

[1] Gérard Cholvy, *Géographie religieuse de l'Hérault contemporain* (1968).

was very quickly established. Their allegiances, however, did not all go the same way. A large number gave their support to the Reds, and engaged actively in politics in the numerous secret clubs that sprang up in many villages. In the Comtat, however, they preferred popular royalism under noble leaders. Elsewhere Bonapartism appeared as a means by which they could win their place in public affairs, against the old ruling cliques. Many factors determined the moment when the masses entered politics: historical traditions—the kind of leadership the notables had provided, the type of conflicts in which the peasants had been involved before they were given a voice; geographical forces—like the isolation of the mountain regions, where indifference prevailed; and economic influences—and here particularly the way the economic crisis of 1848 hit different classes and different areas. A comparison of Vigier's findings with those of some of the other important local studies recently undertaken shows that universal suffrage affected politics in a wide variety of ways and that one cannot talk simply of one class displacing another in power at any given date, certainly not on a national level.[1]

So far, this discussion has used the terms left and right. It is a traditional view of French politics that under the multiplicity of party labels the real struggle has been between two major tendencies, labelled according to the parts of the chamber the deputies of the First Republic occupied. The French invented the notion of left and right, and it has been adopted almost universally. This is the distinction, said Emmanuel Berl, which is by far the most living one for the mass of the French electorate. 'A sure instinct enables us to know if a person is left or right', said André Siegfried, though it was difficult to explain why we knew it. Generally speaking, to be left wing denoted acceptance of the enlightenment, of the idea that man was naturally good, capable of infinite progress, which would be achieved above all by the application of reason, that the world as it was required improvement, and that this 'improvement' should be sought in accordance with the wishes, and in the interests, of the majority

[1] Philippe Vigier, *La Seconde République dans la région alpine* (1963), 2 vols.; André Armengaud, *Les Populations de l'est aquitain 1845–1871* (1961); Pierre Barral, *Le Département de l'Isère sous la Troisième République* (1962); Georges Dupeux, *Aspects de l'histoire sociale et politique du Loir-et-Cher 1848–1914* (1962).

of the nation. To be right wing was generally to prefer to
maintain the *status quo*, or even to bring back the good old days,
to believe in hierarchies, the inequality of men, to doubt
whether free discussion was the way to truth, to place great
emphasis on the wisdom of the past and to look on the Catholic
Church as the greatest repository of that wisdom.[1] Under
Louis-Philippe, the left clarified its intentions by calling itself
the party of movement and the right the party of resistance. The
Dreyfus affair owes some of its fame to the fact that it re-divided
the country clearly once more, when distinctions had been
blurred, so that those who supported Dreyfus were left and
those who condemned him were right. To intellectuals, this
long remained the test case to determine a man's basic allegiance. However, though the great merit of this distinction was
that it seemed to make politics more intelligible, in other ways
it introduced as much confusion and ambiguity. In the course
of the nineteenth century, the left was more successful than the
right, and so more and more people thought it desirable to call
themselves left, however limited their attachment to its principles. Also, more and more people of the left, when they
attained power, found it hard to implement their plans of
reform and spent more time resisting the attacks of new men
who emerged to be more left than themselves. Thus the anomaly
arose of conservative parties having 'left' as a prominent part
of their name; appellations which had once suggested extreme
revolutionary tendencies came to mean the very opposite.
Thus radicals were once clearly left wing, their programme in
1869 was extreme, but by the end of the century they were
sitting in the centre of the chamber, and they are now on the
right. There have been groups, like the Republican left, which
sat on the right, and were conservative in all but their memories.
'Progressist' in 1885 meant advanced, but in 1898 it meant
moderate and by 1906 it was positively right wing and even
clerical. In the south there have been 'anticollectivist socialists'
who are in reality conservatives. There is no consistency in the
content of the distinction either. A man calling himself right wing
was often clerical, but this was not always the case and there
are regions which have been moving steadily to the right in
direct proportion to the increase in their religious indifference;

[1] Cf. E. Beau de Lomenie, *Qu'appelez-vous Droite et Gauche?* (1931).

and in the 1930s and 1940s the Catholics successfully detached themselves from conservatism. A man calling himself left wing might be thought to be liberal rather than authoritarian, but this could be an illusion and is by no means always or necessarily the case.[1]

It is not possible to associate the left wing simply with industrialisation and the rise of a working class. The east of France, after having been left wing for the first half of the Third Republic, became right wing for the second half. Now this is a region which includes some of the largest industrial agglomerations of the country, and yet there has been a peculiar absence of socialism and communism. Clearly the conservatism of the west, so graphically described by Siegfried, is quite different from that of the east. One cannot talk of the influence of the employers dominating the workers in the east, for they are often of a different religion and apart from some famous exceptions, they have been 'egotistic exploiters'. It seems that what has been the determining factor in the east is its position on the frontier, its fear of invasion, its nationalism precisely because its French character is somewhat uncertain. So when nationalism was represented by the left it voted left, but then moved right when nationalism became a creed of the right. It favoured strong and authoritarian government, so its republicanism was always of a special character, and it voted massively in favour of De Gaulle. Industrialisation has had a completely different result in the north, with its strong communist vote, and in the east, where it is tiny.[2]

There are so many differences within each of these two 'temperaments' as they have been called, that it has been suggested that the terms left and right should be used in the plural. The right should, in this view, be seen to be composed of basically three distinguishable varieties, which were originally called legitimism, Orleanism and Bonapartism. With time, the ideologies of these varieties and the support for them have changed, but the new forms of conservatism, like corporatism and nationalism, and movements like the M.R.P., Poujadism

---

[1] René Rémond, *La Droite en France* (new edition 1963), contains an excellent analysis. Cf. E. Weber and H. Rogger, *The European Right* (1965).

[2] *Recherches sur les forces politiques de la France de l'est depuis 1787* (Strasbourg, 1966), cahiers 8 and 9 of the Association Interuniversitaire de l'Est.

and Gaullism, can be linked with them.[1] The left wing should
be divided at least into two, for its extreme wing, ending in
communism, has clearly developed distinct functions. This
modification of the left–right dichotomy certainly makes for
greater clarity, though the danger in it is that it encourages an
over-schematic attitude towards political phenomena, and a
blurring of incongruities in the interests of simplicity. It can
be of assistance in understanding new forces, particularly since
historical traditions play such an important part in shaping
these, but, unless carefully used, it can suggest that the ultimate
aim is to be able to categorise them, and that ultimately there
are only two possible solutions, two basic psychologies.

It should not prevent one from realising that the purpose of
these labels is partly to conceal differences, to make common
action possible, to rally support, and not just to enlighten the
public. Some who adopt a label are mistaken in thinking that
it represents what they would like it to represent. The labels
perpetuate distinctions, feuds, enmities whose origin is almost
forgotten and whose significance is largely historical. Their use
keeps politics in a vicious circle, which makes it difficult to
perceive and assimilate new forces and problems; it keeps the
parties which adopt them at one remove from reality. There is
much to be said for writing the history of Frenchmen not in
terms of what divides them but of what unites them. Apparently
radical reforms, when actually implemented, turn out to be
much more moderate than their proponents made them out
to be, and often to approximate to the common denominator
of public opinion. The Revolution of 1789 is now seen to have
been far less of a break with the past than was once believed.
The separation of Church and state, fought for for so long by
the anticlerical left wing, in the end strengthened the Church.
The equilibrium that seems to be maintained despite the
efforts of either side to tilt the balance in its favour is a useful
pointer to the consensus which party strife obscures. The two
sides have more in common than they are willing to admit.
An understanding of this common factor in the mentality of
political opponents is essential to a proper appreciation of just
how much place politics has in the life of a nation. This common

[1] René Rémond, 261–92, has a discussion of the links. Cf. François Goguel, *La
Politique des partis sous la Troisième République* (3rd edition 1958), 17–29.

mentality, precisely because it was accepted, was often a force of far greater power than anything a party could create. France did indeed appear to be moving leftwards throughout this century, but the cult of originality very often flourished in people who also had, in other ways, a deep hostility to it. The ambivalence of the radical party, which survived so long because it incarnated with such muddle and guile the feelings of the average man, illustrates this well, and Proudhon, who was so sympathetic to large sections of the working classes, was of course simultaneously revolutionary and conservative. It is important to accept these contradictions as real and not to attempt to clarify too much what was confused and hesitant. The political parties did not necessarily fight for the objects they thought they were fighting for. The radicals who tried so hard to destroy Catholic teaching and introduce a lay morality never quite caught up with the fact that the morality they preached was very little different from that of the Catholics. Were they fooling themselves or the electorate?[1]

The real issues about which people cared were not necessarily represented by the parties; and, in any case, it should not be forgotten that France had no parties, in the British or American sense, organised and with clear programmes, until the communists introduced one. To vote for a party therefore meant something different in France. The vocabulary is misleading. So it is not enough to count votes to discover the opinions of a constituency or a region. To assert the opposite is to imply that the whole nation was fully integrated, fully conscious of the options open to it, and that it saw them in the same terms as the politicians. This was clearly not the case in this period. In different regions, in different sections of society, and at the personal level, votes had many different meanings. Some opinions represented ambitions and attitudes which could not really be expressed in political terms. Only with the advent of public opinion polls has it become possible to come anywhere near a satisfactory analysis of the significance of political votes. When one poll in 1952 asked Frenchmen whether they thought France ought to remain neutral in a war, the vast majority answered yes. But when it asked further whether France could

---

[1] See Theodore Zeldin (ed.), *Conflicts in French Society* (1970).

remain neutral in a war, the vast majority answered no.[1] Much
subtlety is needed to distinguish between the theoretical and
the practical content of a vote. In France, the distinction is all
the more difficult to make because people have often been more
reticent in answering public opinion questionnaires than they
are in the U.S.A.; American sociological techniques do not
always produce comparable results in France. But the use of
these polls has suggested that there is more consensus than the
political system leads one to believe.

The violence of party strife has given France the reputation
abroad of being a nation in whose life politics play a very
important part. The number of Frenchmen who have actually
joined a political party is, however, infinitesimal, around 1·5 per
cent in the 1950s, and very much less before when there were
fewer parties which believed they could actually enrol members.
Only the communists have managed to get more than 100,000
party members. There is some justification for the view of those
who have claimed that the political nation in the twentieth
century is no larger than that of the days of Louis-Philippe,
when votes were limited to the rich. Charles Maurras was not
an impartial commentator but his suggestion that only about
20,000 to 30,000 people were really involved in politics may
contain some truth.[2] The vicomte d'Avenel, a social historian
and analyst of considerable merit, whose writings enjoyed
much esteem at the turn of the century and who has somewhat
unjustly been forgotten, began his book on *The French* thus:
'Politics does not at all have, in the lives of each one of us,
the place it holds in the newspapers, in conversation, in the
apparent life of the nation. The public life of a people is a very
small thing compared to its private life. So the modifications of
government do not have the influence on our well-being, on the
material or moral situation of each one of us, or on our un-
happiness, that is commonly believed. They are not matters of
indifference, but in the end they do not matter much. So people
as a whole do not bother a great deal about politics; and this
attitude is fortunate. If it was otherwise, nations would be

[1] P. Fougeyrollas, *La Conscience politique dans la France contemporaine* (1963), 144.
For the results of polls, see *Sondages*, periodical published by the Institut Français
de l'Opinion Publique.
[2] C. Maurras, *Enquête sur la monarchie* (1900), xcii.

ungovernable.'[1] D'Avenel's conclusion may be debatable, but his assertions are supported to some extent by electoral and poll statistics. Between 1815 and 1846 abstentions in elections, even though the vote was limited to a few, were occasionally as high as 30 per cent, and fell to 10 per cent only once, in 1830. After the Revolution of 1848, there were only 16 per cent abstentions in April, but by December, in the presidential election, they were up to 25 per cent, and reached 35 per cent in May 1849. Under Napoleon III they started at 37 per cent and fell gradually to 18 per cent in 1870. Under the Third Republic, abstentions were as high as 30 per cent in 1881, 29 per cent in 1893, 27·7 per cent in 1898, 27·5 per cent in 1910, but in hard-fought elections, when the clash of issues was stressed, they fell to 20 per cent, as in 1881, 1902 and 1906. On the whole, however, abstentions diminished, and in the 1930s they were down to between 15 and 16 per cent. Though some greeted these figures as showing that depolitisation (so noticeable in the content of newspapers) was a myth, the Fifth Republic saw the figures rise again to between 22 and 24 per cent and as high as 31 per cent in the election of 1962. These figures should probably be reduced by 5 per cent—to allow for mistakes in the electoral role, and those physically incapable of voting—to reveal those who voluntarily abstained; but they should also be compared with the abstentions in local elections, which in 1937 were as high as 40 per cent, in 1952 43 per cent, in 1955 38 per cent. These are national totals: in some cantons the majority, even 60 per cent, abstained.

Perhaps France's reputation for interest in politics came to it from the eighteenth century. It could be argued that after 1848 politics ceased to be a major preoccupation. 'People engaged in politics, they discussed them in conversations and newspapers; they published pamphlets and even a few important books. But what a contrast intellectually with the eighteenth century, when politics were a principal concern of the great minds, and when books about the state and its laws were best sellers.' In the nineteenth century, most of the great thinkers, like Saint-Simon and Proudhon, were enemies of politics, anxious to reduce government to the minimum. Demolins wrote a book entitled *Is it worth capturing power?* Until the 1930s,

[1] G. d'Avenel, *Les Français de mon temps* (1904), 1.

young intellectuals dreamed of writing poetry and novels
rather than of emulating Aristotle or Tocqueville. The prestige
of politics was well below that of literature or science. It was
only after 1945 that French political science really established
itself as an independent discipline.[1] In a poll held in 1959 only
9 per cent of those questioned said they were very interested
in politics, 47 per cent said they were interested a little and 42·5
per cent said they were not interested at all. This 9 per cent of
very interested people contained twice as many men as women
(12 per cent men, 6·5 per cent women; 52 per cent of women
as opposed to 32 per cent of men said they had no interest in
politics at all). 35 per cent of men in the upper ranks of management and administration said they were very interested, 22·5
per cent of members of the liberal professions, 15 per cent of
middle management, 14 per cent of people in agriculture, 13
per cent of junior employees in business, 12 per cent of artisans,
7 per cent of industrial workers and 6 per cent of agricultural
labourers. Among the industrial workers, the figure for qualified
ones was 9 per cent, but for labourers 3·5 per cent. In the same
year (which was of course a crucial and exciting one in French
history) 89 per cent of those interrogated said they had attended
no electoral meeting of any kind, 54 per cent had not bothered
to read any electoral posters, 35 per cent had not heard any
political broadcasts. Only 19 per cent said they regularly read
the political articles in newspapers, but 21 per cent said they
never did. It seems unlikely that the interest in politics was
higher in the nineteenth century, in a population with so much
less leisure and far greater illiteracy.

Now, abstention from politics is in France often a political
act in itself. Some conservatives in particular take up the
attitude that parties are ruining the country and when they
stand for parliament they say they are doing so unwillingly,
simply to put right what the politicians have spoilt. They dislike the word party and prefer to organise 'movements', 'unions'
and *rassemblements*. Napoleon III made the criticism of parties
one of the main planks in his platform: parties, he claimed,
paralysed reform and produced only agitation: against them
he offered a return to order and union. Pétain in 1940 attacked

[1] *Revue internationale d'histoire politique et constitutionnelle*, 7 (1957), special issue on
'L'entrée de la science politique dans l'université française', 1–119.

the sterile quarrels of the parties of the Third Republic, which had encouraged the feverish unleashing of personal ambition and ideological passions, with permanent incitement to division. De Gaulle's prime minister, Michel Debré, in the same tradition, positively advocated depolitisation, arguing that the removal of vital problems from partisan discussion was essential in the national interest. The advocates of technocracy, from Saint-Simon and Comte downwards, have been the enemies of unbridled politics. The civil service, the army, certain business circles have all in varying degrees echoed this distaste for and discrediting of politics as something dishonest and futile. Not even the republic's hard-won moral-education classes themselves, which are supposed to instil patriotism into children, seem to encourage a different attitude. A sample of children were asked in the early 1960s who in history had done most good to France. 48 per cent said Pasteur, 20 per cent said St Louis, 12 per cent said Napoleon, 9 per cent De Gaulle, 4 per cent Colbert, 2 per cent Louis XIV, 1 per cent Gambetta and 1 per cent Robespierre. The most popular heroes are not politicians.[1]

Moreover, those people who are interested in politics are not always interested in political questions. At the village level, politics sometimes appears as simply a pastime in which people engage to save themselves from boredom, particularly when there is a rural middle class with a certain amount of leisure and pretension. In the south-west, politics could be ideological but also have an element of game playing in it, particularly when an autarchic economy meant that the election results and the outside world's policy had less material consequences than fluctuations of the weather. In the west, when the social structure was more rigidly hierarchical, the struggle to replace the old élite by a new one could assume a more bitter and angry complexion, as traditional supremacies and a whole view of life were simultaneously challenged. Some villages have their political alignment firmly settled by the rivalries of families, clans and clienteles, and the battles for influence and prestige

1 Jean Meynaud and Alain Lancelot, *La Participation des Français à la politique* (1961); Georges Vedel, *La Dépolitisation. Mythe ou réalité* (1962); J.-P. Charnay, *Le Suffrage politique en France* (1965), 180; Charles Roig and Françoise Billon-Grand, *La Socialisation politique des enfants. Contribution à l'étude de la formation des attitudes politiques en France* (1968), 64.

between them are carried on, under sophisticated labels, with infinite subtlety.

When the results of an election are known, their significance is not easy to assess. Under the voting system adopted during most of the Third Republic, a majority of those who cast their votes were not represented in parliament. In 1881, for example, 4·5 million votes were cast for the deputies elected, but 5·6 million for others.[1] The inequalities of the constituencies accentuated the gap between public and parliamentary opinion.[2] 49 per cent of people questioned in 1963 did not consider that any of the political parties was suited to defend their interests.[3]

The study of political behaviour is, despite all the advances made, particularly over the last few decades, still in a rudimentary stage. The way people acquire their political ideas, the influence of parents, schools and peer groups and of the increasingly varied pressures to which people are subject, has not been satisfactorily unravelled. In the U.S.A., the choice of party is said to be made by children at a very early age. Parties do not have the same position in French society, but divisions on national issues appear to be established firmly in the schools. The interactions of politics and family organisation, and of the models of authority inculcated in childhood with subsequent behaviour, are worth investigating. Meanwhile French politics cannot be seen simply as the clash of two ideologies, or even a number of them. Indeed, judged by the amount politics meant to the masses, it might seem that they should not be accorded too much attention. But, if it is granted that the ideological clash symbolised or revealed other conflicts, the exceptional richness of the political material can yield insights not to be derived from any other source. There are definite limits to what the historian will ever find out about family life. The mass of political archives and newspapers is by contrast almost inexhaustible in its variety. Through a study of politics, this section will attempt to enable the reader to become acquainted with one of the ways in which Frenchmen

[1] Eugène d'Eichtal, *Souveraineté du peuple et gouvernement* (1895), 204. The figures for 1885, 1889 and 1893 were similar.

[2] J. M. Cotteret, *Lois électorales et inégalités de représentation en France 1936–1960* (1960).

[3] *Sondages*, 2 (1963), 69.

expressed their character, their ambition and their frustration. The ideas and the activities to which politics gave rise are fascinating in themselves, but a good deal of their significance and intelligibility depends on their being seen also as part of a wider whole. The links between the parts, between the different sides of life, are elusive, but it is in the search for them that history acquires its universal interest.

2. Kings and Aristocrats

THERE is a great deal of drama in the history of royalism after 1848—secret conspiracies, tense crises, prolonged rivalries. The leading protagonists included colourful extremists, vigorous, stoical and melancholy agitators, and men strangely out of touch with reality. The fate of royalism, at this personal level, is usually presented as the result of individual mistakes, mismanagement and lost opportunities. In 1873 it seemed that the monarchy was *almost* restored; in 1889 Boulanger *almost* staged a *coup d'état* in its favour. In this interpretation, France would have been a monarchy again but for the errors and divisions of the royalist leaders. This chapter will ask just how much part accident played in what was, for many people, the major tragedy of this period. It will attempt to analyse why the leaders acted the way they did, where and why they won support and why they lost it, and whether, if the monarchy had been restored, it could have lasted. One can, by the study of these questions, get a glimpse of a section of society whose preoccupations were considerably more complicated than a loyal devotion to hereditary monarchy.

For royalism was a movement aiming at much more than the restoration of the monarchy and it was backed by forces far more powerful than those of a corrupt court, or a decaying nobility regretting its lost prestige. Its history cannot be written off simply as one of failure. It is true that by the 1890s it had ceased to be a significant political force; that its resuscitation by the Action Française in the twentieth century was the work of a tiny if vocal minority and that today, for all practical purposes, it is dead. However, the men involved were not fighting simply about forms of government, or about ideology. Paradoxically, many of those who worked hardest to secure the king's restoration were, in fact, among his bitterest enemies. The nobles of Brittany were famous in the nineteenth century for the perseverance with which they supported the royalist cause. But in the eighteenth century they had been among the king's principal enemies. They were not inconsistent. In both centuries they stood above all for a view of the distribution of political and local influence, which involved the rule of the countryside by an élite. In the eighteenth century they saw the king as their enemy; after the Revolution they believed the republic was an even more dangerous threat. Royalism was part of this struggle about decentralisation, about the unification of the state, about the evolution of a ruling class within it, and about the way those interested in power balanced themselves between Paris and the provinces. The royalist cause was not entirely lost, if seen from this point of view. The republic, in the form in which it ultimately triumphed, did not secure an unadulterated victory over this movement against the state: on the contrary, the republic triumphed partly because it absorbed the movement. *La république des camarades* evolved its own way of diffusing power and of limiting central authority. It ended the rule of the aristocracy, but it replaced it with a new kind of élite, in which the hereditary element was not totally absent. So deep were the passions involved, that neither side could admit that they had anything in common. The struggle over the monarchy was not one in which the alliances were natural ones, or the enmities as inescapable as they may have appeared.

One of the basic and acknowledged divisions of royalism was between legitimism and Orleanism, between the partisans of the eldest line overthrown in 1830 on the one side and those of the younger branch of Louis-Philippe, overthrown in 1848, on the other. But, to begin with the first of these, it is not always appreciated that the legitimists were themselves divided into three different groups, each advocating different methods of securing a restoration. On the one hand there was the party of violence. These were the successors of the *chouans* of the first Revolution, of the men who had waged civil war against it and against Napoleon, and who believed that the king and his nobility could still raise an army of one or two hundred thousand men, principally in the west, which would be able to restore the fleur-de-lis once more to Paris. These advocates of conspiracy were led by the duc des Cars, 'a small, thickset, energetic, taciturn man, a visionary all the more attached to his chimeras in that he divulged them only to those he knew in advance would approve them ... Outwardly cold, but deep down ardent to the point of temerity, he was impenetrably discreet, indefatigably active, an enemy as much of the salons as of parliament. He never went into fashionable society. His true friends received his visits at five or six in the morning.'[1] His policy was tried out in 1832, by the duchesse de Berri, but the planned rising of that year was discovered before it had actually broken out, and the policy, because it had never decisively been proved impossible, was therefore able to survive. The opening up of Brittany and the Vendée by new roads and then by railways, the establishment of garrisons in formerly impenetrable regions, the economic development which created a new prosperity, new classes and new relationships between the nobility and the people, soon created different conditions to those prevailing during the counter-revolution, but for long there were royalists who continued that tradition. They were associated with absolutist doctrines, but the exposition of doctrine was not their strong point.

Secondly, there was the legitimist parliamentary party, which believed that the monarchy could and should be restored by parliamentary means, by fighting elections and winning a majority for it. Its leader was Berryer, and he was not even a nobleman. Indeed, he was barely a Frenchman. He came from Lorraine if not from Germany, his father's name had been Mittelberger. But just as the Tory party in England bought the Irishman Burke an estate, so likewise the legitimists set up Berryer as a country gentleman. For Berryer, though now somewhat forgotten perhaps because he never held office, was in his day regarded as probably the most powerful orator of the century, in a century which prized oratory as one of the most important political gifts. 'He who has never heard Berryer on one of his good days does not know what eloquence is.'[2] For thirty-eight years (1830–68) Berryer led the sizeable ranks of legitimists who went into parliament despite the pretender's orders to abstain. He stood for a constitutional monarchy, though circumstances were never to reveal just how liberal he intended that to be. One of his associates, the comte de Falloux, wrote a book in praise of Louis XVI as a man who had really understood his times, which suggested that the aim of this party

[1] Comte de Falloux, *Mémoires d'un royaliste* (1888), i. 222.
[2] E. Ollivier, *L'Empire libéral*, i (1895), 439.

was to restore the *ancien régime* but reformed on the lines
envisaged by Turgot, another of their heroes. The legitimists
were far from having clear aims.

Thirdly, there was left-wing or popular legitimism, which was
in some ways a precursor of radical Toryism. Its tactic was to
'dish the Whigs', to steal the thunder of the left and to restore
the monarchy by means of referendum, by legal but extra-
parliamentary means. Their methods were similar to those of
some radical republicans and they were willing to enter into
alliance with these. They were among the first to demand an
extension of the suffrage, and they directed their propaganda
at the masses, hoping for an alliance of the nobility with them,
against the bourgeoisie. They acted above all through the press,
which they made into a vigorous instrument of agitation. Their
leader, the Abbé de Genoude, was editor of the *Gazette de
France*. This remarkable man, again, does not fit into the stereo-
type of the aristocrat. He had made a lot of money under the
Restoration, and after 1830 he used it to finance his newspaper.
When his wife died, he became a priest. Wearing neither ton-
sure nor cassock, he preached at the Chapelle du Temple,
using as his sermons his leading articles, which he read out from
the printed proofs before publishing them the next morning.
His ally, the marquis de la Rochejacquelin, a nephew of the
great *chouan*, once a cavalry officer, but an industrialist after
1830, even preached the sovereignty of the people and made
his main demand a referendum on the question of republic or
monarchy. Under Napoleon III, who adopted this appeal to
the people, he agreed to serve as a senator, to cries that he was
a traitor to his party. He illustrates well how the distinction
between parties was not wholly clear cut.[1]

The division of the legitimists into three types is apparent
mainly when one looks at the leaders; but if one goes a stage
further to examine lesser-known men, a considerably greater
variety emerges. Above all, there were profound differences in
legitimism in the different regions, which the leaders only
partly reflected. Thus in the west legitimism was essentially
rural, drawing its strength from the close relations of the nobles

---

[1] Comte Alexandre d'Adhemar, *Du parti légitimiste en France et de sa crise actuelle*
(1843); C. de Lacombe, *La Vie de Berryer* (1894–5); C. de Mazade, *L'Opposition
royaliste* (1894); C. T. Muret, *French Royalist Doctrines since the Revolution* (1933).

and the peasants, cemented by the Church, but with little journalistic intervention. It showed its strength by a kind of passive resistance. In the south, by contrast, where there were few resignations from the civil service after 1830, the legitimists were most powerful in the towns. Toulouse was their principal stronghold, but they exerted little influence in the country around it, where a rich 'rural bourgeoisie' successfully rivalled it. Far from being abstentionist, the legitimists fought elections with demagogic fervour. In the Nîmes–Montpellier–Montauban region this vigorous attitude was envenomed and impassioned by the conflict against Protestantism. In Marseille, legitimism was different again, based not on traditionalism but on an alliance of a few nobles, but far more businessmen, with the masses: it was an opposition party, against Paris and against the holders of state offices. One of their leaders was Béchard, who was a leading theorist of decentralisation; and it was no accident that it was there that Berryer got himself regularly returned to parliament, to uphold a liberal interpretation of the royal cause. Southern legitimism as a whole could more properly be called reactionary or counter-revolutionary, perpetuating old animosities. In Lyon, by contrast, it was watered down to a respectable conservatism, so moderate as to be ready to ally with any government maintaining public order. In the Nord, it was closely connected with Catholicism and manifested itself as much in charitable work as in political organisation.[1]

To which of all these forms of legitimism did the pretenders adhere? The answer is, to none. This was one of the major sources of weakness for the monarchists, who wore themselves out in vain efforts to win the ear of the pretenders, only to be constantly resisted and discouraged. It is also a result of the paradox of legitimism, that the legitimist party was almost inevitably at loggerheads with the pretender. It wanted to give him power, but at the same time it opposed his exercise of that power, for it wanted decentralisation. This is not the only difficulty the party had with its leaders. Royal power and party organisation are not easily compatible. The pretender always felt the need to appeal beyond his own followers, to appear to

[1] A. J. Tudesq, *Les Grands Notables en France 1840–9* (1964), 1. 130–236, is the best social study of legitimism, though it deals only with Louis-Philippe's reign.

be a national leader. He had to work hard to avoid being en-
slaved by party (as Queen Anne of England quickly realised
when parties were first organised here). These difficulties were
obscured by the mystical devotion legitimists bestowed on their
pretender, existing side by side with their criticisms but for
long triumphing over them. The devotion was essential, for
the record of the pretenders was an appallingly unsuccessful one.
It had been no easy thing to admire Louis XVIII, obese to the
point of immobility, scrofulous, egoistic, conceited, concerned
primarily with his own physical well-being, opportunistic when
it served him but rigidly archaic in his obsession with ceremonial
and court ritual. He had got his throne back and this gave him
a reputation for sagacity, but it was hardly deserved. His
moderation and balancing of the parties had been designed
primarily to keep himself the supreme arbiter in politics. His
ignorance of conditions in his kingdom and of changing opinions
was astounding. Charles X had been more attractive, with far
more grace, even if his genuine benevolence was somewhat
ovine. Unlike his elder brother, he was not concerned with
showing his own importance, and he always had a kind word
to say to everyone. He could win real affection from those with
whom he had dealings. But he too was ignorant and uneducated.
His keen desire to perform his duties punctiliously proved his
undoing, for he did not understand compromise. He believed
that opposition must be met with frontal attack. For all his
devotion to the public welfare, as he saw it, the result of his
reign was catastrophic.

The comte de Chambord (born in 1820), pretender for
forty-seven years (1836–83), was an equally difficult leader to
follow. Educated by conservative noblemen of narrow outlook,
it is said that he was instructed in political economy, cosmo-
graphy, trigonometry and botany, and that he was therefore
alive to the new ideas of his time, but his hagiographers also
add what probably gives a truer picture of his interests—that
he knew by heart the history of all the dynasties of Europe with
their dates and his own genealogy right back to Roman times.
His tutors had been told to teach him no history beyond 1788.
In any case his main activity was hunting. In 1841 he broke his
leg in a riding accident and limped for the rest of his life. He
was not of a particularly prepossessing appearance. He grew

to be almost as fat as Louis XVIII. He was exceedingly hairy (or, as the court sycophants put it, 'his pilose system was very developed'). He was lazy and not particularly intelligent. He could tie neither his own shoe-laces nor his cravat. He maintained the etiquette of the *ancien régime* with a scrupulous devotion, and preserved relics of Louis XVI and Marie Antoinette religiously in glass cases. But his court was sordid rather than grand. He furnished his residences in a drab style which his disappointed visitors found too bourgeois. He obtained relaxation from his hunting by playing cards for high stakes till the early hours; he enjoyed most of all bawdy stories about barrack rooms and Jews. He lacked generosity; he made donations to charity only when pressed for them. His marriage was a gloomy one. His bride, the twenty-seven-year-old daughter of the duke of Modena, was unequivocally ugly, with a face one half of which was larger than the other. She was passionately reactionary; she was ruled by a Jesuit, who, however, is said to have betrayed all her secrets; but then her principal topic of conversation was pilgrimages. The pretender's court was in Austria, at Frohsdorf, where a painful boredom kept a retinue of aristocrats busy with petty intrigues and with the reproduction of the etiquette of the court of Louis XIV. Nevertheless, seeing in the comte de Chambord not a man but the embodiment of a principle, these followers closed their eyes to his defects, his dullness and coarseness, and worshipped him. The ultimate power of decision was left with a man for whose personal qualities his abler followers had no respect.

Because he lived in Austria, Chambord was able to maintain more easily his independence of the legitimists in France, but also to ignore their advice. His policy was determined instead by his constant companions, the comte de Blacas, the comte de Vaussay and above all the duc de Levis. Levis's ideas could be summarised in the word prudence: his great aim was to prevent Chambord from committing himself, and indeed he got Chambord to declare repeatedly that he would make no decisions as pretender, that all controversial questions would be left until he returned to the throne. This attitude could be presented as the one which would make fewest enemies, but it was not one which could rally new support or win the popular imagination. Chambord, however, did not see his role as that of an agitator. He was waiting for the French to see the errors of their ways. His basic principle, reiterated in all his proclamations, was simply that hereditary monarchy was the 'unique port of salvation in which they would at last find peace'. He was asking for a return to a faith, for France to 'confide her destinies' to him. He was confident that no other form of government could take root in France because only monarchy was morally justified, and morality, for him, meant renunciation of personal desire in favour of a divinely preordained order. Republics involved social anarchy, and 'favoured all forms of greed and all forms of utopias'. He would wait till men abandoned their selfish aspirations. Monarchy, as he saw it, was almost identical with religion. There would clearly have had to be a very drastic transformation of French life, as it was in the nineteenth century, before such a restoration could be feasible. Occasionally, it is true, Chambord, under pressure, made some ostensible concessions to his times. He issued denials that he wanted 'power without limits'. 'Why do men still suspect me of wishing to be nothing but the king of a privileged caste, or to use a phrase they employ, the king of the *ancien régime*, of the old nobility and of the old court?' He did indeed hope to be leader of the whole nation. He promised 'the exclusion of all arbitrary rule, the reign and the respect of laws, honesty and justice everywhere, the country sincerely represented, voting taxes and co-operating in the making of laws, expenses really controlled, property, individual and religious liberty inviolable and sacred, communal and departmental administration judiciously and progressively decentralised, and free access for all to honours and social advantages'. But these promises were balanced by contradictions and reservations. Though he talked of 'submitting with confidence the acts of government to the serious control of freely elected representatives', he made it clear that government would remain in the hands of the king. He sometimes mentioned 'judicious liberty' but far more often emphasised the need for 'strong authority', for the first essentials were security, stability and order. Though he denied that he wished to go back to the *ancien régime*, 'no one', he declared, 'under any pretext, will obtain from me that I should become the legitimate king of the Revolution', for the revolutionary spirit was the great obstacle to the kind of liberty he envisaged. He promised decentralisation, but partly to prevent a repetition of 1830, when a Parisian coup had overthrown the dynasty overnight, and partly to 'create amongst us a natural hierarchy conforming to the spirit of equality'. This meant the creation of a new élite of local notables to strengthen the decaying aristocracy. He encouraged workers' associations, but with corporatist intentions; they would become 'important collective interests with the right to be represented and to be heard', but he assumed that they would use this right only to obtain 'efficacious protection' and that they would cease to be 'instruments of trouble and revolution'. He promised, in language which parodied Louis Napoleon's, 'to march at the head of the social movement', but only 'to give it a moderate and useful direction', and ultimately he placed his faith in a general return to religion. 'The Christian worker' was the basis of his dream of 'social resurrection'. He firmly supported the pope's temporal power, because 'the fall of the most august sovereignty in this world would bring down with it all other sovereignties'; but he was so anxious to keep the Church subordinate to him in France that he forbade his courtiers to address bishops as *monseigneur* and ordered that they be called *monsieur*. He alone was *Monseigneur*. It was not all that easy, therefore, for contemporaries to see exactly what Chambord stood for, and their suspicions of a return to the past were not without foundation. Chambord's policy was never clearly expressed: his declaration on agriculture, for example, stated that the sufferings of the peasants 'merited serious attention' but did not give any hint that he had any practical solutions. So when Chambord declared in 1871: 'I bring back only religion, concord and peace', that was, to a great many Frenchmen, probably both too little and too much.[1]

It is doubtful, however, whether legitimism was a political force because of the adherence of many people to this ideology. Those who advised Chambord to remain silent or vague did

---

[1] Pierre de Luz, *Henri V* (1931); comte de Chambord, *Correspondance de 1841 à 1879* (5th edition 1880), 377, 395, 159–60, 283, 357, 209, 267, 396, 155, 330; comte René Monti de Rezé, *Souvenirs sur le comte de Chambord* (1930); Marvin L. Brown, Jr., *The Comte de Chambord* (Durham, N.C., 1967); baron J. G. de Hyde de Neuville, *Mémoires et souvenirs* (1892); baron M. de Damas, *Mémoires 1785–1862* (1922); marquis René de Belleval, *Souvenirs de ma jeunesse* (1895).

so because they appreciated that legitimism was a web of personal and social relationships rather than a party with a programme. The nobility formed its backbone. It might be assumed, therefore, that this was another basic cause of the weakness of legitimism, for the nobility are supposed to have been a dying class in the nineteenth century. This was not quite the case. On the contrary, the nobility survived the Revolution, despite severe trials and heavy losses. In 1789 there were perhaps 12,000 families in the hereditary nobility, making some 60,000 individuals in all. In addition there were about 100,000 people with personal titles not transmissible to their heirs. In the mid twentieth century there were between 3,600 and 4,400 families—about 30,000 individuals—who were genuinely noble. But in addition there were about 15,000 families falsely claiming to be noble, and in most cases accepted as noble by society at large. That is to say, the demand for ennoblement did not cease with the Revolution. Before then the king had been able to obtain very substantial revenues by selling offices carrying ennoblement to a bourgeoisie eager for honorific distinction and for recognition by the state. In the eighteenth century the law courts and the financial civil service succeeded in obtaining recognition that tenure of their posts carried with it ennoblement. Even the regent doctors of universities claimed nobility by virtue of their degrees, but unsuccessfully, except for those of the papal university of Avignon, and there are today fifteen families enjoying nobility by virtue of descent from doctors of law of that institution. The nobility, for all its exclusiveness, had long been a class, membership of which could be bought or won. A large proportion of the real nobles surviving today obtained their titles by this kind of purchase. Only 20 per cent of them can trace their titles to the fifteenth century or earlier. Another 19 per cent go back to the sixteenth, and 17 per cent to the seventeenth century. That leaves 40 per cent who go back no further than the eighteenth century (20 per cent to the eighteenth century, 8 per cent to Napoleon, and 12 per cent to creations of 1814–70).[1] In 1848 titles were abolished and their public use forbidden, but

[1] H. Jougla de Morenas, *Noblesse 38* (1938), 101. These statistics should be regarded as very rough, in view of the numerous inaccuracies in the genealogical dictionaries.

Napoleon III allowed the use of those which could be proved to be genuine. His law of 1858, penalising false titles, has remained the basis of jurisprudence to this day. Numerous bills introduced into parliament to abolish titles have all failed. Napoleon III allowed people to obtain confirmation of their titles by having them scrutinised by a committee of the ministry of justice, in return for the payment of a substantial fee: 5,000 francs for a duke, 2,000 for a marquis or count. (These sums were levied when an *ancien régime* title was claimed. For imperial titles, a dukedom cost only 200 francs and a barony 65 francs.) This proved a useful if small source of revenue, for the Fourth Republic found it worth while in 1947 to increase the fee to a flat rate for all kinds and grades, 100,000 francs a time. In this way, people were able to resuscitate their nobility after the fall of the monarchy.

But in addition there were legal means by which they could give themselves the appearance of nobility. The law allowed the 'rectification' of birth certificates, and large numbers of people continued to appeal to the courts to insert the particule *de* into their names. The particule was not a legal sign of nobility, but it gave the impression of aristocratic descent. It was in this way that a bourgeois called Laurent Delatre in 1829 got the court of Poitiers to 'rectify' his name to de Lattre de Tassigny, supposedly to distinguish him from relatives, by adding the name of a piece of land he owned. It is from this para-ennoblement that the Marshal descended. It was in the same way that a certain Millon in 1864 was allowed to call himself Millon de Montherlant, which is how the writer obtained his name. The war of 1914–18 provided additional means for these changes, for the heirs of a soldier who had died on the field of battle were allowed to add his name to theirs. This is said to have ennobled more people than ever Louis XIV did. Thanks to it the future minister Felix Gaillard became Gaillard d'Aimé; the magnate of ready-made tailoring Thiery became Thiery de Bercegol du Moulin. A person who became famous under a pseudonym was allowed to make it part of his real name and thus Franz Wiener became in 1910 François Wiener de Croisset. Aristocratic lines on the point of becoming extinct were known to advertise for heirs, and it was thus that in 1864 M. Achille Lacroix was adopted by the last

Vimeur de Rochambeau and became Lacroix de Vimeur de Rochambeau. Modification of spelling was not difficult to obtain and it was such modification that allowed the Marshal Franchet d'Esperey to appear noble, though originally called Desperey. The Action Française leader Beau de Loménie obtained his particule only in 1923. The organiser of the employers' federation, the Comité des Forges, Robert Pinot, became in 1922 Pinot-Périgord de Villechenon. Ennoblement thus continued even though there was no monarchy. Since the republic did not enforce the legislation against the false use of titles, these multiplied more vigorously than ever. Many genuinely noble families adopted titles to which they had no legal claim. Different branches of the Chambrun family called themselves indiscriminately marquis, count and viscount, without, as the genealogists claimed, proper justification. But even more vast numbers-of people with no claim to nobility of any kind, adopted the title of their choice to consecrate their social aspirations. The *Bottin Mondain* has been the directory in which more or less anyone who pays for an entry can include his name among the aristocracy, with the title of his choice, giving as his address whatever château he had bought or whatever house he cared to call a château.[1]

This survival and re-creation of nobility would not have been very significant if it had not been allied with a preservation, and in many cases a reinforcement, of the nobility's wealth. The nobles lost land at the Revolution but apparently far less than is popularly assumed. Hitherto studies of noble wealth have concentrated on the *ancien régime* and there is no proper account of it since then; but sample investigations suggest they remained a powerful economic force. Thus in the 1840s, there were 530 electors paying over 5,000 francs in tax; about 238 of these were noble and another 78 had noble pretensions. Of the 58 paying over 10,000 francs in tax, 39 were noble. Louis-Philippe's reign, which is considered as representing the triumph of the bourgeoisie, still had a very strong aristocratic element in it.[2] The fate of these noble fortunes over the nine-

[1] Henry Bellamy, 'Vraie et fausse noblesse', issue of *Le Crapouillot* for Mar. 1937; Philippe du Puy de Clinchamps, *La Noblesse* (1949); G. Chaix d'Est Ange, *Dictionnaire des familles françaises anciennes ou notables à la fin du 19e siècle* (Évreux, 1903–29), 20 vols. but reaching only as far as the letter G.

[2] A. J. Tudesq, *Les Grands Notables en France 1840–9* (1964), 1. 431.

teenth century has been studied in the department of Loir-et-Cher. Here between 1848 and 1914 the nobles lost only about 10 per cent of their land. Small property ownership progressed considerably, but at the expense of only a section of the nobility. A few noble families with large estates disappeared, but it was rather the families with small estates which succumbed. In individual communes noble property fell by between 10 and 50 per cent, but the most powerful families strengthened their position. Thus the largest estate in the department was still owned in 1914 by the family of the comte de Chambord—over 5,000 hectares. The comte de La Roche-Aymond inherited the estates of the prince de Chalais-Périgord and added 600 hectares more to them, so that he had 4,500 in all. The duc de La Rochefoucauld-Doudeauville added 1,100 hectares to the inheritance of 3,200 hectares he picked up from the duchesse de Montmorency. The marquis de Vibraye doubled his estate between 1848 and 1914. The prince de Broglie, a new-comer to the area, bought the property of the d'Etchegoyen family and added to it, so that by 1914 he had 2,079 hectares.[1]

Nor was it only in agriculture that the wealthy nobility prospered. Many of them went into industry and finance. 30 per cent of the directors of the railway companies in 1902 were noblemen, 23 per cent of those of the large steel and banking companies. In the insurance companies which survived nationalisation after the war of 1939–45, 20 per cent of the directors were noble.[2] Judicious marriages brought a considerable amount of new capital. The American heiress had already arrived in Paris in the mid nineteenth century. In 1887 Charles de Talleyrand-Périgord, duc de Dino, having divorced Elizabeth Beers Curtis, married Adele Sampson, widow of Levington Stevens, with a dowry, it was said, of 7 million dollars. In 1888 the duc Decazes married Miss Singer for 2 million dollars. Comte Boni de Castellane made news when his bride Anna Gould brought him 15 million dollars, though she then divorced him and married another Talleyrand, prince de Sagan. Rothschild heiresses were snapped up by the duc de Gramont, the prince de Ligne and the prince de Wagram.

[1] Georges Dupeux, *Aspects de l'histoire sociale et politique du Loir-et-Cher 1848–1914* (1962), 577.
[2] Jesse Pitts, *The Bourgeois Family* (Harvard Ph.D. thesis, 1957), 235 n.

Prince de Chalençon-Polignac married a Mirès, the duc de Richelieu a Heine, the marquis de Plancy an Oppenheim, the marquis de Breteuil a Fould.[1] These were only exceptional windfalls for a class which was constantly recombining its wealth. The family of Rocheouart-Mortemart, in the late nineteenth century, listed 124 noble families to which it was allied.[2] There was little prospect of a noble inheritance falling into a commoner's hands.

Marrying advantageously and judiciously was a major part of the art of being noble; and that is why the principal intellectual activity of the nobleman was often the study of genealogy and heraldry, of family titles and property deeds. A nobleman needed to understand these, since so much of his status and livelihood depended on them. A considerable amount of money was spent in proving nobility, hiring so-called experts to do research and publishing lavishly produced books illustrating obscure genealogies, in a manner reminiscent of the upstart English gentry of the seventeenth century. As a result, the nobles were considered to have an excessively selfish concern with their own family problems, but their concern was justified by their own criteria. Maintaining and adding lustre to their families was inevitable to a class drawing its principal distinction from heredity. Concern with their own style of life became increasingly important after they had lost the fiscal and feudal privileges which had differentiated them, particularly since this was the way they could keep control of their rebellious children. The nobles were associated with the cult of the family, but internal family disputes possibly reached the most bitter and violent levels among them. Under the *ancien régime*, they made enormous use of *lettres de cachet* to control their children. In the nineteenth century, they called in the Church and the schools to help them instil obedience, but these were only partially successful.

To explain the survival of legitimism by the fact that the nobles supported it is to beg many questions. The nobles were the hereditary enemies of the king, whose centralisation they

[1] Vicomte A. de Royer, *Y a-t-il une noblesse française?* (n.d., about 1899), 34–9.

[2] Vicomte A. de Royer, *Nous avons une noblesse française (1899–1901)*, 1. 188; comte Adrien de Louvencourt, *Notices sur les familles nobles existant actuellement dans le département de la Somme* (Abbeville, 1909).

abhorred, of the people, whom they had long oppressed with exactions, of the bourgeoisie, whose urban power they resented and whose enlightenment they feared. The alliance of classes behind legitimism in the nineteenth century was thus not a natural one nor a historical one, and this was an important weakness in legitimism. Even the clergy, who are inseparably linked with the nobles as supporters of the king, had a long history of rivalry with them. Under the *ancien régime*, there had been no spectacular conflicts but a great deal of petty wrangling in the inevitable struggle for dominance in the village, disputes about the tithes the nobles had usurped, hostility to the interference of bishops from outside. The alliance of Church and aristocracy in the nineteenth century was cemented by the latter's return to religion but it should perhaps be regarded as a tactical alliance, inspired by the terrors of the Revolution and a surviving belief that unity was the best way to preserve the authority of both over the masses. In due course the Church would see that there was nothing sacred in the alliance. The same was true of the nobles' alliance with the king. They were old enemies who believed they stood to gain from union against the republican enemy, but the nobles with time learnt how to extract what they really wanted from the republic. They learnt to become magnates of a new sort in a pseudo-egalitarian society. The strengthening of the economic position of the rich aristocracy in the nineteenth century inevitably led to apostasy from the royal cause, even though allegiance might be maintained at the verbal level. The petty nobility who, by the twentieth century, found it difficult to survive on their landed estates made their peace with the centralising state and accepted civil service jobs. Though the nobles had always stood basically for decentralisation, they had never been united about this. Younger sons, left without land, had gone off to join the royal ranks, and sometimes returned to their native provinces to implement state policy against their families. Whether state or aristocracy was dominant in such a situation in a particular area depended on the political situation, on the economic strength of the local nobility, and on how the rivals judged each other. If the state officials felt intimidated by the 'influence' of the local nobles, they would prefer to ally with them, and the civil servants would become part of local clienteles. That is what was meant when certain areas of France were said to be ruled by the aristocracy, but it was a rule preserved by timidity on the part of the state.

For in the age of universal suffrage, ultimately the power of the nobles rested on whether they could get the masses to vote for them. The poor had many good reasons for overthrowing the yoke of their former masters. The legitimists, particularly the backwoodsmen amongst them, feared progress and modernisation, education, luxury and the material benefits brought by the towns. 'Their leisure was haunted', as their own *Gazette de France* said, 'by the phantom of the terrible reactions of the proletariat.' La Rochefoucauld duc de Doudeauville wrote to Napoleon in 1852 urging him to reduce the number of scholarships offered by the state, so as to stop the ambitious from starting revolutions in their search for better jobs.[1] On the other hand the nobles in many regions for long succeeded in retaining their hold on the peasants by the links of patronage. Even if this was to a certain extent resented it was decisive so long as the nobles appeared to be, as members of the local community, safer protectors against the dangerous, unknown forces of the outside world. The liberation of the peasants from their control would come only when the peasants were either integrated into the general life of the nation, or developed institutions of their own to give them an independence which they could not have individually. Until then, the nobles could insist on deference being paid to them as leaders of the local community. The comte de Comminges has described his youth in a château in Haute-Garonne, where 'customs kept their feudal colours'. The peasants, he said, were very attached to his father 'even though he treated them like blacks'. Feudal services were demanded of them long after their legal abolition. 'When my father had need of stones, for example, he had the fact shouted out at the end of mass' and the peasants found it worth their while to help him.[2] The survival of this relationship depended on the efficiency of the nobles in giving the peasants reciprocal protection and help. Their return to the land after 1830 strengthened their bonds with the peasants, for there was much more in this patronage than the economic control the nobles could exert on their tenants.

[1] Halt, *Papiers sauvés des Tuileries* (1871), 7.   [2] Tudesq, I. 122.

The influence of the legitimists depended more than anything else on their activity. In the west their activity was agricultural, social, communal. In the south it was much more
conspiratorial. The nobles there specialised in forming secret
societies. These went under different names, but had in common a hierarchical organisation, elaborate ritual and a secrecy
which was often as fascinating as what any revolutionary group
could offer. The 'Grand Priory' of the south-west had a whole
network of 'Little Priories', run by the rich, but admitting the
poor without subscription, provided they took oaths to obey
orders and keep their secrets. Often arms were distributed.[1]
Occasionally the freemason lodges were captured and turned
into legitimist organisations. In the Vaucluse they called themselves the Association of the Friends of Order, organised in
legions, centuries and decuries, ready for armed revolt. These
clubs were most successful where they could fit into village
rivalries, family feuds and religious animosities. Many villages
welcomed them not for doctrinal reasons so much as because
the republican club called for a counterweight. The constitutional question, of whether France should be a monarchy or
a republic, became the label under which old animosities were
made respectable. The organisation of these clubs reveals as
much about the clan structure of the provinces as about
political opinions.[2] In the towns, the nobles had another
effective way of bringing together the great variety of people
whose personal interests could be organised to serve their
cause. Charitable and mutual benefit societies were frequently
given a political direction. The most powerful of all, the Society
of St. Vincent de Paul, had over 30,000 members by 1859 in
1,300 branches, becoming so powerful a weapon of the legitimist
revival that Napoleon III dissolved it. It recruited people like
shopkeepers, artisans, waiters, cab-drivers, employees of the
Church, clerks, servants and not a few factory workers. In
elections these would often act as a significant army of propagandists, particularly when the societies worked closely with
a politically passionate clergy. Members of the middle class

[1] Jeanne Lesparre, 'Les Partis politiques dans la Haute Garonne à la fin de la
monarchie de juillet', in J. Godechot, *La Révolution de 1848 à Toulouse* (1948), 31–5.
[2] Jack Barnouin, 'Le Parti légitimiste en Vaucluse 1830–1883' (unpublished
D.E.S. mémoire, n.d. (1950s) in Montpellier University Library).

could hope to be admitted into the salons of the aristocracy if they joined.[1] Legitimism could appeal to many forms of snobbishness and interest.

But its appeal was limited for two reasons. First, the legitimists could not always conceal their patronising contempt for the middle classes, contradicting their pretence that they were a national party open to all. Too many of them made it clear that true virtue could be found only among peasants, and that the towns were a source of vice and artificiality. Secondly, they were indecisive in their use of governmental influence to bolster their own. Chambord told them to resign *en masse* from all their jobs and elected offices. Some did. A few of them lost little by their withdrawal, but in most cases this gave their opponents the chance to dangle alternative patronage before the electorate. However, perhaps about a half of the legitimists decided to stay on as *conseillers généraux*. In 1852 there were about 450–500 of them elected out of 2,500.[2] After 1848 they stayed on in local politics with greatest perseverance in the west, and in the 1950s this was still the area where their descendants survived as mayors.

To a certain extent the collapse of legitimism was the result of abdication, of the nobles abandoning their traditional leadership. It was also the result of the state and other classes learning to do what they had done and offer an alternative leadership. The nobles were distributed very unequally over France. There were over thirty departments where there were so few of them that it was a simple matter for the state to monopolise the sources of influence or for professional politicians to emerge as intermediaries. This set up a pattern which spread to other areas. Where the nobles could be played off against other forces, or where they gave up the initiative in politics, they were soon supplanted. The process by which the masses came to look elsewhere for personal advantages was occasionally dramatically rapid—1848 witnessed some complete volte-faces

---

[1] See Austin Gough on Catholic Legitimism and liberal Bonapartism in Theodore Zeldin (ed.), *Conflicts in French Society* (1970), 107–17. On the working-class alliance see Denise Lefort, 'Le Parti légitimiste dans les Bouches du Rhône 1830–1848' (D.E.S. mémoire Aix-en-Provence, 1956, unpublished, kindly lent by M. Pierre Guiral).

[2] A. Gough, 'French Legitimism and Catholicism 1851–65' (Oxford, D.Phil. thesis, 1967, unpublished), 127–8.

KINGS AND ARISTOCRATS47

—but more usually it was slow, as new customs were evolved to go with universal suffrage. In some areas the Bonapartists

MAP 10. Noble Mayors in the 1950s. Based on Fauvet and Mendras: *Les Paysans et la politique* (1958), 35

played a crucial role in the destruction of noble influence, but even they did not always have the self-confidence to see how vulnerable that influence was. The Third Republic of course did not have national parties which put up candidates at elections in every single constituency. The electors therefore

often did not have a choice put before them. That is why the
decline of noble influence was both fitful and slow.[1]

Skilful leadership could probably have postponed this decline.
The politically experienced legitimist nobles complained bitterly
about Chambord's inability to provide any form of leadership
at all. They criticised him for refusing to come out clearly in
favour of any particular tactic, for ruling the party despotically,
ignoring the advice of men with far more knowledge of French
conditions than he possessed; for being a bad manager of men,
incapable of putting to good use the great stores of loyalty
offered to him; for disowning all his really active and zealous
followers by his cautious, inactive prudence; for dealing so
unimaginatively with his public relations, a field in which Louis
Napoleon had shown how much could be accomplished with
quite moderate effort. Chambord preferred to organise his
forces so that they remained firmly under his control. He had
a central committee of twelve, known as the Bureau du Roi,
which met, at least in theory, once a week in Paris. Its members
were selected by him, presided over by the duc de Lévis or in his
absence, the duc des Cars or General de Saint Priest (a replica
of des Cars, but rather more sociable and conciliatory). Far
from considering this as an advisory body, he made it clear
that its function was executive, to carry out his instructions,
and to inform him about opinion in France.[2] Under the Third
Republic the organisation was tightened up. France was
divided into three regions, each placed under the control of
one man. In 1877 these three sections were united and put
under the marquis de Dreux-Brézé, through whom all communications to and from Chambord passed. Under him were
departmental committees of twenty members, nominated
directly by Chambord, meeting every two months in the chief
town of the department to discuss the political situation, to
organise elections, collect funds and stimulate the formation of
a local royalist press. Their minutes were sent to Chambord.
Wherever possible, similar sub-committees were set up in each
arrondissement. The press was given a central party line to follow
by the royalist newsagency. This had been founded in 1848

[1] The excellent thesis of Jean Meyer, *La Noblesse bretonne au 18e siècle* (1966), is the
most comprehensive study of the nobility in the modern period.
[2] Membership in Noailles, *Le Bureau du roi* (1932), 96–9.

by a M. de St Chéron, who every evening sent out reports, in the form of letters, on the political news of the day, to provincial newspapers. By 1867 he had a consortium of seven royalist papers subscribing to his service. Some rich legitimists then combined to make it possible for this correspondence to be sent to all royalist papers in the country, which it continued to do till 1883. Between 1873 and 1883 the *Correspondance St. Chéron* was supplemented by a *Correspondance A–Z* (later known as *Les Nouvelles*) which was set up by the royalist deputies to supply the provincial press with summaries of parliamentary proceedings. To this was soon added a daily leading article, designed to be published throughout the country by papers without the resources to employ their own leader-writers. Equally important was the organisation of banquets, which enabled legitimists to meet and to win recruits. The acceptance of an invitation to one of these, at which a toast to the king was drunk, was one of the regular ways by which outsiders came into the royalist ranks. Funds for all these activities were always inadequate. Only in 1879 was a central party treasury organised, on an original basis particularly suited to French conditions, for it was well known that the regular payment of subscriptions was not a national characteristic. The legitimists were invited to lend Chambord money at 3 per cent interest. They would promise not to ask for their money back, until either Chambord died or became king. It was understood that meanwhile Chambord could do as he pleased with the money. Comte Arthur de Rougé was appointed to travel round France collecting for the fund. Thus did Chambord build up a national organisation completely at his command. Rebels could have no place in it.[1]

When the revolution of 1848 broke out, Chambord was presented with a real opportunity, for that revolution was a triumph for the legitimists as well as for the republicans. Lamartine offered Berryer a ministry in his provisional government. At least a hundred legitimists were elected to the constituent assembly. But by themselves they did not have a majority. They needed, at the very least, the support of the Orleanists, the supporters of Louis-Philippe who believed in monarchy, provided it was constitutional monarchy. Why was their alliance never obtained?

[1] Marquis de Dreux-Brézé, *Notes et souvenirs* (1899), 24–30, 43–4, 55–63.

The Orleanists in theory differed from the legitimists on four crucial points. They denied that the king ruled by divine right, as most of the legitimists claimed. It is true they did not go to the opposite extreme of claiming that sovereignty lay with the people—at least in 1830 they defeated a motion proclaiming this. They took some pains, like the English Whigs in 1688, to conceal the fact that Charles X had been evicted: they declared the throne vacant and put Louis-Philippe on it as his hereditary successor. If sovereignty lay anywhere, they would say it lay in parliament. Secondly, they did not wish the king himself to govern. They increased the power of parliament considerably, giving it the right to initiate laws, they abolished hereditary peerages, they deprived Louis-Philippe of the emergency powers Charles X had used in 1830. But they were divided amongst themselves as to exactly how much power the monarch should have. Louis-Philippe and Guizot thought that he should take an active part in government, while Thiers and his followers wanted him to reign but not rule. All were agreed, however, on some form of parliamentary government. Thirdly, the Orleanists declared in 1830 that the Catholic religion was no longer the state religion and that the king should no longer be instituted in a religious ceremony. They included many unbelievers and Protestants among their numbers—though after 1848 many of the former returned to the faith, or at least came to see the value of religion in maintaining order among the masses. But this new emphasis on religion came at a time when religion was losing its hold on the masses. Fourthly, the Orleanists accepted the French Revolution, while the legitimists on the whole did not. The Orleanists, despite their conservatism, were not a party of the *ancien régime*.

At the personal level, the Orleanists' leaders were ambitious men with whom compromise would not be easy, even if agreement could be reached in principle. There was great variety of character and opinion among them. Orleanism often seems to have some of the qualities of a mirage, or of a chameleon. It is difficult both to locate and to characterise.

Louis-Philippe, though he had served in the revolutionary army, was no radical. He had opposed the elder branch as much from personal rivalry as from principle. Though he loved to talk about his youth, he hardly ever mentioned the Revolution, because his memories of it filled him with horror. He had no wish to set Europe on fire; his dearest wish was to be accepted as a real king by the other sovereigns of Europe and a policy of conservatism at home and peace abroad was the way he hoped to obtain this. He greatly enjoyed being king: he had a passion for power and an immense conceit about his political abilities. He felt he must have power also because if he behaved as a constitutional king and left politics to the politicians, they would produce a terrible mess, revolution, war, and he would be overthrown. That is why he worked so hard to influence policy and why he was so absorbed in intrigues with the politicians, to the neglect of the masses. Since he thought the support of Europe was essential to his throne, he concentrated on foreign policy, and indeed read only foreign newspapers. So far from being content with being a constitutional monarch, he regretted bitterly that the rules of the game forbade him to make speeches in parliament. He cultivated his image as a bourgeois king in order to win popularity. 'I know the French. I know how to manage them,' he confided to an ambassador. His umbrella, his famous wig were publicity stunts. His walks through the streets of Paris, unaccompanied and unguarded, were not the sign of a bourgeois nature, but a deliberate policy by a very brave man, for he probably held the record for attempted royal assassinations. A real bourgeois would have stayed at home. He put on the façade of simplicity in order to conceal his intrigues and ambitions. He had a profound belief in the efficacy of flattery as a means of getting his own way, and he used it constantly on his ministers, and on the nation at large —by his bourgeois act. He had a special employee with card indexes to enable him to greet everybody he met with a friendly inquiry about their family. So far from being a bourgeois, he was one of the richest men in France, largely by inheritance from the duc de Bourbon-Penthièvre, Louis XIV's bastard who had been one of the richest men of his day. He devoted a great deal of time after the Revolution to reconstituting his estates, which he succeeded in doing after a lot of litigation. His principal relaxation was the restoration of the crumbling château of Versailles, where he recreated the ancient glory of his ancestors without the expense or danger of war. So far from being a believer in parliamentary government, he devoted his

reign to preventing its establishment, systematically working
to diminish the authority of the prime minister, playing off the
politicians against each other, so that they were unable to
impose the supremacy of parliament upon him.

Louis-Philippe's most distinguished minister, Guizot, who
survived until 1874, was a Protestant of dour and pessimistic
outlook. He was profoundly convinced of the weakness and
inadequacy of human nature. He believed that the eighteenth
century had been very wrong in thinking that man was naturally
good and omnipotent. Guizot conceived of right government as
the fulfilment of the will of God. This meant the rule of reason
and justice—not of popular sovereignty, which Guizot execrated.
The problem for him was not how to discover the popular will
but how to discover what was reasonable; and he believed that
there was an elect minority with the capacity to judge what
was reasonable. The rule of the upper bourgeoisie was justified
in his eyes because it was the rule of merit, of men who demand
not what they want but only what they ought to want. They
represented the rule of duty and of justice, rather than of will
and of rights. Though Guizot won fame as the theorist of
representative government, his use of that phrase was misleading. He envisaged not the voluntary delegation of rights but
on the contrary the exclusion of individual wills from power
and the prevention of universal suffrage and popular sovereignty. For him liberty meant what is just. He distinguished
between political and personal rights. All men were equal to
him in the sense that they had an equal right to be protected
by the state and to behave as they pleased provided they did
not interfere with the rights of others. But political decisions
concern others besides oneself: therefore they should be exercised only by those who were properly qualified. Guizot confused legitimacy and liberty. For him, liberty was obedience
to the will of God, not to that of man. The revolution of 1830
had therefore created no new rights: on the contrary, it had
created the danger of anarchy, so that though Guizot accepted
the revolutions of 1789 and 1830 he thought they had done
enough and that a halt must be called to the revolutionary
spirit. His famous exhortation, 'get rich', meant earn the leisure
and the qualities needed to make you one of the elect who can
see reason: it was the very opposite of the materialism it was

often taken for. Guizot's major reform was in education, because this was the means to knowledge and reason. He did not however carry this to the point of wanting to turn the peasants into educated men but rather to moralise them, to teach them why they should be contented with their lot. It was not the business of the state to interfere in the social or economic order, but only to establish the free conditions in which God's will should be done. 'Real virtue in institutions consists in calling citizens to the duties which they are fit to carry out.' Guizot could not therefore be forced easily into compromise. His theories could be interpreted as being basically a rationalisation of the *status quo*. He was a doctrinaire, who turned accidents into principles, and who achieved his dominance by providing arguments for salving the conscience of the rich. He was possibly a blind politician, but it should not be concluded that he was wildly out of touch with his age. Rather his weakness was that he represented only one aspect of it. His comment on the revolution of 1848 which overthrew his system was, 'God has spoken.'[1]

There is a great difference between the way Orleanism worked and what it came to stand for. Under Louis-Philippe it was authoritarian, based on a narrow electorate of propertied men, with king, parliament and ministers struggling indecisively for supremacy, no party system in any organised sense and even greater ambiguities in its local manifestations. After 1848 it came to stand for liberalism, parliamentary government and the imitation of England.[2] Its opponents condemned it as egotistically middle class, materialist, timid in its foreign policy and blind in its social attitudes. All these descriptions have some truth in them. Orleanism certainly meant different things when it was in power and when it was not. If it could be summarised in the phrase the *juste milieu*, that meant that it stood for compromise, and so its character depended on circumstances. It was the party of the most vocal and fluent section of the community, which interpreted Orleanism in an infinite

[1] There is a valuable guide to the large bibliography on the Orléans monarchy, which falls outside the period covered by this book, in Douglas Johnson, *Guizot* (1963), 443–56.

[2] See in particular Pierre Guiral, *Prévost-Paradol* (1955), which is a rich source of information about liberal thought under Napoleon III in general, as well as an illuminating biography of an important thinker.

variety of ways. Its theorists—many of them men of exceptional distinction—had a more elevated notion of how it should work than the practical politicians and indeed than they themselves had when faced with the problems of power. It is perhaps better to talk therefore about Orleanists than about Orleanism. It will then at once become apparent how inevitably evanescent this party was.

Some members were monarchists. They were Orleanists because they had been dissatisfied with the way the Bourbons had interpreted monarchy. But by judging the personal merits and policy of the king, they made monarchy so fragile and so open to debate that it became very difficult to win really firm support from them. Some were liberals. But as a result they could not reject a liberal empire or a liberal republic and many of them indeed rallied to one or both of these, however reluctantly. Some were personally devoted to the Orléans family. But among these there were men who had also served Napoleon, and indeed many whose families had emerged into fame and wealth in the upheavals of the Revolution and empire: they had other loyalties too. 1830 had been a triumph for Napoleon's followers—exiled in opposition after 1815—as much as for anyone else. As one moves down the social scale, the Orleanists appear increasingly as notables keen to enjoy local influence but anxious for government backing. In one sense they could be allies of the legitimists, in that some of them favoured decentralisation, though they were of course rivals of the legitimists for local influence. But they also needed a more powerful consecration of their status than mere respect for their personal merits and their wealth, which they saw was increasingly challenged by what they called the forces of anarchy. Their complacency concealed a deeper insecurity. They needed a strong government to check the popular and revolutionary threats to their position. The Orléans monarchy had once seemed just right, but out of power it was of little use to them. These notables, who could be classified as the 'friends of government' would make friends with any government that was willing. With appropriate reservations, they supported empire and republic in turn. Men in business, men in industry, men of ambition, men with pretensions, could not for ever work against a centralised state which had so much to offer.

For all these reasons, the Orleanists were always uncertain allies.

They were also allies of diminishing influence. Orleanists were a corps of officers but it was never clear that they had much of an army. Under Louis-Philippe, they had no occasion to apply themselves to winning a mass following. After 1848 they adapted themselves to the new conditions of politics with varying degrees of success. In about 50 per cent of municipalities the mayors in office before the Revolution were re-elected in July 1848: the greatest change occurred in the south and south-west, but in the north and north-west they survived best. Universal suffrage did not at once destroy their rule. Those Orleanists who were expelled in 1848 often returned a year or two later, on the wave of conservatism or panic that swept the provinces. Conscious of the dangers of division, they often united with the legitimists and conservative republicans as part of a 'moderate' alliance, to fight the red menace. In certain regions, the socialists and the Bonapartists succeeded in putting up new leaders to the electorate and throwing the Orleanists out. The Orleanists survived where there was no such challenge to them, and they lasted so long as they knew how to play politics in these new conditions. In the process, they became less and less Orleanist, or at least their Orleanism became increasingly, as it were, a mere perfume that they could not get rid of, implying a certain family origin, a certain distinction and opinions which were once liberal. If Orleanists were men of substance or education, aspiring to consequence and respect in a mass age, there could not, by definition, be many of them.

The expectation of a monarchist restoration after 1848 was widespread, but it was based on a whole series of illusions. Orleanists and legitimists had more things dividing than uniting them. The leaders of both parties knew they could not work with each other. Thiers could never expect office from a monarchy he had done so much to overthrow. Broglie knew there was no chance of real constitutionalism from Chambord. Chambord for his part had enormous difficulty even in talking to the Orleanists, whom he considered to be rebels. When they sent emissaries to him to negotiate, he refused to discuss the basis for a treaty. Exasperated by Napoleon III's success, and relying on the fact that Chambord was childless, the Orleanists offered to help restore him to the throne, putting up with his deficiencies until their own pretender could succeed him on his death. In this way the breach of the royalists might be healed. But they always had reservations, as can be seen from a letter Louis-Philippe's son wrote to Chambord in 1857: 'In expressing to you our sincere desire to see France summon you one day to its throne, in speaking to you of our wish to devote all our efforts to obtain this result, I did not offer you a blind and indefinite support. A preliminary agreement would have been necessary to determine our conditions. Our conditions could be summarised in three points which our convictions and the respect we owe to our family's past, demand that we should never abandon. First, the maintenance of the tricolour flag, which is today in the eyes of France the symbol of the new state of society—the incarnation of the principles consecrated since 1789. Secondly, the re-establishment of constitutional government. Thirdly, the agreement of the national will to this re-establishment as well as to the restoration of the dynasty.'[1]

The longer the restoration was postponed, the slimmer were its chances. The plots for a legitimist military *coup* in 1849 and for an Orleanist one in 1851 never materialised. Once Napoleon III was in power there was no chance of success in such an enterprise, particularly since the emperor gave the royalists plenty of freedom to continue their agitation and refrained from driving them to desperate acts. In 1871 at last their chance came. The National Assembly had a royalist majority. But this was highly deceptive. The nation elected them because it wanted peace, because the Bonapartists were associated with defeat and the republicans wanted to carry on the war. Had the royalists then succeeded in bringing about a restoration, the nation might well have refused to accept their act. Civil war might well have followed. The failure to bring Chambord to the throne, which is so often explained in personal and parliamentary terms, was probably inevitable, given the way such large sections of society had assumed a new attitude to politics since 1830. The negotiations themselves were in any case conducted on a basis of mutual ignorance and equivocation, so that their collapse in 1873 was not surprising. The dramatic announcement at the last minute that Henry V (as Chambord

[1] Marquis de Noailles, *Le Bureau du roi 1848–73* (1932), 148.

was to be known) refused to abandon his ancestral white flag should not be interpreted as a sudden caprice which ended a movement on the verge of success. On the contrary, Chambord's attachment to his flag had long been known, but it had been concealed by his declaring that it was something he would decide upon after his return and by his seclusion which prevented people from realising just how much it meant to him. In 1871 Chambord had stated that he was determined not to accept the tricolour, but his entourage kept the fact secret to prevent the negotiations from coming to a halt. In reality the negotiations never had a chance, even before they had begun.

This insurmountable difficulty to a restoration—because it was symbolically very important—was matched by equal difficulties on the Orleanist side. The reconciliation which took place between Chambord and the Orleanist pretender, the comte de Paris, did not have the full support of the Orleanists. At least a quarter of the Orleanist deputies in the assembly of 1871 preferred a republic to a monarchy with Chambord as king, whatever guarantees he might give. The duc de Broglie, it is said, was so repelled by Chambord's authoritarianism that he hoped to make such impossible demands on Chambord as a condition of restoration, that the latter would abdicate in favour of the comte de Paris. The duc d'Aumale, fourth son of Louis-Philippe, a man of great personal distinction, sometime Governor-General of Algeria, and a man also of great personal wealth, intrigued against the restoration not only of Chambord but of Paris too, hoping that if it proved impossible to restore either, then the assembly would elect him president of the republic or lieutenant-general of the kingdom. His ambition was to be a stadtholder. He issued a declaration that if France preferred a republic, he was ready to serve it. He got himself elected to parliament in 1871 and mixed with all the deputies as an equal, in a proper republican manner. When he was elected to the French Academy in 1871, he asked to be addressed as monsieur, not monseigneur. He refused to visit Chambord and left most of his money to the nation, not to his family.

Finally, even the personal reconciliation between Chambord and Paris in August 1873 was not as complete as was thought. Chambord consented to see Paris on condition that the latter made an agreed public statement to him, in which were to be included the words that Paris came 'to resume his place in the family'. Paris at the last moment omitted this phrase and substituted one that Chambord 'would have no competitor among members of his family'. The political divisions, that is to say, continued. At their meeting, not a word was uttered about politics. Their reconciliation was superficial. It was perhaps just as well that it all came to nothing. Chambord would have caused far more confusion had he pretended to be what he was not. His honesty spared France a second revolution of 1830. But his failure in 1873 made him more suspicious than ever of co-operating with people who did not share his attitudes and who wished to change him. He ordered his followers to abstain from all electoral alliances. Many of his followers on their side, disheartened by his obstinacy, withdrew from politics, never to re-emerge. When Chambord died in 1883, his party was a weak relic of what it had been, particularly when compared to the republicans, now firmly entrenched in power. His more die-hard supporters proclaimed Don Juan of Spain, who had married Chambord's sister, pretender, creating a new legitimist religion, but one without practical significance. The great majority of legitimists, however, acknowledged the comte de Paris as the new leader. Legitimists and Orleanists were at last united. This ought to have meant that the forces of royalism were greatly strengthened, but the legitimists were not keen to have much to do with Paris. Chambord's organisation was wound up and the funds he had collected were paid back to the subscribers. A new era was opened up.

The comte de Paris, who was pretender from 1883 till his death in 1894, had far more vigour, intelligence and suppleness in him. He was the son of Louis-Philippe's very promising son the duc d'Orléans, who had been noted for his energy and liberalism, and of a Protestant German princess, though he was brought up as a pious Catholic. Born in 1838, he was, from the age of ten, educated in England, for which he developed a great affection and admiration: it was not without significance that he spent most of his life there, whereas Chambord had pre-ferred to live in Austria. He was a well-travelled man. He visited the U.S.A. and served in General MacClellan's army in the Civil War. He toured the cotton factories of Lancashire, which stimulated an interest in social problems. In 1869 he published a book on the trade unions of England, advocating participation in profits. He welcomed as 'one of the finest pieces of progress of our century . . . the raising of charity to the status of a social duty and a political right'. When allowed back to France in 1872, he toured the factories there too. He appeared to be one of the first socialist millionaires—socialist perhaps only in a rather loose sense, but very much a millionaire. He had an income, it was said, of 500,000 francs (£20,000) a year, which increased very considerably thanks to the legacies from royalist supporters, culminating in one bequest of 20 million francs from Madame de Galliera in 1888.[1]

The comte de Paris was the very opposite of Chambord also in that he was above all an opportunist who, far from adhering to his principles as Chambord had done, was determined to broaden his appeal as widely as possible. He cloaked his policy, which came near to being power at any price, beneath a grave and pious exterior and a family life of irreproachable chastity: he had all the appearances, someone said, of a scholarly German professor, but he was profoundly ambitious. To begin with, he converted himself from an Orleanist into a legitimist, in an attempt to make the fusion of the royalists into a reality. After having made his submission to Chambord in 1873, he became an intransigent upholder of heredity and rejected all attempts to put forward his candidature in place of Chambord's. On Chambord's death he assumed the title of Philippe VII instead of Louis-Philippe II. He attempted to unite under him the Catholics who suspected his anticlerical antecedents, the Protestants who expected him to remember his mother's religion, and the sceptics who wanted toleration; to win back the conservatives who had gone over to the republic with Thiers, and at the same time to keep legitimists and Orleanists loyal. It was perhaps an impossible task, but by February 1884 the fusion of the royalists had been successfully achieved in at least 24 departments. On the other hand, the legitimists remained aloof in at least 13 departments and in 13 others there was no

[1] Marquis de Flers, *Le Comte de Paris* (1888), 114; Marcel Barrière, *Les Princes d'Orléans* (1933), 182–3. Eugène Dufeuille (who was in charge of distributing the comte de Paris's subsidies to the royalist press), *Réflexions d'un monarchiste* (1900).

royalist organisation or activity at all. But he captured the
royalist press: 130 royalist newspapers supported him, against
only 13 hostile ones.[1]

Secondly, for Chambord's policy of abstention, Paris substituted one of vigorous action. He became an energetic,
hard-working party leader. He realised that the majority of
Frenchmen were not royalist. It was just possible that they were
conservative. So in the elections of 1885 he ordered the monarchists to stand not as such, but as conservatives, to carry out
a new fusion between monarchism and all the forces of the
right, on the basis of the widespread dissatisfaction with the
republic, its ineffectual parliamentarianism, its financial deficits,
its expensive colonial policy, its menacing anticlericalism. In
October 1885 his *Union conservatrice* obtained 177 seats against
the 129 won by the republicans. This brilliant victory, however,
was made possible by the dissension of the republicans who,
rallying together in the second ballot, succeeded in winning
the elections as a whole. Replying to his threat, they sent him
into exile.

But, from Sheen House near Richmond, he pressed on with
his policy of a programme which would offer something to as
many people as possible. To those who were simply conservative,
he promised to re-establish order and firm government, but to
avoid reaction, to reconcile the principles of historic tradition
with modern institutions, to bring in a monarchy which could
be freely accepted by the nation but which would not be a
slave to 'the sovereignty of numbers'. To the Catholics he
offered liberty of education and the end of persecution. To
please the Bonapartists he proposed to hold a plebiscite, or at
least to summon a constituent assembly, to approve his restoration: indeed he borrowed large sections of their programme.
Attempting to benefit from the disillusionment with parliamentary government (once so dear to the Orleanists, but taken
over by the republicans), he said that universal suffrage made
constitutional monarchy as it had existed between 1815 and
1848 out of date. Parliament would no longer be supreme: the
king would govern with the co-operation of the chambers (a

---

[1] Samuel M. Osgood, *French Royalism under the Third and Fourth Republics* (The
Hague, 1960), 36–7. In 1892, however, an anonymous article on 'Les Anciens
Partis' talked of about 250 newspapers being royalist. *Le Figaro* (2 Apr. 1892), 59.

phrase to be found also in Bonapartist manifestos) and ministers would no longer be at the mercy of majorities. He kept quiet about divine right—and also about his economic and social policy.[1]

The comte de Paris did not wish, however, to return by means of a *coup d'état*. He was not made for conspiracy or violence. He was determined that if he got the throne he should be strong enough to keep it. His hope therefore was that the republic would collapse and that he would then be the man to whom France would look to end the ensuing chaos. In 1888 he played his last card to bring about this situation. Under the influence of two former Bonapartists who had become royalists, the president of the *Union conservatrice*, baron de Mackau, and the journalist Arthur Meyer, he decided to back General Boulanger. A leading royalist lady, the duchesse d'Uzès, put up a large sum of money to pay for the great adventure in which the general would throw the republicans out of office and end parliamentary government. At the last moment, of course, Boulanger lost his nerve. The collapse of his movement was the greatest blow the royalists had suffered since 1873. The prospect of a restoration, which had re-emerged as a possibility, ceased for ever to be a serious one. Not only was there a widespread desertion from the royalists as a defeated party, but there was a fatal split among the royalists themselves. The Orleanist wing, for whom parliamentary government was sacred, realised that the pretender no longer stood for the principles they cherished. They wanted constitutional monarchy and not just monarchy, and the republicans now appeared as the true defenders of parliaments. The Orleanists in any case could hardly continue to support a pretender who, infuriated by their refusal to obey his instructions to support Boulanger, publicly damned them with disgrace, abruptly ending many old personal friendships. Paris was at the same time equally enraged with those who had advised him to join the Boulangists, so that the relations in the royalist party became strained in the extreme. Paris had been an able pretender, but adversity revealed his limitations. He could not bear to take the blame for the disaster and did not know how to maintain hope in his defeated ranks. As one who knew him well wrote: 'He could not bear to be

[1] Text in Flers, 406–10.

contradicted; he enjoyed flattery; he could never admit that
he was wrong. Even the superiority of certain scientists and
great scholars offended him as though he was their rival.'[1]
Perhaps in fairness to him it ought to be added that in this same
fateful year of 1889 his doctôrs told him he had an incurable
disease and could not last long.

Monarchism died finally in the *ralliement*, when the republicans dropped their attacks on the Church and offered the
supporters of monarchy and empire union against socialism.
Pope Leo XIII urged Catholics to accept the republic, which
had proved its solidity. The comte de Paris himself, while
resenting this papal interference, admitted that the royalist
cause was hopeless and put his faith in religion: there was no
chance, he thought, until France became Christian once more.
After 1894, therefore, royalism ceased to be a major force in
politics. It will be seen elsewhere how it was reincarnated in the
Action Française, but that was in response to new conditions,
which require separate examination.

The pretenders who succeeded the comte de Paris stood at
the very fringes of political life. The duc d'Orléans (1869–1926)
educated at Sandhurst, a specialist on hunting in Nepal and
interested more in food and women than in politics, was so
lazy, superstitious and indecisive that he could not be considered a serious pretender. His opinions were anachronistic to
the point of dreaming of the absolute monarchy of the Mero-
vingians, and being unable to bear the mention of democracy.
His entourage, led by the comte Eugène de Lur-Saluces, the
owner of the Château d'Yquem, was composed almost entirely
of legitimists. He had followers who wished to link his name
with the nationalist movement and present him in this refur-
bished guise, but with little success.[2] In 1896 the police estimated
that there were royalist committees in only thirty departments.
In 1908 an article on the royalist movement suggested that
hardly one elector out of ten would know the name of the
pretender. The activities of the duc d'Orléans became a matter
mainly for the social columns of the *Gaulois*. Though he reluctantly came to accept Action Française in 1911, he was never its

[1] Barrière, 161–3.
[2] Eugène Godefroy, *Quelques années de politique royaliste: du ralliement à la haute
Cour 1892–1899* (1900), xii–xiii, 213.

driving force.[1] The duc de Guise, who was the next pretender, 1926–40, led a retired life. His son the comte de Paris (born in 1908) for a time had hopes of reviving the royalist cause. He started a newspaper in 1934, *Le Courrier royal*, resuscitated the royalists' organisation, repudiated Action Française, had himself interviewed repeatedly by the press and published a book expounding his programme in detail. During the war, there was a plan to proclaim him head of a provisional government in Algiers, but Eisenhower scotched it. An opinion poll held on 1 January 1945 showed that only 6 per cent of the nation thought that the royalist party had an important role in France and about 75 per cent thought not.[2]

[1] E. Dimnet, 'The Neo-Royalist Movement in France', *Nineteenth Century* (Aug. 1908), 287–93. Georges Cerbeland Salagnac, *Quatre Règnes en exil* (1947). The Action Française will be dealt with in volume 2, but there is great deal of information relevant to the pretenders in the excellent standard work by Eugen Weber, *Action Française* (Stanford, Cal., 1962).

[2] Comte de Paris, *Essai sur le gouvernement de demain* (1936); Osgood, 137–81, has a good account of this later history.

3. The Genius in Politics

FRANCE in the nineteenth century cannot be understood without an appreciation of the role of the utopians, any more than the Revolution of 1789 can be without a knowledge of the *philosophes* of the Enlightenment. The utopians were historically important because they introduced the *genius* into politics. The genius became the nucleus of a new class, challenging the state, demanding power and threatening to dismember the traditional centralised authority, an élite like the nobles, and with similar pretensions. Genius, men generally believed in this period, could not be acquired; it was something that one was born with, but, as with nobility, one could associate with it and become assimilated to it. One of the marks of genius was that one was understood by other geniuses. So those who accepted their leadership could enter into this new class of *illuminés*. Against the nobles, who spoke as the representatives of local community life, the geniuses spoke in the name of a new community of the enlightened. The genius indeed was a new kind of individual ideal. Hitherto the chivalric hero, the saint, the courtier, the *honnête homme*, had been universal models, but only for private conduct. The attainment of that status brought self-gratification, honour and public respect, but no political power. The genius was much more dangerous. Until the eighteenth century *génie* had meant simply talent or skill. But with Diderot the genius was held up as an exceptional apparition, standing outside his time, almost outside his species, whose importance was that he could perceive truths others could not. He was therefore not subject to common standards, ethical rules or controls. He produced great ideas and 'every great idea', as Lamartine said, 'is a struggle against society, a revolution'.

The basis for this new role for the intellectuals had been laid in the eighteenth century. Around 1700 the 'man of letters' usually lived in a state of insecurity and constraint, shackled by an arbitrary censorship exercised simultaneously by the king, the *parlement* and the Sorbonne. He often had to use pseudonyms or conceal his identity altogether. Only in the second half of the century did a few of them manage to live by their pens. These successes did a good deal to raise the status of what was becoming almost a profession. The government began employing writers to influence public opinion, 'to prepare the way for legislation', as Moreau described his own function. But it was slow to accept advice from them. 'It is not up to an obscure writer,' said L'Averdy, 'who often has not a hundred *écus* to his name, to indoctrinate persons in office.' A book about *L'Homme de lettres* published in 1764, by one of them, admitted with regret that they were 'kept outside the state'.[1] The first stage in their ascent was for them to win honour, respect and security. They did not think of power yet. They solicited the subsidies, pensions and presents, of tiny amounts, which the government gave them—a mark at once of patronage, disdain and fear. They were for long treated essentially as entertainers. Voltaire complained of the 'excessive disparagement attached to this equivocal state' of the writer. Montesquieu was appalled when he learnt that his son was developing a taste for learning: 'He will never be anything', he exclaimed in horror, 'but a man of letters, an eccentric like me.' He had planned to buy him a state office, the mark of respectability (which he of course enjoyed also, as member of a *parlement*). However, as the censorship relaxed, books on politics gave the writers increasing authority. Foreign admirers in particular did much to raise their status. It was the *philosophes*, not the nobles, whom the visitors from abroad came to see. That was one reason why the writers assumed with such vigour the mission of French culture abroad. Frederick II invited Voltaire to his table, to the horror of the French king. On the eve of the Revolution in 1778, Mercier wrote, 'the influence of writers is such that they can today proclaim their power and no longer disguise the legitimate authority they have over men's minds'.[2]

The Revolution confirmed their power in a dramatic way, but not least because its enemies accused them of having been a principal cause of it. Of course historians no longer believe that the theories of the *philosophes* produced the collapse of the *ancien régime*. Much more emphasis is laid on the aristocratic revival and the attempt by the nobles to recapture power from

[1] 'En dehors de l'état': Garnier, *L'Homme de lettres* (1764), chapter 5.
[2] L. S. Mercier, *De la littérature et des littérateurs* (1778).

the king. After the catastrophe they brought about, the nobles put the blame on the writers. However, even at this apparent zenith of their influence, when the democratic ideas some of them preached introduced immense new forces into the political arena, the writers did not claim any direct power for themselves. They had seen themselves as advisers to those in power. Voltaire had supported enlightened despotism. Montesquieu had supported the *parlements* against the king. If they envisaged power, it was only very indirectly. 'If opinion is queen of the world,' wrote Voltaire, 'the *philosophes* govern that queen.' This was the germ from which the pretensions of the nineteenth-century utopians developed. Until then they had not entirely emerged from their inferiority complex or from the antique pretence that love of letters was incompatible with cupidity or ambition.[1]

The literary romantics rationalised this complex into the doctrine that the genius was inevitably doomed to be misunderstood. The genius was a prophet, but a prophet in the wilderness. They accepted that he should be met by incomprehension, that his lot should be suffering and even martyrdom, and that he should obtain acknowledgement of his worth only from posterity. Stendhal thought people would start reading him only forty years after his death.[2] But Saint-Simon broke away from this arrogant modesty by greatly expanding the idea of genius. To the skills of the man of letters and the imagination of the artist he added the new knowledge and new prestige of the scientist. Combining these he produced what was in effect the intellectual. He claimed for him the spiritual power in the state. The romantics had thought principally of themselves as geniuses; it was a tiny group they placed at the apex. Saint-Simon certainly thought he too was divinely endowed, but he greatly broadened the class of those who had the gifts and the wisdom to lead mankind. In effect, he proposed the intellectuals as a new clergy, and not much smaller in number. The amazing thing was that he won

[1] Peter Gay, *Voltaire's Politics* (Princeton, N.J., 1959), 34, 93; Maurice Pellisson, *Les Hommes de lettres au 18ᵉ siècle* (1911), 41, 50, 239–40; C. P. Duclos, *Considérations sur les mœurs de ce siècle* (1751), 263; Lucien Brunel, *Les Philosophes et l'Académie française* (1884); D. T. Pottinger, *The French Book Trade in the Ancien Régime 1500–1791* (Cambridge, Mass., 1958), 353.
[2] G. R. Besser, *Balzac's Concept of Genius* (Geneva, 1969).

disciples of this kind, who did constitute a visible élite and who succeeded in making their mark. His proposals for the rule of the intellectuals were not just a dream, they became almost a reality. The Saint-Simonians were, in some ways, a new aristocracy.

The utopians, more generally, effected the democratisation of genius. New schemes for the reorganisation of society pullulated in large numbers. The socialist utopians, of whom there are about a dozen major ones, are only the better known of a vast host of writers in similar vein, but with lesser talent. New religions, mysticisms, visions, prophecies—new ideas of all kinds and even more new mixtures of old ideas—acquired respectability, when established authority was no longer powerful enough to condemn them to ridicule or oblivion. The Revolution suggested that change was perfectly possible, that utopias need not be purely theoretical. It was now open to any man to have ideas and publish and propagate them. It is in this way that the intellectual in politics arrived. His self-consciousness was stimulated all the more by the fact that he won hostility as well as esteem. In his favour the phrenologists claimed that genius could be recognised in the conformation of the skull. The doctors, however, defending the superiority of their profession, replied that there was no physiological distinction between genius and madness. Dr. Lelut decried genius as a form of hallucination. Dr. Moreau de Tours called genius a neurosis: 'The constitution of many men of genius', he wrote, 'is really the same as that of idiots.' This was a battle, between the genius and the philistine, which was to continue unabated, and to be a permanent limitation on the power of the intellectuals.[1]

The utopians were important also because of their special relationship with public opinion—a relationship which could be compared again with the links of the nobility with the local community. The majority of utopians—and most notably Fourier and Proudhon—became popular because they tried to give expression to widely felt aspirations. There were some precedents for this in the eighteenth century. Rousseau in particular had obtained an immediate echo from a vast audience which recognised something of themselves in him or

[1] See my *France*, vol. 2, part 3, on Anxiety.

reflected his mood. But though most of the *philosophes* had seen themselves as leaders if not creators of public opinion, they had been primarily concerned with creating the conditions in which public opinion could express itself freely; they had on the whole sought to influence governments rather than to investigate the problems of the ordinary man. The latter was the second stage, and the utopians gave a great deal of attention to it. It is important to assess the extent to which the utopians were speaking for a public opinion which pre-existed, and the extent to which they created a new kind of consciousness. This is difficult to do. The utopian message was taken up like a popular song, whose tune one heard repeated everywhere, even if the words were often got wrong. The analogy with songs is not purely metaphorical. A lot of these new ideas were propagated in songs.[1] No one has yet made a proper study of these. They might well contain clues for the formulation of an archaeology of popular sentiment. The utopians were thus significant at two levels, that of the intellectuals and that of the masses. With them a new range of public opinion made itself felt in politics. The extent to which the ideas of the utopians were acceptable in 1848 can be seen from the way so many of them were spontaneously elected to the Constituent Assembly. Buchez was its first president. Louis Blanc and Hippolyte Carnot were members of its first provisional government. Pierre Leroux, Proudhon, the revolutionaries Barbès and Martin Bernard, the Fourierist Considérant were all deputies. It will be seen in due course just how widespread was the participation of their disciples in public life.

The intellectuals had a vital role to play in many of these utopias, because one of the characteristics of the utopias was that they were designed to unite mankind, in a moral harmony of which the intellectuals would inevitably be the priests. The utopians reacted against the eighteenth century's destructive criticism. They represented the longing for order and peace after the Revolution. Unlike the *philosophes* who saw the Church as their great enemy, the utopians were much more favourable towards religion, and they sought only to reform Catholicism. They hoped that this new religion—which they

---

[1] *La Chanson française* (3 vols., published by Éditions Sociales, Classiques du peuple), especially vol. 2, *Le Pamphlet du pauvre*, edited by Pierre Brochon (1957).

variously called the new Christianity or the Religion of Humanity—would provide the spiritual cement to hold the society of the future together. So whereas liberty had been the watchword of the previous century, fraternity was that of utopians. Fraternity was expressed in religious terms as association or co-operation, as opposed to capitalist exploitation. The utopians were concerned with the whole mass of the population and wanted to bring everybody in to share in the new era. But because they laid so much stress on the moral or spiritual basis of this unification, they—as formulators of the new creed—held a key position.

Saint-Simon (1760–1825) was not only a genius who sometimes resembled a madman; he actually spent a period in a sanatorium for mental diseases and received treatment from the celebrated Dr. Pinel. His political ideas represent only one part of a life filled with a large variety of hare-brained schemes. Having lost his mother at the age of seven, he spent his youth torn between rebellion against an aged and authoritarian father and guilt at not deserving affection but repeatedly pleading for it. His was first of all a philosophy for orphans. He had passionate relationships with a Prussian count and former ambassador, with whose money he became a speculator in national lands, and then with a succession of young men, whom he adopted as his pupils. His life was a constant search for patrons to back him and collaborators to assist him in the elaboration of his ideas. He was a man of great warmth, with an ardent longing for its reciprocation, never hesitating to beg for it, but always confident in his own genius and ever optimistic, except for an attempted suicide in a moment when he felt particularly abandoned. His character was reflected in his preaching of fraternity. The summary of his New Christianity was: 'Love one another and help one another.' This plea, which historians tend to interpret in political or religious terms, may have received such widespread adhesion because it was also an appeal against the coldness of contemporary family life, by a generation no longer ashamed of its emotions. 'To do great things', said Saint-Simon, 'it is necessary to be passionate.' He might have been the founder of modern sociology, as some now claim, or even a precursor of *Planification*[1]

[1] Pierre Ansart, *Sociologie de Saint-Simon* (1970); François Perroux and P. M.

but that is no excuse for assuming that his thinking was pre-dominantly rational. His mysticism, illuminism and apocalyptic style were an essential part of him, as they were of so many of his contemporaries. The importance of Saint-Simon, indeed, is that he helped to shift thinking from the theoretical to the emotional.

He also turned away from the political interests of the eighteenth century, to a stress on social and economic forces. He was not interested in party politics, or in increasing the par-ticipation of people in government. Progress for him involved practical achievements: the building of roads, and massive investment for great public works. The aim of every institution should be 'the moral, intellectual and physical amelioration of the most numerous and poorest class'. The way to do this was to stimulate economic development and public education. The condition of the exercise of the rights of citizenship should be the passing of an examination on the 'national catechism'. Saint-Simon was not a democrat. He wished to deprive those who were idle of their leadership of society: the idle nobles, the 'metaphysicians and lawyers' were his great enemies. He pro-posed to give power to the *industriels*, i.e. to those who worked, which included all classes, but he expected policy to be formed by the 'most important' of these, the great manufacturers and leading financiers, merchants and agriculturalists. He never made it clear how they would be chosen, except that he thought that constitutions should reflect economic realities. He wished to abolish inheritance, but not property, nor inequality pro-duced by merit. His slogan was: 'To each according to his capacities, and to each capacity according to his works.' This was meritocracy—and some say technocracy, the foreshadowing of a managerial revolution. But Saint-Simon in his last years moved away from this, since the rich were not appreciating him, and he turned increasingly to the working class. The ambiguities in his theories were never resolved, and that is why he won support from every class except the nobility, to whom alone he was constantly hostile. The ambiguity is partly explicable, however, because government was a matter of little importance to him. He looked forward to the virtual elimination of the

Schuhl, *Saint-simonisme et pari pour l'industrie XIX–XXᵉ siècles* (*Économie et Sociétés*, Apr. 1970).

state, since a harmonious social order would deprive it of most of its usual functions. He was opposed to government regulation; his method of producing change was not revolution, nor violence, but persuasion, enlightenment, and a free rein to economic forces. His ideal was peace (whereas governments fought wars) and prosperity (and governments exacted taxes). This deep-rooted hostility to the state will be seen again and again throughout this period—balancing the fawning on it. Saint-Simon contained the contradiction within him: he begged the king to become 'the first of the industrialists'.

Though Saint-Simon stressed economics, and said that politics was 'the science of production', he also thought that no society could exist without 'common moral ideas'. He wanted scientists and artists to enjoy a power equal to that of industrialists, to provide the latter with inspiration, and to rouse the masses to greater exertions for the mutual good. Whereas the eighteenth-century *philosophes* had seen men as more or less the same, and therefore equal, Saint-Simon, following the doctors Cabanis and Bichat who wrote in the early nineteenth century, believed in their diversity and uniqueness. There were different types of men, suited to different occupations. That is why he distinguished between these three classes. In his view people were not concerned with equality but with the expression of their individuality. Society must therefore aim only for harmony among these inequalities. The equality of the eighteenth century had brought brutal competition and strife, which he wished to eliminate. His whole doctrine was a reaction against the destructiveness of the *philosophes*. The age of criticism was over: Saint-Simon wanted an age of harmony. Hence the importance of the intellectuals, whose duty it was to minister to the new spiritual unity, replacing the corrupt clergy but in some ways perpetuating their functions. The problem of conflict within this new order was never analysed by Saint-Simon, and this might be a justification for calling him a utopian. He blithely assumed employers were the natural leaders of the workers. But this was a problem other utopians tried to solve.[1]

[1] Saint-Simon's main works have recently been republished in 6 volumes (1969–70); there is also a good selection in his *Œuvres choisies* (3 vols., Brussels, 1859). An excellent biography is by Frank E. Manuel, *The New World of Henri Saint-Simon* (Cambridge, Mass., 1956). For a full guide see Jean Walch, *Bibliographie de Saint-Simon* (1967).

Just as Saint-Simon's thought passed through several phases, so the movement which developed his ideas was equally varied. Saint-Simonianism, as it flourished in the mid nineteenth century, laid stress on religion, financial investment, and the emancipation of both the proletariat and that class of whom so little had hitherto been heard in the writings of political theorists, women. But this programme failed to win a mass following. Though bits of it were absorbed into other mass movements, Saint-Simonianism remained the creed of an élite. It was a very remarkable and influential élite. It included about a hundred graduates of the École Polytechnique. Engineers, managers, financiers and writers adopted it with a fervid enthusiasm. As a result, one aspect of it was magnified and it has appeared ever since as a doctrine for technocrats. But some of these men also had emotional problems, and they gave Saint-Simonianism ˉan even more esoteric slant. This was another reason why it did not become a mass movement. These particularly active disciples were men who had failed to enter the traditional ruling class; a good number of them were Jews. Olinde Rodrigues had wanted to go to the École Normale but had been prevented by his Jewish birth and had had to become a stockbroker instead. Gustave d'Eichtal—in turn a Jew, a Catholic and a Saint-Simonian—wrote in 1866 that 'there has perhaps not been a single person among the Saint-Simonians who was not urged to join by some family trouble'.[1] Bazard was illegitimate and had been maltreated as a consequence. Enfantin had been stopped from joining the King's Bodyguard by the bankruptcy of his father. Saint-Simonianism was financed by wealthy men who devoted their inheritances to preaching that inheritance should be abolished.

It was above all Enfantin (1796–1864) who turned Saint-Simonianism into a religion, and almost a monastic order. He was a man of great personal beauty and quite exceptional charm, able to exercise a magnetic fascination, so that highly intelligent men worshipped him and listened respectfully while he talked absolute nonsense. For in a prolonged phase of mystical enthusiasm, Enfantin introduced the strangest ideas into the doctrine. He got his disciples to proclaim him *Le Père*—

---

[1] G. Weill, *L'École saint-simonienne. Son histoire, son influence jusqu'à nos jours* (1896), 21, 47 n.

the 'industrial pope'—a title he had embroidered on his clothes. He got them to follow him first into monastic seclusion at Menilmontant, and then on a fantastic journey to the East in search of the ideal woman, *La Mère*. He got them to wear strange uniforms, which buttoned at the back, to remind them that people were interdependent. The managing director of Le Creusot, the giant ironworks, resigned his job to follow him, in company with distinguished officers, mining engineers, civil servants and a professor of medicine. Enfantin's gifts modified the nature of the movement. He was above all an unctuous confessor, and in no way made to be the leader of a rabble. He therefore objected to his supporters mixing too much with the unconverted world. He preferred a closed society, held together by ardent emotion. The life in this community was 'intense, the feelings of fraternity touching, the exaltation of hopes prodigious; the faithful tasted pure joy and knew unbridled enthusiasm'. Inevitably, however, this put into the background any idea of associating the workers in ending the exploitation of man by man, which represented the socialist side of Saint-Simon's original doctrine. A proposal by a few in 1839 to start a *Social Party* was rejected. Internal conflicts brought an end to this mystical phase. By 1848 Saint-Simonianism had no organisation.[1]

The importance of Saint-Simonianism in the future was to lie in the way of thinking it had imprinted in their youth on many subsequently important individuals. Its direct influence, however, has generally been exaggerated. It is true that in 1848 the ministry of education was run by three Saint-Simonians,[2] but it left no permanent achievements. Their short-lived National School of Administration to produce higher civil servants may look like a Saint-Simonian attempt to train a new ruling class based on merit, just as the lectures for women which they authorised at the Collège de France seemed to implement Saint-Simon's new deal for the female sex. However, when in March 1848 some sixty Saint-Simonians held a meeting to decide what concerted action they should take, they could

[1] Hippolyte Carnot, 'Sur le Saint-Simonisme', *Séances et travaux de l'Académie des sciences morales et politiques*, 28 (1887), 122–55; S. Charlety, *Histoire du saint-simonisme* (1931); Léon Brothier, *Du Parti social* (1839), quoted by Weill, 97 n.

[2] Hippolyte Carnot, assisted by Jean Reynaud and Édouard Charton.

reach no agreement. The master's doctrines had been too variously interpreted; there had been a complete failure to establish priorities. Gustave d'Eichtal thought the moment had come to found a religious democracy, but as a first step he urged the erection of a statue of Moses in the Place de la Concorde. Olinde Rodrigues drew up a constitution for the new republic, abolishing the right to make wills, limiting inheritance to the direct line only, proposing participation in profits for the workers and political rights for women, but at the same time he gave the directing role in the running of the country to the University and the Institut. Prosper Enfantin, for his part, suggested that the state should buy up all the railways, then the mines and then all the factories making products for the railways; and it should take over industrial planning. However, he also said the time had come to establish the Kingdom of God. Since this proved to be not immediately practicable, he founded a newspaper instead, *Le Crédit*. It lost him a great deal of money. He supported Cavaignac but, when he failed, rallied to Louis Napoleon, hoping that he would be strong enough to advance the cause of industrialism. Enfantin's notion that he was called by Providence to give a new place in the social order to the proletariat and to women therefore did not get very far. He ended up a relatively minor business man.

The Saint-Simonians never ran the new industry of the Second Empire, as is too often believed. They never achieved their objective of financing expansion by inflation. The railways they had a hand in were balanced by others in which they played no part. They influenced Napoleon III's Algerian policy perhaps, and also his Mexican adventure, but so did others. Napoleon III cannot really be called one of them. However, they had always used the press in a particularly vigorous manner: they were experts in public relations, and what they bequeathed was not an actual achievement but a myth. Their greatest triumph probably was that some of their doctrines ceased to bear the specific imprint of Saint-Simonianism because everybody came to believe in them.[1]

Charles Fourier (1772–1837) represented a different stratum

[1] Enfantin left enough money for the *Œuvres de Saint-Simon et d'Enfantin* to be published after his death in 47 volumes (1865–78). Cf. Crampon, *La France saint-simonienne à son déclin* (1867).

of society. He looked at the world from an entirely different viewpoint. He was a humble commercial traveller and clerk; his utopia was essentially one for the small man, the consumer, the petty bourgeois. He claimed his discoveries had been started, like Newton's, by an apple: when he saw apples being sold in Paris for a hundred times the price they fetched in the district where they were grown, 'I began to suspect that there must be something radically wrong in the industrial mechanism.' At the age of seven he was punished for telling the truth by his father, a draper, who declared he would never be any good in business; it was then that he swore a Hannibal's oath of eternal hate against commerce. This later hardened into a criticism of the whole social order for which he proposed a complete transformation. 'Harmony' must replace the antagonism of civilisation. Co-operation must replace blind and vicious competition. The parasites of commerce must be done away with. The toil of the peasant, both stupefying and inefficient, must be made a joy. Man was naturally good but society as at present organised corrupted him; it alone was responsible for the conflict between private and public interest, for the repressions and frustrations he suffered. Fourier's purpose was not to improve man, but to liberate him, to allow him to do what he pleased. Unlike his contemporary Robert Owen, who hoped to modify human nature by modifying its environment, Fourier wished to make the environment suit human nature, to satisfy human needs and passions. He denied that any of these passions were vicious and needed to be suppressed (in what was a remarkable foreshadowing of modern psychological theories); in the harmonious state he dreamed of, all of them could be expressed and reconciled. Men wanted principally to eat and drink well, to work in very moderate amounts, at tasks they enjoyed—and not necessarily in the same occupation all the time. They wanted independence and security.

Fourier invented a scheme to achieve all this, without strife, without leaving anyone out and without dispossessing the minority who were well-to-do in the existing order. The world should be organised in *phalanstères*. These would be communities of about 1,600 people, of every variety of age, wealth and character, for the more variety there is, the quicker would harmony be established between them. Ideally the number should be 1,620, for Fourier calculated there were no fewer than 405 different temperaments in each sex. These *phalanstères* would consist of a farm (which would make each one self-sufficient) surrounding a large building (rather like a large eighteenth-century country house or Oxford college in appearance). The building would contain dining-rooms, common rooms, studies and a library; one wing would house the workshops; the rest would be divided into living accommodation, of various types, from the humble room to the luxurious flat. All classes would live a separate family life, but there would be a communal kitchen; meals, available at different prices, would be taken either in the common restaurant, or in private rooms or in the individual apartments. The communal kitchen would not only effect enormous economies in fuel and food, but would also free women from domestic chores; only those who enjoyed cooking would cook; the rest would swell the labour force.

When everyone worked and the waste of competition was eliminated, production would increase fivefold. Only goods of the highest quality would be made, and the most delicious food grown; arduous agriculture would be diminished or mechanised and men would turn rather to horticulture and arboriculture. Far shorter working days would be needed; and men would work only because they enjoyed it. However, men liked to compete and intrigue against each other, so all work would be done in small teams of people who enjoyed being together. Every individual would be a member of different teams, each performing a different job; and he could move around from one to another in the course of the day. The monotony of labour would thus be ended. The team spirit, fostered by prizes, would ensure that work was highly productive. Class distinctions would disappear because no man would be tied to any one occupation. Disagreeable jobs would as far as possible be eliminated. The dirty jobs that were unavoidable would be done by children, who naturally love getting dirty. In civilised society, children were punished for getting dirty, but Fourier finds social use for every human characteristic, however un-desirable it may superficially appear. He was a pioneer of education through activity, of the development of the child's natural inclinations; he proposed that children should learn not by playing useless games, but by helping in elementary industrial and agricultural pursuits. This would enable them to discover their vocations freely, since they would be introduced to a large number of different occupations at an early age. He urged useful professional education instead of formal classical courses, but always offered in response to interest expressed by the child. Fourier in other words sought to enable people to do what they pleased, women as well as men. He was bold enough to apply this to sexual relations: some people wished to live with the same partner for life, and they could do so in his *phalanstère* if they wished, but others wanted variety, as they did in their work, and he allows this too, by ingenious schemes which rule out social discrimination against the promiscuous. Crèches are provided, so children are no problem. He prefers indeed that children should all be educated in what is virtually a comprehensive school (of which again he was a pioneer advocate) so that class prejudices should be eliminated.[1]

Fourier wished these *phalanstères* to be voluntarily established by individuals, each subscribing a share of the capital needed. He offered subscribers 33 per cent interest on their capital. He did not wish to overthrow capitalism but to outdo it, to reconcile it with socialism. He believed that property was what all men longed for; he observed that men working on their own account produced twice as much as wage earners in factories in which they had no interest. In the *phalanstère* there would be no more wage earners: he would abolish the proletariat. All would be both capitalists and workers. Those who had no capital at first would receive a share in the *phalanstère* simply by offering their labour; later they would be able to buy shares. The profits of the community would be distributed between all its members, who would be associate owners of it, though in varying degrees. Capital, labour and talent would all draw dividends. There would not be financial equality, but there would be social equality. A minimum income would be guaranteed to all, and pensions for the sick and old. Competition would be replaced by association. The advantages of large-scale production would be combined with co-operative ownership.

Government would be virtually abolished. Positions of

[1] David Zeldin, *The Educational Ideas of Charles Fourier* (1969).

leadership in the commune would be by election. Fourier was
not interested in politics and thought they could be dispensed
with. He waited for the first *phalanstère* to be founded by some
rich individual; he asked nothing from the state. When his
schemes were universally adopted, he foresaw the establishment
of industrial armies where the young would use up surplus energy
in great public works instead of in war: among these, he foresaw
the piercing of the Suez and Panama Canals and the irrigation
of the Sahara Desert.[1]

Fourier's principal works are in six long volumes. They are
written in a difficult style, with barely understandable neolo-
gisms and numerous eccentricities of presentation; the good
sense and prophetic intuition in them is buried in a jungle of
wild fantasy which sometimes borders on madness. He obtained
few careful readers and was much misinterpreted. His ideas on
the relation of the sexes caused scandal. His *phalanstère* was quite
wrongly thought to involve common ownership and common
living in quasi-military barracks. However, he also won much
sympathy and considerably more disciples than Saint-Simon.
The bibliography of books and pamphlets dealing with
Fourierism is a hundred pages long.[2] The circulation of the
Fourierist newspaper rose to 3,700 in 1848, and among its
readers was Louis Napoleon. However, this paper did not
minister to any closely knit society such as the Saint-Simonians
formed.

The man who took over the leadership of Fourier's followers
after his death, Victor Considérant (1808–93), adopted a
policy which was precisely the opposite to that chosen by
Enfantin. Considérant was a graduate of the Polytechnic who
resigned his commission as a captain of artillery to devote his
very considerable journalistic talents to the cause. He successfully defeated an attempt by one of Fourier's disciples, Just
Muiron, to organise a Union des Phalanstériens, which would
have meant the creation of something like another Saint-
Simonian religious sect.[3] Considérant tried instead to spread
knowledge of Fourier's ideas as widely as possible; and he was

[1] C. Fourier, *Œuvres Complètes* (1841); H. Bourgin, *Fourier* (1905).
[2] Giuseppe del Bo, *Charles Fourier e la scuola societaria 1801–1922, saggio biblio-
grafico* (Milan, 1957).
[3] H. Bourgin, *Victor Considérant, son œuvre* (Lyon, 1909), 41, 81.

a vigorous and effective propagandist. He wrote books which clarified the doctrines of Fourier and presented them in a much more vivid and intelligible style. He founded a journal (with financial assistance from an English admirer, Arthur Young) and in 1843 successfully transformed it into a daily newspaper, *La Démocratie pacifique*. Considérant jettisoned the more ridiculous or inconvenient products of Fourier's imagination. He quietly dropped such ideas as that men would in 15,000 years time grow tails with an eye at the end of them and he explicitly abandoned Fourier's opinions on sex. He strengthened the appeal of his doctrines to the middle classes by making it clear that Fourierist socialism was not revolutionary, but essentially a search for the peaceful reconciliation of the antagonisms and class hatreds of present society. Association, he said, meant 'the organisation of all new rights [i.e. the rights of the masses] without hurting vested interests'. He warned the middle classes that if they continued the *laissez-faire* regime, they would soon lose their property and their small businesses, which would become concentrated in the hands of a very few magnates. 'The French bourgeoisie [must] not allow itself to be sheared and despoiled with impunity of its property and be thrown into the proletariat.'[1] At the same time Considérant made Fourierism more attractive to the lower classes. He rebelled against Fourier's apathy towards politics and he gradually became an advocate of democracy. At first he accepted the constitutional monarchy of Louis-Philippe, and merely held that though all had a right to participate in government, the rights of the masses should be adjourned until they had enough competence to understand the issues: they should be treated as minors.[2] However, on 25 February 1848 he came out in favour of the republic and he soon threw in his lot with the left wing. Socialist unity became his watchword: he was outstanding among the socialists for the generosity and modesty with which he treated the rival schools while still disagreeing with them—in sharp contrast to the vituperative bickering of the others.[3] In 1849 he formed a Democratic and Socialist Committee in Paris in collaboration

[1] Victor Considérant, *Principes du socialisme* (first published 1843, reprinted 1847), 13.   [2] Ibid., 77.
[3] Victor Considérant, *Le Socialisme devant le vieux monde* (1848), 31–110.

with Proudhon and Ledru-Rollin; and on 13 July 1849 he joined them in their call to insurrection, though this was in contradiction to his long preaching of pacific methods.[1]

The Fourierists now also relied less on private initiative and assigned a new role to the state. Considérant asked parliament to finance a phalansterian experiment. Victor Hennequin, who was a member of the legislative assembly in 1849, modified the master's doctrines much further. He argued that the desire to experiment in the commune was out of date. It had been understandable in the apparently secure atmosphere of the July Monarchy, but the chaos into which society had fallen after its collapse meant that a more general programme for total reconstruction was needed. He proposed therefore that the state should take over and itself run industries and commercial concerns in which abuses prevailed, rather than try to palliate their abuses by fixing wages and prices. Thus coal was too expensive, the miners were paid too little; the state should exploit the mines itself, though not necessarily all mines. The state should set an example of how to run an industry efficiently and fairly: it should be like the chief orchestra conductor of industry—'but the conductor must not play all the instruments in the orchestra', only give a lead. The state should also buy out the railways and canals which were the 'blood of society' and the insurance companies which created solidarity between the members of the body politic. For the communes he urged a form of municipal socialism: municipal crèches, old age hostels, butchers, bakeries, public gardens and town planning, rural banks and entrepôts for agricultural produce to eliminate the parasitic middlemen and retailers of commerce. While still believing that the regeneration of society would be achieved through a reorganisation of agriculture, in rural communes, Hennequin nevertheless gave consideration to the problems of industrial workers. He proposed pensions for all and favoured the encouragement of trade unions and mixed associations of workers and employers: these would encounter many difficulties but they would give some satisfaction to 'the moral need of the worker who aspires to the status of associate and who will soon be led, by the failure or by the success of

[1] Felix Armand, *Les Fouriéristes et les luttes révolutionnaires de 1848 à 1851* (1948), 41–2, 56–7.

these elementary forms of association, to seek the conditions for normal [or thorough] association in a regenerated commune'. He insisted that 'confiscation, abolition and destruction are not words in our vocabulary'.[1]

Hennequin concentrated on demanding the 'garantist' state, which was the half-way house Fourier had imagined before 'harmony' was established; but the trouble with both ideals was that they were very expensive to achieve. In France only a few attempts were made to set up Fourierist communes. These were disowned by the leaders of the movement because they were only partial experiments, making many compromises; they failed in any case, from want of capital or perseverance. The nearest approach was that of Godin (1817–88). Originally an ordinary metal worker, he was struck on his *tour de France* in 1834 by the poverty of his fellows and the inefficient way they organised their work. Determining to establish a factory on fairer principles, he set up on his own. He invented a new method of making stoves and of enamelling them, so that his business prospered, and grew into a factory. He read Saint-Simon, Owen, Cabet and finally decided that Fourier provided the best guidance on how to organise his factory. In 1859 he was at last wealthy enough to build a 'social palace' near his factory and to introduce solidarity amongst the workers by sharing the profits. He took 5 per cent for his capital, plus his wages as manager and a share of the profits as a worker. All workers received a share of profits likewise in addition to their wages. This was not quite Fourierist, since wages were not abolished, and there were four different grades of workers. However, Godin was sufficiently popular to be elected to parliament in 1871, and when he died in 1888 he left a large part of his fortune, some 2½ million francs, to the *familistère*. Henceforth the 1,200 workers largely owned the factory themselves.[2]

There were some other experiments which, in varying degrees borrowed ideas from Fourier, like 'Le Travail', an association of housepainters, which distributed profits more or less in accord with his principles; but they all soon foundered. There were never any really successful ones in France to serve as

[1] Victor Hennequin, *Programme de l'École phalanstérienne* (1848).
[2] Charles Gide, *Les Colonies communistes et coopératives* (1927–8), 131, 181–8; Bernardot, *Le Familistière de Guise et son fondateur* (1889).

models.[1] Fourierist experiments were far more numerous abroad: about thirty at least in the U.S.A., the most famous of which, Brook Farm, was described by one of the participants, Nathaniel Hawthorne, in his *Blithedale Romance* (1852).[2] Fourier was also influential in Russia, though it is interesting that the *phalanstère* built by Petrachevsky in 1848 was burnt down by his peasants, too attached to their traditional ways.[3]

Zola's novel *Le Travail* (1901) has an attractive account of a Fourierist commune, and Eugène Sue's *Les Misères des enfants trouvés* (1851) contains a detailed description of one actually established in Sologne. Fourierism thus passed into literature, into the common French inheritance; but it quickly disappeared as a party and only Charles Gide, the co-operative leader, acknowledged Fourier's influence. In 1895 Georges Sorel wrote, 'Nine out of every ten Frenchmen interested in social questions are partial or illogical Fourierists. No one reads Fourier or even Considérant, but the quintessence of their doctrines or rather of their solutions, has passed into the common domain.'[4] Fourier's ideas were shared out between the socialists and the radicals, blurring the dividing line between them. It is interesting how Considérant, who was a man of extraordinary adaptability, prepared the way for this. After spending most of the Second Empire trying unsuccessfully to found a community in Texas, he refused to stand for parliament during the Third Republic; he insisted that he had no wish to repeat his attempts to found the ideal *phalanstère* and that different efforts were now needed, on 'absolutely scientific bases'. He spent his old age instead attending lectures at the Sorbonne and the Collège de France, so as to be able to marry new knowledge and science with the old ideals. Dressed up in scientific garb, some of the principal elements of Fourierism were in fact revived in Solidarism. It was no accident that a statue of Fourier was erected in Paris only in 1900, when Solidarism reached the height of its influence.[5]

[1] C. Bouglé *Socialismes français* (1946), 130.
[2] A. J. Bestor, *Backwoods Utopias* (1950).
[3] Georges Sourine, *Le Fourierisme en Russie* (1936), 59.
[4] Quoted by Hubert Bourgin, *Fourier* (1905), 581.
[5] At the corner of boulevard de Clichy and rue Caulaincourt. Cf. Gaston Isambert, *Les Idées socialistes en France de 1815 à 1848. Le Socialisme fondé sur la fraternité et l'union des classes* (1905), 197.

Fourier's was a utopia for the petty bourgeoisie. Another, which particularly had in mind the problems of industrial workers and of unemployed artisans, was that of Louis Blanc (1811–82). He was considerably less original that his predecessors: he borrowed Fourier's ideas on association and combined them with Saint-Simon's on authority, to produce a state-sponsored socialism; but he is important for then attempting to reconcile their ideas with universal suffrage and the republic, producing the first democratic brand of socialism. Louis Blanc's father had been a civil servant, sacked after 1815; his mother was the daughter of a Corsican solicitor. He obtained his school education thanks to a scholarship; he was then tutor to the son of an iron master of Arras, from whose 600 workers he learnt something of the problems of industry. He entered into Paris journalism in 1834 and quickly rose to a leading position in the party of *La Réforme*. He was an extremely able writer, with a very vivid and vigorous style: his *Histoire de dix ans 1830–40* (1841–4), a solid work in five volumes, highly readable because of its lively detail, would by itself have made him permanently noteworthy. He achieved his popularity with the masses by his *Organisation du travail* (1839), a practical programme for the immediate introduction of socialism without revolution. His ideal was that state authority should ultimately become unnecessary, but meanwhile he saw it as the instrument of the emancipation of the working classes. He proposed to raise a gigantic loan, and with the proceeds establish 'social workshops', i.e. factories in which co-operative association would be practised. The profits would be shared equally by the workers, but a considerable amount would be set aside for pensions and assistance for the sick, and a further amount would be used to help other workers to buy their own tools, and to set up independently in the same way. Gradually the system of association would spread throughout industry. The social workshops would at first exist side by side with capitalist factories producing the same goods, but their superiority would soon drive the latter out of business. The state would only provide the initial impulse and appoint the first managers; after that it would leave all to the workers themselves, who would elect their own managers. Unlike Fourier, Blanc did not offer the capitalists a share of the profits, but only a fixed, though advantageous, interest on their loan; but like Fourier, he hoped to achieve his reorganisation with their help. He argued, like Fourier, that competition was ruining the bourgeoisie as well as impoverishing the workers; that continuance in it would mean 'war unto death' with England, unless France was willing to confine itself solely to agriculture. He was far from proposing the abolition of all private property: he considered it to be a natural right, though it must not be allowed to produce privilege.[1] However he criticised Saint-Simon's formula 'To each according to his merits' and replaced it by an egalitarian one, 'To each according to his needs'. He disliked the hierarchical and authoritarian aspects of Saint-Simonianism, for he believed that no progress could be achieved without universal suffrage—he defined justice as equality.[2] His political ideas had a curious resemblance to those of the seventeenth-century English levellers: he feared long parliaments, which only set up mistrust between people and government. He wanted annual elections, so that those who held power should be perpetually conscious of its popular origins—and he demanded that certain fundamental rights should always remain inviolable, outside their scope.[3]

Louis Blanc was one of the most talked-about men of 1848 because he had found a simple formula 'The Organisation of Labour,' which seemed to offer the solution for the major social problems all at once. However, a period of economic crisis was no time to raise capital for his industrial schemes. The modest workers' associations he set up went largely unnoticed and affected only a tiny fraction of artisans. Unfortunately for him the National Workshops (which had no connection with his theories, since they simply gave useless labour to the unemployed for a very small wage) got confused in the popular imagination with his 'social workshops', and thoroughly discredited him. He was unable to get a ministry of progress or of labour established, or any significant budget vote to enable him to achieve anything. However, he had time to draw up a bill 'to prepare the social revolution and to abolish the proletariat [i.e. wage earning]

[1] L. Blanc, *Le Socialisme: droit au travail*, reprinted in his *Questions d'aujourdhui et de demain* (1873–84), 4. 317–25.

[2] L. Blanc, *Le Pouvoir, ce qu'il doit être* (1841).

[3] L. Blanc, *Du suffrage universel* (1850).

gradually, peacefully and without shock'. The state should buy
up the railways, the mines, the Bank of France and the insurance companies and set up a national wholesale and retail
commercial chain. With the profits of these, it should set
up workers' co-operative associations, which would compete
against private enterprise. Blanc's plans are important for
distilling into a single document the common aims of most
socialists in 1848.[1] However, when in 1870 he returned to
France from more than twenty years of exile in England, he
had completely ceased to hold this intermediary position,
though he was still popular enough to be elected to parliament.
He opposed the Commune, because he was still a believer in
the centralised state. Though he had appealed to universal
suffrage he had never given much thought to the organisation
of the peasantry which comprised its principal part. He became
obsessed with anticlericalism and placed more emphasis on
it than on social reform.[2] He even quoted approvingly from
Thiers's book on property.[3] Though he had been a pioneer
democrat, he disliked the parliamentary democracy of the
Third Republic, and the idea of party organisation was alien
to him. He had always been hostile to the small constituency
which could easily be led astray and he cherished the illusion
that if only 'all France could meet in a single *place publique*', his
ideas would be triumphantly acclaimed.[4] He now called himself a radical and he was no longer on the extreme left. He was
a man marked by the failure of 1848, but on the other hand
some of his ideas were becoming respectable and to that
extent he could claim a lasting achievement.[5]

The most widely known socialist doctrine in 1848 was that
of Étienne Cabet (1788–1856). His book, *Voyage en Icarie*, went
through five editions between 1840 and 1848; even though it
was a closely printed volume of 600 pages, it was much read by

[1] L. Blanc, *Histoire de la révolution de 1848* (1870), i. 161.

[2] L. Blanc, *A mes électeurs* (12 Feb. 1876), L. Blanc, *Discours politiques, 1847 à
1881* (1882), 208, 372.

[3] L. Blanc, *Le Parti radical, sa doctrine, sa conduite* (15 Oct. 1872).

[4] L. Blanc, *Du gouvernement direct, du peuple par lui-même* (1851), in *Questions d'aujourd'hui et de demain* (1873–84), i. 200.

[5] J. Vidalenc, *Louis Blanc* (1848); I. Tchernoff, *L. Blanc* (1904); L. A. Loubère,
Louis Blanc; His Life and his Contribution to the Rise of French Jacobin-Socialism (Evanston, Ill., 1961).

the workers. Cabet was not a powerful thinker, but this did not make him any less interesting. His book attempted to reflect with exceptional directness the ordinary hopes of the common worker. For Cabet held out above all the prospect of prosperity. He sacrificed liberty entirely in order to have equality. He was himself of working-class origin. His father had been a cooper of Dijon, 'an honest and industrious artisan' Cabet called him. Thanks to scholarships, Cabet became a teacher and then a barrister, with the ultimate ambition of being appointed a professor of law. But the Restoration closed the avenues of promotion to him, for he preferred Napoleon to the Bourbons. He joined the Carbonari and was active in the liberal opposition before 1830; but when the July Monarchy was established, he could not find a settled place in it. He was made Prosecutor-General in Corsica but was quickly dismissed for his blind attacks on the powerful vested interests there. When elected a deputy for Dijon, he bitterly criticised Louis-Philippe for not breaking with aristocracy and privilege. He demanded a true republic, with votes, education and a decent living for the masses. His newspaper, *Le Populaire*, was distributed at a very low price to the working class.[1] 'We do not want to despoil the rich,' he wrote, 'but to enable the poor to acquire a competency and to enrich themselves by working.' The rich could build themselves as many palaces as they pleased, so long as all the poor had a cottage.[2] He was repeatedly prosecuted by the government and finally forced into exile.

It was in England that he became a communist. Some say this was due to the influence of Robert Owen; others claim Cabet owed more to Babeuf (whose communism represented the longing of poor peasants for the old common organisation of pre-capitalist open-field agriculture and for the traditional common rights of pasture and firewood).[3] Cabet decided that

[1] Sales in 1846 were 3,600 copies; but in the 1830s on some occasions 20,000 copies were sold. Cf. the entry by Proudhon in his diary for Sept. 1843: 'Getting on badly with everybody, what can I hope? The masses are still too ignorant; and besides Cabet has taken the lead in their esteem.' *Carnets de P. J. Proudhon* (1960), 1. 8.

[2] *Poursuites du gouvernement contre M. Cabet, député de la Côte-d'Or, directeur du Populaire* (1834), 2. 28, 45. A sort of autobiography by Cabet is to be found in the first thirty pages of this volume.

[3] Jules Proudhommeaux, *Icarie et son fondateur, Étienne Cabet. Contribution à*

the basic cause of human trouble was inequality and he deduced that only common ownership could end this. His ideal state he described in the form of a novel, a kind of science fiction for his time. Icaria, as he called it, will be above all a land of plenty. All the luxuries of Paris and London will be found in it in abundance, but no longer as the exclusive possession of a privileged few. All will be owned by the state and the state will feed, clothe, lodge and provide work for everybody. All jobs will be equally esteemed and all equally rewarded. Every man will contribute what he can and draw what he needs. Machines will not be abolished but on the contrary multiplied, for there will no longer be any danger of their depriving anyone of employment: they are designed in fact to lighten man's labour enormously. All homes will be identical, identically furnished in lavish style by the state: they will all have bathrooms and dressing-tables and carpets. Each will be inhabited by one family; larger families will have larger flats in proportion to their size. There will be no hint of Fourierist libertarianism. Strict morality will flourish universally; marriage and procreation will be encouraged; celibacy punished; the 'free unions' of the workers ended. Everybody will wear the same kind of clothes, all lovely because 'bizarre and tasteless designs' will be banished. Every profession, every age, however, will be distinguished by a different uniform, so there will be no lack of variety. Fashion, however, will never change any more, and ladies' hats will be so cunningly designed by the best brains that they can be worn by heads of every size and shape. Commerce will be abolished. Government will be based on democratic elections but the possibility of disagreements is barely envisaged. Truth is one, and so only official newspapers will be allowed; the liberty of the press is necessary only against kings and aristocracies, not in popular democracy. 'Nowhere is the police so numerous,' says one of the characters in the novel, 'because all our public servants and even all our citizens are obliged to survey the execution of the laws and to prosecute or to denounce crimes which they witness.'

Cabet was not a revolutionary. His experiences as a Carbonaro had filled him with hate of secret societies. The second

l'étude du socialisme expérimental (1907), 144; M. Dommanget *et al.*, *Babeuf et les problèmes du babouvisme* (1963), 55 ff.

part of his book describes transitory measures, to extend over about fifty years, while society is gradually made ready to adopt communism. During this period, work would not be compulsory, and private property would continue, though it would be gradually reduced by taxation and by the formation of co-operative associations. Wages would meanwhile be regulated, poverty abolished through state action and the new generation prepared for equality by free education. The attraction of Cabet was that he offered a clear ideal without offending morals or religion; indeed he maintained his scheme was only a development of primitive Christianity. His brand of communism—reformist and deist—quickly became by far the most popular one, outstripping the tiny sect of revolutionary materialists, led by Theodore Dezamy in the tradition of Buonarotti. The government quite failed to distinguish between them. Lumped together, they appeared a terrifying menace. 'The Communists are about to rise', wrote the liberal *Journal des débats* on 20 January 1848. 'Thirty thousand of them are ready to take up arms to overthrow the government. Their chief has even been chosen who will doubtless be in charge of sharing out all property.' But Cabet in fact had surprisingly little influence during the Second Republic. The socialists, and notably Louis Blanc and Ledru-Rollin, vigorously dissociated themselves from him and would not support his candidature to parliament. He obtained only 20,000 votes in Paris in April 1848 and 68,000 the following June—never enough to get a seat.[1] Already before February he had summoned his followers to leave the old country and set up the utopia, as an experimental community, in the U.S.A. The first 69 settlers left France on 29 January 1848. He followed them in December. His authoritarian temperament, his contempt for individual independence, increased the practical difficulties that faced him. When he died at St. Louis in 1856 he was already a man of the past, from the point of view of French politics. But the ideal of which he dreamt was not therefore forgotten.[2]

Pierre Leroux (1797–1871) was another socialist who for

---

[1] Pierre Angrand, *Étienne Cabet et la république de 1848* (1948), 65, 70.
[2] Fernand Rude, *Voyage en Icarie, deux ouvriers viennois aux États-Unis en 1855* (1952), with a valuable introduction on Cabet.

a brief period enjoyed some popularity and then was almost completely discredited. He was very highly esteemed by the generation reaching manhood before 1848.[1] Lamartine prophesied that 'Pierre Leroux will one day be read as the *Social Contract* is read today'.[2] The *British and Foreign Review* for 1843 wrote: 'We think his works far more worthy of attention than those of almost any modern thinker.'[3] The son of a humble café keeper, he was educated at the Lycée Charlemagne, but his parents' poverty prevented him from going on to the École Polytechnique. He became a printer, and later a journalist: he founded and edited *Le Globe*, which was in turn Liberal and Saint-Simonian. In 1831 he broke with Enfantin and evolved his own theories. He was probably the first Frenchman to call himself socialist, though there was nothing sectarian about him at all. He had been a Carbonaro in his youth, but he had disliked its violent methods. He preferred to be, as he called himself, a 'pacific revolutionary'. He saw a growing conflict between proletariat and bourgeoisie but wished to avoid it: he prescribed the granting of special parliamentary representation to the working class as the answer. His aim was always to reconcile. He invented not only the word socialist but also solidarity—the new link between the classes to replace charity, since equality must replace hierarchy. He modestly called himself 'the fourth socialist', for he looked on Saint-Simon, Fourier and Robert Owen as the founders of socialism. For him they stood respectively for equality ('the improvement of the lot of the greatest number'), liberty and practical fraternity. His plan for a democratic and social constitution in 1848 placed even more emphasis than Louis Blanc's on the need for democracy: its sub-title was 'the infallible means of organising the nation's work without hurting liberty'.[4]

Pierre Leroux had at one stage appeared to be the man who best united the aspirations of his age. His Encyclopaedia, modelled on and designed to replace that of the eighteenth

[1] E. Renan, *Souvenirs d'enfance et de jeunesse* (1883), 249; Theodore Zeldin, *Émile Ollivier and the Liberal Empire of Napoleon III* (Oxford, 1963), 5–6, 9.

[2] Henri Mougin, *Pierre Leroux* (1938), 13.

[3] Quoted by D. O. Evans, 'Pierre Leroux and his philosophy in relation to literature', in *Publications of the Modern Language Association*, 44, no. 1 (Mar. 1929), 283.

[4] P. Leroux, *Projet d'une constitution démocratique et sociale* (1848).

century, raised great hopes that a new creed of action was about
to be evolved. But Leroux took a turning into a blind alley. His
Religion of Humanity, though in keeping with the prevalent
view that Christianity needed to be regenerated and that society
required a new moral basis, turned into an amalgam of
mysticism and nonsense. He came to preach reincarnation
(though breaking with his friend Jean Reynaud when the latter
decided reincarnated spirits travelled from planet to planet) and
a method of food production using human manure. The constitutional bill he introduced as a deputy in 1848 was *unanimously* defeated. Fat, round, puffed up, red faced, wrapped in
a vast shaggy frock-coat, his head covered with bushy and
unkempt hair, he appeared like a wild creature from the woods,
and though he had more wit in his little finger than ten of his
parliamentary colleagues put together, he was the victim and
butt of perpetual jokes.[1] When he died, a subscription to raise
a statue of him obtained almost no support; the Commune
agreed to send two representatives to his funeral but made it
clear it was doing homage to the defender of the people, not
the mystic.[2]

Buchez (1796–1865) created another sect of socialists, which
is principally interesting for the way it moved away from
socialism. Buchez began as an atheist and a revolutionary, and
it was in his room in Paris that the French Carbonaro movement
was founded. He was then converted to Saint-Simonianism
but in 1829 broke with Enfantin when the latter turned it into
a religion and developed his unorthodox ideas on women.
Buchez attempted instead to reconcile socialism with Catholicism. He believed in progress, the improvement of the lot of
the masses and the end of their exploitation, but he stressed
above all the need to produce a moral regeneration and he
thought Catholicism could help in this. He never became a
practising Catholic himself, rather like Maurras, though many
of his disciples ended up as priests. Buchez argued that the
practical application of Christianity would solve the social

[1] Jules Simon, *Premières Années* (n.d.), 386.
[2] P. Felix Thomas, 'Pierre Leroux' in *Entre camarades* (1901), 257–68; id.,
Pierre Leroux, sa vie, son œuvre, sa doctrine (1904); D. O. Evans, *Le Socialisme roman-
tique* (1948); P. Leroux, *L'Égalité* (1838).

question; by this he meant that workers should pool their savings and borrow to found associations, in which they would all be equal, their own masters and drawing equal wages. By dint of economy and austerity they would soon repay their loans and would then swell the associations' capital, which, he insisted, should always be indivisible. These were in effect production co-operatives and Buchez in practice helped to found several, of which the most famous, the Gilt Jeweller Workers, lasted from 1834 till 1873, prospering so that it had no fewer than eight branches in Paris. The snag was that the workers remained in great poverty themselves while the association flourished and the indivisible capital increased. It was too much an association of saints to appeal very widely.

Buchez was highly esteemed by two different sets of people. The moderate republican newspaper *Le National* favoured his ideas, and particularly Garnier-Pagès, Jules Bastide and Recurt, who all became ministers in 1848. Buchez was accordingly appointed deputy mayor of Paris immediately after the Revolution, and in April he was elected president of the constituent assembly, with his disciple Corbon as vice-president. He owed his position, however, to the support of the moderate conservatives, not to any wide popularity among the workers. This patronage from the bourgeoisie only alienated him still further from the socialists.

There was, however, a small group of workers who were devoted to him and who are remarkable because they ran a journal uninterrupted for ten years propagating his ideas. *L'Atelier* (1840–50) was, as its sub-title stated, 'The Special Organ of the Working Class, edited exclusively by workers'. It defined socialism in a rather vague way as 'an instinct, a sentiment, a need . . . an energetic desire shown by the working classes to rise to a better social condition', meaning that none of the doctrines of the individual utopians could be taken as exclusive truth. In practice, however, it meant more by socialism, for it asserted the inevitability of a conflict of interests between workers and employers, and the need for solidarity among the workers themselves. But it did not wish them to fight the employers and it disapproved of trade unions. These could do nothing to end the cause of the trouble, which was twofold. First, workers had a right to the full product of their work

(which was the formula it offered in contrast to Louis Blanc's
right to work) and they believed employers and foremen were
parasites depriving workers of this. Secondly, the division into
master and man was an insult to the workers' dignity. The
paper is extremely interesting on this subject. It complains
bitterly of 'this stupid and humiliating phrase "inferior class" '
which is applied to the workers and of the insults that are
thrown at him, unintentionally sometimes, simply by the way
superiors act towards inferiors. When in 1846 some factory
owners established a prize committee to recompense workers
who distinguished themselves by their 'good conduct' and
'morality', it sarcastically proposed to set up a 'committee
of encouragement' of its own, which would award prizes to
factory owners whose conduct was exemplary in every respect.
The status of master must be abolished: 'The worker must
cease to be an instrument and become a man.' Since property
was the necessary guarantee of liberty and dignity, all workers
should possess property: it proposed common ownership of the
instrument of production, in the form of workers' associations,
but individual property of consumable wealth. Dignity required
that the worker should achieve his emancipation by his own
efforts; so it opposed equally Louis Blanc's faith in the state
and the advocates of participation in profits, which left the
hierarchical organisation untouched. As temporary measures
till the establishment of associations, it demanded wage regulation, easy credit and far greater use of the *prud'hommes*.

The *Atelier* modified Buchez's doctrines considerably, away
from Saint-Simonianism. Buchez had been socialist in the
original sense of being anti-individualistic, and in placing
emphasis on the needs of society. The *Atelier* had followed him
at first but gradually, and particularly after 1848, it emphasised instead 'human values' and the need for individual
liberty. It urged comparison between the Russian serf and the
citizen of the United States.[1] Its Christian sympathies also
got the better of its socialist ones. It thought that moral interests should be given greater weight than material ones. It
sided therefore with the bourgeois *National*, with which it
agreed about morals, rather than with the socialists, to whose
ideas on economics and the organisation of labour it was

[1] Armand Cuvillier, *Un Journal d'ouvriers: L'Atelier* (1954), 73.

sympathetic. This was really its undoing. Its asceticism, its moderation, its awareness of the practical difficulties of emancipation, its Catholic tendencies, all repelled the workers. So paradoxically the readers of this workers' journal (never more than 1,500) were mainly middle class. Proudhon wrote of it that it lacked 'any real and sound popularity' among the workers because instead of making itself the echo of the people's feelings, it mistrusted them, 'in too learned a language, with excessively peremptory theories'. It enjoyed only indirect influence because in 1849 its editor, as president of the legislative assembly's committee on labour, was able to pack the council for the encouragement of workers' associations with his friends. This body was charged with distributing 3 million francs to workers seeking to establish production co-operatives. It imposed the Buchez principle of indivisible capital upon them and so perhaps helped to discredit the scheme. In 1848 Louis Blanc enjoyed a little power: in 1849 the followers of Buchez had their day.[1]

But they did not contribute to the development of later socialism. One of them, J. P. Gilland, a locksmith, declared 'I like my trade, I like my tools and even if I could live by my pen, I would not wish to cease to be a locksmith.' He published a collection of stories and poetry, to which George Sand wrote a preface, and he remained faithful to the democratic cause. Others among these worker-journalists evolved differently. Anthime Corbon (1808-91) was successively a weaver, sign writer, surveyor, compositor, sculptor in wood and marble. 'He has worked at all trades and succeeded in all', but though able, he was not friendly, and rather cold and peevish. A deputy in 1848 and again in 1871, he became a permanent senator in 1875, and eventually lived by journalism. He published a curious book called *The Secret of the People of Paris* (1863), with the object of revealing the real nature of the working class, but it is disappointing, and not very informative. By then he had really broken away from his class and abandoned both his socialism and his Catholicism. One of his colleagues in the editorship of *L'Atelier*, Quénot, a hatter, became an employer and by 1865 had one of the largest factories in Paris: he likewise forgot all his old beliefs and even started a paternalistic

[1] Armand Cuvillier, *P. J. B. Buchez et les origines du socialisme chrétien* (1948), 73; and the theses of F. A. Isambert.

friendly society to compete against the old-established and exclusively working-class Hatters' Society.[1] Buchez's school in effect proved to be a diversion of the workers' efforts from socialism: it offered them alternative experiments and it was a failure.

Proudhon (1809–65) was the most genuinely plebeian of the early socialist thinkers. He was the son of a rural artisan—cooper, innkeeper, small-scale brewer, smallholder. However, he did not follow in his father's footsteps, for reasons which show why traditions of resignation were breaking down. Proudhon's father lived on the borderline of subsistence: he was ruined by his lack of business sense: he too honestly sold his products for just enough to cover his costs and keep his family, leaving nothing in reserve for bad times. His plight made a profound impression on Proudhon, whose political philosophy was in consequence designed above all to make it possible for artisans like his father to survive, for honesty to pay, for fair prices to be charged. As a boy, his intelligence was spotted by a local *curé* who got him a place in the lycée of Besançon, but because of family misfortunes he had to leave before he could complete the course. He became a compositor. In this trade he was able to indulge his passion for books and to become a leading example of that new class of men, the autodidact artisan, self-confident, basically conservative but innocently open to all new ideas.

A school prize when he was fourteen, Fénelon's *Proof of the Existence of God*, had first sown some doubts about religion in Proudhon's mind. As a printer and proof-reader of mainly theological works, he learnt the art of disputation, as well as accumulating a mass of half-digested erudition, and a knowledge of Latin, Greek and Hebrew. He began questioning everything. He printed Fourier's *Nouveau Monde Industriel* and for a while was his enthusiastic supporter. 'There was no system, no heresy in which, as I discovered it, I did not believe.' When the crisis of 1830 threw him out of work, he went on a tour of France: his repeated difficulty in finding work exacerbated his hostility to the existing order. The printing firm he eventually succeeded in establishing soon collapsed when his

[1] A. Cuvillier, *L'Atelier* (1954), 61.

father committed suicide. He avoided bankruptcy by obtaining a scholarship to study in Paris, but the fruit of his study, a book entitled *What is Property?* lost him this support. It was in this unusual way that Proudhon became a polemicist and a journalist, but despite the enormous bulk of his writing, he was never able to support himself properly by it. It is possible, indeed, that he might never have become a rebel had his life not been so much of a struggle and had he not been so harshly rejected by bourgeois society. 'I hoped to find a refuge in some honourable commercial employment', he wrote, but 'I am repulsed everywhere as if I had the plague.' He would have been willing to compromise with Louis-Philippe or Napoleon III had they shown more sympathy for his economic ideas.[1] His failure as a practical politician in 1848 and again in 1863 intensified his attacks on the established order, even though, as will be shown, he was not as much its enemy as he appeared to be. The combination of radicalism and conservatism in Proudhon's thought is highly significant, for it helps to explain also the ambiguities of later French socialism.

There was no subject on which Proudhon did not have an opinion. He loved talking and he wrote with great facility: he had no inhibitions about making asides or digressions. He published 26 volumes in his lifetime, 12 more appeared posthumously, as well as 14 volumes of correspondence. It is not surprising that he was seldom original. His importance indeed derives partly from the very fact that he was not original. Proudhon was popular because he expressed the feelings of the masses, or at least a very considerable section of them. He freely admitted that he had no higher ambition. 'We are the monitors of the people, asking it to speak, interpreting its acts. To interrogate the people is our whole philosophy and all our politics.' The most he pretended to do was to 'widen the people's horizon and clear paths for them'. His mind was more analytical than constructive. He showed up the significance of received ideas, pushed home to their logical conclusions, seeking to create, as he said, 'a people's philosophy'. He pointed out the weaknesses of the society of his day far more than he offered

[1] Daniel Halévy, *La Vie de Proudhon 1809–1847* (1948), 412–21; but G. Gurvitch, *Pour le centenaire de la mort de P. J. Proudhon: Proudhon et Marx, une confrontation* (1964), 59 ff., disagrees with my view.

alternatives to it. In any case, the people, he claimed, had no wish for utopias. He epitomised the scepticism of the Paris *frondeur*, the eternal critic.[1] Proudhon was wrongly accused by Marx of misunderstanding and misapplying Hegelianism. Proudhon showed up the contradictions of the world but he had no hope of reconciling them into a synthesis. His world was a pluralistic one, in which truth had several faces, and in which the problem was to enable inevitable differences to co-exist side by side. The variety and ultimate paralysis of the Third Republic found a true prophet in him.

Proudhon considered the principal aim of the masses to be the attainment of independence, self-respect and a sense of their own dignity. His main concern was that society should be organised to make this possible. He believed that the qualities it needed were justice, equality and liberty. Justice he defined as mutual respect for other people's dignity, which meant that men should have dealings with each other only on a basis of strict reciprocity: in this way there would be no more oppression. His passion for equality distinguishes him from Saint-Simon, who believed in a hierarchical society, from Fourier, who reserved special rewards for both capitalists and men of ability and also from Cabet, who wanted complete uniformity in wealth. What Proudhon cared for most was social equality. He believed, it is true, that, given education and equal opportunity, men would become increasingly equal intellectually, but he did not demand equal pay, only that every man should receive the whole of what his labour was worth. Nor did he extend his demand for equality to women. Advanced ideas did not attract him as much and he said the masses were not really attracted by them either. Woman's place, he said, should be in the home. He was deeply influenced by biblical ideas, by the Napoleonic Code, by the scraps of Roman law he had picked up, and by the unemployed workers' fear of female competition. Women, he argued, were inferior to men on all counts; they must find their fulfilment in chaste marriage and their pleasure in obedience to their husbands. Proudhon was a puritan. Adultery he considered to be the greatest cause of the decay of modern society. Sexual intercourse should be reserved for procreation. The father's power should be 'almost unlimited' in

[1] P. J. Proudhon, *Correspondance* (1875), 7. 10, 10. 12, 14. 161.

his family. Family life he regarded as the basis of dignity and he never considered that it might be an obstacle to liberty.[1]

After a family, where he was complete master, a self-respecting man must have property. Proudhon made his name by proclaiming that 'Property is Theft',[2] but in fact he had no wish to abolish property. All he meant was that landlords who did no work themselves were guilty of stealing, because profit obtained without labour was theft. What he wanted was to give the land to the peasants who cultivated it and to establish more or less equality between them. He condemned absolute property but proposed something only slightly less absolute, 'possession' or usufruct—ideas he picked up again from Roman law. Full ownership should remain with society, to ensure fair distribution and to prevent profiteering by landlords at the expense of their tenants. At first he identified society with the state but later he proposed that the control of the land—its allotment and the levy of taxes on it—should be in the hands of the communes, so that neighbours could settle these questions freely and amicably amongst themselves. With time, however, he grew increasingly suspicious of the social controls on property he had originally favoured and he came to insist that 'possession' should be hereditary (so as to avoid destroying the family), and even that it should not be withdrawn if the land was neglected or left uncultivated. In the end his major proposal for real reform was the enfranchisement of tenants: after a tenant had paid the equivalent of the value of his land, plus 20 per cent, in rent, he should be considered to have bought out the landlord. By the time of his death, Proudhon had abandoned his early flirtation with the fief and declared the superiority of allodium. He calculated that a peasant family needed about twelve and a half acres of varied arable, pasture and vine land, with rights of common and forest and this—clearly derived from his memories of his native Franche-Comté, where this variety existed—was his ideal. He wanted a balanced society of small peasant proprietors. Communal ownership was anathema to him. 'The peasant', he wrote in

---

[1] P. J. Proudhon, *De la justice dans la Révolution et dans l'Église* (1858), 1.98, 175–6; on women 3. 181 ff.

[2] Proudhon was not the first to use this phrase. Brissot said something similar in the 1789 Revolution. But Proudhon was probably unaware of this when he wrote it.

a passage which says much about himself also, 'is the least romantic, the least idealistic of men. He loves nature as a child loves his wet-nurse, he is less concerned with its charms (though he is aware of these) than with its fertility. The peasant loves nature for its powerful breasts, for the life it disgorges.' Proudhon fully accepted the peasant's selfishness and he was never a utopian building a system on any hoped-for altruism.[1]

But for all his conservatism—and he called himself a conservative—he was also an enemy of many established values. The property he was attacking, it should be remembered, was that of the early nineteenth century, untramelled by any social restraints, with no possibility of compulsory purchase and no rent control. His contemporary Laboulaye called property a divine institution. The Convention had decreed the death penalty for any one proposing a law which endangered property. Proudhon's views on property were linked with his hostility to the Catholic Church: he criticised it for holding that poverty was inevitable, that property for all was not one of its aims, that charity was commendable—attitudes he considered incompatible with human dignity and equality.

However, the peasant and the worker, even when they owned property, were still far from free, because they lacked the capital to make use of it and were usually in debt. The first step to liberty was economic liberty, and for this cheap credit was needed. Proudhon claimed he had discovered a system which could provide it almost by a stroke of the pen. The tyranny of money should be ended simply by abolishing money. Instead, a system of exchange should be instituted: goods would be valued by the amount of labour put into them. A central bank would give credit to all who were able to produce anything. Interest would be abolished, or at least reduced to $\frac{1}{2}$ per cent. Public and private indebtedness would be extinguished. Virtually free credit would be available to all; tenants would gradually become owner-occupiers; workers would get the full value of their production. This was Proudhon's *mutuellisme* designed to bring justice into economic relationships.

[1] P. J. Proudhon, *Qu'est-ce que la propriété?* (1840); Aimé Berthod, *P. J. Proudhon et la propriété. Un socialisme pour les paysans* (1910).

The men he hoped to save by it, however, were the independent small peasants and artisans whom he considered to be the healthiest element of French society. His economic views were in many ways backward looking, hostile to expansion and industrialisation. For a long time he even opposed workers' production associations (which was one reason why Louis Blanc called him antisocialist). Proudhon's people's bank was designed to give individual workers independence: he feared the associations would restrict it. With time, however, he came to accept the general view, as he so often did: he agreed that the associations were a useful preparatory step towards the reciprocal system; he then even saw them as the ideal form of replacing large capitalist companies, like mines, where individuals were powerless on their own.[1] Proudhon, it is important to note, wished to destroy only the top section of rich idle capitalists; for the rest, he was very keen to conciliate the mass of the bourgeoisie and the proletariat. He hoped that an appreciation of the dignity and joy of work, made more varied and interesting by a wide education (on which he laid great stress) would, in a society where work never involved exploitation of others, lead to true social equality. He wanted not just the right to work but the emancipation of work.

This reorganisation of economic relationships would make governments of the traditional kind superfluous. He carried Saint-Simon's idea of the administration of things replacing the government of men to its logical conclusion, and it is in this sense that Proudhon is the father of French anarchism. He hated all authority, all control on his independence and believed this to be an innate characteristic of man (and it probably was of a great many Frenchmen). He wanted a loose federation of autonomous communes or cantons to replace the centralised state which he saw only as an oppressor, not as an instrument of progress. He was, therefore, hostile to the unification of Italy and Germany into centralised states. He advocated that all arrangements between individuals should be based on free contracts between equals. He attacked Rousseau's *Social Contract* because it involved the surrender of responsibility and power and the creation of a government over the individual.

[1] Aimé Berthod, introduction to P. J. Proudhon, *Idée générale de la révolution au 19e siècle* ([1851] 1923), 32–46.

He was a bitter critic of democracy, of universal suffrage, and of violence and revolution. Political action was never adequate for him. He was hostile likewise to the Church, which represented authority and oppression to him: he was one of the most vigorous pioneers of anticlericalism. He wished to deprive the Church of its control of education, but he wished to transfer this not to a state system but to the free enterprise of parents. State education would in any case, he thought, be too expensive. He longed to reduce taxation, not to institute a welfare state. In many ways, therefore, Proudhon differed fundamentally from contemporary socialists.

Proudhon had ambitions to be an active politician but no talent for it. After being defeated in the parliamentary election of April 1848, he won a seat in a by-election in June but he never became a party leader. His journalism won him numerous convictions, including repeated imprisonment and exile, which he devoted, perforce, to writing. The political line he adopted was erratic, and almost perversely paradoxical. He was unenthusiastic about the revolution of February 1848 (because it did not accept his ideas), but hopeful after the *coup d'état*. His flirting with the empire discredited him for a time. In the election of 1863, consciously opposing the policy of all other republicans, he changed his tactics and urged mass abstention from the polls. His call went unheeded: how few his contacts with the workers were was seen when he tried to find some to serve on his electoral committee. It was in fact only in his last book (unfinished and published shortly after his death) on the *Political Capacity of the Working Classes* that he finally succeeded in grafting his ideas on to a political movement. He changed his tune somewhat when he developed a philosophy out of the manifesto of sixty Paris workers (1863) demanding that the workers should stop voting for bourgeois candidates and elect only men of their own class to represent their interests. He announced the dawn of a new age, in which the working class was for the first time self-conscious, separated from the bourgeoisie and with ideas in complete contrast to theirs. Just as atheists did not go to church, so the workers should stop going to the church of bourgeois politics. They should concentrate on effecting economic change. They should try not to take over the power of the centralised state, but to abolish it.

Proudhon has apparently been highly influential since his death. He was frequently referred to as a source of inspiration in many quarters. He seemed to be to the second half of the nineteenth century what Rousseau had been fifty years before, and like Rousseau, he was interpreted very variously. The French section of the First International constantly quoted from his works and their mutualism was identical with his in most respects. The Commune of 1871 has been looked upon, in one interpretation, as the fulfilment of his thought. The revolutionary syndicalism of the Trade Union movement was considered to draw many of its precepts from him: both Pelloutier and Jouhaux talked reverentially of him. The Anarchist movement of course considered him, with Bakunin, as their founder. Gambetta acknowledged him as his master and he clearly had many links with the radicalism of the late nineteenth and early twentieth century. His name was then taken up by the Action Française and he was one of the patrons of the Vichy regime. A society, Les Amis de Proudhon, was founded to further the study of his works, which have been painstakingly reprinted over the last thirty years in a grand new edition. It is important, therefore, since his name is to be found in so many corners of French history, to be clear exactly how influential he was and to what extent his name has simply been taken as a cloak.

'The masses do not read me,' said Proudhon himself, 'but without reading they hear me.'[1] In the 1860s the cobbler Rouillier always carried a volume of Proudhon in his pocket: its pages were uncut, but he considered himself a Proudhonist all the same.[2] For Proudhon said what these artisans rather incoherently thought. If this is realised, it becomes clear that Proudhon's direct influence was far smaller than has hitherto been believed; and modern research is increasingly taking the view either that the events and ideas were moving in a Proudhonist direction in any case, or that, where he did have influence, it was far from complete. Thus the memoir of the Parisian workers to the Geneva Congress (1866) of the First International was full of Proudhon's views; but these workers did not slavishly follow them. Proudhon condemned strikes but

[1] *Correspondance*, 21 May 1858; M. Harmel, 'Proudhon et le mouvement ouvrier' in *Proudhon et notre temps* (1920), 33.
[2] Maxime Vuillaume, *Mes cahiers rouges au temps de la Commune* (1910), 313.

they, as practical union leaders, finding strikes necessary, used them; he condemned political action during most of his life, but they engaged in it when they saw opportunities. Soon they adopted attitudes which seemed to support an acceptance instead of the influence of Marx or Bakunin, but there was no real influence there: the practical problems of organisation led them to adopt new politics—which in turn led them to the adoption of modified or new ideologies.[1] The same will be seen in the Commune, the limited socialist and Proudhonist elements in which will be discussed below.

The effect of the utopians on political life was thus not to create a series of coherent new parties, but on the contrary to uproot tradition, to sow confusion, to stimulate hope, to construct dream-worlds which alienated Frenchmen from the present and consoled them for its shortcomings. The attitudes they encouraged were perhaps more important, from the long-term historical point of view, than the precise details of their schemes, because men mixed up and recombined their ideas in a large variety of ways. What they achieved was to give a high status to ideals and theories. They made people feel enlightened when they indulged in theorising, rather than when they belonged to a certain party. They thus helped to undermine the stability and prestige of ordinary political life. They placed themselves, as their intellectual successors increasingly did also, outside organised society, whose doom they predicted. But they also claimed a role of direction and influence in the society they condemned. The tradition they established became one of the most powerful forces in French life. Their idealism, even if it was seldom implemented in practice, reflected widespread aspirations, and playing with idealism, verbally or more deeply, was a constant feature of this century.

[1] J. Rougerie, 'Sur l'histoire de la Première Internationale', *Le Mouvement social* (Apr.-June 1963), 41-3. See also R. Bancal, *Proudhon* (1970) and above all the important forthcoming work by John Hooper, *The Ethical Socialists*.

4. Republicanism

THE significance of republicanism is that it reflected changes in social relationships which gave a new dimension to politics. It was through republicanism that popular political organisation appeared as an alternative to the system of patronage and clientage on which the nobles and royalists had based their power. The republicans thus mobilised another force in French society. The nobles and the notables had dominated politics because of their wealth, their connections and their active search for power. The republicans counter-balanced their influence with that of the electoral committee, the political party and many kinds of societies in which ordinary men, by getting together, were able to stand up to the notables and challenge their monopoly of public office. They offered the masses an alternative they had not had before, because they united local resistance under a national banner.

However, republicanism was not a mass movement in a simple sense. There were several varieties of it and it produced contradictory results. While appealing to the masses, it also developed a new class of notables. Its ambiguities explain why it attracted so much support, and also why so many myths have been generated about it to cloud over its confusions. There was a mystique about republicanism which long discouraged impartial investigation. The subject has only recently emerged from the realm of partisanship and passion, now that the republic—after tottering in 1940—has established itself as a generally accepted form of government. There are thus many legends about it which need to be dispelled.

The first concerns the way the republic of 1848 was established. This poses the problem of how far the proclamation of the republic was the spontaneous expression of the popular will, in what ways that will was influenced by the economic crisis which struck the whole of Europe in those years, and why the monarchy collapsed. Now it is clear that the monarchy was weak long before the economic crisis. It is quite conceivable that even if there had been no economic crisis, Louis-Philippe might have abdicated all the same, in a row with his own supporters.[1] On the other hand, the events of 22–4 February 1848 suggest that it was by no means inevitable that Louis-Philippe should have been overthrown at that particular time. All the banquets of the opposition involved less than 17,000 people spread over 70 different meetings.[2] The demonstrations of 22 February were started by little over 1,000 students and workers, and the crowd swelled to only about 3,000 in the course of the day. Its slogans were directed against the police, not the monarchy. Its wrath was exacerbated when troops were called in, but a rapid withdrawal of these might have produced a very different turn of events.

The republicans were prepared to accept a regency,[3] for they were under no illusions about their strength: they were a small minority party. The victors in these events could have been the dynastic opposition. But they lost control. It was as a result of the withdrawal, rather than the overthrow of the old ruling class, that the republic was established. It was established in Paris, which had been lost to the government some years already, for most of its deputies were in the opposition. There were no fights in the rest of France. The old administration withdrew. This might be taken as an admission of their weakness, or alternatively as proof of the superficiality of the republican victory. In these three days of February, about 350 people were killed and 500 admitted injured into hospitals. It was the least bloody of French revolutions.[4]

Tocqueville had predicted the revolution but this should not be taken as a sign of extraordinary political perceptiveness. A large number of people had predicted it too—indeed the prediction was a commonplace of discussion. The king himself was worried by its imminence more than anyone. Nevertheless when it came many people were startled by it. Garnier-Pagès, a participant in it and a member of the provisional government

[1] Douglas Johnson, *Guizot* (1963), has an excellent and very fair chapter on 'Guizot and 1848'. Cf. Paul Thureau-Dangin, *Histoire de la monarchie de juillet* (1884–92); P. and T. Higonnet, 'Class Corruption and Politics in the French Chamber of Deputies 1846–8', *French Historical Studies*, 5 (1967), 204–24.

[2] J. J. Bingham, 'The French Banquet Campaign of 1847–8', *Journal of Modern History*, 21 (1959), 1–15; L. Girard, *La Deuxième République 1848–51* (1968), 34.

[3] L. A. Garnier-Pagès, *Histoire de la révolution de 1848* (1861–72), 5. 213.

[4] C. Seignobos, *La Révolution de 1848, le second empire* (1921), and P. de la Gorce, *Histoire de la seconde république française* (1887), contain detailed narratives.

of 1848, thought that if Louis-Philippe had yielded promptly, if he had withdrawn his troops from the capital, if he had been, in other words, willing to be a constitutional monarch, there would have been no revolution.[1] The royalist Falloux, another acute observer, thought the revolution was 'an effect out of all proportion to its cause'.[2] In England, Lord Brougham, fulfilling for this revolution the role Burke had performed for that of 1789, declared that it was 'the sudden work of a moment—a change prepared by no preceding plan—prompted by no felt inconvenience—announced by no complaint . . . Without ground, without pretext, without one circumstance to justify or even to account for it, except familiarity with change and . . . proneness to violence . . . It was the work of some half-dozen artisans, met in a printing office . . . a handful of armed ruffians headed by a shoemaker and a sub-editor.'[3]

The opinion of Guizot on his own fall was not quite so extreme but he found the explanation within the middle class. It had been divided and this division had ruined the monarchy. Granier de Cassagnac, a protégé of Guizot but later one of Napoleon III's supporters, agreed that the rivalry and ambition of the politicians had been disastrous, but he concluded from this that parliamentary government was unworkable: therefore Louis-Philippe was trying to do the impossible. No section of the country supported the regime of July with enthusiasm. That is why a riot was enough to topple it. Thiers, for his part, who had distinguished himself repressing similar riots earlier in the reign, argued that the revolution would have been avoided if the troops had been withdrawn from Paris and later taken the city by assault. This is what he successfully did in 1871 with the Commune.

But Louis-Philippe himself had no such optimism. In an interview with a journalist after his fall, he saw the revolutionary movement as being much stronger than these supporters allowed. He considered that his regime had been very weak, because freedom of the press had produced so many attacks on him (he was very sensitive to them) that the authority of the monarch, and indeed of monarchy, had been greatly diminished:

[1] Garnier-Pagès, 4. 368.
[2] Comte de Falloux, *Mémoires d'un royaliste* (1888), 1. 254.
[3] J. S. Mill, *Dissertations and Discussions* (1859), 2. 339.

it had therefore been easy to overthrow. In 1848, said Louis-Philippe, public opinion was no longer behind him, as it had been in 1830. He had spent his reign trying to repress the spirit of revolution, while securing the gradual development of the principles of 1789. To have allowed the reform movement to triumph would have been to allow the revolution to come to power and to plunge Europe in war; and he preferred to abdicate rather than be the king of the revolution. He would not use force, because he had as much horror of civil as of foreign wars. Louis-Philippe did not analyse why public opinion had abandoned him, for he had come to see all opposition as part of the revolution.[1]

In contrast with these interpretations, which concentrate on the disputes of the middle class, other historians have attempted to claim the republic as the result of far deeper causes. The comtesse d'Agoult, aristocrat turned republican, mistress of Franz Liszt, author under the pseudonym of Daniel Stern of one of the best contemporary histories of the revolution, hailed it as a product of the spontaneous union of the people and the bourgeoisie. It was not an accident but the natural result of several powerful forces. The eighteenth-century *philosophes* started it all with their movement for free thought. The masses became increasingly keen on winning political power after 1789. The industrial proletariat, rendered increasingly miserable by repeated economic crises and unemployment, stood out in sharp contrast as the prosperity of the other classes waxed. 'At first', she said, 'hardly anyone was aware of this conflict.' Fourier and Saint-Simon alone pointed out these injustices: but their views went unheeded: 'There was blindness everywhere.' However, that section of the bourgeoisie which had not yet become rich gave expression to the confused sentiments of the masses through its parliamentary opposition. The corruption of the government 'brought forward the hour of conflict . . . When the battle was joined, instinct triumphed over science, popular sentiment over political cleverness. Democratic France, in an outburst of indignation, overthrew the government of the French bourgeoisie and proclaimed itself free under a republican government.' This was a very subtle analysis. Madame d'Agoult introduced social and intel-

[1] E. Lemoine, *L'Abdication du roi Louis-Philippe racontée par lui-même* (1851).

lectual factors but very astutely limited their role as actual causes of revolution. She did not quite offer an explanation. On the one hand she said that public opinion demanded a republic, but on the other hand she concluded it soon became clear that the revolution had come too early. She did not explain why, as she put it, the people lost confidence in the republic and why in June 1848 the republic finally repressed the people. She contradicted herself by implying that the republic was not as popular as it had appeared in February, and that the people were not masters of it.[1]

Karl Marx, who wrote some brilliant journalism about the revolution, gave the proletariat only a very modest role in it. He argued that the monarchy of Louis-Philippe was dominated by the 'financial aristocracy'—bankers and large landed proprietors: it was 'nothing other than a joint stock company for the exploitation of France's national wealth, the dividends of which were shared among ministers, Chambers, 240,000 voters and their adherents'. The opposition to it came from what he calls the industrial aristocracy, and it is this group which captured power in 1848. The revolution for Marx was therefore not a proletarian one. The proletariat obtained no power from it and it was duped again, as it had been in 1830. February 1848 was nothing like as important as 1789. The real significance of the revolution, for Marx, derived from the June days when the bourgeoisie repressed the workers and by thus destroying the alliance of the two, prepared the ground for the genuine struggle of the proletariat against the bourgeoisie, which he predicted would come at the next economic crisis. Marx placed only limited emphasis on the crop failure, and the agricultural and commercial crisis of 1845–7, by which the revolution had only been 'accelerated and the mood of revolt ripened'. It is much more his disciples who have stressed this economic aspect and it is thanks to them that a great deal of research has been undertaken to reveal the extent of popular distress.[2]

The idea that the revolution was an accident was vigorously attacked by Albert Crémieux in 1912, in a detailed study of the

---

[1] Daniel Stern, *Histoire de la révolution de 1848* (1850–3).

[2] K. Marx, *Class Struggles in France 1848–50* (English trans., 1924); J. Dautry, *1848 et la deuxième république* (1957); G. Duveau, *1848* (1965); and the Sorbonne lectures of E. Labrousse. Good analysis in R. Price, *The Second French Republic* (1972).

four days 21 to 24 February 1848. He condemned previous historians who had concentrated on the role of ministers, deputies and political parties and pointed out that the barricades were put up not by their orders, but spontaneously by the people. 1848 was therefore essentially a popular revolution. He brought forward a mass of evidence from police reports of the agitation during these days and statements made by participants. He attributed the intervention of the masses in politics to the economic crisis, the spread of socialist doctrines and general dissatisfaction, but he did not discuss just how far these factors directly affected their behaviour on the crucial days.[1]

Recent research has shown that no single explanation of the revolution of 1848 will hold water. The agricultural crisis began after the harvest of 1845. By the spring of 1847 the price of bread was at about double its normal level—but there were large variations in different parts of the country. In May 1847 for example the price of a hectolitre of wheat was 34 francs in Var, but 49 francs 50 in Haut-Rhin. The harvest of 1847 was a very good one. By the time of the revolution, prices had tumbled everywhere to levels below the previous average and they remained so throughout the republic. The revolution was therefore not a revolution of hunger in the direct sense of there being a shortage of food. There had been some bread riots in 1847 but they had been very minor and had had no political consequences. Not all the population suffered equally. The large wheatgrowers were compensated for the bad harvests by high prices. Smaller producers who could not afford to hold back their wheat till prices were favourable suffered. Tenant farmers who had rented their farms at high rents during the years of prosperity found themselves in difficulties. It was the labourers who were hardest hit, particularly when they were not lodged and fed by their masters. Sacked by their impoverished employers and unable to obtain, because of the general crisis, the supplementary industrial employment which was essential to their survival, they experienced some of their worst years in the century. One of the great problems of 1848 was unemployment. Not only people on the borderline of starvation,

[1] Albert Crémieux, *La Révolution de février: étude critique sur les journées des 21, 22, 23 et 24 février 1848* (1912). Cf. Pierre Quentin-Banchart, *La Crise sociale de 1848: les origines de la révolution de février* (1920).

but large sections of the population were plunged into debt. So even when the harvests were normal again, the difficulties were by no means over. When wheat prices did fall, they did so in a way the peasants could not recall the like of since 1787. The labourers now benefited but the producers got derisory returns. The crisis continued therefore for several years after 1848, with varying groups being affected. The winegrowers, for example, had done well in 1847, but then suffered four consecutive years of unprecedented severity, as this table of their income shows (for Loir-et-Cher):

1843	96	1849	66
1844	96	1850	41
1845	176	1851	59
1846	87	1852	136
1847	143	1853	143
1848	72	1854	87

It should not be thought that the crisis brought prosperity to a sudden halt. The farmers had had problems throughout the previous reign, some more than others. What made this crisis so catastrophic was its extension over the whole of the economy.

The textile industry had been reducing wages for some years and had been heading for disaster because of uncontrolled overproduction. Now demand collapsed. 35 per cent of textile workers are estimated to have been sacked, the same proportion of metal workers, 20 per cent of miners. Work stopped on the construction of railways; orders for house building dried up; and many small rural industries found their markets disappearing. Metal production fell by 50 per cent. The financial crisis was perhaps the most serious of all, because it made recovery impossible. The stock market collapsed. The 3 per cent *rente*, which was 75 francs in February 1848 remained at between 56 and 58 francs for three years. The volume of discounts at the Bank of France fell by 40 per cent and was still a third below normal in 1851. In desperation manufacturers dumped their goods on the market at knock-down prices, with disastrous results on the small shopkeepers. 'Hence', said Karl Marx, 'the innumerable bankruptcies among this section of the Paris bourgeoisie and hence their revolutionary action in February.'[1]

[1] K. Marx, *Works* (1950), i. 133.

The significance of the doubling of bankruptcies should not be exaggerated, however. In Paris in 1845, a normal year, there were 691 bankruptcies, between August 1846 and July 1847 there were 1,139. These were not a massive class. But together the agricultural, industrial, commercial and financial crises created not only a whole new mass of unemployed and hungry men, but also a middle class in severe distress, and an upper class conscious that the very basis of society was being shaken. In January 1847, the comte de Castellane noted at the ball of the duchesse de Galliera, wife of one of the richest of railway magnates, that people prophesied the pillaging of châteaux: 'We are threatened', he noted, 'by social upheaval.'[1]

It does not follow, however, that those men who suffered most, the starving unemployed, played an important part in the revolution. Research into the industrialised regions of France has revealed little subversive activity among them. In Lille, the number of poor in receipt of public assistance did increase from one in six in 1828 to one in 4·2 in 1846, but the attitude of the working class to this seems to have been not anger and sedition, but submission and resignation. The Church retained its hold here and successfully preached acceptance of misfortune by the poor. In 1848 the workers did not revolt. Their political activity—if it can be called that—was confined to demonstrations against foreign workers, particularly Belgians, who were serious competitors for work in periods of depression. The revolution seemed an opportunity, above all else, to expel the foreigners. The only political riot by the workers of the Nord occurred on 5 December 1851, after the *coup d'état*, and this was confined to some fifty miners of Anzin.[2] In Alsace, socialist ideas were confined almost exclusively to the bourgeoisie. The workers' material conditions were appalling but there was no evidence under Louis-Philippe of agitation by them. 'The population of Alsace', concluded Mme Kahan-Rebecque in her thorough study of the years 1830–48 in the province, 'did not feel very strongly the need for profound social reforms, first because the industrial employers themselves

[1] E. Labrousse, *Aspects de la crise et de la dépression de l'économie française au milieu du 19ᵉ siècle* (Bibliothèque de la révolution de 1848, no. 19, 1956).

[2] André Lasserre, *La Situation des ouvriers de l'industrie textile dans la région lilloise sous la monarchie de juillet* (Lausanne, 1952).

carried out some reforms, and secondly because the Alsatian was very respectful of the established order.' Even during the crisis of 1847, which hit the workers very hard, there was only one insurrection, in June, when some 300 or 400 workers demonstrated against the high price of bread.[1]

The workers in France as a whole were far from being incapable of protesting against their conditions. In the eighteen years of Louis-Philippe's reign 382 strikes have been counted (and there were probably more) occurring in 121 different places. But it was not the large industries which went on strike most often: building workers, followed by tailors and carpenters were the most militant. It was the privileged silk weavers of Lyon who provide the one case of workers taking up arms to further their demands. There certainly was much organisation and planning of industrial action, especially by miners and woolworkers. The government often used troops to repress these strikes and sentenced many workers to imprisonment for their participation. But the links between industrial and political action were still only embryonic. These strikes prepared some workers for active participation in the Second Republic, but they had not gone far enough to give the workers as a whole the initiative in politics. It was in any case the urban artisans, not the factory workers, who were most active; and it was precisely in areas where conditions were worst that protests by factory workers were almost non-existent. Likewise, the agrarian disturbances of 1846-7 produced by the high price of bread occurred mainly in the west, not in regions which voted socialist in 1849. The uniquely free conditions that prevailed during the republic made possible the manifestation of grievances which had remained concealed, and which were by no means always the same as those revealed before the revolution.[2]

The republic was thus established first because the monarchy lost its nerve, lost its self-confidence and its belief in its own mission. It did so under the influence of a demonstration of popular discontent of a very exceptional kind—not just a press

[1] Mme Kahan-Rebecque, *L'Alsace économique et sociale sous le règne de Louis-Philippe* (1928).
[2] R. Gossez, 'Carte des troubles en 1846-7' in E. Labrousse, *Aspects de la crise* (1956), 1-3; J. P. Aguet, *Les Grèves sous la monarchie de juillet* (Geneva, 1954); Peter N. Stearns, 'Patterns of Industrial Strike Activity in France during the July Monarchy', *American Historical Review*, 70 (Jan. 1965), 371-94.

campaign, nor party agitation, but unorganised, uncommitted, ordinary Parisians breaking the habits of routine and protesting in a way for which few comparisons can be found. It is this that needs to be explained, which can be done only by looking far more widely than simply at the economic distress or the immediate events of February. The character of the Second Republic cannot be understood just by examining the sparks which set it alight. Precisely because the revolution was so much an expression of anger, its significance was by no means clear. The nature of the republic still had to be worked out.

It was, moreover, a Parisian revolution. In the provinces there was no real struggle for power, and no similar mass demonstrations. The local authorities, the prefects, put up no resistance. In the north and west many towns accepted the republic without enthusiasm; the old monarchist officials proclaimed the new regime and continued to govern as before. In Bordeaux, where the opposition to Louis-Philippe was weak and where a prosperous upper class of Orleanist wine merchants and shipowners was firmly installed, the republic was not inaugurated until 29 February, and then only by the general of the garrison, acting under orders from Paris. In Lons-le-Saulnier, the national guard remained loyal to the king and for several days the monarchist prefect and a revolutionary committee coexisted as rival claimants to authority; it was only on 3 March that the republic was finally triumphant, when the colonel of the national guard accepted a compromise and reluctantly embraced the republican leader.[1]

There was a long tradition of republican thought before 1848 and of considerable agitation and organisation, but it was con-

[1] For the revolution in the provinces see Albert Charles, *La Révolution de 1848 et la seconde république à Bordeaux et dans le département de la Gironde* (Bordeaux, 1945); E. Dagnan, *Le Gers sous la seconde république* (Auch, 1928–9); A. Desannis, *La Révolution de 1848 dans le département du Jura* (1948); P. Muller, *La Révolution de 1848 en Alsace* (1912); G. Rougeron, *La Révolution de 1848 à Moulins et dans le département de l'Allier* (1950); Élie Reynier, *La Seconde République dans l'Ardèche* (1948); G. Rocal, *1848 en Dordogne* (1934); J. Godechot, *La Révolution de 1848 à Toulouse et dans la Haute Garonne* (1948); *La Révolution de 1848 dans le département de l'Isère* (Grenoble, 1949); F. Dutacq and A. Latreille, *Histoire de Lyon*, vol. 3 (1952), and the works of Tudesq, Vigier, Chevalier, Armengaud, and Dupeux already cited. There is a large amount of information in the publications of the Société de la Révolution de 1848, appearing under different titles since 1905.

fined to relatively small circles. The importance of 1848 is that
the masses were drawn into politics, and won over to this
movement. This did not occur uniformly over the whole country.
The republicans succeeded in winning the peasants over only in
some regions. They made least impression in the west, where
many continued to accept the leadership of the nobles, and to
ally with them against the cities. The south, by contrast, they
managed to convert from a stronghold of royalism into a steadfastly republican region. The process by which this was done
can best be illustrated by looking at a single department. In
1815 the department of the Var was a region where the White
Terror raged with a passion that revealed the political leadership of an active nobility. In December 1848, however, it gave
12·2 per cent of its votes to the republicans, in May 1849 27·4
per cent, and in March 1850 31·5 per cent. It was the department in which the largest uprising against the *coup d'état* of 1851
took place. It remained for the next century in the vanguard of
the republican movement. In 1936 it elected two communist
deputies. Yet this was a rural department with no large-
scale industry. Its conversion to republicanism can be explained
by the development of different forms of independent popular
action in the early nineteenth century. Until the 1830s villages
had little hope of preventing the descendants of their feudal
lords from usurping common rights in the woodlands around
them, which meant so much to the poor; but after that date an
increasing number of communes brought lawsuits against the
rich and more often than not won them. A new sense of local
power developed. Poor communes could not afford the legal
fees—but the richer ones were able to carry on the struggle, not
only against the lords but even to extend it against the state
also, which tormented them with its Forestry Code and its
endless taxation.

There were villages in this region with populations of between
1,500 and 5,000, often including small industries like tanneries,
paper-mills, silk weaving, cork and oil manufacture. They had
strong artisan elements, and so differed from the towns only
slightly: the transition from one to the other was imperceptible,
with no real change of type. These villages—if they can be
called that—had ancient traditions of combination in religious
fraternities. In the nineteenth century these developed into new

forms of association and in particular friendly societies and drinking clubs. The latter, known as *chambrées* or *chambrettes*, were a peculiarly southern institution, men's clubs devoted to drinking, gambling and conversation. They acquired a political complexion because they quickly came into conflict with the government over their avoidance of wine duties and of the laws restricting gambling and public meetings. Precisely because they served an important social purpose, they grew in numbers despite all attempts to repress them. Under Louis-Philippe there were between one and seven in every commune.

The tradition of young men getting together in groups was an old one, but their clubs had usually been ephemeral. Now the *chambrées* became more permanent organisations, for men of all ages, modelled rather more on the bourgeois club, into which the upper classes had for rather longer organised themselves. This increasing imitation of the bourgeois was perhaps a natural outcome of the spread of education. The number of army recruits who could read and write in this department increased between 1831 and 1851 from 33 per cent to 60 per cent. The peasants were gradually acquiring the means of participating in national life. Knowledge of French was spreading. The village theatres began acting classical plays in addition to the old folkloric ones. Musical societies were founded, going beyond the ballad to perform choral works in French. Their musical activities were often combined with more practical ones, particularly mutual insurance, so that they were doubly social institutions, and some called themselves 'philanthropico-harmonic' societies. Thus in 1842 the single village of Cabris had five different clubs: the literary club (to which the professional men and largest landowners belonged—the notary and the doctor), one artisans' *chambrée*, and three peasants' *chambrées*, each catering for a different area. All these channels for southern sociability provided an excellent breeding-ground for popular political involvement.

However, the transition from the influence of the notables to the independence of the masses did not take place in one step. The societies were made political to a considerable extent by the intervention of dissident members of the bourgeoisie. One of the classical types of popular hero in the mid nineteenth century was the barrister who had represented the commune in its lawsuit against the descendants of the feudal lords. Another is the bourgeois philanthropist who was worshipped for the benefits he brought to his village, particularly if he was self-made. But it was above all the 'bohemians of the village, the failed graduates, the doctors without patients, all sons of peasants who had become rich and who, tired of emaciating work in the towns, retired and used up the income of their papas, who were stupidly proud of this strange progeny'. So wrote a mayor of Toulon in 1870, about the youth of the 1840s. The rise of this class of 'young petty bourgeois, idle and intellectual, libertine and sociable' was very important in spreading the ideas of Paris to the provinces. Important too were the bourgeois bachelors, ostracised from the society of their equals because of their liberal opinions or their moral conduct, because, unable to marry for fear of dispersing their families' wealth, they lived with concubines. Such men frequented the cafés and clubs and created links between the classes. Many of these peasant and artisan clubs had honorary bourgeois members who provided leadership or advice. Established manufacturers naturally supported the government under Louis-Philippe, but there were many cases of small ones, still almost artisans, who challenged their domination equally in business and in politics. The well-to-do, or those rising on the social scale, were not necessarily all on the same side. In particular the sons of manufacturers, educated beyond their fathers' station, often came back to their villages to side with the workers and provide a republican leadership. Once again family problems can be seen to have a significance for politics.

But republicanism can be connected with traditional forces too: the risings of 1851 had much in common with the old *jacquerie*. What changed now was the method of expressing it. Before 1848 the peasants acted through municipal channels. After 1851 they learnt to act through political parties. That was the achievement of the republicans; but it was not the doing of any party organisation. Often a village which emerged with a large vote for the Reds was converted by the isolated activity of a single enthusiast, who subscribed to a Paris newspaper and set himself up as a local sage. There was much accident in the way the seeds thrown to the wind sprouted over the country. The seeds did not all necessarily come from Paris.

One of the complications of republicanism was that local plants adopted national names, but did not lose their individuality because of that. 'The Paris revolution', Louis Chevalier has written, 'was only the occasion for these troubles' in the rural areas of France. 'It was not really their cause. It did not communicate to them either its rhythm, or its preoccupations, or its ideology. It only allowed a sudden reawakening, on a more violent scale, of that agrarian fever that goes back to the great revolution and before that, whose scarcely extinguished ardours Balzac, Tocqueville and Proudhon have described.'[1]

The role of young people and of students in the creation of republicanism was an important social development and it also had an interesting theoretical basis. Students entered politics long before 1968. The first *Political History of Students* in France was published in 1850.[2] Just as after the war of 1945 the number of university students doubled and trebled, creating new problems and a new class, so in the mid nineteenth century the *bacheliers* and *licenciés* more than doubled in a single generation. The number of men awarded the *baccalauréat* annually rose from 3,200 to 7,200 between the 1840s and the 1870s, and the number who got the *licence* rose from 338 in 1842 to 865 in 1876. This new intellectual élite was still small enough for personal relations to be possible within it. Each batch of graduates from Paris (and from every major town) could know one another. Common ideas and common action were possible. The ties of friendship or common experience gave these groups a unity. There thus grew *la jeunesse républicaine*, including past students even more than actual ones. Nor should one omit to include in this failed students, for about half the candidates at the *baccalauréat* were rejected. Paris also had many '*ex-jeunes gens*, known as students in their seventeenth year ... recognisable by their untrimmed beards, their unkempt clothing and their

[1] Louis Chevalier, 'Les Fondements économiques et sociaux de l'histoire politique de la région parisienne (1848–51)' (1950, unpublished, but very important thesis), 196; id., *La Formation de la population parisienne au 19ᵉ siècle* (1950); Maurice Agulhon, *La République au village: les populations du Var de la Révolution à la Seconde République* (1970) and id., *Pénitents et francs-maçons de l'ancienne Provence* (1968) both outstandingly original; Lucienne A. Roubin, *Chambrettes des Provençaux* (1970).

[2] Antonio Watripont, *Histoire politique des écoles et des étudiants* (1850). Only volume 1 was published. The manuscript of volume 2 was, however, seen and briefly summarised by the author of the interesting article on students in P. Larousse, *Grand Dictionnaire universel du XIXᵉ siècle*, 7 (1870), 1085.

eccentric hair-styles' who rarely went to lectures except those of political celebrities like Michelet and Quinet.[1]

As students these men had been something of pioneers, the first of the meritocrats, but the state, which had brought them into being, alienated them by simultaneous neglect and repression. The students had high pretensions. They claimed that their presence made Paris 'the most powerful centre, the most active agent of civilisation . . . a home of discussion, a vast laboratory of ideas'.[2] The great artists, scientists and writers of France, and the great statesmen of the revolution, had risen from their ranks. Already in 1830 they had played a significant part in the revolution. Balzac had spotted that these young men, whom literature liked to portray as lazy, eccentric and devoted to pleasure, were a new force to be reckoned with. The monarchy of July, he said, had been brought into power by 'intelligence' and by 'youth', but it had then forgotten what it owed them, it had refused them the right to sit in parliament or even to vote. 'Youth', he prophesied, 'will explode like the boiler of a steam engine . . . The new barbarians are the intellectuals.'

The government could not provide enough openings for this increasing class. Its fiercely competitive system of recruitment, vitiated by nepotism and political bias, made frustrated ambition a common fate. It could not find docile teachers to indoctrinate the young. A great deal was demanded of the teachers, but they were rewarded with the most meagre salaries and the minimum of status and respect. In the secondary schools, 55 per cent of the teachers were of peasant, artisan or shopkeeper origin: and only 14 per cent of them married into the liberal professions.[3] The children of the bourgeoisie were thus taught in the *lycées* by the bright children of the working classes, an anomaly which inevitably created tension. At this stage, the teachers had not been absorbed into middle-class society: they lived on its fringes, often unmarried, insecure in their jobs as well as socially. They were in some ways interlopers, brought in by the state against the clergy, and they were thus a threat to the traditional order at the same time as they were supposed to

---

[1] Alphonse Lucas, *Les Clubs et les clubistes* (1851), 122–3.
[2] Larousse, loc. cit.
[3] P. Gerbod, *La Condition universitaire* (1965), 110, 629, 636.

bolster it. The paradox of the situation was that these poor teachers were most of them at bottom intellectually quite conservative, passionately attached to the classics, and with their horizons normally quite restricted. Because they were so conservative, they denounced the materialism and corruption of their times—much like the clergy. The state did not know how to handle them. It allowed this idealism, which reflected a sense of unease and isolation in the world, to develop into political opposition. The republicanism born among the teachers was savagely persecuted, which exacerbated its tone and made it appear more revolutionary than it really was. Once the persecution was over, republicanism revealed its true colours. Republican radicalism came to mean conservatism. This was not a betrayal, but a proof of an attachment to traditional values, which had always been there.

A distinguishing characteristic of student agitation in the early nineteenth century was that it was led by teachers. Persecuted professors were often the heroes of demonstrations. Guizot had begun life as a liberal professor, and one has only to read his lectures to see how they could be taken as political programmes. There were many others who used their position to preach doctrines the government in power disliked. Just before the revolution of 1848, the two Paris student newspapers, *La Lanterne du Quartier Latin* and *L'Avant-garde, Journal des Écoles*, had been organising demonstrations to protest against the closing of the lectures of Michelet, Quinet and Mickiewicz. It was not uncommon, during the Restoration and July Monarchy, to find crowds of students outside parliament, applauding the opposition deputies; nor for students to go on strike. It was not surprising that on 22 February 1848 they should have provided the nucleus of the demonstrators who started the revolution. Michelet's lectures to them in 1848, at the Collège de France, encouraged them to act, rather than to study. He told them that they had a mission to fulfil which no other class could. As young men, they had the time, the warmth of feelings, and the ability to mix freely with all classes. They alone could start the reign of fraternity, the moral union of the nation, by taking the ideas of the intellectuals to the people. They had not yet been limited and narrowed by the responsibilities and outlook of a specialist profession. They could still be interested in men for their own sakes. They should therefore be the intermediaries, the 'mediators of the city', for it was the young who could best bridge the great abyss between the masses and the bourgeoisie. The trouble with men of letters, said Michelet, was that they wrote for other men of letters, and even workers who wrote books wrote in the style of the men of letters, not for the people. The masses were still isolated, divided by a hundred different patois. The young should seek them out. They should translate for them the message of the geniuses.[1]

The persecution of professors like Michelet turned them into heroes. During the Second Republic and the Second Empire some outspoken professors, dismissed for their independence, or resigning from their chairs rather than take an oath of loyalty to the regime of Napoleon III, became martyrs of the young. Vacherot, who had acquired great influence as deputy director of the École Normale, and Jules Simon, who resigned from the Sorbonne, are only the most famous of them. A host of lesser-known ones retired from the state educational system to humbler posts in private schools. Sainte-Barbe, one of the best cramming establishments in Paris, became a haven for them. Some 700 secondary teachers were sacked or resigned during the Second Republic alone. In the primary schools, the *instituteurs*—who likewise began by being on the whole conservative—were regimented and victimised in the same way. This is the origin of the *république des professeurs*.

Republicanism also attracted many doctors and barristers, partly because theirs were professions in which political independence was possible. The problems of the doctors have already been discussed. Those of the lawyers were not dissimilar. A normal liberal education in the mid nineteenth century ended with the study of law. The legal profession was therefore vastly overcrowded. Young barristers without clients, living from hand to mouth by private tutoring or literary hack work, were a principal ingredient of the intellectual proletariat of most towns. They were the natural champions of the underdog. Rhetoric was the common language of the Bar and of politics. Barristers were another of the intermediaries between the

[1] J. Michelet, *L'Étudiant* (Lectures of 1848 not printed till 1877, reprinted 1970), 57, 67, 76.

centres of power and the masses. It was no accident that when
the republic was at last established, they should have occupied
so prominent a role in it. In 1881 41 per cent of the members of
the chamber of deputies were lawyers, or 45 per cent if one
includes those with a legal training who had not practised. In
1906 the figure was still 37 per cent (or 40 per cent). 52 per cent
of all ministers between 1873 and 1920 had legal degrees. But
a legal education, of course, was no stimulus to innovation or
imagination. The skill of these lawyers was in effecting compromises, in acting as interpreters between classes and powers
which could not understand each other, in administering and in
bringing a semblance of order in anarchic situations. That is
why they were so highly valued in the early years of the Third
Republic. They helped to consolidate it. But by winning
leadership of it, they also prevented it from becoming genuinely
radical. It was no accident that the proportion of lawyers in
parliament fell after 1920: they were of less use when new
challenges demanded change. A republic of lawyers was even
less of a threat to established values and traditional ways of
thought than a republic of professors. But their oratory and
their youth made it difficult to see just what they were aiming
for.[1]

In 1848 and in the three succeeding years several different
forms of republicanism manifested themselves. First, there was
the utopian, fraternal republicanism over which Lamartine
presided. This blossomed out in the first months of the revolution of 1848, in a situation of unprecedented anarchy. The disappearance of the monarchy created a totally new sense of
freedom, because the government that replaced it was, at
least in name, that of the whole people. There was suddenly
the liberty to speak as one pleased, without fear of the police,
to publish any book one liked, to issue newspapers without
tax, caution money or censorship. Three hundred newspapers
appeared in Paris. Seventeen new ones were founded in the
department of Nord alone. By May, the circulation of papers
produced in Paris simply for the working class was 400,000.[2]

[1] Statistics in Y. H. Gaudemet, *Les Juristes et la vie politique de la Troisième République*
(1970), 15, 18.
[2] Claude Bellanger *et al.*, *Histoire générale de la presse française*, 2 (1969), 208;
J. Godechot, *La Presse ouvrière 1819–1850* (Bibliothèque de la Révolution de 1848,
no. 23, 1966), 185.

People could meet and form associations without restrictions. Within a month 145 clubs were established in Paris; and there were probably 300 three months later. In the provinces they multiplied rapidly. Those which had been informal or secret assumed a new importance, and often developed into electoral organisations or even went beyond discussion and became production associations—firms run by the people. The corporations of the artisans enjoyed a sudden revival, and at public ceremonies the different trades were solemnly represented. The juxtaposition of a powerful government and isolated individuals was replaced by groups of every size, who could believe that they held their destiny in their own hands. Social, professional and traditional animosities were swamped by a wave of fraternal good feeling, the 'solidarity' the utopians had called for. The proletariat, for a brief period, were no longer looked on as outcasts, but were idealised as heroes of the revolution. Some bourgeois ladies even thought it fashionable to wear clumsy workers' boots; men covered their fine linen with artisans' blouses, allowed their beards to grow and called each other citizen.

Lamartine, head of the provisional government and minister of foreign affairs, epitomised and represented this ecstatic atmosphere better than anyone else. The hope of this kind of republicanism was not the triumph of one class over another, but the fusion of classes and their abolition altogether. Lamartine was particularly suited to lead this movement because he stood above the clash of faction and even of the conflicts of class. He was an aristocrat, but a bankrupt one, who liked to say that he was simply a winegrower. He had nationwide popularity as a poet. He could hold out a hand to all parties, because he had served all and none. After having been a diplomat under Charles X, he had first accepted Louis-Philippe and then turned against him. He had proclaimed himself a democrat under the monarchy, but he had consistently kept outside the established parties. He claimed that his principal political gift was his instinctive sympathy for the masses, his ability to commune with them in some mystical way, so that he, better than anyone else, understood the 'fundamental idea of the time'—reconciliation. He had always believed that he had been picked out by Providence to give effect to the popular

will: he had even 'longed for the storm, in order to be brilliant
and heroic in the struggle'. He did not deny that for him
politics was essentially a matter of sentiment, for he insisted
that all the great achievements of history had been the product
of a sentiment moving the hearts of the masses. He believed
there was a popular yearning not so much for political or
economical change as for the moral regeneration of mankind,
a return to primeval virtue and innocence, and the solution of
all problems by love, which had hitherto been shackled and
frustrated by society. He had great faith in the power of oratory
to bring this about. As a result he often believed that he had
achieved his purpose simply because he had proclaimed it in
fine language. But his naïve enthusiasm was echoed by a large
mass of people. In the elections of 1848, a quarter of a million
men voted for him in Paris, and one and a half million in
the nine other departments where he was spontaneously
put up. He was the first hero of universal suffrage: no one then
could equal his popularity. Within a very short space of time,
however, he was seen to be incapable of dealing with the realities
and he lost power as suddenly as he acquired it. But the attitude
he represented was tenacious. His brand of republicanism,
even though it had proved so inadequate, did not die, because
it was the reflection of a widespread idealism and generosity.
Lamartine's search for popularity among the masses, rather
than among the party politicians, his contempt for parliamentary government, his ideal of a mixed republic, popular at its
base but heroic at its summit, led by a great man with a passion
for the idea of his generation, using a strong centralised state
to improve the lot of the poor, following a foreign policy at
once glorious and disinterested, based on the principle of
nationalities and aiming eventually at a federation of European
states—this together formed a programme which has survived
him. Napoleon III's policy echoed it in many ways. The Fifth
Republic had much in common with it. Between these two
periods, many politicians have admired Lamartine—Ollivier,
Waldeck-Rousseau, Combes and Barthou for example—but,
beyond individual cases, his tradition constitutes a not insigni-
ficant element in the subconscious of the republican party.
Republicanism always harboured a penchant for bold humanitarian gestures and generous action which served no class or

private interests. On occasion it could move very close to Bonapartism. These ambiguities often brought internal discord and sometimes catastrophe for the movement, but they were never exorcised, because they appealed to a temperament with deep roots. Republican politics continued to attract poets, orators and dreamers, even if, after 1848, they paid lip-service to science and realism.[1]

The republicanism of the democratic socialists, who made republicanism Red, was in some ways equally woolly and vague. It derived its inspiration partly from the Revolution of 1789 and partly from the utopians. The former was a confused memory and the latter, as has been seen, attracted relatively few adherents. However, Red republicanism went beyond utopianism. It turned it into a mass movement, by grafting it on to the traditional institutions of the workers and the peasants. It made it not just intellectually or emotionally attractive, nor simply a novelty—resistance to which was always strong—but part of the community life of ordinary people. In this form, republicanism brought the masses into politics, in a way which the mere proclamation of the republic and of universal suffrage did not. It organised them in such a way that they were able to overthrow—even if only temporarily—the notables who had hitherto ruled them.

The republic of 1848 was to begin with a largely urban phenomenon. Historians have concentrated on the events in Paris, but the permanent consequences of what happened there were limited. Before 1848 the workers of Paris had already developed many forms of organisation. They had artisan corporations which still had life in them. They had mutual benefit societies—262 in 1846 (60 per cent of them linked with trade associations, and counting 22,000 members). They had clubs for self-improvement and recreation, evening classes and choir singing. They had gone on strike under the July Monarchy five times more often than any other city. They had been touched by the writings of the utopians, and they even had

---

[1] There is a good selection of Lamartine's speeches and writings in *La Politique de Lamartine*, ed. L. de Ronchaud (1878); see also A. de Lamartine, *La France parlementaire* (1865); E. Harris, *Lamartine et le peuple* (1932); C. Latreille, *Les Dernières Années de Lamartine* (1925); Gordon Wright, 'A Poet in Politics: Lamartine and the Revolution of 1848', *History Today* (1958), 616–27; and G. Flaubert, *L'Éducation sentimentale* (1869).

their own newspapers. The republic of 1848 was to a considerable extent their creation.

They entered political life with enthusiasm. On some occasions their response to calls for united action was profoundly impressive—as in the demonstration of 17 March, when as many as 200,000 of them marched through the city. In the Luxembourg—where once the peers of France had met— they had a Government Commission for the Workers sitting, which between 150 and 200 representatives of different trades attended, with a view to evolving a new order for them. In the clubs and cafés also, they gave themselves up to interminable discussion, and some pretty effective organisation. Paris was alive in these days in a way which has only been repeated in two or three critical periods since then. But at first the majority of the workers lent their support to the lyrical republic of Lamartine. They did not foresee how difficult it would be to redress their grievances. The petitions they sent in to the government confused ephemeral and fundamental aims, and hesitated between nostalgia for the past and vague longings for change. Counterbalancing their humanitarianism, they were keen on expelling foreigners, on limiting work by women and by convents, on controlling apprentices—because all these were rivals and what they wanted above all else was employment. The Right to Work was their slogan. Somehow they thought the government could give it to them. Their other slogan was the Organisation of Work, which meant the participation of workers in running industry, but again they were not clear whether they intended this to be started or assisted by the state, and what the place of capital in it would be. In the immediate present, they negotiated for higher wages, improved methods of payment and minimum scales.[1] In the elections of April 1848, Lamartine came head of the poll in Paris by a wide margin, with 259,800 votes. The moderate republicans in his ministry got over 200,000 each. But Ledru-Rollin came twenty-fourth with 131,000, Louis Blanc got only 121,000, Barbès 64,000, and Cabet 20,000. The workers of Paris were not won over unanimously to an extreme form of republicanism. Paris was an active breeding-ground for revolutionary ideas and for advanced doctrines; it was so before and remained so

[1] R. Gossez, *Les Ouvriers de Paris*: Livre 1: *L'Organisation 1848–51* (1967).

after 1848. But once universal suffrage was proclaimed, it could no longer decide the fate of France. And it was too varied a city, with too many complicated relationships and traditions, for it to have a single will.

The rising of June 1848, which took place when 100,000 unemployed workers were told that society could do nothing more for them, was one of the most frightening episodes of the century, but it was not a class war in simple terms, with workers fighting the bourgeoisie. The researches of Remy Gossez in the files of those arrested after it have shown that there was no class war. There were workers on both sides of the barricades. The national guard which suppressed the rising contained a complete cross-section of the population, proprietors, shop-keepers, workers and intellectuals. At the barricades raised in the rue Soufflot, the partisans of order were led by the scientist Arago and the typographer Pascal (one of the writers for *L'Atelier*, the workers' paper): their discussions with their opponents showed mistrust by the manual worker of the intellectual much more than envy by the poor of the rich. The intellectual could be more of a stranger to the worker than his employer, with whom he lived and worked. A leading role in the repression was played by young workers, especially those from the provinces. They were natural enemies of the older workers who held the jobs, and whom they, being bachelors, could undercut. Many of them had enrolled in the *garde mobile* simply because they needed work. The interests of young students and young workers did not always coincide. The rebels, moreover, were not, on the whole, Parisian workers at all. Only one-seventh of them, and only one-ninth of those arrested, were born in Paris. They were not necessarily underprivileged workers either, but often men who had come to Paris to complete their professional training, to rise in the world—and a good number of them had done so: there were foremen and even employers among the insurgents. It is true that there was more approximation to a class war in the large factories of the mechanical construction industry and the railway workshops, whose workers took a leading part in the insurrection, but here there were also cases of foremen, engineers and even directors leading their workers out to revolt. All sorts of unemployed, vagabonds, journalists, even *déclassé* aristocrats and bankrupt bankers were found on the rebel side. There were representatives of every class in both parties. The leaders were by no means predominantly proletarian. Women took a very important part in the rising: it was a rising as much of women as of men, but this side of it has been forgotten and cannot easily be investigated further because few of them were arrested or made depositions. If there was one single category which the insurgents were united in hating, it was their landlords. Most of them were behind with their rents: the revolution of February had given them an excuse to postpone paying. In the arrests which followed, denunciation by landlords was the principal source of information used by the police. The conflict of generations, the animosities between workers and shopkeepers, tensions between individuals and the frustrations of housewives all played their part in this holocaust. The workers certainly paid the price for it: 11,000 of them were imprisoned or deported and another 1,500 shot without trial. The aftermath of the repression was probably almost as damaging as the insurrection itself. The clubs, the right to strike, the freedom of speech were brought to an end. The exhilarating and enervating experience of freely organising themselves and planning their future could not be forgotten. The trade union and the republican movement were both deeply influenced by the experiences of 1848. Paris was confirmed as a centre of revolution. But not the whole of Paris, nor all the workers, were converts to democratic socialism. In December 1851 Paris rose again to protest against the *coup d'état*. It showed its republicanism with a massive vote of 80,000 against the plebiscite—but 133,000 voted for Louis Napoleon.[1]

The really dramatic gains which the Red republicans made in 1848–51 were among the peasants. In the election of May 1849, the democratic-socialists got 34·8 per cent of the votes cast, 2,357,900 votes in all. In 16 departments they won a majority, with a vote rising to as high as 67·6 per cent in Saône-et-Loire. In 27 other departments they got between 34·8 and 50 per cent of the votes. These victories were won above all in rural areas. Paris itself cast only 37·8 per cent of its votes for them.[2] What is so interesting about this rural protest is the way

[1] R. Gossez, 'Diversité des antagonismes sociaux vers le milieu du 19ᵉ siècle', *Revue Économique* (1956), 439–58.
[2] Jacques Bouillon, 'Les Démocrates socialistes aux élections de 1849', *Revue*

the peasants became conscious of the possibilities open to them only gradually, and then methodically and deliberately took advantage of them, producing a sense of an immense power being slowly unleashed. In the first days after the revolution, they were aware only that the government had gone. Their first reactions were not political. They invaded the commons and forests, claiming back the traditional rights they had lost to the rich: they sacked the houses of those who resisted them; they drove tax collectors and policemen into hiding; they refused to pay taxes and tolls. This was behaviour similar to that which took place in towns, where textile handloom weavers destroyed machines which were threatening their livelihoods and where carriage drivers and boatmen burnt railway stations and tore up the track of the new invention that was ruining them. But as a whole the peasants were slow to see the implications of universal suffrage. In the Constituent elections of April 1848 they took no independent initiative. The real change occurs in the local elections a few months later. Over half of the mayors and deputy mayors in office appointed by Louis-Philippe were re-elected by popular suffrage. The peasants in many areas accepted the traditional hierarchy. But in certain parts of France, mainly the south-east, the south and the Paris region, these local elections were an extraordinary revolt by the masses, who expelled the notables from office and took over themselves. In the election of the president in December 1848, this was turned into a public declaration of independence, when the peasants, ignoring the instructions of the notables, who were largely in favour of Cavaignac, voted Louis Napoleon in with a decisive majority.

It could be said that the republic of peasants dates from this, except that the peasants were divided as to what kind of republic they wanted. A majority made a deal with authority and accepted the Bonapartist version of the republic, and it was left to the next generation—that of Gambetta—to draw them away from this. A sizeable minority, however—about one third of the total—chose the democratic socialism of Ledru-Rollin. He obtained only 5 per cent of the votes in the

française de science politique, 6 (1956), 70–95, correcting the earlier calculations (still to be found in most textbooks) made by G. Génique, *L'Election de l'assemblée législative en 1849* (1921).

presidential election, as against Cavaignac's 19 per cent and Louis Napoleon's 74 per cent but he made enormous gains in the following year when the extent to which Napoleon was in league with the notables became clear. Ledru-Rollin's disciples toured the countryside, visited the *chambrées*, made converts in village after village. They resurrected the old Carbonaro traditions[1] but widened them beyond their élitist, exclusive character. Secret societies with a mass recruitment, with a full complement of passwords, secret signs and initiation rites, developed out of the drinking clubs and friendly societies, driven underground by government repression. The *Société des Montagnards*, the *Solidarité républicaine* and other regional associations, with remarkably active teams of propagandists, made these essentially local clubs into a force of national significance. Their strength came in part from the fact that they effectively combined peasant and artisan activity with intellectual leadership. Red deputies elected in 1849, who led this movement, included 127 'intellectuals' (76 lawyers, 25 doctors, 13 journalists, 13 teachers and men of letters) out of a total of 211 about whom details are available.[2]

The Reds believed they could win the election due to be held in 1852. They were probably over-optimistic, since their successes were confined to only certain parts of the country. But their judgement of their strength was vindicated in December 1851, when a veritable peasant rising, complementing that of the towns, followed immediately on the *coup d'état*. The departments in which the largest number of arrests were made were precisely those in the south and south-east where they had implanted themselves. These arrests deprived the Reds of their leadership for at least ten years. But during the Second Republic the Reds of these regions had effectively challenged the rule of the notables and they had introduced a new kind of politics, with genuine popular participation.[3]

They had, however, failed to capture power at the national

[1] On the Carbonari in France see Alan Spitzer, *Old Hatreds and Young Hopes* (Cambridge, Mass., 1971), which is a very thorough investigation of all that can be discovered about them, and, on secret societies in general, John Roberts's book (in the press).

[2] J. Bouillon, op. cit. A further 19 were in agriculture, 19 in commerce and industry, 11 were workers, 11 soldiers, 9 civil servants, 7 mayors, 8 miscellaneous.

[3] P. Vigier, op. cit., and A. J. Tudesq, op. cit.

level. The responsibility for this must be partly borne by their leaders. Ledru-Rollin was the son of a well-to-do physician; he inherited a very decent private income (30,000 francs a year); he could afford to buy one of the privileged barrister's practices at the court of appeal (for 300,000 francs). As soon as he had reached the age of eligibility, he had tried to enter politics under the patronage of Odilon Barrot, leader of the 'dynastic opposition' under Louis-Philippe (that is, of the opposition which accepted the monarchy). Eventually, however, he was adopted by the republicans of Sarthe as their candidate to succeed Garnier-Pagès, one of their leading figures who had died prematurely. He alone was rich enough to subsidise their local paper but also willing to issue a manifesto radical enough to suit them. Already in 1841 he could have made the famous statement with which he is always associated: 'I am their leader, I must follow them.' He used his wealth, augmented by the dowry of his half-English wife, to subsidise *La Réforme*, the principal democratic newspaper. He had a loud voice and an imposing presence; he was amiable, impetuous, easily given to declamation. His manifesto in his first election was considered so bold that he was prosecuted for it; but he was no innovator, for he owed at least some of his popularity to his sharing the prejudices and superstitions of the working class. He demanded universal suffrage, proportionate taxation, more equality in the army conscription system and the pursuit of glory in foreign policy. He saw the social problem principally in the industrial workers of the city. 'Thanks to the immortal revolution', he said, 'the workers on the land are in a comparatively tolerable material position, even though it is still very imperfect. They are less dependent than workers properly so called.' This real proletariat should be given the right to form trade unions and to strike, and higher wages; but ultimately it should be, as far as possible, abolished. Ledru-Rollin was hostile to large-scale industry, which he considered to be the product of cupidity. As England's experience of it showed, it caused too much suffering. France should remain essentially agricultural and industry should be relegated to a secondary role, in the same way as France considered herself militarily as a land power, and limited her navy to minor proportions. He advocated that industrial workers should be repatriated to the country and given smallholdings: this would revive agriculture, which was being ruined by emigration into corrupting towns. When all workers were made owners of property, they would be 'more tranquil and more moral'. He rejected communism, and vigorously dissociated himself from it. He was hostile to state interference: 'I do not wish to abolish liberty of industry. I do not wish to make the state either a producer or a manufacturer. I wish to make it only an intelligent protector.' He had little use for parliamentary government either: he wanted the direct rule of the people, in the tradition of 1793. His ideas were all those which could appeal to the small man, seeking a modest rural existence—radicalism was already a doctrine of the small man—but this was forgotten in the fury of his rhetoric and in his resurrection of memories of the Terror. He was one of the very few who took the republic's civil uniform seriously, and actually wore suits in the style of Robespierre. 'You are agents of a revolutionary government', he wrote to his prefects when he became minister of the interior, 'and you are revolutionaries too . . . You ask what your powers are: they are unlimited.' Ledru-Rollin had a genius for frightening the middle classes, without meaning to. His flamboyance concealed lack of subtlety and, some have even said, of intelligence or will-power. He was responsible to a considerable extent for making his party into bogy-men.[1]

At the popular level, republicanism contained elements which made it a form of permanent revolution. One of the great problems of the movement was to reconcile this with capturing and holding power. As soon as the republic was successful and became a government, it inevitably came into conflict with supporters whose temperaments made it difficult for them to be on the side of authority. Much of this popular basis was therefore lost in turn to the socialists and then the communists. This happened particularly because a new class of republican notables grew up, who developed (as opposed to the utopian and the popular types) the third variety of republicanism. Republicanism thus represented three contradictory things: a belief in an ideal government which could not exist, a popular

[1] A. A. Ledru-Rollin, *Discours politiques et écrits divers* (1879), 1. 4–5, 20, 46, 2. 99, 420–9; *De la décadence de l'Angleterre* (1850); R. Schultz, *Ledru-Rollin et le suffrage universel* (1948); A. R. Calman, *Ledru-Rollin après 1848* (1921).

opposition to all government, and a new establishment party, accepting responsibility, honours and compromise. This latter willingness to compromise had deep roots. The word radical sometimes meant extreme or revolutionary, but under Louis-Philippe it also meant moderate republican, because the word was borrowed from the English and signified a democratic concern perfectly compatible with monarchy and parliament-ary forms. One had to distinguish between the 'radicals' and the 'exclusive radicals'. Only the latter were total enemies of Louis-Philippe. In 1847 Carnot (of unimpeachable republican descent) published a pamphlet, which publicly offered the king support in carrying out democratic reforms, which, said Carnot, could perfectly well be achieved within the framework of the monarchical constitution. A good number of republicans would have accepted the monarchy if it had widened the franchise and turned its attention to improving the lot of the masses, just as, under the leadership of Émile Ollivier, a good number were to accept the empire of Napoleon III. This willingness to compromise has naturally always been played down by republican historians, because it has been seen as treachery.[1]

When invested with power, these republicans behaved in a manner which was not all that different from their monarchist predecessors. The rivalry for jobs and promotion, the expulsion of political opponents and their replacement by friends and relatives of the new masters of the country, were as pronounced among the republicans as they had been under Louis-Philippe, whom they had attacked so bitterly for corruption and nepotism. From the point of view of the masses, the new republican prefects, mayors and civil servants often represented simply one clique taking over from another, perhaps less wealthy and less experienced, but still usually bourgeois. This clique, once possessed of power, was as difficult to deal with, for the small man with no strings, as any other. Surrounded by friends and acolytes, it could become as exclusive as the aristocrats had been. It did not hesitate to use the very same pressure in elections, which it had denounced the authoritarian regimes for employ-ing. It was even willing to use force in a very vigorous way to repress popular agitation. The question arises therefore why, if

[1] Cf. A. Bonnard, *Les Modérés* (1933); H. Carnot, *Les Radicaux et la charte* (1847).

there were republicans with this sense of reality and with an
ability to use power, the republic failed to get established in
1848. These men would perhaps have created something like
the republic of Washington or that of Thiers, respectable,
solid and safe. They did not do so for several reasons.

First, they never won a majority in the country. The republicans were still a small group before 1848. They held office for
a few months after February only while a vacuum of power
existed. In the elections of April, contrary to general belief,
they were not successful. It is usually said that the majority of
the Constituent Assembly was republican, but one can make
this calculation only if one considers as republican everybody
who said he was one. Many conversions were purely superficial. Recent research has shown that only one third of the
assembly consisted of men who had been republican before
1848—285 out of 851 deputies. Of these about 55 were extreme
republicans or socialists, so the moderates, whom the influential
historian Seignobos has made out to be the victors of the election, were in fact only 230. More than half the assembly were
monarchists of one kind or another.[1] The moderate republicans
held power under sufferance, because the monarchists were
not ready to attempt to resume it: they were in disarray,
divided and confused by universal suffrage. It would take a
long time for these new notables to establish themselves, let
alone permanently oust the old set.

Secondly, their great weakness was that they were unpre-
pared for government office. They were not just an opposition
party, but one which had not worked out an identity to deploy
in these new circumstances. There were no men of outstanding
ability or exceptional personality among them. Cavaignac was
after all summoned to become chief of the executive not because
of any particular merit—though he had been a decent general
in Algeria and he was an upright and worthy man—but
because he was the brother of Godefroy Cavaignac, one of the
best-known republican journalists of the monarchy, who had
died in 1845. This Godefroy, moreover, was a republican, as he

---

[1] Frederick A. de Luna, *The French Republic under Cavaignac: 1848* (Princeton,
N.J., 1969), 110–13. This shows the errors of the essay on the elections of 1848 by
a student of Seignobos, J. Tournan, on which Seignobos based his statement. It
is also a well-argued reconsideration of this neglected period of the republic.

himself said, through filial loyalty: he was the son of the regicide member of the Convention. Carnot, minister of education, was in the same position. Republicanism had this element of family tradition which made it the perpetuation of family feuds, at the centre of government as at the village level. Garnier-Pagès, another member of the government, also owed his office to the fact that he was the brother of another dead hero, a Marseillais of humble origin, one of the republicans' most brilliant orators. These men had yet to win popularity for themselves, or to establish more widespread networks, to draw more people into their still restricted cliques. As a result, the policy they followed was cautious, exploratory, indecisive. They arrested vast numbers after the June riots, refused an amnesty, but in practice gradually released all but about 250, who were gaoled, and 450, who were transported to Algeria: they thus earned a reputation for being both repressive and weak. Their opinions about the social question were not all that different from those whom they repressed: they believed in workers' co-operatives and state aid for the unemployed. Even after the June days, they continued to spend money on both of these, and they developed advanced programmes for agricultural credit, education and representation, for free public and lay primary schools. The germs of the Third Republic legislation were all here.

The Cavaignac government (June–December 1848) is wrongly thought to have been a reaction against the provisional government of February. It continued its work, and retained many of its personnel. There were thus about eight months of office by which to judge the republicans. What they showed was that they had not learnt the art of government. They lost the opportunity of winning the loyalty of the peasantry by a dramatic gesture on taxation. They would have liked to have carried out reforms—they promised them—but ultimately they were too intimidated by orthodox financial theories. They had inherited a whole series of deficits from the monarchy. They refused to declare bankruptcy. On the contrary, instead of reducing taxation, and while simply talking about the merits of a progressive income tax, they levied an additional land tax, known as the 45 centimes. They refused to exempt the poor— as Ledru-Rollin demanded—and so one of their very first actions was to penalise the peasants, while the townsmen went scot-free. There was a great movement of discontent: many refused to pay: some departments paid about three-quarters of what they ought to have but others paid only 2 per cent: by mid July less than half had been collected. Other tax measures showed a similar lack of political skill. The salt tax was abolished but only as from 1 January 1849. The tax on alcoholic drinks was ended but was replaced by another levied in a different way, so transferring discontent from the wine merchants to the producers and consumers. The abolition of the tax on butcher's meat had almost no effect, because the slaughterers did not pass much of the benefit on to the retailers. The feeble attempt to tax the rich, by a 1 per cent duty on mortgages, could not be enforced: it would have involved borrowers denouncing their creditors to the tax collectors. The republicans would have achieved far more if they had instead done something to help the peasant free himself from his debts.[1]

Their attitude to press censorship was similarly equivocal. The freedom allowed in the first months was soon brought to an end. The caution money was reintroduced for newspapers—earning them the enmity of the press, even if the new tax was at a much lower level than that imposed by Louis-Philippe. Finally, they paved the way for their own doom, by helping to draw up a constitution which brought about most of the things they wished to avoid. This constitution proclaimed the sovereignty of the people, and naïvely assumed that this would guarantee their freedom. It declared that the separation of powers was the first condition of a free government, and so it established on the one hand an executive president and on the other a legislative assembly of 750, both elected by the people, but each independent of the other. Reacting against Louis-Philippe's supposedly English-style parliamentary government —which had brought only weak and corrupt coalitions—it made the president more powerful than the king with the ministers entirely dependent on him. The president could hold office for only four years and the constitution could be revised only with difficulty. Within a very short space of time, president and parliament were at loggerheads. Only force could decide between them and that was in the president's hands. Thus,

[1] Alfred Antony, *La Politique financière du gouvernement provisoire, février–mai 1848* (1910); M. Marion, *Histoire financière de la France depuis 1715*, vol. 5 (1928).

almost inexorably, the constitution produced a dictatorship. As a result of this, the Third Republic went to the other extreme and concentrated all powers in an assembly, but this had equally disastrous results.

No less important was the republicans' failure to deal with the problem of the Church. They were on the whole no enemies of religion. They believed in the need, if not for Catholicism, at least for a religion of some kind—the new Christianity of Saint-Simon, the religion of humanity of Leroux, the Christian socialism of Buchez. Many of them defined fraternity as the implementation of the ethics of primitive Christianity. Universal suffrage reinforced the political power of the Church, but the republicans hovered on the bounds of anticlericalism. The alliance of the clergy with Louis Napoleon was, in due course, to clinch this matter and make the republicans firmly hostile.[1]

These mistakes were made, thirdly, because moderate republicanism was the product of very diverse origins and had not been welded into a coherent ideology. The distinction textbooks usually make, between the followers of the *Réforme* and the *National* newspapers, is superficial. The differences between these papers were largely ones of personality. Far more important were the different sources from which they derived their republicanism. There were some who saw the republic as the rule of virtue and whose heroes were the ancient Greeks. For many republicanism meant patriotism, the revival of national glory, French leadership of the world. Such men, of whom perhaps Carrel was the most eminent and vocal, were often distinguishable only with difficulty from the Bonapartists. Until 1830 republicanism and Bonapartism were closely allied. Then vast numbers of the generals, civil servants and admirers of Napoleon I were given office by Louis-Philippe and partially absorbed into Orleanism—the distinction between the parties was by no means clear cut. Those who remained in opposition continued to flirt with the Bonapartists, and it was a republican paper which published the writings of Louis Napoleon when he was in prison. Carrel (whom Jules Simon in his memoirs was to

[1] Paul Bastid, *Doctrines et institutions politiques de la Seconde République* (1945); Jacques Cohen, *La Préparation de la constitution de 1848* (1935); Georges Cogniot, *La Question scolaire en 1848* (1948); O. Festy, *Les Associations ouvrières encouragées par la Deuxième République* (1915).

describe as 'all powerful over the minds of the youth' of the
1830s and 1840s) was the first man to call himself a 'conservative
republican'. He was opposed to revolutionary methods and to
violence. He declared that he would prefer a monarchy with a
little liberty to a republic with none. The young Bonaparte
was his hero and in his ideal constitution he would have had a
first consul at the head of state, or a president modelled on the
U.S.A., with strong powers.[1] The American revolution indeed
was as much an ideal in France as the French one.[2] The First
Republic was so bathed in unpleasant memories that people
preferred to forget about it; ignorance about it was extraordinary, even if vague family feuds dating back to it continued
to smoulder. Thiers—an Orleanist—began its rehabilitation
under the Restoration, but it was only in the 1840s that histories
of it became really numerous. Till then it was synonymous
with the Terror. But now every writer stressed a different aspect
of it, and division among its admirers was bitter.[3]

These internal enmities were linked with the increasingly
numerous interpretations republicans formed of the Enlightenment. Voltaire was read avidly: 36 editions of his complete
works were published between his death in 1784 and 1877, 22
of them under the Restoration. Some editions involved as many
as 125 volumes, and these filled the bookshelves of men of intellectual pretensions who could afford them, but there were also
available *The Cottage Voltaire* and *The Small Property Owner's
Voltaire*, at more modest prices. The single work reprinted most
often was his *History of Charles XII* (74 editions, 1815–80); his
theatre was far more popular than his *Philosophic Dictionary* or
even *Candide*. So it is by no means clear what people made of
him. A Voltairian could be either an Orleanist or a republican.
His tendency to sarcasm and rebelliousness, to doubt and

---

[1] *Œuvres politiques et littéraires d'Armand Carrel*, ed. Littré and Paulin (1857), 3.
58, 122, 176, 4. 137, 5. 366; Jules Simon, *Premières Années* (n.d.), 181; R. G. Nobe-
court, *La Vie d'Armand Carrel* (1930); Angus MacLaren, *Armand Carrel* (Ph.D.
thesis, Harvard, 1970).
[2] René Remond, *Les États-Unis devant l'opinion française 1815–52* (1962), 2. 640–1.
[3] Thiers's history appeared 1823–7 (10 vols.). Among other histories of the
revolution were Félix de Conny, 1834–42 (8 vols.); E. Cabet, 1840 (4 vols.); L.
Blanc, 1847–62 (12 vols.); J. Michelet, 1847–53 (7 vols.); Abbé de Genoude, 1845–8
(7 vols.); A. Esquiros, 1847 (2 vols.); A. Gabourd, 1846–51 (10 vols.); A.
Laponneraye, 1845 (3 vols.); A. de Lamartine, 1847 (8 vols.); and the parliamentary history edited by P. Buchez, 1834–8 (40 vols.).

frivolity but also to strong definite opinions made it difficult for him to be unreservedly on any one side.[1] It was even more the case with the disciples of Rousseau that they could draw divergent interpretations from his writings, and besides many republicans, converted to positivism, turned altogether against Rousseau in the second half of the century.[2] Dupont de Bussac showed the complicated amalgams which could be formed when he said that he thought of himself as continuing the tradition of Condorcet and Turgot, Price and Priestley.[3]

In their attitude to the common man, the republicans placed varying emphasis on the improvement of his material lot and on his education; but some tempered their democratic leanings with a certain élitism. Vacherot, for example, argued that 'free thought' was the ultimate goal which the human mind, in perfect maturity, could reach, but only a rare élite had the 'philosophical spirit' necessary to achieving this, to freeing itself completely from all prejudice, passion and self-interest. Moderately intelligent people could only approximate to it if they had a developed critical sense. But even they were pretty rare: they were found mainly among male Aryans: there were very few among the Chinese, negroes and women. Vacherot distinguished between the doctrines fit for the élite and the watered-down, simple proverbs which the masses were capable of understanding, and he wrote rather contemptuously of the prejudices of the bourgeoisie who had received no classical education.[4] This élitism, again, was linked with the Protestantism which, as will be seen later, was one of the constituent elements in republicanism. Some republicans, even if they were not Protestants, felt sympathy for its attack on Catholic dogmatism;

---

[1] Georges Benesco, *Voltaire: bibliographie de ses œuvres* (1890), 4. 163, 195; J. F. Nourrisson, *Voltaire et le voltairianisme* (1896), 656–7; Abbé Berseux, *Le Voltairomanie* (Lanenville, 1865); Pierre Guiral, in *Hommage au Doyen E. Gros* (Gap, 1959), 193–204.

[2] J. F. Nourrisson, *J.-J. Rousseau et le rousseauisme* (1903); J. R. Talmon, *The Origins of Totalitarianism* (1952); J. Jaurès, 'Les Idées politiques et sociales de J.-J. Rousseau', *Revue de métaphysique et de morale*, 20 (1912), 371–81; Harald Höffding, 'Rousseau et le 19e siècle', *Annales de la Société J. J. Rousseau*, 8 (Geneva, 1912), 69–98. For an example of a Rousseauist republican see Demosthenes Ollivier's views in Theodore Zeldin, *Émile Ollivier* (Oxford, 1963), 3–4.

[3] G. Weill, *Histoire du parti républicain en France 1814–1870* (new edition, 1928), 111.

[4] E. Vacherot, *La Religion* (1869), 255, 267, 411–13; cf. his social doctrines in *La Démocratie* (1860). For a life of this very interesting man, E. Boutroux, 'Notice sur la vie et les œuvres de M. Étienne Vacherot', *Mémoires de l'Académie des sciences morales et politiques*, 21 May 1904, 25 (1907), 83–114.

but there were also complex and tortured Calvinists who found in republicanism an outlet for their search for salvation. Religion, however, is so large a question in the making of republicanism, that it must be left for separate treatment.

The nature of the moderation of these republicans can be illustrated with the case of Alexandre-Thomas Marie, minister of public works in the provisional government and of justice under Cavaignac, and president of the Constituent Assembly in June 1848. Few people have heard of him now, but he was popular enough in 1848 to be elected to parliament by Paris, with more than twice as many votes as Lamennais received. He came of a family which had been lawyers for two centuries, but his father, a younger son, was an impoverished archivist who soon left him an orphan. Marie worked his own way up as a barrister, until in 1840 he became *bâtonnier* of Paris. He had had to wait a long time to earn the money to become an elector: he felt the insult, and he joined the republicans to demand universal suffrage. He did not differ profoundly from Guizot in his general views; he agreed that reason should be sovereign, but he thought that it manifested itself not through an élite but through the masses. He deplored the 'mad dreams' of the 'new aristocracy' of bourgeois. He argued that democracy was a 'social necessity' because the masses had, after many centuries, at last freed themselves from the powers which had dominated them and had learnt their strength: they now demanded respect, and it could not be denied to them. But Marie hated the agitation of the clubs and the revolutionaries. He was an enemy of violence. He had not pressed for the immediate proclamation of the republic, because he did not believe that a party had a right to impose a particular form of government on the nation. He agreed to join the provisional government because he wanted to help maintain order and to prevent anarchy, and he looked back with pride on its repression of successive popular risings. The people were children who had to be shown that their utopias would not work: he therefore approved trying out the National Workshops, and then ending them when they got out of hand. 'A lot of blood had to be shed', he wrote, 'to dethrone the false gods.' The masses, more than any other class, needed to be strongly governed. 'The despotism of a thousand heads is a thousand times more odious than the despotism of a single man.' Liberty had to be combined with order. He supported the freeing of the press, but then agreed that it had gone too far and needed to be controlled when it abused its liberty and attacked the very basis of society, 'insolently calling into question all the traditions of the past'. He was all in favour of democracy, whose function was to develop the moral and material interests not of some but of all, but he was also for realism. Universal fraternity was a 'sublime idea' but 'is man's heart large enough to contain so much charity, devotion and heroism?' He thought national groupings were probably more practical. The fatherland was like 'a great home' in which the citizen found all the protection and all the love that in his private capacity he found in the family home. One can see in Marie how the moderate republicans were still in the process of working out their relations with the masses.[1]

The republicans had a great deal to learn from the other parties before they could discover how to establish themselves. Their experience of defeat and their tribulations under Napoleon III, were to have a profound effect on their attitudes and thinking. In 1870 they emerged in many ways transformed.[2]

[1] Aimé Cherest, *La Vie et les œuvres de A. T. Marie* (1873).
[2] Compare I. Tchernoff, *Le Parti républicain sous la monarchie de juillet* (1901), and id., *Le Parti républicain au coup d'État et sous le Second Empire* (1900).

5. Bonapartism

FOR over a hundred years, Bonapartism has been the intellectual's nightmare. It has represented the silencing of free discussion, the domination of the military and the rule of a heavy-handed bureaucracy. It has implied the discrediting of the man of letters, in favour of the industrialist and even the peasant. So though Bonapartism has, at times, won more votes than any other party—whatever may be said about how it obtained these votes—it has been always vigorously and almost unanimously attacked by writers. There have been some able Bonapartist propagandists, but only of the kind who have addressed themselves to the masses. There have been— with few exceptions—no serious Bonapartist historians or theoreticians to create an intellectually respectable doctrine, or to defend the programme of the movement in universal terms. As a result, the Second Empire has been studied far less than other regimes—as a glance at the sparse entries in the annual bibliography shows—and there is still no full history of Bonapartism as a movement.[1]

The simplest definition of Bonapartism is that it is the perpetuation of the ideas of Napoleon I, the cult of his genius and the appeal to his methods for the solution of France's problems. Guizot summed up the secret of its strength in its ability simultaneously to represent national glory, to guarantee the maintenance of the achievements of the Revolution and to affirm the principles of authority and order. Bonapartism, that is, reconciled democracy and authority in a way which was neither reactionary on the one hand nor parliamentary on the other. It offered itself as the answer to the rule of anarchic and discredited parliaments. It provided a leader to appeal to the whole nation—against the parties and factions which monopo-

[1] The main histories are Pierre de La Gorce, *Histoire du Second Empire* (7 vols., 1894–1904); C. Seignobos, *La Révolution de 1848. Le Second Empire* (vol. 6 of E. Lavisse, *Histoire de la France contemporaine*) and *Le Déclin de l'empire et l'établissement de la Troisième République 1859–75* (vol. 7 of the same series), both 1921; Albert Thomas, *Le Second Empire* (1906, in Jaurès, *Histoire socialiste*) and Émile Ollivier, *L'Empire libéral* (18 vols., 1895–1918).

lised power for their own benefit—elected by the nation, and responsible to it. Unlike royalism, which claimed equally to be national, to maintain order and to provide security for property, Bonapartism aspired to preserve the work of the Revolution, by affirming the equality of men, careers open to talent, and the abolition of the privileges of castes and corporations.

However, it is a great mistake to assume that Bonapartism meant the same thing throughout the nineteenth century. The fact that its leaders paid homage to Napoleon I should not conceal the variety of their interpretations of his message, nor the changing circumstances in which they tried to apply it. Some political scientists and historians have attempted to find the essence of Bonapartism, to isolate its individuality, as though they are studying a disease, which erupts from time to time; and if they discover that it is not always identical, they dismiss any deviation as an aberration. Thus H. A. L. Fisher, in his eloquent and influential lectures on Bonapartism, asserted that the First and Second Napoleonic Empires were 'to a large extent inspired by the same principles, rested upon the support of the same intellectual and social forces, appealed to the same appetites, flattered the same vanities'. However, he did not investigate in detail exactly what these forces and appetites were, beyond quoting with apparent approval Tocqueville's summing up of the Second Empire as 'the paradise of the envious and the mediocre'. More recently, parallels have been drawn between Napoleon III and de Gaulle. Jacques Duclos, the Communist leader, has written a book placing them both in the same tradition, of authoritarianism, contempt for public opinion, thirst for power, pride and egocentricity. The use of plebiscites has been seen as the essential damning feature of Bonapartism. When de Gaulle achieved his sweeping triumph in 1962, L'Express recalled the words of Émile Ollivier in 1870: 'One is never weaker than when one appears to be supported by everybody.' André Siegfried, one of the ablest of commentators, distinguished between 'true' Bonapartism, which was that of Napoleon I, and Bonapartism as it evolved, 'and in my view became corrupted', under Napoleon III and Eugénie, for in this second phase it was clerical, aristocratic and reactionary. In his opinion, therefore, Bonapartism for most of the century was not proper Bonapartism at all. It ceased to be national and

was a party like any other. When it tried to become liberal and
parliamentary in 1870, it was contradicting itself and denying
its 'true character'. It discovered in fact that if it allowed free
discussion of its government, it would commit suicide, but if it
did not, its repression deprived it of the support of many liberals
and workers, so that it was forced into alliance with the reactionaries. It thus ceased to be democratic and left wing and became
a prisoner of clericalism. It is difficult to see when Bonapartism
was 'its true self'. One might indeed wonder whether there
ever was such a thing as Bonapartism. Is not Napoleon III
supposed to have said, 'The empress is legitimist, my cousin is
republican, Morny is Orleanist, I am a socialist; the only
Bonapartist is Persigny and he is mad'?[1]

One has only to glance at some maps of the regions of France
from which Bonapartism derived its strength at different dates,
to realise at once that its support was not constant. Under the
Restoration Normandy was royalist but in the early Third
Republic it was staunchly Bonapartist. Under the Restoration the
east of France was Bonapartist, and it voted for Louis Napoleon
in 1848, but after 1870 it was a bastion of republicanism. The
west of France, which was always regarded as the stronghold
of royalism, elected considerable numbers of Bonapartists in the
Third Republic. The south was uniformly hostile throughout
the century; but the south-west, which had virtually no Bonapartist party in 1848, became the fief of whole dynasties of
Bonapartist deputies, until it was transformed once again into a
major centre of republican radicalism. These variations need to
be explained. They certainly show that one is not dealing with
an unchanging clientele or a static doctrine; and they raise the
question of whether Bonapartism meant different things in
different parts of France.

When it is suggested that liberal Bonapartism was simply
a corrupt form of Orleanism, it is assumed that Orleanism
was distinct and different from Bonapartism. From the ideal,
theoretical point of view it might have been, but in practice
they were rather like estranged brothers, offspring of the same

---

[1] H. A. L. Fisher, *Bonapartism* (Oxford, 1908), 3, 87; André Siegfried, *Tableau
politique de la France de l'ouest* (1913), 473–95; Jacques Duclos, *De Napoléon III
à de Gaulle* (1964); *L'Express*, 5 Apr. 1962; M. Rubel, *Marx devant le bonapartisme*
(1960).

father. For some time after 1815 the distinctions between the
opposition parties under the Restoration were not clear. Men
who were later labelled as Orleanist, Bonapartist and republicans all contributed to establishing the monarchy of Louis-
Philippe. Before 1830, the Bonapartists often called themselves
liberal, in the same way as their allies did.[1] The first consequence
of the revolution of that year was to bring back into power the
vast horde of Napoleonic generals and civil servants who had
been dismissed in 1815. Orleanism is one of Napoleon I's
unacknowledged legacies. It was Napoleon I who invented the
société censitaire, the rule of notables selected on the basis of
a property qualification. It was he who abolished universal
suffrage, who established the rule that only men with private
incomes should enter the higher ranks of the civil service.
Napoleon I gave his nobles no fiscal privileges, but when he
gave titles, he allowed them to become hereditary provided the
recipients were rich enough. He, perhaps even more than
Guizot, could have been credited with the injunction to 'get
rich'.[2] If Orleanism was liberal, so too were the Additional
Act of 1815 and the legend of a constitutional monarchy which
Napoleon created on St. Helena. What distinguished Louis-
Philippe's reign from Napoleon's was that the notables got the
upper hand after 1830. They obtained far more power from the
king whom they installed on the throne, than they had been
able to exercise under the shadow of the military conqueror.
But they became even more loyal to Napoleon's memory once
he was safely dead. It was under Louis-Philippe that they
brought back Napoleon's ashes to France and raised monu-
ments to his glory. However, they steadfastly refused to end the
exile imposed on Napoleon's family. The trial of Louis Napoleon
in 1840 was conducted by a court of 4 former ministers of
Napoleon I, 6 of his marshals, 56 of his generals, 14 of his
councillors of state, 19 of his prefects, 7 ambassadors and 21
chamberlains who were then members of Louis-Philippe's
chamber of peers. It was these men who created the Bonapartism of the future by their treatment of Louis Napoleon, who
might have been content with a modest share of the spoils

---

[1] Cf. Balzac, *Le Député d'Arcis*: *Œuvres*, ed. Bouteron and Lognon (1949), 283–4.
[2] See Jacques Godechot, *Les Institutions de la France sous la Révolution et l'Empire*
(1951), 496–7, 502–3.

which they refused to share with him.[1] Louis Napoleon had to transform the Napoleonic legend, to base himself on universal suffrage, in alliance with the republicans, in order to get back into France. Bonapartism could be called an Orleanist heresy.

Alternatively, it could be seen as a variety of republicanism. Militarism, the passion for glory and foreign adventures was, before 1848, essentially a characteristic of the republicans. The army was considered a dangerous hotbed of liberalism and revolution. It was only later that the republicans accused Bonapartism of militarism, when the army, like the notables, developed an independent *esprit de corps*, forgot its revolutionary origins, and became the defender of hierarchy and order. Louis Napoleon modified the interpretation of Bonapartism produced by the Orleanists, by grafting on to it two republican doctrines, universal suffrage and an active foreign policy.[2] The republican leaders had little use for him, but he was far from being looked on as an enemy by the lower ranks of their party.[3] His break with them came only after 1848, when he allied with their enemies, and after 1851, when he persecuted them with unprecedented severity. When he obtained power, both his doctrine and his support were altered. Bonapartism was continually evolving. It is important not to create stereotypes for it, any more than for Orleanism or republicanism. These became increasingly differentiated with time: what one needs to ascertain is why. In this way, one will see whether the divisions of French politics were inevitable, necessarily embedded, as commentators have argued, in irreconcilable 'temperaments', and inescapably following from incompatible

[1] J. Taschereau, *Revue rétrospective* (1848), 140–1; *Aux Mânes de l'Empereur, la patrie reconnaissante. Notice biographique des 192 pairs de France ayant reçu des faveurs de l'Empereur et qui aujourd'hui sont les juges du prince Napoléon* (1840), Bibliothèque Nationale shelf-mark Lb(51)3137.

[2] See the views of Thiers, a 'Napoleonist', on the republicanism of Louis Napoleon, *Moniteur universel* (1851), 185, and those of Crémieux, ibid. (1845), 884. Douglas Jerrold, *Life of Napoleon III* (1875–82), 1. 250–1, letter of Louis Napoleon to Vieillard, 29 Jan. 1836; P. Thureau Dangin, *La Monarchie de juillet* (1897–1904), 1. 594, Baron Gustave de Romand, *De l'état des partis en France* (1839), 23–5. Jean Vidalenc, *Les Demi-Soldes. Étude d'une catégorie sociale* (1955), shows that Bonapartism was not common among these former soldiers of Napoleon I. G. Perreux, *La Propagande républicaine au début de la monarchie de juillet* (1931), shows the interrelationships of the parties.

[3] See Carnot's denunciation in *Moniteur universel* (1841), 1538.

principles. It is worth asking whether, on the contrary, the party's divisions were created gradually, and adopted principles to give respectability to animosities which often had personal or fortuitous causes; whether, that is to say, the politicians and the theorists helped to produce the divisions. It will be suggested that Bonapartism was the intermediary for the effecting of social changes which republicanism was unable to carry out on its own and that it contributed a considerable amount to the evolution of republicanism, which became its bitterest enemy. Polemic has obscured its work.

First, it is necessary to see how Napoleon III stood in relation to the masses, the notables, the parties and what effect his reign had on these. Napoleon III ruled France for twenty-one years, longer than anyone else in the country's modern history. The usual view is that he was a well-meaning visionary out of touch with reality, a confused charlatan, a feeble parody of his uncle, an adventurer whose bluff and gambles were doomed to a catastrophic end. He owes this reputation partly to the repeated fiascos of his foreign policy and partly to the fact that the majority of intellectuals of his day were opposed to his regime; he has never quite recovered from their witty and pungent attacks. In the twentieth century, there has been, almost inevitably, a reaction to this hostile interpretation. Some historians have instead painted him, not as aping the past, but as a man far ahead of his time, principally concerned with the economic development of his country, a precursor of technocracy and of the modern dictators. This is to go too far in the opposite direction. For Napoleon III cannot be classified accurately in any single category. One should not assume that he was a man with certain set ideas, which he described in his books and which he then put into practice when he became emperor. For if his books are read with care, it will be seen that they contain contradictions on nearly every subject. In his writings he was a republican, an opponent of nobility, a protectionist, a believer that colonies were unnecessary and that the Church should be kept out of education. Once in power he proclaimed the empire, created dukes, made the free trade treaties with England and many other nations, established an empire in the Far East and supported the clericalist Loi Falloux. There are those, nevertheless, who claim that Napoleon was basically a

Saint-Simonian: they point to his concern for the lot of the poor, his stimulation of industry, his interest in communications and in the Suez and Panama canals, his belief in a hierarchical society and his advocacy of agricultural colonies. They argue that he must have got his ideas from Louis Blanc and the *Atelier* newspaper he is known to have read, for he never actually mentions Saint-Simon; they think he may have read Enfantin's *Colonisation de l'Algérie*, because this contains ideas similar to his own; they suggest he may have been influenced by Vieillard who was a Saint-Simonian. There is no direct evidence for any of these suppositions and there is much that throws doubt upon them. For in his writings Napoleon was an enemy of the industrial revolution; his agricultural colonies were designed to send town workers back to the land; he himself later said that they were modelled on the example of experiments in foreign countries (presumably van der Bosch's in Holland and Belgium); his economic aim was not to produce as much as possible but to keep the masses in employment; he did not want the country to be ruled by industrialists; and as for his famous statement that the government was not a necessary ulcer but the beneficent motor of society, there were more numerous declarations by him praising individual initiative and holding England up as the ideal. The fact that many Saint-Simonians were successful industrialists in his reign does not necessarily mean that he belonged to their school. On the contrary he frequently criticised doctrinaires, party men and utopian theorists.[1]

Napoleon III's political ideas were essentially opportunistic. His most fervent belief consisted in a deep admiration for his uncle, but this was not an uncritical admiration, for he considered Napoleon I a great man because he gave the people what they wanted as well as what they ought to have. Likewise he admired William III of England for ending a century of revolution in that country by giving it the liberties and religion it sought. Politics for Napoleon III was not the slavish imitation or revival of the past but, as he himself said, the application of

[1] Napoleon III, *Œuvres* (1856), 2. 5, 31, 125, 367; 3. 27, 54, 59, 118, 148, 162, 182, 236; Douglas Jerrold, *Life of Napoleon III* (1875–82), 2. 280. The evidence on his familiarity with Enfantin's book suggests he was introduced to it by Urbain only in the late 1850s.

history to the present.[1] That is why the majority of his works
were historical: studies of Napoleon I, William III, Julius
Caesar, the history of artillery. History revealed why statesmen
had succeeded or failed and it also showed that there were great
irresistible currents, such as the movements for economic
progress, liberty and nationality, which it was the function of
great statesmen to assist. His romanticism produced in him
enormous veneration for such men and his mysticism convinced
him that he was destined to be one himself. 'I believe', he
wrote from his prison in Ham, 'that there are certain men who
are born to serve as a means for the march of the human race
. . . I consider myself to be one of these . . .' He added: 'The
history of England says clearly to kings: March at the head of
the ideas of your century and these ideas will follow and support
you; march behind them and they will drag you after them;
march against them and they will overthrow you.' The mark
of a great statesman is that he can discover the wishes of the
people, identify himself with them and lead them to the attainment of their goal.[2]

This is not to say Napoleon had no programme of his own, or
that he envisaged his role as that of a passive intermediary for
that of the people. He insisted that the duty of a government was
to lead only *right* ideas and the establishment of universal
suffrage—the first plank in his platform—would not necessarily
produce a mandate in favour of right ideas, for as Switzerland
showed, the masses were really conservative, attached to old
prejudices and rejecting every improvement.[3] Though he was
always to watch public opinion closely and to pay great attention to it in formulating his policy,[4] he did not expect it to take
the initiative in dictating policy to him. Liberty he defined as
'a chief ruling according to the will of all' and by *will* he
understood something very like Rousseau's General Will.[5] He
considered that democracy existed once the people were the
source of power, even if they did not control its exercise. The
popular election of the ruler was therefore the main requirement
for good government. In this sense Napoleon's ideal was a

[1] *Œuvres*, 2. 243, and 1. 98.   [2] Ibid. 1. 342; 1. 31–2.
[3] Ibid. 1. 398.
[4] See L. M. Case, *Public Opinion on War and Diplomacy during the Second Empire*
(Philadelphia, Pa., 1954).
[5] Cf. *Œuvres*, 2. 83.

popular dictatorship, but it does not follow that he stood for absolutism as opposed to the liberalism of the republicans. Under Louis-Philippe very few people distinguished between liberty and democracy; universal suffrage, it was generally believed, would secure both. During this period Napoleon differed from the republicans only in preferring the government of one man to that of a party committee. However, he quoted his uncle as saying that constitutions should be flexible; it was impossible to leave too many chances open for modifying them. With time indeed the strong government of one man would develop respect for law and a public spirit such as existed in England; this would provide a basis and a demand for more liberty, the ultimate establishment of which had always been his uncle's aim.[1]

Napoleon's social aims naturally therefore incorporated the most commonplace ideas of his time: careers open to talent, the fusion of classes, the ending of all privileges except those based on merit, prosperity for all, but not at the expense of the rich, employment and social benefits for the working class, cheap credit and less taxation for the mortgaged peasantry, property ultimately for all men, great public works and improved communications which would be self-financing because they would increase the national wealth, peace but also glory. Napoleon's view of popular pyschology was that the masses would be content with nominal sovereignty, with political equality between classes, with opportunities to rise in the social hierarchy and to make a better living.

However, Napoleon was elected president in December 1848, confirmed in December 1851 and became emperor a year later not because his programme as a whole was approved by the electorate but because so many sections of the electorate placed their hopes in him. Napoleon was not simply the emperor of the peasants, against the industrial town workers and the bourgeoisie. Many peasants did vote for him but many also did not, particularly in the clerical west and the republican centre and south. Some town workers voted against him but a great many more voted for him. There was opposition to him from artisans, rural as well as urban, but again this was by no means the case everywhere. In 1848 many parliamentary leaders

[1] *Œuvres*, I. 44, 52–5.

supported him for the presidency but a considerable section of the bourgeoisie seems to have preferred Cavaignac. In 1851 and 1852 these leaders went into opposition, but their rank and file, terrified by the threat of another revolution, largely accepted his dictatorship. Again many legitimists supported him in 1848, as a conservative against the republican Cavaignac; but later, when he seemed to be about to become emperor, abstained. Everywhere the vote was complicated by local issues, the vital significance of which will be explained in due course. Napoleon's success was due to spontaneous reactions much more than to the effect of propaganda. A. J. Tudesq has produced some very interesting maps showing on the one hand how the different regions voted in December 1848 and on the other whom the local newspapers supported. There is little correlation between the two.[1] Napoleon's election did not represent the triumph of a programme. The significance of Bonapartism still had to be worked out. It was to depend very much on interaction with events and opinion.

In any case, Napoleon III, as emperor, did not possess the power to do as he pleased. He inherited institutions, customs and legal practices from his predecessors, so that his was a modified rather than a completely reshaped version of previous governments. The three major constitutional changes were the reduced independence of ministers, the diminished powers of parliament and the increased vigour in censoring and suppressing opposition. But Napoleon had to act through individuals of widely different backgrounds and ideas. There was thus possibly even less coherence in his government than in the chaotic struggle for influence that prevailed under the July Monarchy. It is true that he commanded a great deal of personal allegiance from those who worked with him. He had a strange charm for those with whom he came into contact. He could flatter without seeming hypocritical; he was generous; he was a good listener. But there was always something opaque about him, so that it was no easy matter following his lead. His silent meditations and his mystical communion with public opinion made him—when he was successful—a kind of wizard.

[1] A. J. Tudesq, *L'Élection présidentielle de L. N. Bonaparte, 10 déc. 1848* (1965); R. Pimienta, *La Propagande bonapartiste en 1848* (1911); A. Ferrère, *Révélations sur la propagande napoléonienne faite en 1848 et 1849* (Turin, 1863).

In his old age, sick and racked by pain, his judgement, though often shrewd, was clouded even more by the languor which always interrupted his moments of energy. Communication between him, his government and the masses was never simple.

In 1852 Napoleon may have appeared to be the absolute master of France but the history of his reign cannot be summarised in his own biography. Certainly, he determined personally the general direction of government policy but he was not sufficiently assiduous in administration nor sufficiently attentive to detail to get his will regularly enforced in practice. It is true the constitution gave him complete control of the executive: the ministers were grand civil servants responsible to him alone and he insisted that they should do nothing important without his approval. He regularly presided over cabinet meetings, led their discussions and made the final decisions in them. He changed and moved his ministers around frequently. But that he had to do this indicated just how little they were pliable tools in his hands.

The duc de Persigny, for example, a bankrupt petty aristocrat and Napoleon's fellow conspirator in his early days, was fervently devoted to him but his zeal led him to adopt a policy more extreme than Napoleon desired. In 1852, as minister of the interior, he organised demonstrations demanding the proclamation of the empire and so made Napoleon move towards it faster than he had intended. In his conduct of the elections, particularly in 1863, his wild attacks on the clericals, his blatant use of administrative pressure was judged by Napoleon to be excessive and he was dismissed. Persigny worked to create a coherent Bonapartist party, to whom all power and all rewards should be confined; but the emperor wished also to make some sort of compromise with the notables, to win over Orleanists and legitimists, even if their loyalty was not as religious as Persigny's: most of his ministers were in fact of this kind.[1]

Morny could be called a typical Orleanist. He was a grandson of Talleyrand and Napoleon III's illegitimate half-brother. He had been a soldier and a sugar manufacturer under Louis-Philippe. He was a patron of the arts, a rake and a speculator but he was also a man with enormous ambition and sang-froid

[1] V. F. de Persigny, *Mémoires du duc de Persigny* (1896); H. Farat, *Persigny* (1957).

behind his languid exterior. He played a decisive role in ensuring the success of the *coup d'état*. He never obtained the leading position in the empire to which he aspired, but as president of the legislature (1854–65) he contributed a great deal to increasing that body's constitutional importance and powers, and to hastening the advent of the liberal empire of which he was a persistent advocate. Achille Fould (minister of state 1852–60, minister of finance 1861–7), a Jewish-Protestant banker, had been an Orleanist too. He and Pierre Magne (minister of finance 1854–60, 1867–9), a barrister who had been a civil servant under Louis-Philippe, both influenced Napoleon's financial policy, though in different ways, and attacking each other.[1] Baron Haussmann (prefect of the Seine 1853–70) was in perpetual dispute with these two men because of the way he raised money for rebuilding Paris. In planning the new city Haussmann followed Napoleon's personal instructions for many details but the authoritarian methods of execution were his own.[2] The marquis de Chasseloup-Laubat (minister of Algeria and the colonies 1858–9, minister of the marine and colonies 1860–7, minister president of the Conseil d'État 1869) came of an old noble family, was the son of a general of the First Empire, a councillor of state and a deputy under Louis-Philippe and then a leader of the independents in Napoleon's first parliament of 1852–7. The principal achievement of his long ministry, the annexation of Cochin-China, was his own work, to which he converted Napoleon by means of a strongly argued memorandum. In 1869, when asked to prepare a constitution for the liberal empire, he followed Napoleon's instructions but also went beyond them, giving deputies the right to initiate legislation. Chasseloup so retained his independence while serving the empire, that he was one of the few Bonapartists to be elected to parliament in 1871, and he was then appointed *rapporteur* of the important Army Law of 1872.[3] Victor Duruy (minister of Education 1863–9), the anticlerical historian and

---

[1] A. Fould, *Journaux et discours* (1867); J. Durieux, *Le Ministre Pierre Magne* (2 vols., 1929); R. Pflaum, *The Life of the Duc de Morny* (N.Y. 1968).

[2] J. M. and B. Chapman, *The Life and Times of Baron Haussmann* (1957); G. Lameyre, *Haussmann* (1958); D. Pinkney, *Napoleon III and the Rebuilding of Paris* (Princeton, N. J., 1958).

[3] J. Delarbre, *Chasseloup-Laubat* (1873); memorandum on Cochin-China in his private papers, which his descendants have kindly allowed me to examine.

inspector of schools, served the emperor without abandoning his well-known republican ideals: he was another whose individuality was widely acknowledged.[1]

Baroche[2] and Rouher[3] were the two principal barristers in the government, and they were accused of advocating in turn every different policy that Napoleon adopted. Baroche was indeed a fairly docile instrument of Napoleon's will, who executed decisions rather than helped to make them; but then he had a great admiration for the emperor, whom he genuinely looked upon as the saviour of society against the socialist menace. Even so he did on occasion resist his sovereign: he spoke firmly against the Crimean War; in 1862 he offered his resignation as a protest against concessions to the clericals and by this means he was able to obtain their attenuation. Rouher's attitude was even more pronouncedly conservative, and though he continued to serve Napoleon after the liberal concessions of 1860 and 1867, he made no secret of his opposition to them. His vast capacity for work, his ability to master the details of the most complicated legal and economic questions, his vigour as a speaker, made him increasingly indispensable to Napoleon. People called him 'the vice-emperor'. Rouher entrenched himself in power with a veritable clientage of dependants distributed throughout parliament and the civil service: it was said that he suffered no job, no decoration, no favour to be given without his advice. When ultimately he had to retire in 1870, with the final advent of the liberal empire, he was still able to organise strong opposition to it. He did much to impress an authoritarian stamp upon the regime.

The legislation of the reign was prepared by the Conseil d'État. This body was nominated by the emperor, but he himself complained that it was very difficult to carry reforms through its conservative committees. That his laws were such pale reflections of his ideas was due in no small measure to it.[4]

[1] V. Duruy, *Notes et souvenirs 1811–1894* (1901); Jean Rohr, *Victor Duruy, ministre de Napoleon III* (1967). Cf. in general Roger L. Williams, *Gaslight and Shadow* (1957).

[2] Minister of interior 1850–1, vice-president of the Conseil d'État 1852, president 1853–63, minister of justice 1863–7, 1868–9. See J. Maurain, *Baroche* (1936).

[3] Minister of justice 1849–51, vice-president of the Conseil d'État 1852–5, minister of agriculture, commerce and public works 1855–63, president of the Conseil d'État 1863, minister of state 1863–9, president of the senate 1870. See R. Schnerb, *Rouher* (1949).

[4] Vincent Wright is writing a book on the Conseil d'État in this period.

The law on workers' combinations (1864) is a good example. Napoleon intended it to be a concession, the Conseil d'État hedged the concession with so many provisos as to render it worthless, and an intrigue between Napoleon, Morny and Ollivier was needed to give it some meaning. The conservatives soon discovered that the easiest way to obstruct change was to hold up technical legal objections, before which Napoleon nearly always yielded. Many parts of the civil service, apparently an instrument of the emperor's omnipotence, were of equally limited pliability.

The Second Empire has been called a police state, but its police force was little different in size or structure from that of preceding and succeeding regimes. An attempt was made in 1852 to create a ministry of police, but it collapsed within fifteen months, foiled by the resistance of the prefects who refused to submit to it; and in any case it was mainly a supervisory institution with only a small staff. What was significant was its creation, and the authoritarian character it gave to the early years of the empire. Apart from it, however, Napoleon kept the disorganised and complex variety of police forces he inherited, in the same way as the Third Republic kept most of what he bequeathed to it. The different police forces were responsible to different ministries and co-operated unwillingly. Until 1854 Paris was patrolled by only 450 men, and even after the reforms of that year, it still had no more policemen than London, about 4,000 in all. Marseille, with 300,000 unruly citizens, had only 213 policemen. Napoleon's most important change was to double the number of *commissaires de police*—who had hitherto existed only in towns of over 5,000 inhabitants—to 1,745, but they were still very unevenly distributed and some had to cover an area larger than a canton. They were poorly paid and enjoyed little prestige or respect. In the villages, the government relied on the *gardes champêtres*, who worked part-time (paid a couple of hundred francs a year), men without uniforms and usually stooges of the mayor or the local notable. Compared to modern totalitarian regimes, the Second Empire's police was amateur and muddled. The prefect of police from 1858 to 1866, Boittelle, conducted his operations from an office crammed full of paintings, mainly of beautiful women, with a studio behind where he amused himself restoring them. The police needed to be feared not for its efficiency but for the arbitrary and haphazard way it used its power. It could repress political opposition with grim violence, but it does not appear that it was particularly active in the control of petty crime. It incarcerated its political enemies, often without trial, but this was still an age when the enemies of the government could write books against it from prison: they were allowed to publish their attacks and usually punished afterwards, sometimes with prolonged trials which gave them valuable publicity. The police was supplemented by the *gendarmerie*, composed of former army non-commissioned officers, run by the ministry of war, and used mainly in the countryside. Louis-Philippe had about 14,000 of them, which he used, for example, to keep order in the royalist west. Napoleon III raised their number to about 25,000, and employed them unashamedly as electoral agents, to obstruct political agitation. They (and indeed the police too) thus became, in the popular imagination, one of the principal ingredients of Bonapartism. But in the really decisive crises—such as the mass arrests of political opponents in 1851 and 1858—Napoleon also needed the army.[1]

What was original about the Second Empire was not its police but the new place the army came to occupy in national life. This does not mean that it was a militarist regime, for the army did not run the country. However, until June 1848 public order had been maintained, in periods of crisis, by the national guard. Under Louis-Philippe this had the reputation of being a bourgeois force, but bourgeois should be understood in a very wide sense, for it recruited its members from all except the 'dangerous classes', the vagabonds who were the terror of peaceful citizens. The problem of personal security was a very real one until the mid nineteenth century; only when it was solved did the 'social question' replace it as the new scourge. The national guard was almost the nation in arms designed to keep peace at home, while the army had the task of defending

---

[1] Howard C. Payne, *The Police State of Louis Napoleon Bonaparte* (Seattle, Wash., 1966). For the repression in 1851 see Eugène Tenot, *Étude historique sur le coup d'état* (new ed. 1877–80) and for that in 1858 E. Tenot and A. Dubost, *Les Suspects en 1858* (1869). For the *gendarmerie*, A. Germond de Lavigne, *La Gendarmerie* (1857), H. Delattre, *Histoire de la gendarmerie française* (1879), 126, 144, 163, 165, baron Cochet de Savigny, *Gendarmerie: notice historique sur la révolution du mois de décembre 1851. Coopération de la gendarmerie dans la répression des troubles* (1852).

France on her frontiers. But in 1848 the national guard showed that it could not preserve order. It had decayed under Louis-Philippe; the middle classes had used all sorts of stratagems to avoid fulfilling the tiresome obligations it imposed. Instead it was the army which emerged as the guarantor of society, both in the June days and again in December 1851. The bourgeoisie seemed to prefer to allow professionals to deal with revolution, rather than do it themselves. That is how a militarist state became possible.

But it should be remembered that the first 'militarist' regime was that of the republic: General Cavaignac was the republic's saviour, assisted by General Lamoricière and by officers trained in military rule in Algeria. When Louis Napoleon became president, he had General Changarnier placed at his side by the *burgraves* in command of both the army and the national guard. The Second Empire was in fact an interim period. In due course universal military conscription, adopted by the Third Republic, put the nation in arms but in a new way, for now these soldiers were placed under military discipline, and they did not elect their officers, as the national guard had done. Previously the army had been liberal and revolutionary. In raising its prestige, Napoleon III was fulfilling the demands of the liberal patriots. But in the course of his reign, because the army became a pillar of his autocratic regime, for the first time it was denounced as reactionary. Participation in the repression of December 1851 was counted as one year of active service. Numerous favours were granted to the army, to win its allegiance to Bonapartism. In 1858 the colonels of the Paris garrison declared to their troops: 'The army is called upon . . . to play a political role in moments of crisis.' The Imperial Guard, with its splendid uniforms, appeared as a new pretorian bulwark of the regime.

But, paradoxically, the greatest defenders of the military system as it existed in this period were the Orleanist opposition. Napoleon, very conscious of the defects of his army, wanted to establish universal military service, copying the Prussians. Men like Thiers, however, protested that to do this would be to turn France into a huge barracks. The bourgeoisie valued its right to buy itself out and the peasants cherished the hope that they would draw a lucky number in the lottery which would exempt them altogether. Military service for all, it was said, would be the re-establishment of a new *corvée*. The most vigorous support for a professional army came not from the Bonapartists but from Thiers. The whole notion of militarism was changing its face in this period, but this is a large subject, which must be left for fuller treatment in the second volume. It will be seen also, in due course, that in Algeria, where the question of military rule was directly posed, Bonapartism did not mean a strengthening of army control so much as of capitalist dominance, with large companies being given incredible privileges to start off public works on a huge scale.[1]

Parliament under Napoleon III consisted of a senate of loyal dignitaries and a 'legislative corps' of only some 260 members (as against 750 under the republic). This lower house was indeed elected by universal suffrage, but its powers were considerably less than those of the legislative assembly created by the constitution of 1848. Its approval was necessary for the budget and all laws, but it was deprived of the power to initiate bills. It was allowed to suggest amendments, but the government was not required to accept these. It met for only three months every year. Its debates were—for the first eight years—published only in a colourless summary. Since press and public meetings were also severely restricted, its role was a very secondary one. Yet by 1870 it re-emerged as a major power in the state. This evolution is one of the central features in the development of Bonapartism, and it needs to be understood, for this did not represent simply the collapse of the system, as some have argued. The pressures which were exerted on Napoleon from within the parliament were very varied, and they illustrate just how many different interpretations there were of Bonapartism among the men who were either its adherents or agreed to collaborate with it. Some insisted that Bonapartism was essentially 'conservative', that politics was not a matter for the masses, who should delegate the affairs of state to responsible men and then get on with their work. They thought liberty was necessary, but by it they understood the abolition of privilege;

[1] L. Girard, *La Garde nationale 1814–71* (1964); R. Girardet, *La Société militaire 1815–1939* (1953); M. Howard, *The Franco-Prussian War* (1961); J. Bouillon, P. Chalmin, *et al.*, *L'Armée et la seconde république* (Bibliothèque de la Révolution de 1848, vol. 18, 1955).

they were in favour of reform but they thought that the first and overriding requirement was order. Many saw Bonapartism as a rejection of Louis-Philippe's timidity and caution, a national revival, a great patriotic movement for glory, in foreign affairs, and in the material sense too. This patriotic element was very strong, but not everybody accepted its social consequences. There were those who insisted that 'the present empire is not democracy incarnate, it is not the republican idea crowned . . . it is a real monarchy.' Some wanted this monarchy to be tempered by aristocracy, with decentralisation, sharing power with the notables who were supposed to bolster the 'moral force of society'. On the other hand there were men who claimed Bonapartism as being essentially democratic, the rule of the parvenus, destroying the influence of the old cliques, but saving universal suffrage from demagogy by leading the people towards material improvement and prosperity. Some thought a strong central power was essential to bring this prosperity, others believed in *laissez-faire*.[1]

Centralisation

If one concentrates on the parliamentary history, the foreign policy or the court intrigues of the Second Empire, one would be inclined to conclude that this was a reign so muddled in its objectives and so blundering in its actions that it has no permanent significance in French history, beyond showing once again the inability of an authoritarian monarchy to deal with the problems of the nation. The importance of the Second Empire lies elsewhere. It was a catalyst in the meeting of democracy and centralisation. Centralisation is well known as being one of the most distinctive features of French society. Tocqueville's famous book showing that its origins go back to the *ancien régime*, and that it was not a creation of Napoleon I, has led historians to investigate those origins, and some very interesting studies have been published about the increasing power of the old monarchy. There is no similar analysis of what happened to centralisation in the nineteenth century, when it was faced with a peculiarly interesting crisis, the proclamation of universal suffrage.

[1] T. Zeldin, *The Political System of Napoleon III* (1958), 46–51, gives quotations and references.

Bonapartism was in fact the means by which centralisation solved the problem, at least in part. It was able to do so because the newly enfranchised peasants—through Bonapartism—found in the centralised state the means of liberating themselves from the rule of the nobles and the notables. In the towns and the quasi-urban villages of the south, the liberation occurred, as has been seen, directly through republicanism. In the rural areas where the possibilities for popular union were more limited, the Bonapartist state provided a lever by which the old hierarchy could be overthrown. The price paid for this was that centralisation survived, side by side with the democracy which emerged. The Third Republic had to absorb the traditions of the old monarchy and the empire. That is why Bonapartism cannot be regarded as something radically different from republicanism: it remains encapsulated in it. That is why, also, neither it, nor republicanism, can be regarded as always signifying the same forces: the Second Empire effected social changes of a kind the First Empire did not, and likewise the Third Republic made compromises which did not tempt the more naïve and optimistic pioneers of 1848. The apparent enigma of why one of the leading republican advocates of universal suffrage under Louis-Philippe, Cormenin, author of the celebrated pamphlets of 'Timon', should also have defended centralisation and then become a senator under Napoleon III becomes clear if viewed in this light. Cormenin said that centralisation gave independence if not liberty. Independence seemed the necessary first stage.[1]

The key to the power of Bonapartism among the peasants was the poverty of the villages. The principle of centralisation was that all villages were equal, at least in their institutions. France was divided into 36,000 communes. The average size of each was about 1,000 inhabitants.[2] 8,000 of these communes, under Napoleon III, had fewer than 300 inhabitants. Only 1,300 had over 3,000 people in them. The possibility of the small ones having an independent civic life was negligible, particularly since they had very little money to carry on any independent activity. The amount of taxation a commune

[1] See L. de Cormenin, *Reliquiae* (1868), *Pamphlets anciens et nouveaux* (1870), and P. Bastid, *Cormenin* (1948).
[2] In Italy, by contrast, the average was 2,845.

could raise for its own use was strictly controlled by the prefects. The bulk of taxation paid by Frenchmen went to the state. A tiny fraction, known as *centimes*, was added to this taxation for the benefit of the communes. The larger towns could levy duties on consumption, known as *octrois* (only some 1,500 did). The villages for their part had another ancient tax in *prestations*, by which every inhabitant had to give three days' labour annually to road mending, or to pay a tax to enable the commune to find a substitute. Only in 1903 was a law passed to convert this tax in kind into a money one, but it remained optional, and in 1911 17,947 communes still had the old *prestation*. Together these formed the tax revenue of the communes. In addition they were variously favoured by income from communal property, which, for France as a whole, provided them (in this period) with 11 per cent of their total income (though some villages, as has been seen, were much luckier in their inherited wealth: private incomes produced inequalities among the supposedly equal communes as much as among the people). The final source—at the discretion of the government—was subsidies, which of course greatly reinforced the domination the state could exert.

The communes could not spend their money as they pleased. The state worked out for them what they ought to use it for. It decided that certain public services should be considered the responsibility of communes and the communes had to pay for them. Thus certain expenses involved in primary education, police, road building and the repair of public property were placed on the shoulders of the communes. The job of the prefects was to ensure that the communes paid. The more state legislation was introduced in the name of progress, the more burdened were the communes: but their power was not proportionately increased. It was the prefect who appointed the schoolmaster (whom, after 1833, every commune had to employ), the state paid him, but the commune had to find him lodgings and a school. Obviously a village of 500 could not afford to build a school, and it was therefore dependent on the state for subsidies. Its own tiny resources were increasingly absorbed in incidental expenses, each of them insignificantly small but together enough to be a heavy burden on the commune. While the power and activity of the state increased, an outdated and totally inadequate system of local taxation kept the communes in bondage. If a village wished to raise and spend money which it was not compelled to, it had to obtain the authorisation of the state to the levying of additional *centimes*—but the law placed strict limits on the number of these, as it did on its power to borrow.

The Council of State kept a watchful and jealous eye to make sure that the communes did not develop excessive ambitions, usurping functions reserved for the state. It long remained the enemy of municipal socialism. The result was that the communes did not borrow a great deal, compared with other countries. In 1890 the communes of France had a debt of 84 francs per inhabitant, compared to 180 francs owed by English local authorities. But most of this borrowing was by large towns: 84 per cent of the local debt was owed by 246 towns. If Paris is left out, the French communes owed only 37 francs a head. Paris owed 798 francs a head, Rouen 389, Marseille 285, compared with New York's 288, Boston's 650 and Rome's 398. In general the rural commune made its terms with the state for subsidies, while the cities got embogged with the capitalists. This goes far towards explaining their different histories.[1]

The financial problems of the villages may be illustrated by taking one individual case. Plibou in Deux-Sèvres (population 801 in 1846 and 522 in 1911) had a municipal life which centred around the provision of successive forms of progress, each involving frightening expenses. First there was the question of the priest. The village did not have one until 1840, when at last they got their own (instead of using the services of the *curé* in the next village), but this meant 100 francs a year to pay for his rent. Decency required that he should have a presbytery. For twenty years they argued about this. At last in 1851 the municipal council voted to buy him a house for 2,962 francs— but this was an enormous amount, equal to its whole annual budget. It did not think it could afford more than 1,500 francs itself, and it proposed to levy this through taxation, in additional *centimes*. All depended on the goodwill of the prefect—who provided first 1,000 francs as a state subsidy, and then 1,087 francs from departmental funds. After the purchase had been com-

[1] L. Paul-Dubois, *Essai sur les finances communales* (1898); M. Himbourg, *Des finances communales* (1891).

pleted, it emerged that expensive repairs would be necessary
and the business developed into a nightmare. Further appeals
were made to the bishop, who persuaded the prefect to ask the
state for 2,000 francs, but only 500 was granted. So further
taxation was needed. Only in 1860 was the bill of about 7,500
francs finally paid. The commune had had to go through ten
years of heavy financial strain. At times, when funds ran out, the
mayor had to advance money to the workers and to the vendor
(who happened to be his uncle) out of his own pocket. The key
roles of the mayor and the prefect in this crisis were naturally
full of political implications: they had led the villagers to
civilisation, and had also saved them from the bankruptcy
this would have entailed, but for their help. And the new
luxury the villagers had acquired turned out to be as difficult
as an expensive wife. When a new *curé* was appointed in 1859,
he declared that the house was too small, or at least he wanted
the commune to buy the one next door for him also, so that he
would not have his conversations overheard by it and so that
the danger of its one day being turned into an inn or a 'house
of scandal' should be prevented. To have obtained this would
indeed have shown the power of the priest to be at a high point.
But the municipal council, overwhelmed by the expenses it had
borne 'principally', as it said, 'under the inspiration of its
priests', rejected the demand, adding that it did not know
what a house of scandal was and that in any case it was not
customary for other householders to buy up neighbouring
properties to prevent a purely hypothetical possibility of
contamination. Nevertheless the priest succeeded in getting,
again after twenty-five years of debate and procrastination, a
vote to repair the church in 1878. 2,300 francs were provided
by state subsidies and a further 3,152 from voluntary subscriptions. The cost, as usual, trebled in the course of the work,
reaching 9,852 francs, to which the commune contributed 2,217
francs. This shows once more how every major village improvement depended on state aid.

The great school-building programme of the Third Republic
between 1878 and 1888 cost the communes about 300 million
francs, to which the state added 216 millions in subsidies.
Plibou drew up plans for its school in 1878, at an estimated cost
of 35,800, the largest undertaking it had ever envisaged. The

sub-prefect told them to start it off by getting a loan of 12,000 francs, which they could repay, at a cost of 18,000 francs, over thirty-one years, by levying 14 additional *centimes* on themselves. The municipal council with prudent thrift refused to bind itself for a whole generation, and voted to borrow only 6,200. It successfully obtained 10,000 francs subsidy from the department's *conseil général* and 20,000 from the state. By 1910 the loan was paid off. The school was like a palace in their midst. It is a good example of the way the state on the one hand encouraged the communes into extravagant expenditure, but also of the way the communes for their part were able to use the subsidy system to embark on projects far more grandiose than they would have ever dreamt of if they had been financially independent. Still, the building of the school raised the *instituteur* to the zenith of his importance. He now lived splendidly. In 1840, when the priest had been paid 100 francs a year to rent a house, the *instituteur* had been given a lodging allowance of only 40 francs, raised to 50 francs in 1855, 90 in 1856 and 120 in 1870. His salary, paid in equal shares by commune and state, was 200 francs in 1834 and 1,444 francs in 1872. He was, unlike the priest, partly a servant in the pay of the villagers, until the Third Republic turned him fully into a state functionary.

But they spent much less on him than they did on what was always the major item in their budget, the maintenance of roads. Between 1,000 and 1,400 francs were voted for this every year, but mostly this tax was paid in kind, for the villagers had plenty of leisure in winter, and they thus kept up their roads very cheaply. But they were quick to seize on government subsidies to build new ones. When they made roads for themselves, little money changed hands. When parliament voted a great road-building programme, with lavish credits (10 million francs a year for ten years in 1868, 80 million francs in 1880, etc.), the villages put in their claims, approved plans, raked in their subsidies (500 francs a year for Plibou after 1868) and took care to claim all possible compensation when the new roads went through their land—which they seldom did if it was a purely communal venture. Plibou got its roads for about 20 per cent of their cost, plus the individual benefits from increased property values. It should not be thought, however, that it was only these large grants that mattered to the villagers. A lot of effort was spent obtaining very small favours from the state, particularly for the benefit of the poor. Public assistance was another function of the commune, but here too it begged subsidies from the prefect. In 1855 it obtained 150 francs (i.e. £6), in 1865 and in 1869 as little as 50 francs. The commune itself voted 15 francs in 1884 to help one old man. The great bureaucratic system could reach out to and influence the humblest pauper.[1]

The municipality was the creation of the state and part of it, a geographical unit rather than a traditional organism. The idea of the unitary state meant that local government was not in the hands of autonomous bodies but was an outpost of the central administration, and that all authority was arranged in a hierarchy, with a clear chain of command. Thus though there was an elected municipal council in the village, its functions were limited, its agenda was prepared for it, it met only briefly (and not publicly) at fixed times or when summoned by the mayor, its deliberations could be annulled if it exceeded its attributions, and if it blocked the state's plans, it could be dissolved. The real power in the village was the mayor. He wore a tricolour sash (not the arms of the corporation as in England) to indicate that he was primarily the representative of the state, as well as being head of the commune. His function was to carry out the state's laws, as much as to defend the interests of the commune. He was originally appointed by the state. After 1831 he was chosen from inside the municipal council, so that an elective element was introduced during the July Monarchy. The Second Republic maintained this system for towns of over 6,000 inhabitants and for capitals of departments and *arrondissements*, but elsewhere allowed the free election of mayors. Under Napoleon III the appointment of all mayors was resumed by the state, so that the authoritarian character of the office was enhanced. Even when after 1871 the election of mayors was revived (Paris remaining a special case), the force of the centralising tradition maintained their supremacy over the municipality. The council now elected the mayor for the same period of six years as it itself sat, and it could not dismiss him. In the

[1] Marcel Denieul, *Histoire des finances d'une commune rurale* (Poitiers, 1912). Cf. R. Brun, *Le Budget de Montmarlon: étude d'une très petite commune* (Lyon thesis, 1919).

event of a quarrel, it was the council which usually lost. Every year there have always been many dissolutions of councils, ordered by the prefects, so as to resolve deadlocks between them and their mayors.

Under the Second Empire the mayors were more than ever conscious of their role as the government's representatives, and they were a major instrument in its control of the masses. They were always unpaid, but this gave them an even greater sense of their own importance. One of them, a doctor in a village in Lot, wrote a book in their praise, in which he described their function as 'a kind of priesthood, with which one cannot be invested without feeling oneself transformed, that is raised above oneself and having to win respect for something other then a mere individual . . . Either to meet general expectations, or because of the feelings which his position naturally gives him, the mayor sometimes takes on a certain grandeur.' This man, being possessed, as he put it, of a noble intelligence, allied to a great fortune, undertook 'to discipline the village', and he achieved a lot so long as he was supported by the favour and aid of the government. But it was no simple matter getting on with the prefect, who too often treated him as a mere office boy. Besides there were three powers in the village, the mayor, the *curé* and the teacher, and their rivalry complicated the mayor's task. The mayor had no difficulty with the municipal council: 'the government rightly allowed them to be ignored.' But when the mayor tried 'to make himself master of the terrain on every point', he inevitably aroused opposition. This particular mayor was dethroned following a battle with the *curé*. He rightly pointed out that the mayor was most successful when he was supported and consecrated by the priest, and when he could either act as the arbiter between priest or schoolmaster, or best of all when these two united and made the school an instrument of their joint supremacy. The mayor's aim should be to 'destroy factions, dominate the masses and make this domination loved through the good that it spread in the village'.[1]

The state gave the mayor a great deal of influence which, with skill, he could use so that the villagers saw in him their protector against the forces of the outside world and their

---

[1] Paul David, *La Commune rurale. Observations et études* (Toulouse, 1863), by the mayor of Saint-Matré (Lot).

representative in it. In a society with a large number of illiterates, and when even many municipal councillors might be illiterate, he had obvious advantages. He could make life very difficult for anybody who refused to co-operate with him: he could, for example, be obstructive in signing documents, or he could prevent a man getting a road up to his farm. The sign of his success was that the village voted as he asked it to. As one Bonapartist sub-prefect said, 'A mayor who has not enough influence to get his subjects (*administrés*, that is how mayors referred to the inhabitants of their village) to vote for an official government candidate should not remain mayor.'[1] The mayor had to explain to them that only if they voted the right way could they hope to get their subsidies. 'Mes chers administrés,' wrote one mayor on a poster he placed outside his office, urging the village to vote for the government candidate, 'I feel I can give you this advice with the most profound conviction that it is that which a wise father would give to his children.'[2] In a rural situation, it was not difficult for a mayor to see every one of the electors and show them exactly what material and local issues were at stake in elections. To help him he had a small army of officials—his deputy mayor, the village constable, the road mender, the tax collector, the postman, the innkeeper who depended on him for his licence, the tobacconist whose trade was part of the state monopoly, and not least the schoolmaster, who was often also mayor's secretary. Together they formed an electoral machine which no opposition party could easily rival, and which could reach every village. That is why so many villages voted almost unanimously, in the way they were asked to by the government, and the mayors took care to point out that they did so in the expectation of material rewards, in the form of subsidies and favours. If the post of mayor was given not to the family which had ruled the village for generations but to a new man, with tact and a gift for winning popularity, then the balance of social forces in the village could be radically altered. Bonapartism could then mean the building up of a new kind of clientele system, challenging that of the nobles and the notables.

[1] Archives Nationales, C. 1347, protest by Anatole Lemercier, Charente-Inférieure.
[2] A.N., C. 1368, Loire-Inférieure file; cf. C. 1351, Ille-et-Vilaine file.

The patron of the clientele was the prefect. The Second Empire raised him to new heights of power and prestige. 'In the prefect's hands', wrote one of them, 'are concentrated all the powers of the state, all the moral force of the country, all the municipal liberties of the communes.' He represented the principles of unity and equality proclaimed by the Revolution. He was 'the guardian of the communes', maintaining their rights, but preventing their mistakes, treating them like minors. He had to approve all the budgets of the municipalities; he could impose taxes on them when they neglected to fulfil their compulsory obligations; he supervised all the printing, publications, bookshops, fairs and prisons in the department. It was through him that all projects on roads, railways and bridges, which the local engineers drew up, had to pass on their way to the ministry of public works, for though he took his orders from the minister of the interior, he was head of all the services in his department. He appointed the mayors, 'an immense right, which by itself gave him the widest sphere of action a man can exercise'. Napoleon rightly called the prefects 'little emperors'. Even when they lost their complete dominance over the mayors in 1871, they remained extremely powerful. The elected departmental *conseils généraux* with which they were then supposed to share their power were never to acquire great importance. Few were ever dissolved, because they were seldom able to be obstructive. The councillors tended to act privately, making individual deals with the prefect for the canton they represented. The standing committee the decentralisers of 1871 tried to establish, to keep the council alive as a watchdog outside its brief sessions, never became anything like a local government. In 1964, when the reforms of the whole system, promised for almost a century, at last became law, the prefect was not only confirmed as the head of the department, but his role as co-ordinator of all the other services in it was strengthened.[1]

Under the July Monarchy, the prefect's supremacy was challenged by the members of parliament, who in return for giving their votes to the government made a bid for its favours to be channelled through them. The same challenge was to occur under the Third Republic. Because the electoral element

[1] A. Romieu, ancien préfet, *De l'administration sous le régime républicain* (1849).

flourished in these two periods, the prefects' task became much more difficult, but during the Second Empire, the prefects were sometimes able to effect an important shift in the balance of social forces, so that after 1870 their problems were no longer quite the same. The deputies of Louis-Philippe's reign were powerful partly because they were notables, capable of exercising influence on others through their social position, independently of the government. When universal suffrage was proclaimed, there was some uncertainty as to whether the masses would remain subject to that influence in the same way. Napoleon III inevitably had to employ as prefects many men trained in the civil service under Louis-Philippe and they naturally tended to assume that the notables could not be ignored. Such prefects saw their task as the conciliation of the notables, rallying them to the empire, in the belief that the masses were still under the influence of the notables and that the government could get the votes of the masses only with their support. They helped former Orleanist and legitimist deputies to get elected under a Bonapartist label, simply because they thought they were bound to win, and it was better to have them at least nominally for the empire rather than against it. As a result of this timidity, dynasties of notables were assisted in establishing themselves even more firmly. In this way, the parliaments of the empire were infiltrated by men whose allegiance was very doubtful, so that it is not surprising that, as soon as the danger of revolution abated, they pressed the emperor for a more liberal constitution. There were some prefects, however, who had the ambition of destroying the influence of the notables and substituting their own. 'Until now', wrote the prefect of the Haute-Loire in 1852, 'the administration has been under the thumb of the factions, now of one, now of the other . . . The time is ripe to recapture the high position which the government ought never to have lost; it must control the passions of the masses and not follow them or elude them . . . The mediocrities who for forty years have exploited power will never forgive the prefect who will reduce them to impotence . . . but the confidence of our rough peasants can be won by an energetic authority which proves that it knows how to punish and to protect.'[1] Persigny, the minister

---

[1] A.N., F (1c) II 100, 14 Jan. 1852.

of the interior in 1852 and 1863, who, having long been an
exile, had not been contaminated by Orleanism, encouraged
such prefects to destroy the notables where they could. 'It is
the masses', he declared, 'who make elections today, and not
the old influences . . . What matters is that there should be no
canton where the hand of the government has not at least
sapped the foundations on which the old influences rested.'[1]

The effect of this kind of Bonapartism was that the peasants
were accustomed to ignoring the nobles and the wealthy men
of their village. When a prefect was able to find an able,
possibly self-made man to become mayor, in preference say to
the legitimist noble, after twenty years of such government, of
favours and public works being channelled through him, the
noble's status was seriously diminished. These prefects paid
little attention to ideological indoctrination. They interpreted
the aspirations of the peasants in largely materialistic terms,
and believed they were profoundly indifferent to politics. The
prefects could succeed in this kind of policy, indeed, precisely
in those areas where the peasants did feel like this, which is why
they did not make much impression in the south, where the
peasants had their own institutions for political argument and
agitation. But in the depressed regions of the west, they were
able to detach many peasants from their allegiance to the local
lords by assiduously holding out the bait of local improvements,
roads and railways, to open new and profitable markets,
education and jobs for those who wished to get on in the world,
cheaper credit for those who were in the clutches of the usurers.
A sub-prefect in the west wrote in 1853, 'The peasant who
sixty years ago owned nothing, is today everywhere a landowner.
Henceforth his interest prevails over old traditions. When the
wastelands were divided . . . he nearly always found the old
aristocracy as his antagonist, either because it revived old
claims, or because it exhumed old title deeds, or because it used
the fact of its possessing extensive properties to claim a proportionately larger share. The peasants have preserved the memory
and the grudge. They are happy to reach municipal office
which gives them some authority over the descendants of their
lords. The influence of the nobility in the countryside received
a first blow in this way. Every electoral defeat [of the legitimists]

[1] A.N., F (1c) II 58 and 98.

has reduced it further. Forced to live on their capital, obtaining no part of the profits of commerce or industry, or from the salaries of administrative offices, the nobility has gradually fallen into debt—the registry of mortgages tells how much. Finally, by refusing the oath [of allegiance to Napoleon III] and abdicating all participation in the deliberations of our councils and our assemblies, it has given itself the final blow. All these circumstances do not escape the perpetual attention of the peasant. . . . Placed between the promises which have for over twenty years announced an ever-postponed restoration, and the acts of the empire, at once energetic and benevolent, he is almost converted to new ideas which daily effect new progress and new benefits for him under his own eyes.'[1] In areas where the clergy did not have a powerful influence, the peasants, through the lever of the administration, often emancipated themselves from the control of the nobles. The way Bonapartism was sometimes a kind of half-way house to republicanism is seen in the winegrowing areas of the Nantes region, an enclave of small proprietors surrounded by large legitimist estates: some turned republican to assert their independence, but some, for the same reason, became Bonapartist. Likewise, in those areas of the Vendée where large and wealthy monasteries flourished as alternatives to noble land-lords, the fear of the revival of the tithe was an important cause of the peasants allying with the administration against royalism. These were often the descendants of the peasants who had opposed the royalist rebellions at the time of the Revolution, who had bought Church lands or made money out of state employment. The Bonapartists in the region of Sables warned the peasants that if they voted for the royalist comte de Falloux, they should expect the tithe to be re-established. These traditional fears were more important here than any simple correlation with small peasant landownership, for many small proprietors continued to vote Catholic and royalist; but once a breach had been effected with the old oligarchs, it was difficult for the peasants to go back.[2]

The south-west, likewise, was still dominated by legitimists

[1] Sub-prefect of Ancenis, 28 Feb. 1853, F (1c) III Loire Inf. 8.
[2] L. Girard, *Les Élections de 1869* (1960), 149–62, article by M. Faucheux on Vendée.

in 1848, with some influential Orleanists, but virtually no
Bonapartists and only a nucleus of republican middle-class
militants. This situation was transformed by the Second
Empire. Its prefects worked hard to destroy the power of the
notables. 'Our aim', wrote Pietri, prefect of the Haute-Garonne,
'is to remove all that can give importance to the party or
coterie leaders and to create a direct communion between
[Napoleon] and the people, which can admit of no intermediary.
Every attempt at oligarchy, at patronage, outside the administrative hierarchy, is an evil: if it appears a source of strength
now it will certainly be a danger later.' So he took great care
in the appointment of civil servants, down to the lowest ranks
of primary teachers, forest guards and village policemen. He
watched their actions closely, prevented them from being
arbitrary or vexatious, particularly with regard to taxation and
forest offences, insisted on their treating all equally and fairly,
protecting the humble, provided of course they repaid the
protection with respect for the prefect's authority. Every job,
every public enterprise was awarded with a view to the same
purpose.[1] As a result, the legitimist influence was gravely
weakened and in the 1870s this was a major area of Bonapartist
success. The republicans of course benefited also from the destruction of the influence of the old cliques. When they obtained
power after 1871, they in effect adopted in modified form some
of the techniques of these Bonapartist prefects. That is partly
why the south-west, after a period of allegiance to Bonapartism,
became in due course a stronghold of radicalism. The significance of these two doctrines was not all that different. The
Gascons in due course became such staunch radicals partly
because the Third Republic developed the policy of subsidies
to a peak of perfection far beyond anything the Second Empire
was able to achieve. It should not be assumed that the Second
Empire spent more *money* in indirect electoral corruption of this
kind: on the contrary the Second Empire's subsidies were
meagre indeed compared to those of the Third Republic,
which rose from 18 million francs in 1880 to 28,800 million in
1947, as the solidarist, welfare state made progress. Only
gradually were rules developed to apportion the subsidies

---

[1] André Armengaud, *Les Populations de l'Est-Aquitain au début de l'époque contemporaine 1845-71* (1961), 351, 398.

between local bodies on some fixed criterion, such as population, or territory, or wealth. It will be seen in due course how the republicans modified rather than completely rejected the methods of the Bonapartists.[1] During the Third Republic, the south-west was the region which supplied a larger share of the civil servants than any other. The government provided the peasant with the means to escape from his bondage to the soil. The great ambition of the peasant here was to get himself a horse and cart, to stop walking, to get away from the land, to set himself up as a pedlar, to get a job in the transport industry or in commerce. 'There were villages in which it was difficult to find an able-bodied man at certain times of the year':[2] peasants often left their women to work on the land while they travelled around in search of speculative gain. The jobs of the civil service and the railways inevitably made a great appeal here.

Reliance on government favours meant of course that once the Bonapartists lost power, their survival as a party became precarious. This can be seen in Corsica, which might be considered the most loyal home of the cause. And yet by 1881 it had abjured its allegiance and sent Gambettists to parliament. The explanation of this is that the decisive period in Corsican history was the First Empire. Napoleon I gave Corsica very important fiscal immunities which lasted throughout the century. In 1910 a commission appointed to inquire into them discovered that the island was saved a total of over three and a half million francs each year thanks to reduced succession and sale duties, lower indirect taxation and concessions on tobacco taxes and customs duties. The Corsicans had good grounds for avoiding trouble with the government in Paris. For long, indeed, they did not demand any large public works. The Second Empire did not grant them any special favours in the form of large public expenditure on roads or railways. Corsica remained appallingly poor and underdeveloped. What the inhabitants wanted was the chance to get out. Corsica exported large numbers of people to France—not to industry, commerce, or domestic service—but to the police, the army and the civil

[1] Jean Boulois, *Essai sur la politique des subventions administratives* (1951).
[2] Edmond Desmolins, *Les Français d'aujourd'hui: les types sociaux du midi* (about 1898), 157.

service, where the Corsican could enjoy a position of command and dignity which his warlike traditions caused him to hold in highest esteem. Bonapartism was attractive because it boosted the prestige of these official jobs. But then the Third Republic offered identical opportunities and the Corsicans could not afford to cut themselves off from them. Corsican Bonapartism was another variety of Bonapartism absorbed by the republic, whose police force continued to be filled by Corsicans perpetuating the authoritarian traditions of the Second Empire. As a political force, Bonapartism vanished from Corsica and turned simply into a kind of saint-worship. When the Bonapartist mayor of Ajaccio, Napoleon's birth-place and the last refuge of his cult, wanted to get into parliament in 1910, he had to transform himself into a republican. Corsica became such a safe radical seat that even Arthur Ranc, Gambetta's old friend, and Émile Combes were elected to be its senators.[1]

The theorist of centralisation as the instrument of the liberation of the masses was Dupont-White (1807–78), who wrote a number of closely argued works defending the intervention of the state in the life of the nation. He was also the man who translated J. S. Mill into French, and he argued that centralisation was compatible with liberty. Against Tocqueville, he maintained that local self-government did not necessarily prepare men to take a more responsible part in national affairs, because it fostered the 'spirit of locality' which made them incapable of seeing large issues. Against the admirers of the English constitution, he pointed out that England was moving increasingly towards centralisation. Against Lamennais, who described the French system as 'apoplexy at the centre and paralysis at the extremities', he defended centralisation as necessary to destroy privileges, castes and the evils of *laissez-faire*, and he argued that Paris could produce a political élite more suitable to lead a democracy than the rotten provincial aristocracies. He praised Paris as the source, the battle ground and the school of the parvenu.[2] Centralisation thus appeared

[1] Thadée Gabrielli, *La Corse: ses luttes pour l'indépendance, son annexion à la France, ses représentants 1770–1937* (1937); Marcelle Stromboni, 'Le Parti bonapartiste à Ajaccio de 1889 à 1914', *Corse Historique*, 34–5 (Ajaccio, 1969), 5–45.
[2] C. B. Dupont-White, *L'Individu et l'état* (1856), *La Centralisation* (1860), *La Liberté politique considérée dans ses rapports avec l'administration locale* (1864), *Du progrès politique* (1868).

to many people as the safest bulwark against the 'revival of feudalism' and the return of aristocracy. Centralisation, wrote Troplong, president of the Cour de Cassation, 'is the most important and most magnificent feature of our history. Rome produced an outline of it; only France has been able to realise it in its full power.' Centralisation has survived because too many people have feared that national unity would be endangered by its abolition, and that the forces of reaction would be the only ones who would profit from such a reversal of the distinctive characteristic of French history over many centuries. When a few republicans joined the leaders of the Orleanists and legitimists to demand decentralisation ('the programme of Nancy', 1865), they were attacked by several of the main republican newspapers as dupes of reaction. Alphonse Peyrat, who in 1871 became president of the *Union républicaine* in the National Assembly, denounced them on the ground that it was to centralisation that France owed 'the cachet of her incomparable nationality. It is through centralisation that those things, which make our nationality a unique type in history, have been achieved.' All the republican commissions, both in 1848 and after 1871, which were set up to promote decentralisation, produced minimal results. The second volume of this work will attempt to explain the deeper causes of this timidity.[1]

Paradoxically, the Second Empire, while on the one hand raising centralisation to new peaks, at the same time did almost as much as any regime to advance the cause of decentralisation. No one was taken in by its laws which simply transferred some powers from the central ministries to the prefects. But Napoleon III, it should not be forgotten, was a believer in *laissez-faire* as well as in strong government. 'Possibly the greatest danger of modern times', he had said, 'is this false opinion with which people have been indoctrinated that a government can do everything, and that any particular system must meet all needs and remedy all evils.' He had urged that 'the number of jobs in the gift of the government should be limited, for this often turned a free people into a nation of toadies. That disastrous tendency should be avoided which causes the state to do itself

[1] Odilon Barrot, *De la centralisation et de ses effets* (1861); Louis Blanc, *L'État et la commune* (1866); A. Simiot, *Centralisation et démocratie* (1861).

what individuals can do as well and better than it. The centralisation of interests and initiatives is in the nature of despotism.'
After the failure of the 1849 commission on decentralisation to
achieve anything, Napoleon III in 1863 asked his government
to revive the question. 'Our system of centralisation,' he
wrote in a public letter to Rouher, 'despite its advantages, has
the grave inconvenience of bringing with it an excess of regulations', so that a small commune wishing to perform a very
minor service to which no one raised any objection had to ask as
many as eleven authorities and wait two years for permission
to proceed. As a result two laws were promulgated extending
the power of both departmental and municipal councils. These
did not touch the political question of the method of nomination
of mayors and presidents of *conseils généraux* and have therefore
been forgotten; but they marked an important stage in the
financial emancipation of the communes. In 1802 the communes
had been allowed to vote additional *centimes* within narrow
limits and subject to the prefect's veto. The law of 1867 gave
them the right to spend their money more freely once they had
fulfilled their compulsory obligations. They were allowed to
borrow to finance schemes of their own invention, to buy
property without the prefect's approval, to embark on repairs
and maintenance, to grant leases—all within limits, but at
least limits fixed by law and not by the prefect's whim. In 1870
the liberal empire, while waiting for the report of a grand
commission on decentralisation, passed a law requiring mayors
to be chosen from among the municipal councillors. Decentralisation was a very live issue during the Second Empire: at
least seventy-seven books were published on it in the 1860s
alone, not counting pamphlets and articles.[1]

These hesitant half-measures reflect a fundamental ambivalence in Bonapartism. There were limits to the extent to which
it would go in destroying the provincial oligarchies. Some of
these limits were involuntary. Thus Bonapartism failed to make

[1] Napoleon III, *Œuvres* (1856), 3. 119; *Larousse du XIX siècle*, article on centralisation; Maurice Block, *Les Communes et la liberté. Étude d'administration comparée*
(1876); P. Molroguier, *Du régime municipal en France* (1849); Étienne de Toulza,
De l'administration des communes en France (1869); Jacques Droz, 'Le Problème de
la décentralisation sous le second empire', in *Festgabe für Max Braubach* (Münster,
1964), 783–94; Ferdinand Béchard, *Du projet de centralisation administrative annoncé
par l'empereur* (1864); A. Pougnet, *Hiérarchie et décentralisation* (1866).

much impression on the towns, though it tried hard. As soon as its mayors were faced not with a few hundred electors to manage, but several thousands, they were helpless. The empire never found a way of getting round the difficulty. The only alternative it could use was the press, but despite all its efforts to repress that of the opposition, it failed to win control of the city newspapers. Thus in 1861 in Paris, the five pro-government newspapers had a circulation of only 52,000, to which might perhaps be added the 17,000 copies of the *Journal Officiel*, which published mainly laws and parliamentary debates. Against this the 'progressive' newspapers of Paris sold 91,000 copies, the Orleanist ones 36,000 and the legitimist and clericals 38,000. This was a very different picture from that in the provinces where the government had 202 newspapers favourable to it, with 207,000 subscribers, while the republicans had only 13 with barely 23,000 subscribers, the Orleanists 13 also, with 20,000 subscribers, and the legitimists 34 with 31,000 subscribers. But when the press law of 1868 relaxed the censorship, 150 new newspapers were founded in the provinces within a year, 120 of which were hostile to the government.[1] How far newspapers were effective in converting people is doubtful, but they certainly acted as a focus for agitation and it was round them that the middle and lower ranks of the bourgeoisie, led by the barristers and the journalists, organised their opposition committees, with their newspaper sellers and bar keepers as their electoral agents.

The urban masses as a whole were not necessarily hostile to the empire. Industrialisation, by increasing the numbers of the proletariat, did not automatically reduce Bonapartism's clientele. On the contrary, in Paris, the new suburbs which contained the large factories were not hostile. The opposition in Paris was led by Belleville, where there were very few factories. The people who lived here were—far more than the factory workers—Parisian-born, exiles from the centre of the city, where the rents had become too high for them. Most of them went into the centre daily to work in small artisan establishments: their protest was that of men battling against modern transformations, from a slum quarter known as the

[1] A.N., F (18) 294 (for Paris), 294 (for the provinces' 1862 figures), 307 (for 1869).

Siberia of Paris.[1] The wave of strikes that swept France between 1869 and 1870 has sometimes been interpreted as revealing an explosion of dissatisfaction by the workers with the empire, particularly since some members of the Socialist International were involved. The strikes, however, were only marginally political, and were primarily a protest against the rising cost of living. The magnitude of some of the strikes—as many as 15,000 came out in Alsace in July 1870—and the activity of the press gave them unprecedented publicity, but, as a careful historian of these events has shown, the workers were far from all being republican, and they got little sympathy from the republican deputies, who were as frightened by their activities as everyone else. It was the government—particularly in Alsace, and partly so in Le Creusot—which proved to be the workers' best supporters: the prefects were cheered by the workers when they went to negotiate with the employers, and to such an extent that the Bonapartists were accused of using the strikes as a tool against the industrial magnates, who were often members of the liberal opposition. Napoleon III never lost the reputation he derived from being the author of the *Extinction of Pauperism*.[2] The causes which led the workers to become republican were not simple, for though Marx identified Bonapartism with speculative big business, the workers did not always do so. Thus Marseille was a city in which Bonapartism never made any headway. But then it was a city with a consistent record for abstention (35 per cent in 1969, 33 per cent in 1958), an old tradition of legitimist hostility to centralisation, a constant flow of immigration, very rapid growth, exceptional problems in assimilating its heterogeneous population. Bonapartism could not mean much here, except to the Corsican colony, quite apart from the class struggle.[3]

The Bonapartist system often failed in the villages also, because its success depended on a formula which could rarely

[1] See J. Rougerie's brilliant article on Belleville in L. Girard, *Les Élections de 1869* (1960), 3–36.

[2] Fernand L'Huillier, *La Lutte ouvrière à la fin du second empire* (1957), 70, 78.

[3] L. Girard, *Les Élections de 1869* (1960), contains a detailed study by A. Olivesi of Marseille in 1869, 77–123; P. Corticchiato, *Les Corses et le parti bonapartiste à Marseille en 1870 et pendant les premières années de la république* (Marseille, 1921); Chambre de Commerce et d'Industrie de Marseille, *Marseille sous le second empire* (1961), 75–88, 143–64.

be carried out perfectly. The mayor had to be on good terms with the other officials of the village for it to work properly, but this was not easy to achieve. The *curé* and the schoolmaster often had pretensions of their own. Every debate in the village could produce disagreements and discontents, exacerbated by men who had personal jealousies or grudges to satisfy. A former mayor, evicted from office, often provided the focus for opposition. As political discussion revived in the 1860s, the whole system was liable to be challenged ideologically by men whose horizons extended beyond the village's boundaries. The prefects were by no means always tactful or judicious in their choice of the faction they supported, nor always consistent in their support. The unitary conception of village life therefore could not always be maintained. That conception, in any case, was not the only one the government adopted. For though Bonapartism, as Napoleon III defined it, aimed at satisfying the interests of the most numerous classes, it also sought to win the support of the upper classes.[1] Even Persigny, who said that the emperor had 'no friends except below' among the masses, wanted to bring 'the highest ranks of society' to his aid.[2] As a result, the policy of dethroning the notables was not always followed. It depended on the energies and ambitions of the prefect. So in many cases the mayor of the Second Empire was the same man who had held the office under the July Monarchy or the republic. Unfortunately, no one has yet undertaken the enormous task of analysing the changing politics and status of the mayors. No statistical statements can be made about the proportions in which the Bonapartists confirmed the notables in their influence or destroyed them.

The *conseillers généraux* of 1870, a more manageable number, have, however, recently been put on a computer, from which some very interesting facts have emerged. Of course, these people were not as significant as the mayors; they were not as powerful and formed as it were the upper house of the department, so that it was natural that eminent dignitaries should be chosen for it. Nevertheless, it is very striking that 27·6 per cent of the *conseillers généraux* in 1870 were nobles. In 1840 only 17

---

[1] E. d'Hauterive, *Napoléon III et le prince Napoléon* (1925), letter by Napoleon III, 58–9.
[2] G. Goyau, *Un Roman d'amitié* (1928), letter of Persigny to Falloux, 160.

per cent of them were noble, and after the revolution of 1848
21·5 per cent were noble. This stresses the fact, which has
already been suggested, that the nobles should not be thought
of as a class whose significance ended with the Revolution or
the Restoration. The rich ones among them survived with
remarkable success, and got richer still. There were some among
them who augmented their prestige by accepting jobs and
honours from the empire: 45 per cent of the generals in 1869
were (or claimed to be) noble, 32 per cent of the staff colonels
and lieutenant-colonels, 34 per cent of the officials of the
Conseil d'État, 34·5 per cent of the members of the legislative
body. In 1870 there were 317 noble *conseillers généraux* with
incomes of over 30,000 francs a year. Some 26 per cent of them
had residences in Paris, so that they could still appear to be a
national élite. They were on average far richer than the non-
noble members of the *conseils généraux*. One can interpret this fact
in two ways. Either it meant that the domination of the notables
survived and was acknowledged in the *conseils généraux*. Or it
meant that nobles had to be twice as rich as commoners to get
into these councils. Nevertheless, the Bonapartism of Napoleon
III, like that of Napoleon I, clearly involved an alliance with
that section of the old aristocracy which was willing. And there
were plenty of Bonapartists who were ready to turn themselves
into aristocrats. The domination of the National Assembly of
1871 by the nobles should not be regarded as an aberration,
and it should not be assumed that they lost power finally with
the end of the 'republic of dukes'. In 1882 they still survived
on the *conseils généraux* and by judiciously accepting the republic,
many survived very much longer. The Second Empire did not
effect any profound change in the social composition of these
bodies:

Conseillers généraux

	1840	1848	1852	1870
Businessmen	14·3	14·1	14·5	15·5
Liberal professions	23·7	35·8	30·4	29·95
Lawyers	38·2	36·5	33·2	30·5
Civil servants	28·2	17·5	19·2	20·95
Landowners	33·8	32·6	35·8	33·6

(The above percentages add up to over 100 because of multiple professions.)

It is remarkable that manufacturers and bankers did not gain more than 1·5 per cent. The 'couches nouvelles' of Gambetta thus did not enter these bodies before 1870, nor did the Second Empire represent a take-over by speculators. However, too many general conclusions should not be drawn from these statistics, for the *conseils généraux* were always the bodies which were slowest to reflect political or social change, but it is useful to be reminded just how slowly policies proclaimed in Paris took to alter the customs of the provinces.[1]

The problem of Bonapartism was the same as that of republicanism in 1848. It lacked leaders. The vast majority of the educated population had served other regimes and made their careers thanks to their favours. Thus the parliament of 1852, which has often been dismissed as a collection of puppets, contained less than a third of people who could in any way be called Bonapartist and besides, many of these had been Orleanist before 1848. The few who could claim to be unsullied in their cult of the emperor were either Napoleon III's personal followers, or men of modest social status whom the heirs of the marshals and prefects of Napoleon I had little use for. The Bonapartist committees which these petty agitators started under the Second Republic were dissolved by the duc de Morny, as minister of the interior, because they interfered with his policy of attracting the magnates. There were quite as many legitimists and Orleanists in this parliament as Bonapartists—rallied it is true, but altering the nature of the regime by supporting it. The new self-made men, merchants, industrialists, lawyers and others on whom the empire pinned some of its hopes comprised a mere sixth of the total. The flirtation of Bonapartism with legitimism is most significant. The legitimists were sometimes used by the Bonapartists to destroy their common enemy, the educated liberals, and sometimes as dupes, playing them off against each other, to undermine the traditional bases of royalism. Sometimes, however, both they and the Orleanists were left in place because the Bonapartists felt unable to dislodge them. The implantation of Bonapartists therefore varied very much from region to region; and under the Third

---

[1] L. Girard, A. Prost, R. Gossez, *Les Conseillers généraux en 1870* (1967), 47–8, 116–31 and *passim*. This (mainly the work of M. Prost) is a most remarkable and instructive example of computer techniques being applied to historical research.

Republic they never even tried to contest half the constituencies where they had never made much impression.[1]

Moreover, though in certain departments the prefects increased the authority of the administration and obtained political advantage from centralisation, the influence of the old notables did not always devolve to the government. The Bonapartists also created their own new class of notables. As the empire entered its more liberal phase, and as the government relaxed its control of the provinces, its supporters found that they had to fend more for themselves. The clienteles they built up became more independent, even personal. The allegiances they had built up became the nuclei of a new kind of fief. The Bonapartism which was entrenched firmly enough to survive into the Third Republic was often that in which personal contact with the electors had been assiduously cultivated over a long period. Some prefects in particular had exceptional gifts in contact with the masses, which rivalled those of both the nobles and Napoleon III. Janvier de la Motte, for example, gave huge banquets for the peasants, whom he enrolled as village firemen, in what was almost a private army, rivalling the religious societies of the legitimists and the clubs of the republicans. He had an extraordinary memory for names; he was always ready to do favours for anyone who would accept his leadership; he spent the fortunes of two wives and ran his prefecture into a large deficit so as, as he said, 'never to refuse anything'. He transformed his Norman department, which had once been subject to the Orléans, Passy and Broglie families, into a Bonapartist stronghold, which he then represented in parliament after 1876. In other regions, when the prefect was weak, members of the legislature subordinated him to their purposes, and used the power of the state in the same way. The Bonapartists thus added to the repertoire of methods by which notables could influence the electorate, at the same time as they helped to destroy the very notion of a notable.

The Liberal Empire

In republican histories, the Second Empire has been regarded as a gap in French history, an interruption in the development

[1] Theodore Zeldin, *The Political System of Napoleon III* (1958, paperback reprint, N.Y., 1971), 10–45, contains an analysis of the parliament of 1852.

of parliamentary government, and a period of reaction during which liberty was repressed for nearly twenty years. This view can no longer be maintained. The Second Empire, in the first place, was responsible for a number of gains in civil liberty which were no less important because they contradicted the restrictions on political liberty which were reinforced at the same time. France had, for most of its history, been a protectionist country. In 1860 Napoleon III made a commercial treaty with England, by which import duties on English goods were reduced to a maximum of 30 per cent, and in return French wine was admitted at lower rates into England. This was followed by free trade treaties with Belgium, the Zollverein of Germany, Italy, Switzerland, Spain, Holland, Austria and Portugal. The Third Republic rapidly restored protection: it is only in recent years that Napoleon has come to be seen as a precursor of the Common Market. His intentions were partly political—he wished to strengthen his alliance with England—but mainly economic, to stimulate agriculture and industry in France by competition and to benefit the masses through lower prices. However, this experiment in free trade was badly mismanaged, for totally inadequate measures were taken to prepare industry for this radical change or to derive political capital from it. As a result, the strains involved in adapting to it produced a vast and uncomprehending opposition. Exports of wine to England more than doubled as a result, but affected almost entirely wine of fine quality: the mass producers of ordinary wine derived little benefit. The silk industry also reaped great rewards, particularly because the closing of the American market during the Civil War and then its limitation by high tariffs made the English market more important than ever. The Cognac, Armagnac and Sauternes regions long remained Bonapartist under the Third Republic, but it is uncertain how much this should be attributed to the Second Empire's commercial policy, for Charente had voted enthusiastically in favour of Louis Napoleon in 1848, long before; and on the other hand, the Lyon silk workers remained steadfastly hostile to him.

French industry in general was in a state of transformation; the construction of railways was providing a great boost to the iron producers, and drastically reducing transport costs. After 1860, the efficient iron firms were able to hold their own against the British and even to export large quantities of iron goods, especially locomotives and other machinery, but there were loud protests against free trade from the firms which had been slower to modernise, or which were held back by high production costs, bad transport and mines nearing exhaustion. In the cotton industry, the issue was confused by the American Civil War, which stopped the supply of raw cotton, and required changes in machinery to take cotton from India. Many small firms did not have the capital to carry these out; rapid fluctuations in prices also put them at a disadvantage; and there were numerous bankruptcies, which were naturally blamed on the ending of protection. In the Rouen region, in the 1860s, 12 out of the 32 printing mills closed down, but this had little to do with competition from England, which had similar problems. Free trade stimulated the wool and worsted weaving firms to install power looms—the number in Roubaix increased tenfold from 1856 to 1867—and Roubaix, by specialising in particular cloths, was able almost to quadruple the value of its exports to England. But in Elbeuf more conservative manufacturers failed to adapt to the new conditions, and it was they who led the complaints against free trade. The free trade was only partial; it left enough protection to prevent the French market being flooded by English goods; but it was enough to discredit Napoleon with a large section of the business community. They, who were active in the liberal movement for political liberty, were not necessarily liberal in other respects.[1]

Napoleon followed the English lead in several other respects, but again failed to obtain credit for what he did. Thus in 1864 he passed a law allowing workers to combine and to strike to improve their conditions (which the first Napoleon had of course rigorously forbidden). The industrialists were horrified and were violent in their protests. The workers' leaders complained that it was damaging to trade unions, because (following the English Combination Act of 1825) it allowed the 'liberty to work' as well as to strike, i.e. it protected blacklegs, and because it included a phrase forbidding 'fraudulent manœuvres' in the organisation of strikes, which seemed to be a loop-hole. In fact, the main mistake Napoleon made was in the tactless way he

[1] A. L. Dunham, *The Anglo-French Treaty of Commerce of 1860 and the Progress of the Industrial Revolution in France* (1930).

passed this law: he chose a renegade member of the left, Émile Ollivier, to get it through parliament, and failed to bring in the workers and republican leaders by adequate consultation. In the circumstances of the reign this was almost impossible. Ollivier had even wanted to introduce compulsory arbitration but could not get his way. The limitations which the law of 1864 imposed on strikers were removed in 1884, but the economic historian Henri Sée was right to recognise it as 'a law of major importance in the social history of France'.[1] Equally important, from the economic point of view, was the law of 1867 which allowed limited liability companies to be formed freely, without need for government favouritism. A host of other minor measures 'freed industry from the restrictions in which preceding governments had entangled it', as for example the need to obtain state approval to install a steam engine in a factory, or to open a foundry. Butchers, bakers and taxi drivers were liberated from the complicated controls to which they had been subject.[2]

Bonapartism, as it developed under Napoleon III, deeply influenced the character of republicanism, which emerged considerably different after 1870. Before 1848, the republicans had been very divided as to the kind of constitution they wanted. There was a strong element among them, led by Blanqui and Comte, in favour of some kind of dictatorship. Ledru-Rollin advocated direct government by referendum, in the tradition of 1793. The constitution of 1848 had balanced the Legislative Assembly by a strong and independent president. England was regarded by the democrats as aristocratic and feudal, no model for France, and the parliamentary government of Louis-Philippe as chaotic. Napoleon III discredited the republican visionaries of 1848 and largely eliminated their influence from practical politics, by showing their *naïveté*. But he also, by bringing into being a constitution, in the latter part of his reign, which in many ways fulfilled these old republican dreams—for he too

[1] É. Ollivier, *Commentaire de la loi du 25 mai 1864 sur les coalitions* (1864); P. L. Fournier, *Le Second Empire et la législation ouvrière* (1911); J. Barberet, *Les Grèves et les coalitions* (1873); L. Barthou, 'Des atteintes à la liberté du travail', *Nouvelle Revue* (1 Feb. 1901), 321–34; H. Sée, *Histoire économique de la France* (new edition 1951), 2. 342.

[2] E. Levasseur, *Histoire des classes ouvrières et de l'industrie en France de 1789 à 1870* (1904), 2. 495.

was heir to the traditions of the Revolution and of the romantic age—made the republicans, in a process of reaction, give up their interest in strong presidents and plebiscites.

The liberal empire of 1870—far from being a belated triumph for Orleanism, as political scientists like Maurice Duverger have claimed—was a resurrection of the peculiar regime France had adopted in 1815, under the inspiration of Benjamin Constant. It sought to establish not parliamentary government, but representative government. This idea was that the cure for despotism was not to transfer power from a monarch to a parliament, which could be just as dangerous to individual liberty as an aristocracy, but to divide power. The executive should be kept independent, the legislature should be freely elected but confined to legislation, imposing 'principles but not ministers' on the executive.[1]

The gradual increase in political liberty which characterised the 1860s has usually been interpreted as a concession forced on Napoleon III by mounting hostility to his despotism. There can be no doubt that opposition to him, silenced in the crisis of 1851–2, when the threat of a socialist take-over was a source of real terror to a large section of the population, revived when the threat seemed less imminent, and that it was augmented by dissatisfaction with Napoleon III's methods of government. His conservative and clerical allies became disillusioned; his nationalist supporters were appalled by his foreign policy; every industry that suffered a depression blamed its troubles on him; the revived political activity of the working class and then the hostility of the press, which was gradually freed from censorship; the return to active politics of the old party leaders: all this combined to make Napoleon feel that his star was waning, that he was losing popularity, and that he had to do something very striking if he was to save his dynasty and indeed avoid a revolution overthrowing him. However, the forces working independently for a liberalisation of the empire, from within the regime itself, should not therefore be overlooked. Napoleon had always seen himself as not simply giving expression to public opinion, but sensing its development almost before it became self-conscious. He had always seen politics as the art of compromise and the relative. He had a belief in liberty as well

[1] B. Constant, *Principes de politique* (1815).

as a fear of it. He had always admired England for giving 'unrestricted liberty to the expression of all opinions [as well as] to the development of all interests', for maintaining 'perfect order in the midst of the vivacity of debates and the perils of competition', and for making possible, through private enterprise and individual initiative, its vast commercial and industrial prosperity.

The duc de Morny likewise believed that, just as the *coup d'état* had been necessary to save society from the radicals, so in the 1860s a liberal transformation was needed to dish them, to destroy them permanently and establish the dynasty on 'imperishable foundations'. He was convinced that obstinate refusal to change would inevitably lead to a repetition of the revolutions of 1830 and 1848, which had been brought about by just that, and each of which postponed stability for another generation. He was particularly keen on civil liberty, because he thought that in France the government was so powerful that the individual needed to be protected against it. He did not want a revival of Louis-Philippe's parliamentary government but simply an increase in the legislature's power, the easing of restrictions and the ending of abuses like nepotism. He dreamt of winning fame for himself as 'the Richelieu of liberty'.

He found an important ally in the leading journalist of the reign, Émile de Girardin, who invented the phrase 'the liberal empire' to mark the new ideal of Bonapartism, and who, after having supported the autocracy, now urged Napoleon, in the new circumstances of the 1860s, to transform himself into a constitutional monarch. The many supporters of Napoleon who had enjoyed considerable power as members of the parliaments of previous regimes, who had accepted the despotism as necessary in the crisis of 1852, increasingly felt that they could help by sharing some responsibility. In the 1869 elections, they rejected the title of official government candidate, which they had previously valued, and formed a new party, intermediate between the opposition and those led by the empress, who continued to resist change. Adolphe Thiers might have been the leader of these liberal Bonapartists. Had he not done as much as anyone to restore the glory of the first Napoleon? In 1840 Louis Napoleon had appointed Thiers prime minister when he had landed at Boulogne to claim his uncle's throne. Discussions took place, but Thiers's terms were too high—he wanted both a complete abandonment of Napoleon III's championship of nationalities and a total restoration of Louis-Philippe's parliamentary government, with a prime minister in command. Had his arrogance not been resented so much, more efforts might have been used to persuade him, and Thiers might have led the empire on a new path, just as later he emerged as the saviour of the republic, a regime he had long opposed.

Above all, the liberal empire was brought to fruition through the collaboration of Napoleon III with Émile Ollivier. Because Ollivier involved France in the war of 1870 and particularly because that war was lost, he has been treated severely by posterity. Because he abandoned the republicans to join the Bonapartists, he has been condemned as a traitor to the cause of liberty. Had the war not occurred, Ollivier might well be remembered now as the author of one of the most original political experiments of the century. As a young man, Gambetta had seen in Ollivier a combination of 'the passion of Fox with the political genius of Pitt'; later, he abandoned him as being unrealistic, the most striking representative, he said, together with Lamartine, of that execrable kind of politician, the brilliant orator with a fascinating command of language, but totally blind to the realities of the world. Ollivier was the son of a republican Carbonaro. In 1848, at the age of twenty-two, he was appointed prefect of Marseille. He showed himself to be one of the purest examples of the spirit of 1848, seeking the unity of all parties and the fusion of classes, preaching Christian fraternity and improving the lot of the workers, but he failed hopelessly, for old antagonisms could not be ended by rhetoric. In 1857 he was elected to parliament, as a member of the republican opposition, but he was more intent than ever to avoid purely partisan criticism of the regime. He was convinced that it was futile to work for a revolution to overthrow the empire, even though he hated its despotism, because revolutions inevitably led to reactions, and the cycle of instability which had plagued France would be resumed. Since the ultimate aim of republicans was liberty, he wished to advance its cause before all else, and he was willing to support any regime which worked for liberty. He would not place the capturing of power by his party as his first objective. His ideal was not Danton nor

Robespierre, but Washington. Intellectually, he was an eclectic. He knew Enfantin, the Saint-Simonians and Proudhon, but he also read Benjamin Constant, de Maistre and Montalembert; he had a horror of sectarianism. Culturally, he was a European: Italy, on whose painting he wrote several books, and which he toured with Édouard Manet, was his 'second fatherland'; he was one of the first to welcome Wagner's music to France; he married the daughter of Liszt. He deplored Napoleon III's foreign adventures. But he did believe in the need for a strong executive and he became convinced that Napoleon, if pressed by public opinion, could well become the founder of liberty in France. The two men met, got on well and after a series of hesitations, the liberal empire was inaugurated on 2 January 1870. For the first time under the empire the government was composed of ministers drawn from parliament, having a majority in it, and with Ollivier at its head. The *Revue des deux mondes*, normally sceptical, declared of this transformation of the despotism that 'if it is not the greatest of all revolutions, it is at least one of the most interesting, one of the most salutary and most opportune'.

The liberal empire initiated a vast programme for the reform of the country's institutions. Commissions were established, on the English model and with distinguished members from all parties, to prepare laws to end centralisation, to give self-government to Paris, to destroy the monopoly of the university, to set up a programme of technical education for the new industrial age, to improve communications, to revise the inquisitorial criminal code, and to establish institutions of 'social peace' to bring employers and workers together. The government introduced bills to abolish its own rights of arbitrary arrest, to repeal the stamp duty on newspapers, establish trial by jury for press offences and free the workers from the need to carry *livrets*. It created a new ministry of fine arts, to end the 'contempt for taste and intelligence' which had alienated so many writers and artists from the empire. The French Academy responded by electing Ollivier a member, with rare unanimity. In a plebiscite, 67·5 per cent of the electorate ratified the new constitution and transformed regime. The Napoleonic dynasty seemed to have been given a new lease of life, and a new image.

There were certainly limits to the liberalism, and ambiguities

in the whole idea. The liberal empire was rejected by the republican leaders, and violent demonstrations were organised by the
extreme left wing. The police was brutal in its repression. The
arrest of all members of the Workers' International was ordered.
The threat of a revolution by the left was used to create a sense
of crisis, and to rally the support of reactionaries, who proved
treacherous allies. Once the plebiscite was won, the reactionaries, led by the empress, set to work to undermine the new
regime. The emperor himself could not completely abandon his
old friends of his autocratic days. Ollivier's parliamentary majority became precarious. The constitution left the question of
where ultimate power lay unclear. Ollivier in fact had intended
this, for though his first principle was that government should
be based on popular approval, he was anxious that absolute
power should rest neither with parliament, nor with the
emperor, nor even with the people. He believed in the division
of power and the working of checks and balances to prevent
despotism by any one force. His theories were too subtle,
however, for most people, who feared that Napoleon, still
declared to be 'responsible to the French people' might take all
the concessions back. The Franco-Prussian War prevented
this liberal version of Bonapartism from receiving more than
seven months of trial.[1]

Bonapartism, in its most simple interpretation, meant
prosperity. It has been claimed that basically this was what
Napoleon's domestic policy was aimed at, and certainly it was
as much for its prosperity as for anything else that the Second
Empire was regretted after 1870. Whereas diplomacy, justice
and police had been the principal activity of the state before
the empire, the economic development of the country was a
major preoccupation under Napoleon III, bringing dramatically visible results. 'The Napoleonic idea', he had written, 'is
not an idea of war, but a social, industrial, commercial and
humanitarian idea.' The economic side of the despotism was
complete government control over public works and their
financing, and government approval for the appointment of
the directors of all large companies and for the formation of new
businesses open to public subscription. In this way, there was

[1] T. Zeldin, *Émile Ollivier and the Liberal Empire of Napoleon III* (Oxford, 1963).

central economic planning and control. Financiers and industrialists acquired a new prestige, in what seemed like a realisation of Saint-Simon's dream of giving them the leading position
in the state. The July Monarchy had wasted years in interminable discussions as to whether railways should be built by the
state or by private enterprise (and some people—Thiers among
them—were frightened of railways altogether). In 1848 only
1,931 kilometres had been completed; in 1852 only 3,000, and
this by twenty-four different companies, each building independent, unconnected lines with inadequate finance and frequent
bankruptcies. Napoleon III did not worry about great capitalists
becoming too powerful. He grouped these numerous railways
into six regional companies, gave them the backing of a state
guarantee for their shares, and so made possible the systematic
construction of the principal arteries covering the whole
country. By 1870 almost 18,000 kilometres were in use, that is
roughly half the lines ever to be built. Telegraph stations, of
which there were only seventeen in 1852, with 2,133 kilometres
of wire, were increased by the end of the reign to 1,500 stations
with 37,000 kilometres. Thus not only were the communications
of the country dramatically altered, and new possibilities
opened up for commerce and industry, but a new prosperity
and importance was brought to the towns the railways linked
up. The reduced costs of transport were far more important for
economic development than the protectionist tariffs, which, for
example, might add 15 centimes to the price of a quintal of
coal, whereas to transport it used to cost between 2 and 6 francs.

Paris was transformed under the direction of Haussmann.
Large, straight tree-lined avenues, with classical perspectives
were cut through the chaotic mass of small streets, so that rapid
movement across it was made possible for the first time. New
systems of water supply and drainage removed the foul odours
which had pervaded it; parks on the English model were laid
out both in the centre and at its fringes in Boulogne and Vin-
cennes. Most of the private buildings on the Île de la Cité were
demolished and the present official ones substituted; the Opéra
and Les Halles were constructed; the Polytechnic, the Fine Arts
and Mines schools, and the National Library were rebuilt. On
a lesser scale similar reconstruction took place in the great
cities, notably Lyon, Marseille and Le Havre. Nothing like

this, as Taine observed, had been seen since Roman times. The unemployed masses were replaced by scurrying builders; it was a heyday for architects and engineers. At the peak of the activity, 20 per cent of Paris's labour force was engaged in the reconstruction. All this, however, brought Napoleon little reward in terms of support. Though a vast number of people made a lot of money—and some of them very large amounts of money—out of all the speculation, the compensation for expropriation and the business opportunities, the whirlwind of activity also brought havoc, jealousies and new problems. Property values in the cities were turned topsy-turvy, there was plenty of unfairness—dishonesty in allocating compensation, businesses were ruined as well as made by the new streets, taxation and rents rose. The workers were expelled from the centre of the cities to ghetto suburbs, and the vast influx of immigrants (Lyon's population for example rose from 258,000 to 350,000 between 1854 and 1865) increased the pressures and the competition. The rebuilding of Paris cost about 2,500 million francs, which was forty-four times the city's normal annual budget at the beginning of the reign. The money was raised, as far as possible, by bypassing the legislature, avoiding its control by all sorts of stratagems, some of them illegal, so that Haussmann's work came to be regarded as epitomising the irresponsibility and arbitrariness of the despotism. The work was completed only by mortgaging the city to an extent which was quite unprecedented. The orthodox financiers refused to accept the idea that this should be looked on not as a loan but as an investment, and that the interest could easily be repaid from the higher values and taxes which would follow. In 1855 Haussmann borrowed directly from the public; later he obtained aid from the renegade Crédit Mobilier, so that all the traditional powers of the financial world were against him. The cities benefited most, at least directly, from the Second Empire, but they were the source of the greatest opposition to it.

It was the same with the railways. The state did not and could not pay for them, but it lent its support to speculators and to corporations who were thus able to mobilise the savings of all classes, and rake in large profits in the process. All this roused hostility. The government could reply that the only works undertaken by traditional financial methods—the canals, ports and roads—made relatively little progress. Nevertheless the notables, after having opposed the railway building in the name of legality and economy, eventually captured control of it, and in its second stage after 1857 succeeded in getting the concessions of the lesser lines given no longer to the court favourites, but to themselves.[1]

The Second Empire was a period of prosperity in over-all terms. There have been calculations suggesting that the national income rose by more than half, that the income of French industry rose by 73 per cent and that of agriculture by 58 per cent. There is some disagreement among economists over the figures, which are inevitably extremely difficult to work out in view of the inadequacy of the material. There is disagreement over the question of when prosperity reached its peak, some placing it as early as 1857, others 1859 or even 1868. There seems no doubt, however, that, by contrast with the stagnant 1880s, the Second Empire was a period of boom. Different sectors benefited in unequal proportions. Proletarianisation had not yet gone very far. In 1865 about 70 to 75 per cent of the industrial labour force was still artisan. The value of the artisan's production increased by 22 per cent. That of large-scale industry doubled. In some industries the average annual increases in production were very high—6·1 per cent in coal, 8·2 per cent in printing, 11·8 per cent in gas, 12·5 per cent in rubber. The increase in all indutrial products was 2·3 per cent p.a. (These are figures for the first dozen years of the empire.)[2]

However, the upper classes seem to have benefited much more from this prosperity than the masses:[3]

	Profits	Wages	Real Wages
1850	100	100	100
1860	220	113	97·4
1870	386	145	128

[1] L. Girard, *La Politique des travaux publics du second empire* (1952); D. H. Pinkney, *Napoleon III and the Rebuilding of Paris* (Princeton, N.J., 1958); J. M. and B. Chapman, *The Life and Times of Baron Haussmann* (1957); G. E. Haussmann, *Mémoires* (1890–3); C. M. Leonard, *Lyon Transformed: Public Works of the Second Empire 1853–1864* (Berkeley, Cal., 1961).

[2] T. J. Markovitch, 'Salaires et profits industriels en France sous la monarchie de juillet et le second empire', *Économies et Sociétés* (Apr. 1967), 79–87.

[3] E. Labrousse, *Le Mouvement ouvrier et les idées sociales en France 1815–1900* (Cours

Thus, whereas the wage of a miner at Anzin rose by about 30 per cent during the Second Empire, the dividend paid by the Anzin Mines Co. tripled each year.[1] It is true that, just as under the First Empire the myth was that any soldier could hope to become a marshal, so under Napoleon III people believed that ordinary workers could still rise to independence. This was confirmed by the inquiry of 1872, already mentioned, which showed that 80 per cent of employers were former workers and 15 per cent were the sons of workers.[2] The number of men paying the *patente* tax rose by 16 per cent in the Second Empire, which meant that there were a quarter of a million more people with independent commercial or industrial establishments. However, the actual number of factories did not increase in this period, though the value of their buildings tripled, which suggests that the large firms did best, and that they were generally beyond acquisition by the rising worker. The number of savings accounts (some of them working class) rose from 742,000 to 2,079,000.[3] What made the Second Empire appear an age of prosperity was that some people prospered, and the rest could nurture the hope of prospering too. But it is not at all certain that the prosperity was all that widespread. In the towns 'the material situation of the worker rarely improved; it sometimes got worse but most often it remained stable'.[4] Men in skilled occupations and in new industries did well, but artisans were frequently in distress. In Paris, over half the working population was in debt and only a quarter managed to save. The city is said to have contained over a million people living in a state of poverty verging on starvation. However, by contrast with the crisis of the last years of Louis-Philippe and of the republic, the Second Empire was indeed a golden age. Although economic depressions did occur, in 1857 and after 1866, there was no repetition of that catastrophic unemployment which was the masses' most terrible scourge. It is in this sense that the Second Empire meant prosperity: it brought full employment and expanding markets.

de la Sorbonne, 1949); id., *Aspects de l'évolution économique et sociale de la France et du Royaume-Uni 1815–80* (1949), 99.

[1] G. Duveau, *La Vie ouvrière sous le second empire* (1946), 410–11.
[2] Ibid., 415.   [3] Levasseur, 2. 735, 688.   [4] Duveau, 410.

Paradoxically, the peasants who gave Napoleon more support than the town workers, did not necessarily always prosper more than they did. In the Ardèche, for example, the prefect reported in 1859 that the workers were doing well, but that the peasants had had bad harvests for six years and were in distress; in 1866 he was still reporting very mediocre conditions in agriculture. In the Charente-Inférieure, the peasants did enjoy great prosperity, cabarets opened up in large numbers for them to spend their money and their leisure in, but some of the most prosperous of these peasants were hostile to the government. It is unfortunate that no study has yet been made of the peasantry under Napoleon III, so that no general picture is really possible.[1] It is certain, however, that Napoleon failed to give the peasants the 'credit' he, and many others, had diagnosed as their main need. The *Crédit Foncier* put very little money into the land; it gave none at all to small men, and quite failed to replace the mortgage system controlled by the notaries. The railways did open up new markets for agricultural produce, but they also attracted the peasants away from the land. The support Napoleon got from different classes cannot be simply correlated with the material benefits they derived from his rule.

In the same way, the Second Empire did a great deal for the Church. It increased the salaries of priests (as it did those of soldiers); it allowed their numbers to increase from 48,000 to 52,000. It helped the Church multiply its schools and even gave it some authority over state education. The Second Empire, to begin with at any rate, was based on an alliance with the Church. The priests recovered their dominance, at the expense of the professors, now silenced and disciplined. It was, however, a very uneasy alliance, in which both sides soon ceased to feel the goodwill they had protested at the outset. Napoleon aided the new kingdom of Italy, which annexed the papal states, but did not dare go the whole way, and supported the pope's temporal power in Rome. In the 1860s he was in constant conflict with the clergy, whose ultramontanism, political ambition and reactionary tendencies, raised to new levels by the Syllabus of 1864 condemning liberalism, made co-operation impossible. Nevertheless Bonapartism remained ambivalent

[1] G. Kulnholtz-Lordat, *Napoléon III et la paysannerie* (Monte Carlo, 1962), is a brief though useful sketch.

and divided towards the Church. Its bitter, broken-down
marriage with it was ultimately a serious source of weakness.[1]

Again, in its foreign policy, the Second Empire was unable to
find a clear direction which could unite the nation or even win
widespread approval. All sorts of explanations have been given
of Napoleon III's diplomatic aims. Some have argued that he
had a single deep-rooted objective, though there is disagreement as to what this was. The principle of nationalities is one
theory. The desire to extend France to the Rhine is another.
The ambition to unite Italy is a third.[2] It is impossible to be
certain. Napoleon III carried on his foreign policy in a mysterious way, so that often his own ministers did not know what he
was up to. He employed, to head the ministry of foreign affairs,
people who do not seem to have shared his ideas. Drouyn de
Lhuys was an Orleanist diplomat who believed in order and
tradition and opposed the whole idea of a revolutionary policy.
Walewski was a Catholic, favourable to the pope and hostile
to the Italian kingdom Napoleon helped to create. Thouvenel
was another career diplomat, who was willing to follow the
emperor's instructions but he was not kept for long. Numerous
influences battled round Napoleon urging him in different
directions, from the empress who advocated national honour
and respect for the pope, to Prince Jerome-Napoleon who was
against the pope, to the businessmen who cared only for peace
and commercial expansion. Napoleon seems to have used his
gift for silent rumination and secret intrigue to resist all these
pressures. His upbringing had impressed a number of deeply
felt hopes and fears upon him. Thus, he hated war very sincerely.
When, in typical paradox, he got involved in one in Italy, he
hastened to end it very rapidly, and he surrendered in the
Franco-Prussian war even more speedily. He differed profoundly
from his uncle in this respect. He believed that the best way to
settle international disputes was by conferences, and he was
always calling them. He was not willing to be led here by public

---

[1] Jean Maritain, *La Politique ecclésiastique du second empire* (1930), is a full masterly
treatment of the subject—one of the first detailed theses on the Second Empire.

[2] See, e.g., the review of theories by A. Pingaud, 'La Politique extérieure du
second empire', *Revue historique* (1927), 41–68; P. Henry, *Napoléon III et les peuples*
(Gap, 1943); H. Oncken, *Die Rheinpolitik Kaiser Napoleons III von 1863 bis 1870*
(Stuttgart, 1926); Richard Millman, *British Foreign Policy and the Coming of the
Franco-Prussian War* (1965).

opinion. Indeed, he repeatedly flouted it: the Italian and Mexican wars were not the result of popular pressure and were opposed by most of his entourage. Only after 1867 did he feel that patriotic pride compelled him to take a different line towards Prussia and he did so hesitantly. He was a European in a profounder way than most who shared this sympathy, for he was a cosmopolitan who had lived outside France between the ages of seven and forty. He declared that for European nations to fight was to engage in civil war. He was, however, also a patriotic Frenchman, with an expatriate's zeal, enhanced by what he felt he owed to his name. He was determined to erase the disgrace of 1815, to restore France to its old prestige, to end Louis-Philippe's timid policy. He combined these views in a vague hope of regenerating Europe on the basis of nationalities, with possibly an ultimate aim of a European federation of national states.

Napoleon was thus a supporter of French glory, but also opposed to a purely selfish national policy. He had grand ideas, but they were inadequately connected with the realities around him. If he had simply pursued his aims by normal methods, he would have failed, modestly. What led him to disaster was that he was carried away by the grandeur of his objectives, so that he was unable to see the obstacles. He had a sense of mission which made him refuse to stop in the face of difficulties. He had won his throne by this kind of fanaticism, against all odds, and as he said, he could not have done it had he not had the mentality of a martyr. He tried to ensure himself from the same fate as had befallen his uncle, by assiduously cultivating friendship with England, but he never overcame its suspicions of him. He was attracted by too many grand causes for his policy to be coherent. He wanted France to lead the world, in the Jacobin tradition, but also to protect Catholicism, in that of the monarchy of the *ancien régime*, and at the same time to bring material prosperity to Europe by economic development. There is no need here to analyse the complicated history of his foreign adventures, which has been treated in another volume of this series.[1] The confusion of aims and the very personal methods by which they were advanced meant that Napoleon

[1] See A. J. P. Taylor, *The Struggle for Mastery in Europe 1848–1914* (Oxford, 1954).

was brought to his downfall by what, ultimately, was incompetence.[1]

Bonapartism after 1870

Bonapartism was by no means a hopeless cause after 1870. It is not clear that its chances were all that poorer than those of the royalists; for despite the catastrophic way the Second Empire ended, there was still much loyalty to it. Twenty years of rule had created a strong Bonapartist clientele. The terror caused by the Commune and the political chaos resulting from the inability of the other parties to found an alternative regime, produced a nostalgia for order and strong government. The Bonapartists were quick to recover from their overthrow. Half a dozen successfully got into the National Assembly in 1871. A party organisation was speedily set up, under Rouher, with a house in the Champs Elysées, owned by the empress, as its headquarters. Though police spies disguised as street cleaners worked night and day sweeping the pavement in front of it, it was able to develop without molestation. Rouher was assisted by Pietri, the former prefect of police, and Chevreau, one of the empire's most vigorous prefects. All were men who had exerted enormous power in their day. In 1872 a regular party committee was formed, of former ministers, prefects, generals and deputies, meeting twice weekly. Correspondents were appointed in the provinces, at the level of the canton and *arrondissement*. Able men were selected to command whole regions, as for example Eschasseriaux, who was given the task of organising nine departments of the south-west. Napoleon was convinced the press had a vital role to play in his restoration and asked for the support of numerous papers to be obtained. Already in August 1871 the owner of one important daily, *Le*

[1] The bibliography on foreign affairs is enormous. A guide can be found in Taylor, op. cit. Some particularly useful recent works include L. M. Case, *Public Opinion on War and Diplomacy during the Second Empire* (Philadelphia, Pa., 1954); W. E. Mosse, *The European Powers and the German Question* (1958); Pierre Renouvin, *Histoire des relations internationales*, vol. 5 (1) (1954); L. M. Case and Warren F. Spencer, *The United States and France: Civil War Diplomacy* (Philadelphia, Pa., 1970). (Professor Spencer is now writing a biography of Drouyn de Lhuys.) N. N. Barker, *Distaff Diplomacy, The Empress Eugénie and the Foreign Policy of the Second Empire* (Austin, Texas, 1967); Harold Kurtz, *The Empress Eugénie* (1964), the best biography of her.

Gaulois, declared his conversion to Bonapartism. One hundred thousand francs were given to Clément Duvernois, who had been one of the most effective journalists in the emperor's pay, to start *L'Ordre* (significantly named), which became the official party organ. The provincial press was placed under the direction of Giraudeau (who had been head of the press service of the ministry of the interior) and then of Mansard, who started a *Correspondance Mansard*, providing articles, written by an able team of journalists, for local papers to reproduce. By 1874 there were over seventy Bonapartist newspapers, including twenty-seven dailies.

Various levels of the literate population were reached in this way, but even more effort was put into the simplest kind of propaganda—the distribution of portraits of Bonapartist heroes, and in particular of the prince imperial. In 1874, on the occasion of the prince's coming of age, 300,000 were authorised, and a lot more printed in England and Belgium and distributed freely to serve as a kind of religious relic.[1] Old soldiers, dismissed civil servants, and indeed civil servants still in office, worked as hawkers of these pictures and of the pamphlets which were also produced. The Bonapartists still had many sympathisers in the administration and in particular in the police. The famous story of Renaudet, the prefect of police, discovering a footman asleep, clutching a copy of the Bonapartist daily *Le Pays*, in the house of the royalist minister, the duc Decazes, simply illustrates how after 1870 it was as difficult to remove Bonapartists from government service, as the Bonapartists themselves had found it to get rid of Orleanists after 1848.[2] It was the same in the army, which the Bonapartists actively courted. Friendly societies were formed to bring sympathisers in it together; two colonels were given the task of creating clubs for retired officers; *L'Ordre* was sent free to serving officers; imperial eagles were distributed and signatures collected for letters to the prince imperial. The Paris working class was stirred up by Jules Amigues—a shady character who had previously moved on the fringes of opposition to the empire and support of the Commune, and who was accused of dishonesty and worse. He

[1] Article on 'Appel au peuple' in P. Larousse, *Grand Dictionnaire universel* (supplement), 16 (1877), 172-84.
[2] Pierre de Witt, *L'Épuration sous la troisième république* (1887).

organised Bonapartist committees in cabarets and cafés, with a radical Bonapartist paper to back them, and a central committee to hold together what became an important propaganda machine, even though the conservatives were horrified that a man so near socialism should be employed. But that had always been one of the faces of Bonapartism. Amigues was successful, not so much with the native workers of the city, as with the provincial immigrants 'who still believed in sorcery'.[1]

The petty bourgeoisie, likewise, was encouraged to cultivate a nostalgia for the prosperity of the empire, as is revealed by the memoirs of a lady cook of Grenoble who had, thanks to the 'beaux jours' of the empire, been able to save enough money to retire on. She worshipped Napoleon, the army and 'officers of a certain age'. In 1872 she visited England to express to the exiled emperor her appreciation of his reign, which had meant that poor people like herself could now wear silk dresses. A fruit seller in Les Halles remarked: 'In those days we used to complain out of habit, but now we do so from necessity.'[2] Every grievance was exploited with this expurgated history of the good old days, which was a new version of the soldiers' tales of Napoleon I's campaigns. The small savings of pensioners, retailers, peasants and civil servants were solicited by the Star Insurance Company, whose agents formed yet another Bonapartist network.

This propaganda was very effective in certain regions. In departments which Bonapartist prefects or deputies had mastered under the Second Empire, they were often able to keep their hold on those whom they had obliged. In Charente, Eschasseriaux had always been an expert in politics based on personal relations. He had a card index of every voter in his constituency, so that he knew exactly how to please each one.[3] The Bonapartists were pioneers in this kind of electioneering, applying Orleanist techniques to universal suffrage. However, the weakness of their position was that there were many departments in which, even at the height of their power, they had never succeeded in creating a party or local notables of their own.

[1] Jules Amigues, *Les Aveux d'un conspirateur bonapartiste* (1874); Georges Lachaud, *Le Prince Napoléon et le parti bonapartiste* (1880), 15.

[2] Rosalie Berruyer, *Les Mémoires d'une Bonapartiste, ou le souvenir de mes voyages en Angleterre* (Grenoble, 1894), 33, 48, 51.

[3] John Rothney, *Bonapartism after Sedan* (Ithaca, N.Y., 1969).

Thus in 1876 they put up only 320 candidates for 525 seats, as against the 400 or so put up by the royalists and conservatives, and the 600 republicans. They thought they had a chance of success in only thirty-three departments. Though they collected money from wealthy supporters for propaganda purposes, they never had a great deal, and the sums they were able to distribute to candidates in elections were usually small.[1]

Even more serious were their internal divisions. After the Second Empire, Bonapartism fell apart into its constituent elements and was unable any longer to hold together its contradictions. Napoleon III himself postponed acting until the German troops had withdrawn, so as to avoid foreign interference. He waited for the chaos, which he thought was bound to occur, to discredit the provisional regime. He had plans to go secretly into France through Switzerland, rally some regiments on the border which he knew to be loyal, and march on Versailles. But he could not ride a horse, owing to a stone in his bladder. That is why he had his operation, though he knew it to be risky. His death destroyed the Bonapartists' chances of a quick return from Elba, and ended the unity of their movement, which only a quixotic character like himself knew how to hold together. The new leadership made it far more conservative and indeed reactionary. Rouher's policy was to unite with the legitimists to destroy the republic, and then, when the legitimists found they were unable to restore their king, to get their support—and that of all conservatives frightened by the growing anarchy—for a proclamation of the empire. He hoped, that is, to repeat 1848. In 1873 it was the Bonapartists who, accordingly, provided the decisive votes (there were about thirty of them in the assembly by then) which enabled the royalists to get rid of Thiers and to install Marshal MacMahon who was probably a royalist but who had also served Napoleon and been made a duke by him.[2] The new prime minister Broglie gave the Bonapartists their reward in the form of three ministries.[3] After the failure of the Restoration, they conspired to overthrow Broglie, and were again rewarded with two posts.

[1] See private papers of Segris, letter of Berger to Segris, 16 Jan. 1875, showing the local newspaper being run on a budget of only 3,200 francs.

[2] J. Silvestre de Sacy, *Le Maréchal de MacMahon* (1960).

[3] Magne (Finance), Général du Barail (War), de Seilligny, nephew of Schneider (Agriculture and Commerce).

However, these successes, increasing victories at the polls, and the discovery of the strength of the Bonapartist organisation, through a police raid on their headquarters, created a scare and at the election of 1876 they had to fight hard against all sides. Nevertheless, they won about seventy-five seats, which made them larger than either royalist party. In 1877, profiting from a revival of the official candidate system and from alliances with royalists and conservatives, their number rose to 105 deputies, more than the Orleanists and legitimists put together. Though these tactics paid off in the short term, it is not at all certain that they were not ultimately disastrous, for, as a result, the Bonapartists lost the most important source of their strength, their ability to appeal to both left and right. They became the main minority group, but also condemned themselves to remaining a minority.

It is said that the alliance with the royalists went so far as a proposal that the childless comte de Chambord should adopt the prince imperial. It may be that the prince would have accepted such a deal, but it is very difficult to get at his real opinions. There are those who claim that he was a liberal but others who quote die-hard reactionary letters from him.[1] It is undisputed that he was a pious Catholic, though not necessarily a clerical. His education did not enable him to make friends outside the upper classes. As a boy, he did not go to school, but teachers from the leading Paris *lycées* came and taught him privately the very same syllabus they taught to their public pupils, they marked his work in competition with his absent classmates and gave him a secret, unofficial place in class. He was at first rather backward educationally, showing no particular talent except in drawing (and particularly caricaturing), but after the fall of the empire, as though stimulated by the tragedy, he suddenly blossomed out into an energetic, hardworking and ambitious youth. His father sent him to study physics at King's College, London, but he was not advanced enough to keep up and could not make friends there. So he went as a cadet to Woolwich, where he at last found his true vocation, got on well with the others and caught up on his studies by not playing games. He emerged a soldier above all else. 'The army'

---

[1] Comte d'Hérisson, *Le Prince Impérial* (1890); Fidus [E. Loudun], *Journal de dix ans: souvenirs d'un impérialiste* (1883), 2. 133.

he wrote, 'will be the keystone of the social edifice, the great school of the nation . . . I love the French army not merely because I am a soldier and a Frenchman to my very marrow, but because I consider that in it alone dwells the force that can first save French society and then restore its greatness.' He opposed parliamentary government but also absolute monarchy, because the inheritance of genius could not be guaranteed. Stability should be sought by basing government on 'the only social forces: religion, the army, the magistracy and property'. Reactionary commentators claim that he was for complete press censorship, for an Estates-General every seven years and provincial assemblies. Whatever truth there is in these statements, at any rate they show that some of his supporters were scarcely distinguishable from the most outdated of Chambord's followers.

The prince himself, however, had no illusions about what he could achieve by his own actions. He accepted that the majority of the nation was indifferent to politics and wanted only quiet. He thought that if he suddenly appeared in Paris, he would not have a popular rising in his support but would simply get arrested. He decided to wait till 'the government of Gambetta becomes detestable to the nation, which will then look round for a saviour . . . It is not our efforts that will overthrow the republic, but it lies with us to take advantage of its fall.' He was not afraid of waiting, for the masses did not forget the first Napoleon between 1815 and 1848: he could afford to wait ten years. After 1877, he said that the party could achieve nothing by its electoral activities. He was, in any case, not keen to be restored by a parliamentary intrigue, for it would make him 'the slave of certain men and of a whole party. I would never have accommodated myself to such a position and I dreaded rather than desired it . . .' All depended, therefore, on what he himself could do. If he could make himself popular, or great, 'the strength of the imperial party would increase tenfold'. He was tired of entertaining politicians and journalists and 'working with them to stir up social problems', which is what his advisers urged on him; he refused to tour Europe with his retinue 'like a fairy-tale prince, to view all the princesses and boast of my political elixir . . . I have not cared to let my wings be clipped by marriage and my dignity refused to stoop to the part of princely commercial traveller. When one belongs to a race of soldiers, it is only sword in hand that one gains recognition.'[1] So he went to fight in the Zulu war in South Africa. Had he survived, it is possible that he might have made the Bonapartists a much more effective challenge in the late 1890s, and enabled them to take advantage of the Boulangist crisis. As it was, after 1879, the Bonapartists ceased to be a significant political party.

The way Bonapartism bequeathed at least part of its inheritance to the radicals can be seen in the career of Jerome-Napoleon (known as Plon-Plon), son of King Jerome Bonaparte and cousin of Napoleon III. He was a man of considerable intelligence, deep ambition and impulsive energy, though all his gifts were thwarted by his lack of tact, moderation and self-control. He was the member of the family who interpreted its mission in the most democratic way. At the age of fifteen, when sent to a military school, he had rejected its discipline, 'thinking it silly, contrary to the rights of man and offensive to his democratic principles'. He was a rebel from earliest youth; he was a brilliant and sarcastic conversationalist, a merciless critic, excelling in pulling characters and actions to pieces, loving to entertain men of letters and artists, even if they opposed his dynasty. Though officially married to the daughter of the king of Italy, he lived openly with a mistress, after discovering, too late, that his wife's main ambition was to achieve beatification if not canonisation. He was a violent anticlerical, to the point of being called an atheist, though he was simply a spiritualist, a Gallican and an admirer of Napoleon I's Church settlement. He had a profound cult of the Napoleonic principle, but he constantly quarrelled with Napoleon III and even more with Eugénie, behaving with furious and undisguised jealousy when, by giving birth to a son, she deprived him of the succession. He was unpopular in the army, but he longed for military distinction. In 1848 he got himself elected to parliament and sat on the extreme left. He opposed Napoleon's policies almost consistently, receiving public rebukes in return; one of them was even inserted in the *Moniteur*. He represented the tradition of Bonaparte as first consul. He was quite happy that France should be a republic, provided it had strong

[1] A. Filon, *Memoirs of the Prince Imperial, 1856–1879* (1913), 187–8; cf. Alain Decaux, *Connaissez-vous le Prince Impérial?* (1958).

government, with a president elected by the people, having the right only to recommend a successor to them.

Jerome-Napoleon became the leader of the party in 1879, to the horror of the conservative wing. He made no attempt to keep their loyalty, or rather to win it, for he had never made his hate of them a secret. In 1880, in the crisis over the republic's educational policy, he publicly supported the anticlericals, and denounced the Bonapartist alliance with the conservatives. He founded a new paper, *Le Napoléon*, to preach a programme of a lay society, the abolition of the temporal power of the pope, the destruction of the tyranny of the great financiers, the improvement of the lot of the masses, democratic taxation, free trade and revision of the republican constitution so that both president and senate should be elected by the people. He accepted the republic, and, even worse for the conservatives, the anticlerical republic. There were only about ten Bonapartist deputies willing to follow Jerome-Napoleon in this path.

The majority of the party disowned him. Jolibois, deputy for Charente-Inférieure, formed a syndicate of Second Empire dignitaries which raised 40,000 francs a year as an income for Jerome-Napoleon's son, Victor, whom they proclaimed leader of the Bonapartists, against his father. Victor's opinions were precisely the opposite of those of his father. Through his mother he was descended from Louis XIV and Marie Thérèse of Austria and he was a cousin of the Emperor of Russia. The Bonapartists were thus split between Jeromists and Victoriens. In the election of 1881, they stood as opposing parties. The former, 'democratic Bonapartists', attempted to negotiate an alliance with Gambetta, on the basis of a division between those who accepted the Revolution and those who did not. Gambetta was too suspicious, but Jerome-Napoleon nevertheless asked his supporters to vote for the republican whenever there was no Bonapartist candidate. He adopted a programme which was virtually that of the radicals (divorce, a political amnesty, the abolition of compulsory Sunday closing) summarised thus: 'We want the Republic, Revision, Election of the president by the people: our candidate is Jerome-Napoleon.' However, he was poor; he had only one newspaper and he put up little more than thirty candidates. Only a dozen were elected, and none of them were his personal friends; Lenglé, who was to have been their leader in parliament, was defeated, and so they lost all significance. In 1885, Jerome-Napoleon did not put up any candidates at all, urging his supporters to become republicans. Several of his main supporters, indeed, had already joined them. When, in the following year, all pretenders were exiled, Jerome-Napoleon's parting cry at the Gare de Lyon was: 'Vive la république quand même.' He now demanded simply a revision of the republican constitution, not an empire. 'The incurable weakness of the republican party', he said, 'is its fear of executive power. It is perpetually haunted by memories of Brumaire and December . . . My aim is to reform the republic, not to abolish it. How can you think that an old democrat like myself should agree to exchange this glory for the outdated pomp of a restoration in which I do not believe?' He negotiated with Boulanger, but not for a restoration. He saw his mission as being to found the republic on a permanent basis, just as Napoleon I had consolidated the Revolution. He insisted that the republic was the logical consequence of universal suffrage. He did not even have any particular fetishism for plebiscites, saying that they were in many cases democratic only in name. How authoritarian his rule would have been it is impossible to guess.[1]

Jerome-Napoleon died in 1891: his remaining followers became republicans. After the prince imperial's death, one of the latter's closest friends, Tristan Lambert, had become a royalist and many had followed the example. Still, though Bonapartists now lost all importance, a rump continued to be active for another fifteen years. Prince Victor continued to hold meetings, to issue circulars and to receive reports from groups which organised lectures and celebrated anniversaries. It was claimed in 1886 that the party still had over forty newspapers; in 1891 it still had seven.[2] It had exceptionally vigorous propagandists in the Cassagnac family whose newspapers continued to be Bonapartist, in one way or another, till the war. The Cassagnacs, father and son, were violently anti-republican,

[1] F. Berthet-Leleux, *La Vrai Prince Napoléon* (1932); Jules Richard, *Le Bonapartisme sous la république* (1883); Paul Lenglé, *Le Neveu de Bonaparte, souvenirs de nos campagnes politiques avec le Prince [Jérôme] Napoléon Bonaparte 1879–1891* (1893); Émile Sauvage, *Le Clergé et le bonapartisme* (1886); Georges Lachaud, *Bonapartistes blancs et bonapartistes rouges* (1885); P. Cordier, *Boulangisme et bonapartisme* (1889).

[2] *Le Gaulois* (2 Apr. 1892), 56–7 and *Le Figaro* (7 May 1892), 77, contain interesting studies of Bonapartism at this period, of uncertain reliability. Mr. Keith Underbrink of St. Antony's College, Oxford, is engaged in research on this subject.

because they considered the republic inescapably demagogic; its anticlericalism made them more irreconcilable then ever because they were 'Catholic first of all'. 'My main aim', wrote Paul de Cassagnac, 'is the destruction of the abhorred republican regime.' He wished to replace it by authoritarian government, with 'only necessary liberties preserved', that is those which give the country material and physical prosperity (reduced taxes, improved roads, local railways). 'Luxury liberties' of the press, speech and public meetings concerned only a tiny minority and should be postponed till the masses had been satisfied. 'Liberty to live well must come before liberty to talk and to write.' But he was too independent himself to do as the pretender asked and in 1894 he declared that since he could not obtain a restoration of the empire of 1852, he would accept a monarchy. The empire was the modern form of monarchy, but 'in view of the pretender obstinately adhering to his contemplative attitude, passively waiting, like the Indian Buddhas, for the mountains to come to them', he had lost hope in him. 'The place of a pretender is not at the tail of his party but at its head.' Cassagnac called himself an imperialist rather than a Bonapartist. In 1917 he suddenly discovered the incarnation of the principle of authority in Clemenceau and accepted the republic.[1]

This was the final, deathbed marriage of Bonapartism and radicalism, though both were very altered with age. It is significant that even Émile Ollivier, who stood at the extreme liberal end of Bonapartism, had talked, when organising his electoral campaign in 1875, of rallying the conservatives against the 'reds'.[2] Now the radicals had come to feel the same about the socialists, and Clemenceau was repressing strikes just as the Bonapartists had done. The marriage between Bonapartists and conservatives was more than a marriage of convenience. They had more in common than they had known. Henceforth, the cult of the Bonapartes survived only in a spirit of antiquarianism. But Bonapartism left descendants, though under other family names.

[1] Paul de Cassagnac, *Articles du Pays et de l'Autorité* (1905, 8 vols.); André Martinet, *Le Prince Victor-Napoléon* (1895); Charles Faure-Biguet, *Paroles plebiscitaires 1906–1913* (1913); Paul de Cassagnac, *Faites une constitution, faites un chef* (1933); Dr. Flammarion, *Le Bonapartisme* (1950); K. Offen, *Paul de Cassagnac* (in the press).

[2] Ollivier to Segris, 28 Mar. 1876, Segris private papers.

6. The Politicians of the Third Republic

THE Third Republic was one of the most confusing and paradoxical of political regimes. It was supposed to mark the advent of democracy, but it produced disconcertingly little fundamental change in the structure of the state, which remained monarchical, or even *ancien régime*, in many ways. Its vision—as Allain-Targé, one of its founders, expressed it in 1867, and as many others continued to repeat with much rhetorical embellishment—was a free, egalitarian and fraternal society, in which constant discussion of common interests would lead all classes to a higher sense of solidarity and justice. But in practice it gave power to an oligarchy of discredited professional politicians, who maintained their dominance by placating the particularist interests of their more influential constituents and by closing their eyes to the corruption which surrounded them. The exceptional longevity of the regime is difficult to reconcile with its equally unprecedented instability. The endless succession of barely distinguishable ministries provides little clue to the evolution of policy or the implementation of reform. There was an extraordinary gap between the principles which were proclaimed as guiding the politicians and the legislation actually passed. Even when laws were at length enacted, as often as not they failed to be implemented. Lip-service to the glory of the fatherland was balanced by bitter criticism of it, more devastating in France than anywhere else. Confused and inconsistent programmes were advocated in the name of logic and rationality.

The chronicle of repeated crises and scandals, though often entertaining and sometimes dramatic, thus inevitably leaves the reader bewildered. It does not help matters that the right-wing parties call themselves left wing, and that the radicals turn out to be conservatives. It can be claimed that this is a purely nominal confusion, that basically France was divided into two clear groups—those for the Revolution and those against it—and that all that is needed is to decide who fits into which group: the struggle was always the same one. In this perspective, the triumph and development of the republic represents the progress of 'Movement' against 'Reaction', each successive generation advancing the same cause. However, there were so many ambiguities in this supposed progress, so much ambivalence in the attitudes of the progressives, that it soon becomes uncertain whether change and reform were the real issues in politics. The principles invoked in the battle between the two sides were too far divorced from the realities to be accepted as the guiding lines of action. They clearly had a more subtle purpose. In many ways it is more instructive to consider what politicians did not talk about than what they did. Indeed it is perhaps easier to see from these silences why the apparently chaotic system was tolerated and even popular. For it protected values which were deeply cherished, even if they were not publicly admitted.

The politics of the Third Republic were governed by a constitution which lasted far longer than any other French constitution. This longevity is explained by certain unusual features. The constitution lacked the qualities which most theorists had recommended and generations of statesmen had striven for: logic, clarity, order, completeness. But it achieved many of their aims, paradoxically, by not trying to. It was not designed as a permanent constitution at all. Its purpose was to temporise, to prepare, as some hoped, the way for a monarchy. It was the first constitution therefore not to require an oath of loyalty from all who served it, with the result that it excluded no one unnecessarily from the start. It was essentially a compromise; both monarchists and republicans gained something from it, and so it had few really implacable enemies. Since its authors came from different parties, it was unable to begin with a proclamation of principles or fundamental rights, on which they held diametrically opposed views.[1] It was thus a

---

[1] There was some debate, consequently, as to whether the Declaration of the Rights of Man remained part of the law of the land. After the triumph of the republicans, there was no serious doubt about this, but it might have been otherwise had the monarchists been victorious. The matter was only officially settled in 1911 when the Conseil d'État quashed, in the name of the principle of equality before the law, exceptions made in favour of individuals in some sanitary regulations. (Case of Roubeau, judgement of March 1911.)

constitution without a label—revolutionary or reactionary, and also it was the shortest of French constitutions. It consisted of only three laws—thirty-four articles[1]—making it one-third the length of the constitution of 1848, one-half those of 1814 and 1830, and one-tenth that of 1795. It was more a guide to procedure than a proper constitution and contained the minimum to quarrel about. The Third Republic was quite unique in coming near to having an unwritten constitution.[2]

The result of this state of affairs was that on the one hand the nature of the institutions which people thought ought to be created continued to be a major theoretical preoccupation, and politics continued, on the surface, to revolve around fundamental questions of principle. But on the other hand, the constitution allowed unprecedented free play to the prejudices, private interests and local customs which formed the basis of personal relations. Its fluidity enabled it to mould itself around these traditions. It based itself on *débrouillage*, the art of getting by somehow. It allowed people to find a corner where they could be more or less comfortable, and where, so as not to be disturbed, they took care not to disturb others. Naturally all this could be unreservedly condemned in the name of efficiency and so it was. The parliamentary machinery creaked and clogged. Vested interests were respected in a way which made the Third Republic almost medieval in its acceptance of the *status quo* and its respect of privilege. But the institutionalisation of inefficiency was so organised that more people stood to gain than to lose from it. It was sustained by the enormous strength of inertia; but because the rewards it yielded could not be respectably defended it compensated for its theoretical weaknesses by passionate attachment to grand principles, though little was ever done about these in practice. The turbulence and rhetoric of politics were necessary to draw a veil over the more sordid and humdrum reality, in which people agreed to live and let live. The relationship between the ideal and the reality

[1] Eight of these articles were repealed in 1884; one was added in 1926.
[2] Text and contemporary comment in F. A. Hélie, *Les Constitutions de la France* (1880), 1348–1456; amendments in L. Duguit, H. Monnier and R. Bonnard, *Les Constitutions et les principales lois politiques de la France depuis 1789* (7th ed. 1952), 286–319; cf. A. Esmein, *Éléments de droit constitutionnel français et comparé* (5th ed. 1909); M. Sibert, *Les Constitutions de la France, 1870–1940* (1946); J. Barthelemy and P. Duez, *Traité de droit constitutionnel* (new edition 1933).

is in many ways much more revealing than the conflicts of ideology.

Liberty was the republic's first principle. There were indeed certain liberties which it both proclaimed and allowed. The Napoleonic Code had forbidden meetings of more than twenty people without police permission; but after 1881 a simple declaration of an intention to hold a meeting was adequate; and after 1907 even this was abolished. As a result of laws of 1884 and 1901 Frenchmen could form associations freely. The abolition of censorship in 1881 brought complete freedom of the press. But all this did not amount to full individual liberty. The methods of the police and the rights of the judiciary were not radically altered. Though the *lettre de cachet* was gone, it was still possible for men to be imprisoned without trial and without charge, to be beaten up, and to be subjected to endless interrogation. In 1899, for example, there was a case of seventy-five people being arrested in the middle of the night under the pretext that they were plotting a conspiracy. Most of them, after being detained for between three and six weeks, were released, without a charge being made. In the end, of those who were kept for several more months, only three were convicted. The police continued to confiscate letters in the post, to conduct searches and inquiries with their traditional brutality— and often ignoring the law. They systematically collected damaging information about everybody, paying informers and tolerating people on the fringe of the criminal world in return for their gossip. But they used their power with a fine sense of discretion, which prevented an effective protest against it. They seldom beat up people who could made a fuss, and they were indulgent to those with influence.

The free citizen of the Third Republic thus continued to live within the powerful and authoritarian state Napoleon had organised. In some ways he was even more exposed, because the formal abolition of censorship was not balanced by any control of libel. The freedom of the press gave journalists, or those who could buy them, immense power to slander reputations, with virtually no means of redress. A libel law introduced in 1894 proved virtually impossible to enforce. The Action Française was able to preach the murder of socialist politicians with impunity; and one minister was indeed driven to suicide by a press campaign. Though everybody was nominally equal under the law, some were better than others at knowing how to get round it, for the rule of law was established with a certain amount of flexibility. A host of moral and economic tyrannies survived. Wide toleration was balanced by a tradition of bitter and malicious polemic. The battle for freedom was far from having been won in the supposedly easy-going *belle époque*. But there was a little more freedom than the country had ever had before, and people *felt* a lot freer.[1]

It was the system of parliamentary democracy, incapsulated within the traditional centralised state, which spread this feeling. The people could consider themselves sovereign. It is uncertain whether they were right, because there was some legal debate as to whether it was not parliament which was sovereign. Still, there was universal suffrage, and it was used in a way which gave people a sense of their individual importance. In fact, not all men were quite equal. A certain amount depended on where they lived. The system of election used for most of the Third Republic was that of the *scrutin d'arrondissement*, by which each *arrondissement* was represented by one deputy. However, they differed widely in their population, and one constituency (such as Barcelonnette) might have only 3,000 electors. *Arrondissements* with over 100,000 inhabitants were given a second deputy, those with 200,000 a third and so on, but even so the sparsely populated regions were considerably over-represented. In these, 275 deputies were elected by 15,320,000 inhabitants, but the rest of the country had only 251 deputies to represent 20,782,000 people. Attempts were made to take into account demographical changes, and some 58 constituencies were abolished between 1889 and 1936, but despite some modifications in 1926, the old constituencies survived tenaciously, and in 1939 there were 347 constituencies (as opposed to 275 in 1875) which were over-represented. In 1931 the first *arrondissement* of Paris had one deputy for 42,166 people, but the sixteenth *arrondissement* (first constituency) had a deputy for 108,501 people, and Saint-Denis (1) one for 143,093. This was a system which gave the rural inhabitants a feeling of privilege, to counterbalance their poverty, and it also gave a sense of resentment to the suburban workers, so that there was

[1] Maurice Claudel, *Nos libertés politiques* (1910).

a constant agitation to abolish it all.[1] Between 1885 and 1889 the *scrutin de liste* was tried, whereby each department elected a number of candidates, and the parties presented lists of names for wholesale nomination by the electors. This turned out to be so advantageous to the enemies of the republic, who were thus able to unite their forces, that it was quickly abandoned. From 1919 to 1927 a modified form of the *scrutin de liste*, combined with proportional representation, was used. This was so complicated, and often so doubtfully fair—for candidates failed to be elected after winning more votes than others, because the average vote of their list was low—that it too was abolished. The majority parties had again lost by the reform.

An important feature of the single constituency system was that if no candidate obtained an absolute majority, a second ballot was held a week later, when a simple majority was all that was needed. Between the two ballots, the candidates bargained as to who should desist in whose favour. Sometimes parties made agreements to support whichever of them got the largest vote on the first ballot. This was the basis on which the republic survived, for the fragmentation of parties meant that the number of candidates was enormous. In 1928 there were 2,763, in 1936 4,815 (that is, between 5 and 8 for each seat). On the second ballot, the left could rally to defeat the monarchists. The main beneficiaries of this arrangement were the radicals, who, poised in the centre, could make deals with either side. They were the beneficiaries also of the electoral inequalities as a whole, for they tended to represent small rural constituencies. Thus it was calculated that, in 1932 for example, they got 42 more seats than they would have done under proportional representation, while the communists got 38 fewer. With time, the importance of the second ballots increased, for there were 227 of them in 1910, but they rose gradually till in 1936 there were 424: in that year only 3 departments elected all their deputies in the first ballot.[2] In the political sense, the deputies were thus far from faithfully reproducing the opinions of the electorate. Intrigues and compromises between the candidates frequently determined the issue.

[1] J. M. Cotteret, C. Emeri and P. Lalumière, *Lois électorales et inégalités de représentation en France 1936–1960* (1960).
[2] W. R. Sharp, *The Government of the French Republic* (New York, 1938), 60–3.

The republicans were thoroughly confused as to what they wanted from elections. Because the empire had had single member constituencies, the republicans turned against them and declared the *liste* to be the only proper system, emphasising principles rather than personalities, and discouraging improper pressure, which was more difficult in a large constituency. However, once the single-member constituency was established by the monarchists in 1871 and the republicans learned to manipulate it and obtained victory despite it, so most of them became attached to it. As a result, the republican system was not very different from the monarchical and imperial one; it preserved the influence of traditional forces, local considerations and personal pressures. The republicans had to stress the unity of the state because in practice they allowed sectional and village interests so much weight. The deputies were supposed to represent the nation, but they came to devote themselves above all to their own small constituencies. The emphasis on principle in their rhetoric was counterbalanced behind the scenes by constant attention to the individual complaints, demands and threats of each constituent. 'We are obliged', said Poincaré in 1926, 'to use the largest part of our efforts in petty errands and unrewarding solicitations. Under the pressure of local influences we find ourselves considering our daily meddling in administrative questions as vital to keeping our seats.'[1] The deputy maintained very close contact with his constituents. He prided himself on knowing their ambitions and needs. He asked for their votes on the basis as much of his personal qualities and his personal relations with them, as on his political opinions. As a result, they looked on him as being obliged to them for their votes and for his living. They pestered him shamelessly for favours. They asked him to use his influence with the authorities to obtain the favourable settlement of all their dealings with them. He had to spend most of his mornings running round the ministries to press their suits, to obtain subsidies for every village improvement. He had to devote a great deal of time simply to writing letters, replying to his constituents, forwarding their requests to the ministers, and reporting back on the results of his efforts. The deputy became the constituents' Paris agent. The stock joke was that he could even be asked to

[1] A. Tardieu, *La Profession parlementaire* (1937), 43.

buy an umbrella for them at a department store, to find a job for their daughters as a servant in some wealthy household, to trace the wills of relatives who might have bequeathed them some money. For much of their time, deputies were concerned not with large issues of policy but with the satisfaction of petty particularist interests.[1]

It is not surprising therefore that being a deputy became a profession. Parliament was not composed of a typical cross-section of the population. In 1881 there was only one peasant and one worker in it. 50 per cent of the deputies were members of the upper bourgeoisie (108 proprietors, 85 former senior civil servants, 44 bankers and industrialists). There were 120 barristers, 15 solicitors and notaries, 60 doctors, pharmacists and veterinaries, 10 merchants, 10 engineers, 20 journalists. The colourful Thivrier used to wear a worker's blouse over his frock-coat but he was an innkeeper not a manual worker. Twenty years later, in 1902, the working classes still had not penetrated in any number: the rich bankers, company directors and landowners still had 160 seats, the senior civil servants 52, the middle classes and liberal professions 252.[2] The deputies received a salary (9,000 francs in 1875), the equivalent of a university professor, a colonel or an appeal court judge. After thirty-two years they could retire on something almost equal to their salary. Till 1914 their pension was paid by a friendly society, but it was then turned into an official one, subsidised by the state. A certain *esprit de corps* developed among them, so that the variety of their opinions, which they exhibited in public, was muted by a camaraderie which they shared after their debates. It became customary for them to *tutoyer* each other. In elections they gave the impression of being the irreconcilable enemies of their opponents. In the chamber they got on well enough. They formed groups of all sorts which cut across the official party labels they gave themselves—they sometimes had as much in common with other representatives of, for example, the metal industry or colonial interests, or sardine manufacturers, as with their co-religionists. They sometimes joined groups as a result of personal relations they formed when they arrived in

---

[1] Max Bonnefous, *Le Scrutin d'arrondissement et la politique* (1926), gives a good summary of arguments for and against the system.

[2] Roger Priouret, *La République des députés* (1959), 85, 180.

Paris, for the first time lonely and bewildered and were be-friended by ambitious colleagues anxious to build up a following. Some joined groups simply for the advantages this gave in appointment to commissions: there was even a 'group of deputies not members of any other group', and another of 'young deputies', who had only their age in common. The political labels a man used in order to get himself elected as deputy were therefore often no indication or guarantee of how he would behave in parliament.[1]

This *esprit de corps* made the deputies pretty indulgent towards each other in judging the way they voted. It was accepted that a man sometimes had to vote a certain way 'to satisfy his constituents'[2] and they often supported each other in defending their independence against party discipline. For long they turned a blind eye to corrupt practices in elections, out of deference to the peculiar difficulties of each constituency. The deputies judged the validity of the elections themselves, and began each parliament with protracted debates of validation, listening to petitions from aggrieved candidates. This washing of dirty linen in public, which served to dampen somewhat the idealism of the electoral months, revealed that many considera-tions apart from politics determined the results. Government pressure, so effective under Napoleon III, did not cease to be exerted. The most notorious example was in the elections of 1876 and 1877, when Broglie, who as a high-minded liberal had criticised the Second Empire for this very failing, reproduced its methods almost exactly and with almost equal vigour. The direct and open support of official candidates by the prefects was soon abandoned, but it survived in a modified and more moderate form, particularly in the more backward constituen-cies.[3] Since governments came and went, what the candidate had to show to his electors was that he knew how to obtain the official favours they coveted. The title of official candidate was dropped because the roles of prefect and deputy were reversed. The deputy now took the initiative in acting as the intermediary

[1] Robert de Jouvenel, *La République des camarades* (1914).
[2] See, e.g., Bernard Lavergne, *Les Deux Présidences de Jules Grévy 1879–1887* (1966), 31.
[3] L. Puech, *Essai sur la candidature officielle en France depuis 1851* (Montpellier, 1922); G. D. Weil, *Les Élections legislatives depuis 1789. Histoire de la législation et des mœurs* (1895).

between the government and the village, the individual and other interests. Thus in 1909, in an election in Saint-Affrique (Aveyron), in which the economist Paul Leroy-Beaulieu was trying to evict the radical Fournol, who had given excellent service as a distributor of government favours, the local news-paper published an article showing the achievements of the two candidates in this respect. In one column they recalled the favours won by Fournol: subsidies for school building, an increase in the number of new teachers, the establishment of a post office, benefits to the old people's home, the building of bridges, more books for the schools, and so on. In the other column, under the name of Leroy-Beaulieu, they wrote in large letters 'Nothing'. The article ended with the conclusion: 'Long live Étienne Fournol, the government's friend.' This article was read out in the chamber by the supporters of Leroy-Beaulieu, who were trying to get Fournol invalidated, but it aroused only laughter. Fournol's friends retorted by reading out one of Leroy-Beaulieu's own electoral circulars: 'M. Leroy-Beaulieu can render considerable services to his electors. Everybody knows that it is in Paris that all important business is decided, concerning schools, railways and indeed everything. Look then at the ministries in turn. First, the ministry of finances. Is not M. Léon Say, who has been minister of finances four times and who will doubtless be back as minister again soon, the colleague of M. Leroy-Beaulieu at the Institut, his collaborator at the *Journal des Débats* and an old friend of his? Next look at the ministry of education. The director of secondary education, M. Buisson, was his school-friend at the lycée Bonaparte. Go to the ministry of public works. One of the main directors, M. Cheysson, the engineer-in-chief, is a colleague of his at the School of Political Sciences. At the ministry of justice, one of the main directors is a close relative. At the ministry of the interior, one of the main directors, M. Herbette, was a friend at the lycée Bonaparte and at law school. In the Midi Railway Company, the president M. d'Eichtal is one of the oldest friends of the Leroy-Beaulieu family . . . This list could be continued endlessly. We ask our readers whether all these contacts, all this support, which cannot be denied, are not useful for the schools, roads, railways and all the personal services electors can hope to expect.'

Right-wing and opposition deputies worked in the same way as the left-wing ones, though a deputy in good standing with a government could arrange rather more dramatic use of Parisian influence. Thus he could get all the subsidies the constituency was waiting for to be announced immediately before the election, as for example Georges Leygues did in 1898, in Lot-et-Garonne, when over 80,000 francs were distributed to orphanages, churches and old people's homes in three months. 'A rain of decorations', 'kilometres of purple ribbon' could be poured into the constituency at the right time. Government favour could also be used to force the issue by less scrupulous means. In an election in 1889, the prefect was accused of defeating a candidate by fiddling the electoral registers, refusing to show them to him and getting all the mayors to ignore his complaints about the honesty of the vote.[1] Several other fraudulent registers were discovered: in Nîmes in 1902 they seem to have contained the names of over 2,000 electors who were dead or had left the town; in Lille in 1914 an enormously inflated register, involving many thousands of false names—almost a fifth of the total—was uncovered.

Money played an increasing role in elections. Jules Simon, writing in 1901, recalled how in 1848 the expenditure of 3,000 or 4,000 francs seemed enormous, but people were now spending 100,000.[2] There had been millionaires in politics under the Second Empire, and there were others under the Third Republic, who used much the same methods. The wealthy sugar manufacturer Lebaudy, for example, made arrangements with the mayors of his constituency in Seine-et-Oise by which they distributed bread and coal coupons to poor electors, who would remember the fact in their vote. He placed the mayors under an obligation to him by giving them private loans for urgent municipal needs, circumventing the delays of the state and as it were substituting himself for it. The electoral largesses of the Rothschilds in the 1920s were notorious. The village firemen were invited by one Rothschild to present themselves at the town halls of his constituency on polling day, to have their measurements taken for new uniforms to be made at his

---

[1] Paul Leroy-Beaulieu, *Un chapitre des mœurs électorales en France dans les années 1889 et 1890* (1890).
[2] Jules Simon, *Premières Années* (1901), 338.

expense. Every friendly society, hunting club, charity and good cause received a gift at the appropriate time. Those who did not have ready cash, as he did, promised it: one candidate had his election invalidated in 1928 because he had undertaken to distribute the whole of his parliamentary salary to his constituents. Free drinks were considered a perfectly proper part of electioneering, provided they were offered discreetly and individually. A great deal of wine was consumed, but the candidates who got into trouble were only those who tried to make too dramatic an impression of generosity. Thus in 1906 one sent the *garde champêtre* to announce, to the beat of his drum, that free drinks were being offered. Another placed barrels of wine in the polling station itself. In 1902 in Montreuil (Pas-de-Calais) it was calculated that each elector consumed 500 glasses of wine, over and above the normal intake, in the two months preceding the election. The chamber of deputies, in considering complaints about this, took the view that 'though they deplored intemperance, they did not consider it was their task to reform the customs' of regions which liked drinking; and even the Conseil d'État ruled that 'if libations did take place in the taverns . . . the complainants cannot prove that this affected the liberty or the sincerity of the vote'.

Votes could be bought for ready cash, particularly in the poor mountainous regions. They normally cost not less than 10 francs each, though the poor in the Doubs sold theirs for only 2. In 1890 there was a notorious case of a certain Bouttain who formed an association to collect together all men willing to sell their votes. He found 1,600 of them, and then made a contract with the banker Bischoffsheim to sell them to him for 20,000 francs. This was discovered after the election when Bouttain blackmailed Bischoffsheim by asking a further 8,000, and on being refused, denounced him to parliament. What was more, one could buy not only electors, but even candidates. There was a gentlemanly convention—it is not clear how long it lasted—that a candidate who desisted in the second ballot should have his election expenses refunded by the beneficiary. This practice could be extended so that rivals were paid to desist, or alternatively to stand as candidates, in order to take votes away from more serious rivals. Thus the respectable Leroy-Beaulieu paid an opponent in 1906 1,000 francs to desist in the second ballot, half to be given before the vote and the other after, and this was done literally with a 1,000 franc note cut into two.[1]

Elections were not generally invalidated for this kind of corruption and pressure, unless there were quite exceptional abuses. Invalidation was reserved as a political instrument by the republicans to expel notorious opponents of the regime: it was indeed one of the methods used to help establish the republic. In 1876–7 102 opponents were invalidated, 90 of them for being official candidates of the fallen regime of 'moral order'. Between 1881 and 1902 85 more were invalidated, nearly all of them royalists or clericals. Between 1906 and 1939, however, there were only 22 invalidations. The most notoriously corrupt of all elections, which were those of the colonies, were never even examined, because it was accepted that nothing could be done to change things. The respect of local custom was the rule. It is in this context that the famous scandals of the regime should be placed: they were simply the extension of common practices from a local to a national scale.[2]

It was only in 1914 that a law was passed to establish secrecy in the voting booths; and no limitations on financial expenditure or libel in elections were ever imposed. Money, however, never became the decisive factor in politics. Businessmen did occasionally spend very large sums (for example Coty against Blum, the banker Octave Homberg in Cannes, the industrialist Loucheur in Avesnes) but an American political scientist, investigating money in politics in different countries, came to the conclusion that, on average, French candidates spent considerably less than English or German ones. They spent very little indeed on nursing their constituencies, compared to their neighbours. Expenditure on printed propaganda was also far less. Very few of them maintained offices. Their meetings cost them virtually nothing since they held them in schools or cafés, and their most effective work was done in conversations over drinks. The state provided them with free advertising space for their posters. Their largest items of expenditure were for travel around the constituencies, and for the buying up of newspapers.

---

[1] A. Pilenco, *Les Mœurs du suffrage universel en France 1848–1928* (1930).
[2] J. P. Charnay, *Les Scrutins politiques en France de 1815 à 1962. Contestations et invalidations* (1964), 117–20.

Unlike American candidates who bought space to advertise themselves directly in newspapers, the French preferred to buy editorial support, or to set up their own newspapers, though they often distributed these free. Before 1914 posters played a major part in elections: General Boulanger is said to have put up 1,300,000 of them in 1889 in the seventh *arrondissement* of Paris, and his opponent could only afford to order half a million of his own—less to read, of course, than to cover up the other's. The law of 1914 put an end to this papering of whole cities. Newspapers then became the influence which candidates particularly valued. Parties, of course, never had much money, and gave only small sums to help their candidates. The radicals gave least of all (in 1928, they apparently assisted only 90 candidates). The contributions of big business still remain largely a mystery, though it seems that in that same year they might have involved some 10 million francs.[1]

The really important financial scandals occurred not in elections but afterwards. The deputies, conscious of their dignity as sovereign legislators, occasionally protested vehemently against accusations that they were in the pay of the rich; occasionally they uncovered scandals even though these brought great discredit upon them. Their links with the business world, their acceptance of directorships and consultancies, have already been described.[2] The deputies knew very well that even the puritan campaigns of Clemenceau against corruption and inefficiency were based on shady support from financiers like Cornelius Hertz. The public scandals erupted when the system, practised by most people, got out of control, through excessive zeal, righteousness or carelessness. The Wilson affair of 1887 did not involve anything new. Wilson was not the first man to sell decorations, but people had other grudges to settle against him. The Panama scandal of 1892, in which it was revealed that deputies sold their votes and accepted money in a dubious speculation, evoked the protestation from Rouvier, accused of dishonesty: 'What I have done all politicians worthy of the name have done before me.' No one could deny this. The list of

[1] J. K. Pollock, *Money and Politics Abroad* (New York, 1932), 279–319.
[2] Above, pp. 55–7. R. Mennevée, *Parlementaires et financiers, répertoire des senateurs et députés directeurs ou administrateurs des sociétés financières commerciales, industrielles et économiques* (2nd edition 1924), lists over 140 deputies and over 100 senators.

public scandals[1] was considerably shorter than the minor ones which continued privately, as a normal part of the political game: the scandals were, to a certain extent, a method of getting rid of rivals who were too successful in it. Parliamentary democracy did not rid France of the corruption and the pressures which its partisans had criticised in previous regimes.

What distinguished the Third Republic was the dominance of the deputies. Parliament was kept in almost constant session: it was required to meet for five months, but since it never completed its business on time, and indeed seldom got round even to passing the budget, extraordinary sessions prolonged it for a further three or four months so that it became as permanent as the government. It never quite accepted the idea of delegating its powers to the government or allowing the government a separate existence. The tradition that parliament was the enemy of the government, rather than the source of its strength, survived from the theories of the *philosophes*, and from the traditional struggle to win power for parliaments from the monarchical regime. 'Every legislator', Mably had written, 'must start with this principle, that the executive power has been, and will always be, the enemy of the legislature.' New traditions were quickly evolved after 1871 to subject governments to strict control, which is a partial explanation of the inability of the latter ever to achieve very much.[2] Questioning the government by means of *interpellations* became one of the principal activities of deputies. The question of confidence was frequently posed in these endless discussions which took up a great deal of time, whether they were on minor or on major topics. The practice halted business to such an extent that in 1909 a system of written *interpellations* was introduced, to save time. But the deputies used this to show their constituents how busy they were on their behalf (every question and answer was published in the *Journal officiel*). In the parliament of 1919–24, 20,000 such questions were asked, usually about matters of very limited interest, as, for example, why some policeman had not been

[1] Robert Arnitz, *Les Enquêtes parlementaires d'ordre politique* (Paris thesis, 1917), gives a full list, with references to the reports on them; A. Dansette, *L'Affaire Wilson* (1936); on the ineffectiveness of the inquiries see Louis Michon, *Des enquêtes parlementaires* (1890).

[2] Joseph Barthélemy, *Le Rôle du pouvoir exécutif dans les républiques modernes* (1906), 420.

promoted as he deserved.[1] A great deal of energy was expended in this way, safeguarding the rights and ambitions of the individual in his contact with the government, even if it meant that larger issues of policy had to be held up in the process.

A second method by which parliament exercised its power was through the right every deputy had to initiate legislation. Historically this had been a crucial demand in the struggle for parliamentary government and it was kept even though at last parliament had a government fully responsible to it. A deputy had the right to get up in the middle of any debate, ask to speak as a matter of urgency, and propose a bill on any subject he pleased. Thus in the parliament of 1889 to 1893 there were 546 sessions. 873 bills were proposed by deputies in these. There was obviously very little chance that they could even be considered. In the following parliament, 1893–8, with 633 sessions, the number of bills increased to 1,112: in addition the government presented 2,216 bills of its own, three-quarters of them of purely local interest. The effect of this appalling amount of legislation was that most bills were passed into law without debate or discussion. Every session began with the president mumbling the titles of bills no one cared about and pronouncing them carried, because no one opposed them. So though parliament was ostensibly in charge of legislation, the rapid drafting and inadequate scrutiny its laws received meant that their effect depended on the goodwill or interest of the civil servants who had to implement them. Laws were seldom passed in the way the legal experts of the Conseil d'État advised; and they tended to be couched in rather general terms, with the details being left to be worked out by administrative ordinance. It was in this second stage, which escaped both parliament and even ministers, that the civil service was able to exert its power. There is some doubt also whether parliament's control of the budget was really effective, so confused and slow did the processes become. In the first thirty years of the republic, on average two million francs were spent irregularly each year.[2] The passion for legislation was self-destructive. It was possibly at its mildest

[1] Joseph Barthélemy, *Le Gouvernement de la France* (1925), 110. René Bloch, *Le Régime parlementaire en France sous la Troisième République* (Paris, thesis, 1905), 79–83.
[2] Emmanuel Besson, *Le Contrôle des budgets en France et à l'étranger* (1899), 552–61; Désiré Ferry, *Le Contrôle financier du parlement* (Paris thesis, 1913).

in the amendments to the budget which the deputies constantly proposed. The budget of 1895 was subject to 371 amendments, that of 1898 to 547. Many of these involved extra expenditure, and contributed not inconsiderably to the deficits which were such a regular feature of the republic. In proposing a bill, therefore, a government knew that its chances of carrying it unchanged were negligible, and that even its chances of getting it heard or passed in any form were pretty poor. It was not surprising therefore that the proclamation of principles was often looked upon as all that was really necessary: it was not practical politics to try and do anything about implementing the principles.[1]

The third way in which governments were kept in subjection to the deputies was the system of parliamentary commissions. Every bill had to be discussed by a commission of deputies. The old tradition was that the commissions were appointed *ad hoc* for each bill. But then permanent commissions grew up, not to discuss a particular bill, but all bills in a particular field. The first was that on finance, started as far back as 1840; others, for foreign affairs, the army, etc., were added until by 1902 there were sixteen grand commissions.[2] The peculiarity of the system was that the commissions were permanent, so that they were in effect counter-ministries. The president and *rapporteur* were rivals of the minister, and not infrequently succeeded him when he fell. There were thus two conflicting sources of authority in the chambers. The commission of finance was particularly powerful. It was as president of it that Gambetta wielded his influence between 1877 and 1881. On several occasions this commission overthrew ministries. As Tardieu said, 'real power rests no longer with the minister, who frequently falls within a month, but with the *rapporteur* of the budget commission who often continues in office from one legislature into another.' In this way parliament, rather than the government, formulated policy. Because, after having been a *rapporteur*, a deputy inevitably considered himself experienced and capable enough to be a minister, this was a strong inducement to overthrow governments on the slightest pretext.[3]

[1] Louis Michon, *L'Initiative parlementaire* (1898); Émile Larcher, 'L'Initiative parlementaire pendant la sixième législative (1893–8)', *Revue politique et parlementaire* (Apr. 1898), 597–611.

[2] There were 6 in 1893, 11 in 1898; in 1920 the number was increased to 20.

[3] Joseph Barthélemy, *Essai sur le travail parlementaire et le système des commissions*

The chamber of deputies, which ruled France in this way, consisted of 533 members, rising to 602 by 1914. It was a relatively small body, compared with the 1,118 deputies of the Estates-General of 1789, or the 750 members of the assembly of 1849. Altogether 4,892 deputies sat in parliament between 1870 and 1940. Not quite half of these, 2,271, were members for only one legislature. Power was concentrated in those who continued to be re-elected time and again. There were 2,621 deputies who sat for more than one legislature. At any one time, about a quarter of the members of a parliament had served for 20 years, and 3 per cent had served for a third of a century. The stability in the membership of the parliaments was quite exceptional. Only 33 per cent of the total 4,892 deputies left politics because they were defeated in an election. 16 per cent did not stand for re-election. But 19 per cent moved on to be senators, and 13 per cent died while still holding their mandate. 12 per cent survived to be deposed by the Vichy regime. Only 2·5 per cent changed constituencies in the course of their careers. One gets a picture therefore of a long-lived almost permanent group of rulers, closely tied to their local origins, often unknown until they were sent to Paris. It was these men who controlled the fate of ministries, rather than the electorate directly, for three-quarters of ministerial changes occurred while parliament was sitting, and only a quarter from the vote of the masses.[1]

There were 108 ministries between 1870 and 1940. The average length of each was therefore about 8 months. This compares with the mere 44 ministries England had in almost twice the time, between 1801 and 1937, with an average tenure of 3 years and 1 month. France therefore had a reputation for instability, which, it might be added, was not exceptional. Belgium had forty-one cabinets from 1831 to 1937: until 1918 they lasted an average of 3 years and 9 months, but after the war only 1 year and 8 months. Italy's cabinets lasted 1 year and 2 months between 1918 and 1922. Germany's Weimar Republic had 21 cabinets lasting only an average of 8 months

(1934); H. Mauchant, *La Commission des finances de la chambre des députés* (Nancy thesis, 1927); R. K. Gooch, *The French Parliamentary Committee System* (1935).

[1] Mattei Dogan, 'La Stabilité du personnel parlementaire sous la troisième république', *Revue française des sciences politiques*, 3 (1953), 319-48.

each, as also did Austria's from 1918 to 1934. This kind of comparison can easily be misleading. The frequent changes of ministers conceal an underlying stability. First of all, the French electorate was exceptionally consistent in its loyalties: France did not, on the whole, suffer from swings of the pendulum. Secondly, these ministerial changes meant that power was kept in the hands of the deputies, who constituted the stable core of the regime. The deputies, being deeply suspicious of governments were not averse to overthrowing ministries frequently to maintain their supremacy. Whereas in England governments were overthrown not as a result of surprise votes, but on major issues of policy, the French deputies did not hesitate to topple a government on points of detail. They could do so because parliament lasted its full term whatever they did and they did not have to fear dissolution. When a ministry fell, it was frequently reconstituted with many of its old members, as will be seen, but with only a few new members, who quite often were the deputies who had organised the *interpellation* which had destroyed the old ministry.

Ministerial instability followed also from the fact that the office of prime minister was unknown to the law until 1934. Till then (except on six occasions, all of them after 1914) the prime minister held a portfolio which kept him busy, so that he had little time to be anything but the chairman of the government. He had no staff or patronage of his own, apart from that of his portfolio; only in 1934 did he get an independent office. Usually, he was not the elected leader of the majority of deputies, and often not even the leader of any party at all. He could not count on the definite allegiance of the deputies. He was overshadowed to a certain extent by the president of the republic, who, as will be seen, sometimes used his prerogative in choosing the prime minister in such a way as to prevent over-ambitious individuals from getting power. The deputies always kept the upper hand, for they could refuse to approve the president's choice.[1] If one wanted to be a minister it did not on the whole pay to be a party leader. Because parties were so fluid and unreliable as supports, ministers had to work hard to collect support from any source they could, outside their own

[1] As they did, e.g., in 1914 (Ribot) and 1920 (G. Leygues). Jacques Verdeaux, *Le Président du conseil des ministres en France* (Bordeaux thesis, 1940).

parties as well as within them. They stood a better chance if they abandoned partisanship altogether, and offered themselves as arbitrators between the parties, reconcilers of opposition. This meant, of course, that they seldom satisfied everybody, and holding office was like walking a tight-rope. Clear policies were thus difficult to pursue. Deputies who reached office often made their names as radicals, but almost necessarily became moderate once invested with power. In so doing, they lost the support of the extreme wings and often of their very own parties. Party leaders, aspiring to be national figures, thus often turned against the whole idea of party, which constant coalitions in any case diluted. The extremism and radicalism of new parties was a natural reaction to this regular evolution, and should not therefore be taken completely at its face value.

The most successful ministers were those who were most deferent to the wishes of parliament. He who wanted to come back into office most often resigned most often, for a clash with the deputies would ruin his career. Ambition thus encouraged instability still further. Briand carried the art of resignation to the peak of perfection: he even used to resign before a vote was taken; he perpetuated himself at the expense of frequent cabinet crises. So, if one looks at how long ministers, as opposed to ministries, lasted, one discovers that there was in fact a small group of politicians who remained in office for very long periods. There were 561 ministers in the Third Republic, of whom only 217 were minister once. 103 held office twice, 71 three times, 48 four times and 122 more than four times. Of the 94 governments between 1879 and 1940, 74 had at least one member of the previous government in it, and 40 kept over half of the ministers of the previous government. Thus Briand was a member of 25 different ministries and was in office for 16 years and 5 months. The record for the longest tenure was held by Sarraut, the radical, who was minister for 18 years and 2 months. Other notable figures were Barthou (14 years), Leygues (13 years), Delcassé (11), Queuille, Freycinet and Chéron (10), Millerand and Poincaré (9).

The Third Republic thus does not have to be divided into 108 different periods, each with a different set of men and a different programme, but falls naturally into much longer phases. Only 5 out of the 63 ministers who served between

1870 and 1879 continued to hold office after that date. The republic of dukes is a clearly defined era. The years 1879 to 1885 were dominated by Ferry, who was minister of education in 5 of the 8 ministries. There is only a brief break with Gambetta, who lasted 3 months in 1881–2. The continuity of the rule of the opportunists is seen in Freycinet, who was prime minister 9 other times: for 7 of these, he was minister of war and was able to carry out army reforms, just as Ferry was able to pursue his educational changes while riding repeated cabinet crises. Rouvier was minister of finance 4 times between 1889 and 1892 and later prime minister twice, Fallières was minister 7 times between 1882 and 1892. It is possible to understand this clique of opportunist politicians as a group; there is no need to despair in confusion at their constantly changing recombinations. In the middle period of the republic, ministries became longer: Waldeck-Rousseau was prime minister for 3 years (1899–1902), Combes for 2 years and 7 months (1902–5), Clemenceau for 3 years and 4 months (1906–9). Delcassé controlled foreign policy for 7 years, from 1898 to 1905. After that ministries appeared to fall faster than ever, but the same men dominated politics. Between 1920 and 1940 ministries lasted on average only 6 months each, but the continuity between them increased, so that frequently up to 80 per cent of one ministry survived into the next. The small group of the radical left, which had between 32 and 50 members, had a member in every one of the 29 ministries between 1924 and 1936. The radicals controlled the ministries of education and the interior for 12 of the inter-war years and the ministry of agriculture for 10. It became increasingly clear that from amongst themselves, the deputies selected a small group of people to fill the ministerial posts. One could say that the core of this group consisted of only 122 men, the ministers who held office more than four times. These were men, of course, who accepted the system, and the supremacy of the deputies. The rebels against it, however able, seldom lasted very long.[1]

It was the intention of the conservative makers of the constitution that the chamber of deputies should be held in check, at

[1] A. Soulier, *L'Instabilité ministerielle sous la Troisième République 1871–1938* (1939); Jacques Ollé-Laprune, *La Stabilité des ministres sous la Troisième République 1879–1940* (1962).

least partially, by the senate. This body of 300 was designed to give weight to the stable rural backbone of the country against the impetuousness of the towns. It was elected by representatives of the municipal councils. Originally every commune had one vote, whatever its size. In 1884 greater representation was given to the cities, but only to the extent of allowing one elector for every commune with under 500 inhabitants, rising to 24 electors for those with over 60,000. This new arrangement kept the favouritism towards the villages, but added a disproportionate influence for the medium-sized town of 5,000 to 10,000 in which the republican élites were to be found. The cities remained grossly under-represented. In the department of Bouches-du-Rhône, Marseille (with 900,000 inhabitants) had 24 electors, while all the other communes put together, with 250,000 inhabitants, had 313. In Seine, Paris had 147 electors, while its suburbs, with half its population, had 1,032. There were 370 rural communes, each with fewer than a hundred inhabitants, who were given 370 votes, while eleven cities, with an aggregate population of two and a half million, had 264 votes. The average senatorial constituency had 800 voters. 90 per cent of these were delegates from the communes: the local deputies and local councillors had a vote each in addition. Seventy-five of the senators were elected for life by the National Assembly, but this category was allowed to die out after 1884 and replaced by elected members.

The intentions of the founders of the regime were not fulfilled. The republicans at first denounced the senate as undemocratic and some continued for twenty years to demand its abolition. But in practice they quickly infiltrated it and it became one more bastion of the rule of the politicians, for it was a chamber which essentially represented them. The people elected were largely retired deputies and civil servants. After the war, indeed, politicians increasingly preferred its calm debates and the greater certainty of re-election it offered, to the rowdiness and risk of the lower house. It appeared to be a retreat, wrote an English journalist in 1900, 'for elderly men of education, whose faculties are undimmed and whose favourite pastime is to meet in a debating society to recite to one another essays on abstract legal or historical questions, with an occasional reference to topics of the hour. The president takes his seat in a leisurely fashion and gives a tone to the afternoon's proceedings by pronouncing in admirable language an obituary eulogy of one of their number snatched away since their last meeting.'[1] It was a reminder of the survival of the slower pace and gentler life of the provinces, for whom the agitation of Paris was a kind of theatre, to be watched and talked about. 'The senate', said Caillaux in 1938, 'is the assembly of the peasants of this country. This earns it some abuse, but, with the support of its electors, it opposes a perfect serenity to certain attacks from the press and the street, which do not rise to merit even its contempt.' The politics of the senate were accordingly considerably more conservative than those of the deputies—though staunchly republican. The senate was an obstacle much less to the power of the deputies as a group than to the political extremists among them, and to the masses as a whole.

While the republic was being consolidated, little importance was accorded to the senate. Ferry, on having his famous Article 7 rejected by it in 1880, simply turned his bill into a decree. In 1896, however, disapproving of the radical ministry of Bourgeois, the senate refused him credits and he resigned, though as a radical he might have interpreted the constitution in such a way as to allow him to ignore it. Its importance as a brake on advanced or socialist legislation increased considerably after that. It was due to its resistance that the income tax and female suffrage were so long delayed. It prevented the law of 1884 from formally allowing divorce by consent; it buried many proposals for social legislation by consideration so protracted that they were forgotten about. Its work was not just negative, however: though it contributed little to commercial or economic legislation, it was responsible for quite a number of unspectacular but influential measures, like the Nationality Law of 1889, the laws of 1885 and 1891 on the punishment and release of criminals, and it made significant additions to many other proposals. Between the wars it came to be the bastion of conservative republicanism against the demands for modernisation: it overthrew the ministries of Herriot, Tardieu, Laval and Blum. It was the other side of the republican coin, the prudent, hoarding, traditional counterpart to the declamatory oratory of the deputies. To a certain extent the deputies could be so

[1] J. E. C. Bodley, *France* (1899), 267–315.

extremist because they knew that their elders would stop any real change coming about.[1]

The deputies also had to contend with the president of the republic in the exercise of their power, but then he again was one of them. His position was dependent, to a considerable degree, on the character of the individual who filled the office. He was clearly not the most important person in the state (unlike in 1848). The republicans, reacting strongly to the experience of the Second Empire, were now hostile to the idea, which they once considered democratic, of a responsible president elected by the people. The president was purposely made weak: he was elected by parliament, so that he would have little authority against it; he was declared irresponsible, so that he should remain outside politics; and he was given a low salary, making him the poorest head of state in Europe.[2] However, in so far as he was, through the influence of the monarchists, given the powers of a constitutional king on the English or Orleanist model[3] he could play a very important role in politics. He appointed the prime minister. The fragmentation of parties meant that any one man was seldom the obvious or necessary choice and the president was thus able to exclude over-powerful figures whom he feared (like Gambetta and Clemenceau), weaken those he disliked by giving them office prematurely (e.g. the radicals under Bourgeois in 1895) or appoint minor politicians who were his friends (e.g. Carnot's friend Tirard). His choice was not confined to parliament but he had to be careful not to defy it. When Poincaré chose the right-wing Ribot to form a ministry in the left-wing parliament

[1] Gaston Coste, *Rôle législatif et politique du sénat sous la troisième république* (Montpellier thesis, 1913); François Goguel-Nyegaard, *Le Rôle financier du sénat français: essai d'histoire parlementaire* (Paris thesis, 1937); Yvan Barthomeuf, *Les Débuts du sénat républicain* (Paris thesis, 1939). For biographical information see the list of biographical dictionaries etc. in David Shapiro, *The Right in France* (St. Antony's Papers, no. 13, 1962).

[2] 600,000 francs, plus 300,000 francs household expenses and 300,000 francs travelling expenses (£48,000 in all). This was trebled between the wars, so the salary failed to keep up with the rising cost of living. No president was enriched by holding the office.

[3] It is sometimes said that the constitution was influenced by the ideas of Prévost-Paradol's *La France nouvelle* (1868) and V. de Broglie's *Vues sur le gouvernement de la France* (1861). These books expressed opinions held by many of those who took part in the drafting of the constitution, but direct influence cannot be proved. Cf. P. Guiral, *Prévost-Paradol* (1955).

of 1914, he was promptly censured by the deputies and had to give way. The president's influence depended to a great extent on his tact. He presided at meetings of the council of ministers, which were held at the Elysée. Though there were cabinet meetings also, at which ministers met without him (but frequently with junior ministers) these never replaced the formal meetings (as they did in England). The president kept a number of the prerogatives of the restoration monarchy. He could sign treaties of alliance, which, unlike treaties of commerce and of peace, needed no parliamentary ratification. In the history of French foreign policy of this period, the presidents of the republic played almost as important a role as the ministers.[1] Since they were elected for a seven-year term (and could be re-elected) they had a considerable advantage of experience and stability.

The republican parliamentarians therefore on the whole elected second-rate politicians to be president, for fear that they might be faced with too powerful a master or rival. Gambetta, Ferry, Waldeck-Rousseau, Clemenceau and Briand were all defeated, in favour of lesser men. On five occasions the president of the senate was promoted in the hope that an uncontroversial mediocrity would make the supreme office a sinecure for aged politicians. On three other occasions the president of the chamber of deputies—somewhat withdrawn from the struggle for power —was elected. Ambition, however, sometimes triumphed and even the mediocrities proved to have more individuality than had been bargained for. Jules Grévy (1879–87) had in 1848 proposed that the office of president should be abolished altogether, as being dangerous to a republic. When he was himself appointed to this post in 1879, he made a historic declaration which greatly diminished the role of the presidency. Marshal MacMahon (1873–9) in 1877 used for the first and last time the president's power to dissolve the chamber of deputies, of whose increasing radicalism he disapproved.[2] The republicans were returned triumphantly, MacMahon was soon forced to resign and Grévy declared on succeeding him, 'Sincerely accepting the

---

[1] 'Opinions de Paul Cambon sur le rôle, en politique étrangère, de quelques ministres et de divers Présidents de la République', *Revue d'Histoire Diplomatique* (1954), 202–7; L. Rogers, 'The French President and Foreign Affairs', *Political Science Quarterly* (Dec. 1925), 540–60.

[2] Y. Haikal, *La Dissolution de la chambre des députés* (Paris thesis, 1935), 55–61.

great principles of the parliamentary regime, I shall never oppose the national will as expressed by its constitutional organs.' After this the president's power of dissolution was never used again—a fact of momentous importance in making the chamber the predominant power in the country. But Grévy, while appearing to be a purely titular head of state, also took a very active interest in politics. 'He pretended', wrote Freycinet, 'that he did not wish to influence any of his ministers, so as not to shift responsibility from them. So he was careful when a proposal was made in the council, not to express an opinion either for or against it. He allowed the discussion to flow, maintaining an indolent reserve which might give the impression that he was not following it entirely. If he approved, he merely nodded or signed quickly, but he abstained from making any comment. If he did not approve, he appeared to awake from a light doze just before the vote: "You have no doubt, gentlemen, reflected carefully on the hostility this might rouse against you"; and then in a seemingly indifferent tone, he would point out the dangers which would arise and very gently in a quiet and masterly way described them like one who had not missed a word of the discussion. "But it is your business, gentlemen; it is you who are responsible. I only mention this to inform you, in case these objections have not occurred to you. Do as you please." It frequently happened that instead of doing as we pleased, we took the file away, rather abashed by the objections we had just perceived and that we altered the project and sometimes even abandoned it.'[1] Grévy certainly played a major part in causing the French to abandon Egypt, and also in avoiding war over the Schnaebele incident in 1887. Sadi Carnot, his successor (1887–94), in a different way, did much to bring about the Franco-Russian alliance, by choosing premiers, or insisting on his premiers choosing ministers of foreign affairs and of war, who favoured that alliance.[2] He intervened less in domestic politics, which had absorbed and fascinated Grévy, but whereas Grévy had devoted himself to a purely Parisian life of political intrigue, Carnot inaugurated the practice of touring the provinces: his travels during the Boulangist crisis were a significant contribution to republican propaganda.

[1] C. de Freycinet, *Souvenirs 1878–1893* (1913), 75–6.
[2] A. Dansette, *Histoire des présidents de la République* (1953), 77.

The president was shielded from political controversy by a custom that neither his name nor his opinions should be mentioned in parliament and by special protection in the press law.[1] Gambetta was sentenced to imprisonment for his speech urging MacMahon to accept republicanism or to resign; a newspaper was prosecuted for a cartoon showing MacMahon on a horse, with the legend: 'The horse looks intelligent.' Casimir Périer's term as president (1894–5) showed, however, that this protection was useless when it was not backed by public opinion. Gérault-Richard, prosecuted for a violent article against Casimir Périer, was sentenced to one year's imprisonment but Paris at once elevated him to parliament and so freed him. Jaurès, who defended him in court, was able with impunity to call the president's establishment a house of debauchery and worse. The foreign minister Hanotaux systematically refused to consult the president or to show him all dispatches. Within eight months Périer, declaring himself powerless, a prisoner, a mere master of ceremonies, open to blows but unable to return them, resigned. He had been elected after Carnot's assassination as a symbol of order, but as one of the wealthiest industrialists in the country, he was cut off from the people.[2]

After him, men of humbler origin, who could symbolise the triumph of merit, however modest, were chosen. Every man could dream of emulating them. Thus Félix Faure (1895–9) was the son of a chair maker of the rue Faubourg Saint-Denis who started life as an apprentice tanner, built up a sizeable business at Le Havre, importing leather from South America, and then became the city's deputy. But as president he behaved not just like a Napoleonic marshal, but like the emperor himself. He treated sovereigns as equals if not as inferiors; he devoted himself passionately to hunting; he made Rambouillet his summer residence; and acquired the nickname of Le Président Soleil. His pomp was popular, because he could always begin his speeches with the words, 'As the son of a working man, and as a working man myself . . .', even though in reality he was a bourgeois. His father had married the niece of a well-to-do wine merchant and property speculator. With a loan from this

[1] Article 26 of the law of 29 July 1881.
[2] P. Barral, *Les Périer dans l'Isère au XIXᵉ siècle* (1964), 163–4.

uncle Faure Senior established a second factory at Beauvais. Faure served his apprenticeship in Amboise, but completed it by marrying the daughter of the town's mayor, who later became a senator.[1]

Loubet (1899–1906) was the son of a true peasant (though a well-to-do one); Fallières (1906–13) was the son of a legal clerk and *justice de paix* and grandson of a blacksmith. Both had become barristers, mayors of their small towns (Montélimar and Nérac respectively), entered politics and worked their way up by making a lot of friends, till they were president of the senate.[2] Faure, an old freemason (though to please his women-folk, he died within the Church), helped to stimulate the retrial of Dreyfus.[3] Loubet, a moderate, tried hard to hold Combes's anticlericalism in check during the separation of Church and state and steadfastly maintained Delcassé in office as foreign minister for seven years.[4]

However, during this period the president slipped increasingly into the background. Félix Faure said, 'I am criticised for doing nothing; but what do you expect? I am the equivalent of the Queen of England.'[5] Fallières, on taking office, assured the cabinet that he would never pursue a policy of his own and he tamely allowed giants like Clemenceau, Briand and Caillaux to become prime minister.[6]

This diminution of the presidential power began to appear regrettable as men became increasingly worried by the instability of ministries. The parliamentary regime was firmly established by now, the danger of a Boulangist dictator was passed, and so good republicans could safely consider making more use of the president, without fear of jeopardising democracy. Poincaré, clearly thinking that he could be more powerful as president than as prime minister, abandoned the latter office to go to the

[1] E. Maillard, *Le Président Félix Faure* (1897).

[2] Henri Avenel, *Le Président Émile Loubet et ses prédécesseurs* (1905), shows Loubet as a vigorous local administrator and as 'le premier mutualiste de France' because he favoured pension schemes. His origins too, were not quite as humble as was made out. His father was a mayor of Marsanne (Drôme) 1844–8, 1860–82; and Loubet inherited the Château de Grignan from Doctor Loubet (an uncle).

[3] Charles Braibant, *Félix Faure à l'Élysée*, souvenirs de Louis Le Grall, Directeur du Cabinet du Président de la République (1963), 22–3.

[4] Émile Combarieu, *Sept Ans à l'Élysée avec le Président Émile Loubet* (1932), 308.

[5] R. Poincaré, *Au Service de la France* (1826–33), 3. 34.

[6] H. Leyret, *Le Président de la république: son rôle, ses droits, ses devoirs* (1913), 37.

Elysée (1913-20). He had no desire for a revision of the constitution: 'Before revising the constitution,' he had said, 'we might perhaps try to apply it . . . We must first draw from the constitution of 1875 the unused resources concealed within it: henceforth the president of the republic must freely exercise the powers of which he has been deprived by custom.'[1] Poincaré's tenure of the office was inspired by the belief that a strong man could transform it, and for a time he did indeed transform it. 'I will see to it', he told the Austrian ambassador, 'that a man takes my place [as foreign minister] who will carry out my policy. It will be as though I were still at the Quai d'Orsay.'[2] The conduct of foreign policy did remain largely in his hands for several years. When he and the new prime minister Viviani visited St. Petersburg in 1914, it was Poincaré who took the lead in all the discussions, leaving Viviani very much in the background.[3] 'In the council of ministers, as neither Viviani nor Briand presided effectively, he [Poincaré] intervened constantly and with authority', for he worked hard and was better informed than his ministers. He summoned civil servants to brief him directly. To such an extent did he abandon the president's self-effacing role in the council that he engaged in violent argument to get his views accepted. On one occasion he shouted at the prime minister Briand, 'You lie, sir!' 'The latter threw down his portfolio on the table. Doumergue, between them, cried in a ridiculous voice: "There is France!" Finally they were brought together and embraced.'[4] This was very different from the cabinet meetings of Grévy, but Poincaré's dominance continued only so long as his premiers were weak or ineffective. The situation was completely transformed in November 1917, when Clemenceau, replacing Poincaré in the eyes of public opinion as the country's hope for a vigorous prosecution of the war, became prime minister. At once the president was relegated to his traditional obscurity. His advice and his letters were ignored by Clemenceau; the foreign

---

[1] Speeches of 1898 and 1902, quoted by Gordon Wright, *Raymond Poincaré and the French Presidency* (Stanford, Calif., 1942), 23. F. Poincaré, *Questions et figures politiques* (1907), 78-9, 197.

[2] Ibid., 62.

[3] S. V. Gallup, 'The Political Career of René Viviani' (Oxford unpublished thesis, 1965), chapter 5.

[4] Wright, 162 n., 164.

minister Pichon took his orders from the prime minister, not the president; and at the peace conference, despite the president's theoretical right to negotiate treaties, it was Clemenceau who represented France. Poincaré's experiment was thus a failure, in the sense that he was unable to make any permanent change in the president's role. But he had shown its possibilities enough for Clemenceau to seek election to the presidency in 1920—and for parliament to defeat him.

The elegant Deschanel, who was elected instead, had long prepared himself for the presidency of the republic. For twelve years he had served as an impartial president of the chamber of deputies. All his life he refused to join any parliamentary group (he advocated, but never actually created, a 'Tory' party) and he declined all offers of a ministry. He was another of the many politicians who wrote a book in praise of Lamartine, whose combination of literary and political glory he longed to emulate: politics was almost a branch of literature, or of rhetoric, to him. He aimed, like Poincaré, to revive the influence of the president. 'It is a constitutional heresy', he said, 'to consider the president of the republic an inert cog or similar to a constitutional king. An elected chief cannot be like a hereditary prince, the impassive arbiter between the parties.' He must give 'active advice' to the prime minister.[1] Owing to ill health Deschanel had to resign after only eight months (February to September 1920) but his successor Millerand (1920–4) continued his campaign and took it much further. He demanded not simply that the constitution should be enforced in the way that had been planned in 1877 but that it should be revised, to increase the president's powers by new legislation. Millerand, who like Poincaré was prime minister when he was raised to the presidency, tried to keep his own ministry in office, under the nominal leadership of Leygues, so as to be virtually prime minister and president in one. When that failed he continued to intervene actively in day-to-day politics and in the conduct of government, while making public speeches in favour of a revision of the constitution. In the election of 1924 he openly took sides—against the left. He opposed

[1] Louis Sonolet, *La Vie et l'œuvre de Paul Deschanel 1852–1922* (1926), 136–9, 276; P. Deschanel, *La République nouvelle* (1898), *La Décentralisation* (1895), and other collected speeches in many volumes each under different titles; René Malliavin, *La Politique nationale de Deschanel* (1925).

parliamentary rule itself, saying that sovereignty, which belonged
to the people, had been usurped by the chamber; a strong
president, and a supreme court of justice were needed to check
it. He wished to make frequent use of the power of dissolution
and to introduce referenda. The parliamentary leaders retali-
ated by refusing to form a ministry so long as he remained
president. He was forced to resign.[1]

Even this crisis, however, did not diminish the standing of
the president. Gaston Doumergue (1924–31) is said to have
intervened in politics more than any other president since
Grévy—which he was able to do because he had great tact
as well as much experience of the parliamentary world. His
humble origins and his southerner's geniality made him as
popular with the masses as his political skill made him influential. When he was recalled from retirement to be prime minister
in 1934, to save the republic after the Stavisky scandal, he
proposed a revision of the constitution, to enable the president
to dissolve without the senate's consent. His proposal, because
it was made too late after the crisis, instead of as a condition of
his accepting office, came to nothing.

In the last years of the republic the status of the president
diminished again. Paul Doumer (1931–2) son of a railway
worker, president of the senate, was elected to keep out Briand.
He was industrious but too puritan and aloof to be influential;
he was assassinated, in any case, within a year, by a Russian
lunatic.[2] Albert Lebrun (1932–40), again a president of the
senate, and of peasant origin, an efficient and conscientious
Lorrainer, graduate of the *Polytechnique* and the *Ponts et
Chaussées*, took his duties seriously. He prided himself on reading
everything before he signed it and he frequently secured amendments to administrative decrees (which had become increasingly
numerous).[3] He considered resigning after the elections of 1936,
for he disapproved strongly of the Popular Front: he decided
to stay so as to 'moderate its excesses' and to prevent the
election of a socialist president, but in fact he exerted little
influence. It was only in the crisis of 1940, when the ministries

[1] Jean Magnien, 'Alexandre Millerand' (D.E.S. unpublished mémoire, Paris, 1962).
[2] P. Bastid, 'Doumer', *Revue Politique et Parlementaire* (Dec. 1934).
[3] Daniel Brune, *Du pouvoir réglementaire du chef de l'État* (Bordeaux thesis, 1898), 98.

were vacillating and divided, that his role became crucial once more. His case illustrates well what was true throughout the republic, that the president's position in the government varied enormously, depending on his personality and on how the other parts of the constitution were functioning. The generalisation, frequently repeated, that he lost his importance after 1877, is very misleading.[1]

Another force the deputies had to contend with was the civil service. The extent to which they kept it in subordination again varied considerably. A powerful deputy, by assiduous canvassing, could get a favourable prefect, sub-prefect and civil servants appointed to his constituency, and if he was sufficiently active he could ensure that the strings of influence and promotion remained in his grasp. Inevitably, however, the civil service had an *esprit de corps* of its own. The prefects of the Third Republic are less famous than those of the Second Empire, partly because their activities were less dramatic, but partly also because they have been studied less. They were in fact of two kinds. There were some among them who accepted a relatively subordinate role in the political system, regarded themslves as administrators, and pressed for security of tenure, to make them like all other state employees. It is not usually realised, however, that many of them regretted the grand days of more unchallenged authority which they enjoyed under previous regimes. They formed an association to defend their interests in 1907, where the principal topic of discussion was their prestige. Every generation of prefects had its contingent of those who complained that their powers were diminishing, compared to the previous one. Some rejected security and insisted that their role was essentially political: the more risk there was in it, the more they could personally achieve. They maintained the paraphernalia which gave them status as charismatic representatives of national power: they kept up their palatial residences, with a social life surrounded by distance and respect. They insisted that they were unlike other bureaucrats, for their skill lay in their ability to handle men. There is no doubt that, although they could no longer manage elections single-handed, as some had once claimed to do, electoral activities continued to be one of their

[1] Albert Lebrun, *Témoignage* (1945), 223–57.

main preoccupations, and their success in them played an important part in their promotions. Brisson sacked ten prefects in 1898 because he thought they were unfavourable to his brand of politics; Combes sacked eight in 1904; Herriot sacked eight after the election of 1924 and moved one-third of the whole corps around. It is true Combes introduced a custom of treating dismissed prefects very gently and finding them profitable sinecures to retire to; his own son Edgar, who was a prefect and who as secretary general of the ministry of the interior supervised all these matters, ended up himself as director of the lunatic asylum of Villejuif.

There is an interesting book describing the equivocal position of the prefects by one of Gambetta's friends who had served as a prefect himself. He was keen that their status as 'the highest functionaries of the administration' should be restored; he was furious that, in the official order of precedence, he might find himself lagging behind bishops, admirals and judges. (The association of prefects indeed has ever since agitated for more decorations to be given, quasi-automatically, to prefects.) He resented that his right to travel free came from a pass issued by the railway company, not by the state. He lamented that his influence was so dependent on his personal popularity and tact, for he had lost his control of the mayors. (This was partly remedied by a system of *délégués*, whom the prefect appointed in villages whose mayors were hostile to him: he channelled all favours through them and so built up his own party.) He had to use much effort to win the co-operation of mayors by constant friendliness, but then if he became too popular, the local deputies got jealous. They would complain to the minister, who tended to play prefect and deputy off against each other. The prefect therefore had to be very careful what he wrote to Paris, lest it be shown to the deputy. When he moved departments, he usually took with him all personal and political files he had accumulated with the result that his successor had to start from scratch learning about the balance of local forces. Though he had lost control of the mayor, he still appointed the *instituteur*, who was frequently secretary of the municipal council and who could therefore be an invaluable tool. But he appointed him on the nomination of the inspector of the Academy; the whole academic administration was increasingly building up an independence of the prefectoral authority, and its Paris headquarters regularly supported them against the prefects. 'It is not going too far to say that the greatest embarrassments a prefect can experience come to him from the inspector of the Academy, supported by his rector, supported by the offices of the ministry.' The *instituteurs* knew their promotion came to them from their inspectors, and though most of them were republican, the ministry, keen to place the university outside politics, therefore appeared reactionary, because it pursued an independent line instead of backing the prefect's efforts to 'republicanise' his department systematically.

The idea of a united party getting control of the whole country is far too simple. The diversity of the civil service was considerable. Quite apart from the clergy, the prefect often had trouble with the numerous officials of the ministry of finance, who had the reputation of being particularly conservative. Its registrar's department (*l'enregistrement*) was especially regarded as 'the refuge of all that is most clerical and most Jesuit in the administration, and if a prefect known for his inflexible republican opinions denounces an official of this department as a reactionary, that official is almost bound to get immediate promotion'. The ministry of justice was more politically conscious, and prefects could influence the appointment of judges of the peace, but on the other hand magistrates were often conservative. The ambitions of the prefects in turn roused vigorous resistance in others. Liberals denounced them as relics of the *ancien régime* and the empire. 'Like their predecessors,' wrote Gaston Jèze in 1911, 'the prefects of the twentieth century are the natural enemies of political liberties.' The civil servants in the older branches of the administration, like justice and finance, were proud of the tradition of their services, and valued the prestige which they felt they inherited from the dignitaries of the old monarchy, who had bought their offices and who had acquired nobility through them. This, again, is another side of the republican regime that was put somewhat in the shade by the rhetorical declamation. The old authoritarian state survived, despite the Revolution. The deputies were representatives of liberty against it, but when they became ministers they were unhesitating in maintaining its power. The republic exhibited herself in public wearing liberal clothes, but one had grounds for suspecting that she was simply the old Napoleonic state disguised, not altered too fundamentally. What the deputies put into her mouth needs to be examined very closely. The great mistake in studying the Third Republic is to take its polemic at its face value and to believe that politicians who attacked each other were enemies for the reasons they gave, or sometimes indeed that they were enemies at all.[1]

[1] Edgar Monteil, *L'Administration de la République* (1893); Jeanne Siwek-Pouydesseau, *Le Corps préfectoral sous la troisième et la quatrième République* (1969); Henri Chardon, *Le Pouvoir administratif* (1910); Henri Joly, *De la corruption de nos institutions* (1903).

7. Opportunism

REPUBLICANISM is not easy to define, because it had different meanings in different contexts. No generalisation about it can escape being vague or confused if it fails to distinguish between at least four types. At the level of the masses, republicanism was closely linked with old traditions, prejudices, rivalries, some going back a long time, but many of them sharpened and embittered by the Revolution and the struggles it fomented. It reflected developments in social relationships whose origins had little to do with the doctrines which were preached in Paris, though these doctrines were sometimes used to rationalise and make respectable personal, family and local animosities. At a level above this, the professional politicians saw the republic as a defence of the individual against the state, as a means of social ascension, and as an instrument for the emancipation of local communities from traditional tyrannies. But making themselves the necessary intermediaries of this defence and liberation, they assumed the positions of merchants or retailers in the political system. They acquired an ascendancy which gave them some of the characteristics of a new ruling class, but also laid themselves open to jealousy and contempt as profiteers. Republicanism for them was thus both a panacea and a living, an ideal of equality and a source of supremacy. There was tension between them and the masses on the one hand and the government on the other. The republicanism of the ministers they raised to power was of a third kind. The ministers were more conscious of national than of local considerations. They inherited the command of an immensely powerful state. Republicanism for them meant not the defence of the individual but the creation of order, unity, glory, all of which required sacrifice from individuals for the attainment of higher principles. Finally, at the fourth level, republicanism had its philosophers, who provided these principles. These of course had no necessary relation with the realities. They often misled people as to what was going on; they often idealised the Revolution, so that its shortcomings were concealed and they stressed divisions which were more theoretical than real. It is from the interplay of these four elements that the total picture of republicanism must be built up. Previous chapters have discussed the popular origins of republicanism and the role of the deputies in it. This one will examine the ministers, with a view to discovering in what way and to what extent they attempted to reorganise the state or to modify economic and social relations. Their careers will help define the boundaries of republicanism, the limits beyond which it would not go, and the degree to which it was content to preserve the inheritance of the past. It will emerge that some of the most important elements of republicanism were those which sought to bolster traditional forces, values or myths. But it will be seen that its attempts in this direction were not all based on popular demand. When the republicans obtained power, they were so deeply imbued with prejudices instilled by many centuries of monarchical rule, that they often had no desire to break away from them. There was thus a fundamental contradiction within republicanism, between what it was in opposition and what it was in office. This can be explained less by the ambition and greed for power of particular individuals, than by the dominance of deeply ingrained intellectual traditions. Republicans wanted to demolish the state when they were in opposition, but to strengthen it when they became ministers. A study of the lives and ideas of some of the leading ministers will help to show how and why this came about, and why, though they saw themselves as the advocates of popular wishes, they so often proved, almost inevitably, impotent.

The man who did as much as anyone to establish the Third Republic was Adolphe Thiers (1797–1873), who had never been a republican at all. Thiers was one of the most astute masters of the French political game in the nineteenth century. He played a leading role in establishing the July Monarchy in 1830, in having Louis Napoleon elected president in 1848, in destroying the Commune, and in founding the regime of 1871. He gave the impression of unsurpassed clarity of mind. It was said of him that there was no subject, however complicated, which he could not understand. He could certainly give this impression, and since he had firm views on all subjects, he was one of the most persuasive speakers of his time. He had infinite

skill as a manager of men. His inexhaustible energy, his imper-
turbable self-confidence, his dogged determination made him
unsuppressible. He was only 33 when he raised Louis-Philippe
to the throne, he was minister of the interior at 35, member of
the French Academy at 36 and an all-powerful elder statesman
while still in his fifties. His influence came to him partly because
he was willing to accept only supreme power, so that he seldom
held office, but he became the *éminence grise* of several generations. He came of undistinguished origins; he was five feet two
inches in height; he had only his wits to live on. He made himself
one of the most striking examples of the self-made man. He
benefited from the prestige this status could give, but he assimilated rapidly into the ruling class. He became president of one
of the most profitable firms in France, the Anzin Mine Company.
He also enjoyed an independent position as one of the country's
most widely read historians, at a time when history was almost
a branch of political philosophy.

His significance, in the long term, was that he incarnated
certain important prejudices of the early nineteenth century,
and he used his dominant position in politics to preserve and
strengthen them against new currents. The republic he founded
was therefore a dyke against these as much as against anything
else. He reveals particularly clearly what was common to the
different regimes he supported in turn. He had served Louis-
Philippe but, even more, he had quarrelled with him. 'I do not
call myself an Orleanist', he said. 'The Orleanist family have
no claim on me; they have always persecuted me and I have
opposed them. By birth I belong to the people . . . By education,
I am an aristocrat. I have no sympathy with the bourgeoisie
or with any system under which they rule.'[1] He shows how
difficult it was for any particular regime to win a permanent
loyalty, and how partisanship was often a label stuck on by
opponents rather than voluntarily adopted. He illustrates how
Orleanists, Bonapartists and republicans all tried to draw
strength, in different ways, from their popular origins, and how
they moved away from them towards aristocracy or oligarchy.
If he could have his way, he once said, he would distribute the
Coburg family on to the thrones of all Europe. His ideal was
constitutional monarchy, with power firmly in the hands of a

[1] N. Senior, *Conversations with Thiers, Guizot . . .* (1878), i. 39.

prime minister. The nation was sovereign, but only theoretic-
ally, in the sense that it should not be expected to make decisions
on every issue, but should leave these to its delegates in parliament. He tried to abolish manhood suffrage in 1850. He had
only contempt for 'the vile multitude', a phrase that, significantly, made him permanently execrable only to a small
minority on the very fringes of politics. The establishment of
parliamentary government was his main aim. Coupled with
free elections and personal security for the citizens, it provided
all that the country needed.[1]

He had a profound hostility to every form of socialism. In
1848 he published an unflinchingly conservative defence of
property as the basis of French civilisation. Though he represented the triumph of merit, he was also proud of having been
admitted into the inner sanctum of the ruling class, and he had
no desire to diminish its power. He adopted its traditional
pessimism about the possibility of any drastic change and its
scepticism towards reform. He agreed that there were evils
governments should try to remedy, but there were also evils
'inherent in human nature which no imaginable perfection in
governments could spare men'. Railways, when they first
appeared, had roused only suspicion in him and he had thought
the best thing was to avoid them. Though he was an industrial
director or because he was one, he was very gloomy about the
chances of industrial success. 'Failures are much more numerous than successes, and if [industry in France] has created quite
a considerable number of middle-sized fortunes, it has established very few large ones, above all very few capable of in-
fallibly surviving serious crises.' Even if a firm did succeed, it
did so only after having ruined several competitors. Workers'
associations had not the slightest chance of being more successful than capitalist firms. His solution was prudent protection
from foreign competition.[2]

Thiers saw that this was not a programme to rouse enthusiasm among the masses. 'What we do in Paris,' he said, 'what
we say in the chambers, has no impact on the country. But

---

[1] See his speech on Necessary Liberties, *Annales du Corps Législatif*, 2 (1864),
305–16, and on the pre-eminence of political solutions, ibid. 2 (1865), 87–98,
and 1 (1866), 202–15.

[2] A. Thiers, *De la propriété* (1848), 192–204, 241, 363.

when the country learns that they are going to fight . . . and that they have been victorious, . . . children are moved and women cry. Is it too much to spend 60 millions to maintain what is left of moral sentiments and of disinterested passions, to prevent France from huddling over a footwarmer?' National glory was the essential counterpart to parliamentary government, and 'an article of faith' to him. Napoleon I was 'the man who has inspired France with the strongest emotions she has ever felt'. Thiers's books did as much as anyone's to glorify the emperor's genius, for whom he had a profound admiration. If he had a model, it was the first consul. The one thing he could not forgive Napoleon III for was that he had allowed Germany to outweigh and outshine France in Europe. Thiers was a Bonapartist also in his horror of disorder. The riots of 1848 had filled him, as he said, with rage, and in 1871 when 'mob rule', which he hated above all else, seemed to threaten, he showed how ruthless he could be in its suppression.[1]

It was no accident that Thiers should have been called in as the country's saviour in 1871, in the agony of national defeat. The effect of his tenure of power was to stamp an indelible conservatism on the institutions of the regime. First, Thiers repeated the repression of the working-class agitation which he had carried out in the 1830s and in 1848; indeed he saw the Commune as an opportunity to end this menace once and for all. He succeeded, but at the expense of a civil war. The consequence of this was almost to suggest the exclusion of a section of the community from full membership of the nation. Paris was defeated by the provinces but at the cost of making it permanently hostile to the regime. Centralisation was maintained. It no longer represented the dominance of the Parisians, but rather of provincials who had made good and crowned their triumph by capturing the state. The failure of the Commune meant that the methods of the old regime survived, defended and taken over by the provincials who had so long suffered from them. Thiers was one of the firmest supporters of centralisation. He tried his best to prevent the royalists from increasing the powers of the municipal and departmental councils, and he did succeed in retaining for the prefects the right to appoint mayors

[1] On his 'rage' see Bibliothèque Nationale, N.a.f. 20618, f. 597, copy of letter from Thiers to duc d'Aumale, 6 Jan. 1861.

in the larger towns. The republic Thiers founded was thus endowed with the institutions of Napoleon I, his hero.

This can be seen even more clearly in the military system which, after 1871, was immediately called into question. Thiers had very conservative views here too, preferring a professional army which he considered the necessary basis of French prestige. It was his insistence that prevented France following the German model and instituting a conscript army. He wanted soldiers to serve for seven years: the reformers wanted universal service for three years. A compromise of five years was agreed, which meant that not everyone was needed. The democratisation of the army was avoided; the army increasingly became a bastion of conservatism and resistance. Its 'republicanisation' remained a major problem for several decades.

Above all, it was Thiers who prevented the reform of the old system of taxation. He won wide acclaim for rapidly raising the money to pay off the indemnity exacted by the conquering Germans, but he staunchly refused to allow the introduction of the income tax to meet the increased costs of government. He preferred to raise existing taxes, however inequitably distributed they might be, than to introduce new ones. He had assisted the financier Baron Louis in 1830 and never changed the views he acquired then; he saw the experience of the Restoration as a vindication of Napoleon I's financial system. France, he thought, should maintain the institutions which had made it great. He objected to the Second Empire's desire to tax new forms of wealth. He believed governments should concentrate on reducing the national debt rather than raise new taxes. It was he who saved the *rentier* in the 1870s.[1]

The attitude of Gambetta towards the state and its institutions was not as radically different as might be supposed from a man who was held up as incarnating the popular will. Though one of the main founders of the republic, he held office for only three months. By the end of his career he was feared or mistrusted by the leaders of the regime he had done so much to create. He

---

[1] R. Schnerb, 'La Politique fiscale de Thiers', *Revue Historique*, 201 (1949), 186–212, and 202 (1950), 184–220. The fullest biography of Thiers is by H. Malo, *Thiers* (1932).

began his life as an apparently extreme radical and ended it as a mild opportunist, claiming that compromise was the essence of politics. A great deal of myth grew up around him and there is more hagiography about him than almost any other politician of his era. There has even been a *Société Gambetta*, founded in 1905, to cultivate his memory in a spirit of hero worship. He is difficult to evaluate because his popularity was due partly to personal qualities, to a distinctive, captivating charm, which an early death maintained as a pure memory among a host of friends, and to which future generations have paid a rather mystified homage.

Physically, Gambetta both repelled and attracted. He himself said he was ugly. He was coarse and untidy. He had a glass eye. He appears to have suffered from syphilis. His health was poor: in later years he grew fat and his complexion reddened. But he was the most approachable of men, with a gentle and ready smile, simple manners, a warm but soft voice, and he could talk as no one else could. His speeches lacked distinction, harmony or any of the classical perfection so carefully cultivated by his better-educated colleagues; they are full of repetition and banality; but they could captivate mass audiences by their overwhelming impression of sincerity and involvement. He did not measure his gestures, nor grow animated at appropriate and preordained moments, as trained barristers should; he prepared only the first and last phrases of his speeches, but in between allowed himself to be carried away by his emotions. He did not so much impress his audiences as move them. There was no haughtiness in him. He made friends almost with a kind of passion. He was particularly good at encouraging and welcoming young people making their first appearance in public life, with a friendliness and grace which won him dazzled admirers. He found time for all this social activity because he slept very little, staying up into the early hours chatting and playing cards, but getting up at seven in the morning. He combined a vast capacity for work with a deep-rooted laziness, so that he alternated between industriousness and sloth. He was a Bohemian, a bachelor, a foreigner, a parvenu, so that he was never restricted by the traditions of any particular class. His father was an Italian grocer who had settled in Cahors. He had had a hard struggle to get his education; he had been a mediocre student at school; he had some difficulty in passing his law degree; he never read much, though he had a good memory for some things and he could recite whole pages of Rabelais by heart.

The friends he collected round him were of the same kind, most of them of obscure origin, who had suffered failures of various kinds and who found in politics a justification, a purpose and also an income. They were a new class of men, who lived by politics, and who had no private incomes to retire to. Gambetta himself lived with an old aunt in a mean apartment until he moved into the splendid residence of the president of the chamber of deputies; he acquired a small house only in 1878 and had no other property. Spuller, whom Gambetta called his faithful Achates, and whom he made his under-secretary at the ministry for foreign affairs, was the orphan son of peasants of German origin, who also had great trouble getting through his law course and who then scratched a poor living by his pen, in a shabby attic. Eugène Étienne was another orphan in the entourage, who started as a shop assistant and only later acquired a fortune in Algeria. Delcassé again was a parvenu and a man who kept failing his examinations, working as a junior teacher until politics raised him and a rich marriage enriched him. Challemel-Lacour came of a bourgeois family ruined by bankruptcy; he was one of the few who had academic success, through the École Normale, but the advent of Napoleon III threw him out of work. He nurtured a deep resentment against the class from which he issued but which had rejected him, and he consoled himself with the study of Schopenhauer. Several of the followers of Gambetta had tried to practise as barristers and had failed. Few of them had provincial ties, let alone properties: they were *déracinés* making their fortunes alone in Paris. They were bachelors for the most part, or were involved in irregular unions. Gambetta himself lived with Léonie Léon, of mixed black and Jewish origin, brought up in a convent, an orphan while still a girl, and the mistress of an inspector general of Napoleon III's police, before she met him. Challemel lived with a married woman, in a union which cast gloom over his whole life. It was no accident they supported the law on divorce. They had no family life to divert them, though Gambetta's passion for his mistress absorbed him increasingly just when power came to him. They needed each other's company and led a life of close friendship and constant discussion which perpetuated the intimacy of student cliques into middle age.

These men desperately needed hope, and they therefore tried to give it to others who were struggling against misfortune like themselves, who did not have their careers and their dowries laid out before them by their parents. Gambetta was their inspiration and their hero emotionally as well as intellectually. Paul Bert (to be his minister of education) wrote to him: 'You are the man I love most strongly and most completely.' Dionys Ordinaire (who was to run his newspaper for him) wrote to him after hearing him speak: 'You made me cry from love and admiration.' Spuller was said to have found in Gambetta's company the equivalent of mother's milk. 'When Gambetta spoke, he closed his eyes so as to impregnate himself better with his words. He had no thought which did not come from Gambetta, or which did not involve him.'[1]

Gambetta made himself the spokesman of these parvenus who had not quite made good, and interpreted the republic as the form of government which would open the doors of power and of society to them. The republic, he said, meant the advent of the *nouvelles couches sociales*.[2] He meant by that that a revolution must take place in the composition of the ruling class. The old aristocracy, and the wealthy bourgeoisie who had assimilated themselves to it, must make way for humbler men, who had gradually acquired self-confidence since the Revolution and were only slowly taking advantage of universal suffrage. These new men were beginning to make their way into the municipal councils and a few of them even to parliament. The republic must be a regime open to all classes. It must make democracy a reality. Gambetta did not preach class war. He was not asking the workers to replace the employers, for—except on a few occasions towards the end of his life—he denied that such things as classes existed in France, let alone an

[1] J. Chastenet, *Gambetta* (1969); G. Wormser, *Gambetta dans les tempêtes* (1964); P. Deschanel, *Gambetta* (1919); Joseph Reinach, *La Vie politique de Gambetta* (1919); H. Stannard, *Gambetta and the Foundation of the Third Republic* (1921); D. Halévy and E. Pillias, *Lettres de Gambetta* (1938); E. Pillias, *Léonie Léon, amie de Gambetta* (1935); P. B. Gheusi, *La Vie et la mort singulières de Gambetta* (1932); E. Krakowski, *Challemel-Lacour* (1932); P. Sorlin, *Waldeck-Rousseau* (1966); Juliette Adam, *Nos amitiés politiques* (1908); G. Hanotaux, *Mon temps*, vol. 2 (1938).

[2] *Discours et plaidoyers politiques de M. Gambetta* (1881–5), 3. 99, 113.

irreconcilable enmity between them. He considered all elements in society who contributed to its productivity, from the capitalist and the merchant to the peasant, to belong to the same category of men who were making their way in the world. He was their champion equally, because he saw France as composed of 'individuals in the process of rising' in the social order. He spoke with respect of the bourgeoisie as 'those who think, who work, who amass wealth, who know how to use this wealth judiciously, liberally and profitably to the country' and who formed 'the enlightened, active and generous part of the nation'. Though he threatened the rich with an income tax and the destruction of their monopolies, his great ambition was to smooth the path that could lead the poor to independence and leisure. Gambetta described the *nouvelles couches* as having been created, first, by universal suffrage, and secondly by economic development, which had brought into existence a new 'world of industry, commerce, science and art . . . imbued with a spirit of enterprise . . . the soul and nerves of democracy'. Their frontiers were thus vague, but they included both the bourgeoisie and the workers. What Gambetta wanted was their unification by the instrument of property. 'Property is, in our view,' he said, 'the superior, preparatory sign of the moral and material emancipation of the individual.' In some confusion (perpetuating the myth Michelet had spread), he imagined that 80 per cent of the country owned some property, so it was only a question of continuing a movement which was well under way. He saw small proprietors, small industrialists, small shopkeepers as the backbone of the *nouvelles couches sociales*. It was for such men that he wanted more active participation in public life.[1]

His ultimate aim, as one of his disciples explained, was that these new men should be accepted without rancour or contempt into the ruling class, which should not be allowed to remain closed, as it had been under the monarchy with its limited franchise. Having got to the top themselves, they should likewise accept that they would be superseded in turn by younger, abler men. That was life. A constant turnover would be accepted if men saw it as an inescapable, scientific law; and if social barriers were no longer raised to halt this inevitable evolution.

[1] *Discours*, 4. 155–6.

Ultimately 'the rich financier, who today lives withdrawn behind his formidable signature, will see his son acknowledge the grocer round the corner who has become a millionaire. People will get round to receiving their tradesmen socially as guests and the aristocrats will be lucky if one day their former valets do not inscribe themselves for the first dance with madame la marquise.' All France would then form one undifferentiated *couche*.[1] Gambetta appreciated that all this could not be achieved at once. In particular he saw that the peasants were ignorant and prejudiced, many of them hating all that came from the towns. He urged his followers to go to them as 'elder brothers', to win them away from their apathy, to teach them to enjoy 'independence of mind'.[2] He looked forward to 'the indissoluble union of those who work and those who possess . . . the alliance of the proletariat and the bourgeoisie'.[3]

Gambetta thus placed human dignity, social equality, national union as the most important objective of the republicans. This must be achieved not by sentimentalism, as in 1848, but by more effective and positive measures. A military reform must turn France into a nation in arms, with universal patriotism replacing the exclusiveness which had been the officer's hallmark. Education for all classes in the same schools must unite the country in the same way. 'It must teach [the pupil] what his dignity is, what solidarity links him to those around him; it must show him that he has a rank in the commune, in the department, in the nation; it must remind him above all that there is a moral being to whom all must be given, all must be sacrificed, life, future, family, and that this being is France.' Until this civic education has penetrated, 'you will always be in the presence of these two imminent perils, either the exploitation of the people by intriguers, adventurers, dictators, ruffians, or something even more grave, the unforeseen explosion of the inflamed masses, who suddenly obey their blind fury'.[4]

Gambetta's purpose was not revolutionary. But he felt he

[1] E. Monteil, *Les Couches sociales* (1880). This book, which no historian seems to have used hitherto, appears to be the only commentary on Gambetta's theory of classes, by a close colleague.

[2] *Discours*, 2. 27–30, 5. 117.

[3] Ernest Charles, *Théories sociales et politiciens 1870–1898* (1898), 52–3.

[4] *Discours*, 2. 254.

had to wage a war against one of the main pillars of society, the Church, because it stood in the way of this emancipation, it opposed the republic and it flouted its laws, because its monks acknowledged a foreign sovereign and educated their pupils to different allegiances. He was a free thinker, as he publicly admitted,[1] but his quarrel was not with religion as such. His war cry, 'Clericalism is the enemy', should be interpreted in the light of another slogan uttered by Paul Bert, also a free thinker: 'Peace to the *curé*: war against the monk.' This distinction was not maintained, because the secular clergy rallied to the defence of the regulars, and the Church emerged as a formidable obstacle to republicanism. Gambetta wanted the triumph of science over religion but he also preached liberty of conscience. Education was too important to be confided to obscurantist teachers. If properly organised, it would prevent social animosities, class hatreds and revolution, for 'no one is more confirmed in the anger and hatred that poverty necessarily breeds, than the disinherited man who suffers without knowledge or understanding'.[2] This could be interpreted to mean that Gambetta's aim was not all that different from that of the Church when it taught people to accept their lot. Gambetta never urged the people to rise against economic oppression. He vehemently denied that there was a 'social question'. There were only 'economic and industrial problems', and these did indeed inflame rivalry and envy, but they had to be solved one by one, individually, for they varied according to local conditions and local customs. 'Let us remain on guard against the utopias of those who, dupes of their imagination or backward in their ignorance, believe in a panacea, in a formula which has only to be found to bring about happiness in the world. There is no social remedy, because there is no social question.'[3] The republic's function was only to make the individual free and enlightened, to prepare him 'for the struggle and for triumph'. He believed in association, but also in competition. By association, he took care to point out, 'I do not understand those forms of it which confiscate the individual, suppress and absorb him, because I consider legitimate only those associations which leave the individual the plenitude of his free and active

[1] *Discours*, 2. 179.   [2] *Discours*, 9. 376.
[3] *Discours*, 9. 122–3, 2. 263.

individuality'.[1] But 'those who have arrived' should act as the 'elder brothers . . . the initiators, the patrons, the guides, the protectors of those who, placed beneath them, have not been able to receive the benefits of education and of fortune but who have their rights too'.[2]

There were limits to what he hoped to achieve. Human societies existed, he said, not to ensure happiness but to establish the reign of justice. It should be left to the next generation to seek 'the most extreme consequence of the principle of human solidarity'.[3] He even claimed to be a conservative, because he was safeguarding the work of the Revolution, which was already nearly a hundred years old.[4] He had no desire to dismantle the state, but on the contrary wanted to strengthen it, to make it, almost in the Napoleonic tradition, 'a motor of progress, protector of all legitimate rights and an initiator of all the energies which constitute the national genius'.[5]

Gambetta derived his national standing from his vigorous activity, as minister of the interior and of war in 1871, when he organised the military and popular resistance against Prussia. He acquired a reputation akin to that of Carnot in the first Revolution, though his dictatorship and his refusal to make peace also condemned him in many eyes as a dangerous fanatic. He was elected to the National Assembly by ten departments, but he had identified his party with war and it was soundly defeated. However, he learnt the lesson very rapidly, and changing his tactics, he secured victory for it within six years. He showed himself to possess exceptional skill as a political strategist. First, he worked hard to destroy the reputation republicanism had for bringing anarchy and revolution. He made compromise his watchword. He urged his followers to be *sage*. He pointed out that his party sought not the control of the country for a new clique, but the end of exclusiveness. He was willing to admit into the fold old Bonapartists and royalists who were ready to forget the past and to work for concord in the future. He admitted that the rich were bound to play a major part in a republican society, because they had so many advantages of education and wealth; he sought not to dispossess them but to win them over, to make them the guides

[1] *Discours*, 11. 9.   [2] *Discours*, 5. 117.   [3] *Discours*, 2. 262.
[4] *Discours*, 5. 44.   [5] Charles, 48-9, 77.

and liberators of the poor. He accepted Thiers, his former enemy, and allied willingly with hostile parties if it was to the advantage of his cause.

Gambetta, secondly, was one of the greatest of France's election managers. He probably invented the phrase 'electoral geography', for the study of which he had a passion: 'Universal suffrage', he said, 'is the most interesting thing in the social life of France.'[1] By 1874 he had enormous maps or tables showing at a glance the position of the republican party in every municipal council throughout the country, with the name and profession of every supporter. 'I am quite proud of my invention,' he wrote, 'for I believe that no government has yet realised or applied it.'[2] He insisted, however, that a party could only make headway with universal suffrage if it made personal contact with the electors. Universal suffrage, he said, 'will support only those who devote themselves to it without respite or rest; it needs to be visited, enlightened, informed'. He set new standards for party leaders: he toured the country making speeches everywhere and getting to know personally the local organisers and local conditions. Some people ridiculed this and called him the republic's commercial traveller, but the method was so successful that they soon began to worry that it was giving him a popularity that recalled Napoleon's. Gambetta organised the republican campaigns of 1876 and 1877, based on the policy of candidates on a national scale and the simplification of the issues, to make them elections for the expulsion of the royalists. He was a partisan of the *scrutin de liste*, because he believed that a two-party system was impossible if local considerations predominated. He founded newspapers to develop a doctrine and a policy for the republicans. *La République Française*, subsidised by sympathetic businessmen, became not only his official organ, but the instrument of a shadow cabinet. His principal followers were each given one speciality to write about,[3] with the injunction that they should treat it with gravity and responsibility, proposing policies they would

[1] *Discours*, 9. 276.

[2] D. Halévy and E. Pillias, *Lettres de Gambetta* (1938), letter 219.

[3] Challemel, Ranc and Spuller on internal affairs, Proust on foreign affairs, Allain-Targé on finance, Freycinet on war and public works, Paul Bert on education, Berthelot on science, Dr. Lannelongue on hygiene and medicine, Léon Clery on law.

be ready to implement. This was directed to the educated classes. For the masses he had *Le Voltaire* and *La Petite République*, in more popular vein, reproducing his provincial and parliamentary speeches for a wide audience.[1]

Gambetta, however, did not epitomise republicanism, which was too diverse to accept his leadership. The well-to-do members of the party, the rural notables and the successful professional men disliked his coarseness, despised his upstart Bohemian friends, and kept their distance. Grévy, president of the republic, could not abide him, and kept him out of office. The members of parliament feared his ambitions, and with reason. When he finally became prime minister, he attacked their power at once. He did not have a reliable majority behind him, he knew he would not last long and he was not unwilling therefore to martyr himself. There was a strange contrast between his tact in opposition and his blundering in office. He revealed his limitations as a politician when he became prime minister, and he allowed himself to be destroyed by his own creation. In an attempt to increase governmental power, as against that of the deputies, his minister of the interior required all the latter's applications for favours to be transmitted through the prefects, with their approval. Now that the prefects were republican, they ceased to be enemies and could be used to strengthen the republic's authority. Gambetta created new ministries without parliamentary consent. He gave jobs to former royalists, in defiance of the deputies' demands for the spoils of power. He declared war on the whole system on which the deputies based their influence, pressed for the adoption of the *scrutin de liste* and offered a deal to the senate, agreeing to abandon his plans for its reform, in return for their approval of the *liste*. He was accused of plotting a dictatorship for himself, which his popularity in the country seemed to support. In fact he was trying to turn the republicans into a party of government, whereas they were inescapably attached to their habits of opposition. It is significant that Gambetta took the portfolio of foreign affairs, placing the re-establishment of French glory as his prime aim.[2]

[1] C. de Freycinet, *Souvenirs 1848–1878* (1912), 281–2.
[2] J. Reinach, *Le Ministère Gambetta, histoire et doctrine, 14 novembre 1881–26 janvier 1882* (1884).

When Gambetta died at the age of forty, his disciples made out that he had been a deep thinker, one of the main philosophers of the republic. It is true that he had sometimes claimed to base his actions on the latest ideas of the time. He publicly called Comte the greatest thinker of the century; he described himself as an interpreter of Littré; he praised Proudhon and borrowed his dictum that democracy was *démopédie*. He paid tribute to positivism and science. One can also find him praising Montesquieu for advocating a balanced constitution, against the popular tyranny he saw in Rousseau, whose ideas he declared to be no longer valid. All this should not be taken too literally. Gambetta was no doctrinaire and not much influenced by books. He simply talked in the language of his day, adopting phrases from those around him.

Gambetta's *nouvelles couches sociales* were slow to win acceptance and even slower to win power. No one has yet made a thorough study of the municipal councils of France, to trace how and when they entered into them. One investigation, of the city of Bordeaux—which of course cannot be considered typical—suggests, however, that the petty bourgeoisie won a majority in its municipality only in 1925. In the 1870s the city was dominated by the rich old-established merchant families, the industrialists, and the large property owners. The very rich continued to occupy between a third and a quarter of the seats till 1925. By 1888 an equilibrium was established between the classes, the rich, the middle class and the petty bourgeoisie each holding a third. In 1896 the petty bourgeoisie (i.e. junior civil servants, artisans, shopkeepers) for the first time had more seats than the *moyenne bourgeoisie;* their numbers rose steadily after that, till they reached a peak in 1925. By then, however, those who took part in politics were no longer the same. The ordinary workers no longer stood and small contractors replaced them; the old dynasties of wholesalers were replaced by more aggressive *nouveaux riches* ones. It is not easy to draw a general conclusion from this example, but it appears that though the exclusiveness of politics diminished slowly, it was replaced by new forms Gambetta had not foreseen.[1] In any case, one should not exaggerate the effect of the intellectual

[1] Jacqueline Herpin, 'Les Milieux dirigeants à Bordeaux sous la Troisième République', *Revue Historique de Bordeaux*, 15 (Oct.–Dec. 1966), 145–65.

content of Gambetta's programme on the electorate. It is by no means certain that his peasant audiences took it all in. In the 1950s one of France's leading rural sociologists, Henri Mendras, asked the peasants of the Haut-Rhin: 'What *couches sociales* are there in French society?' The majority of those interviewed said they did not understand the question.[1]

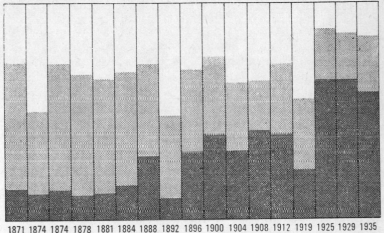

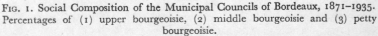

FIG. 1. Social Composition of the Municipal Councils of Bordeaux, 1871–1935. Percentages of (1) upper bourgeoisie, (2) middle bourgeoisie and (3) petty bourgeoisie.

The republic, therefore, for men like Gambetta, meant fraternity, but fraternity took on a different appearance if it was approached from above rather than below. For Gambetta it meant the opening of doors and the breaking down of barriers. For Jules Ferry, fraternity was also the aim, but he interpreted it in a different way, seeing the problem from a different angle. He was not so much interested, as Gambetta was, in social mobility. He came of a family which had arrived, and was very solidly bourgeois. In the seventeenth century his forbears had been artisan bell founders, but his grandfather, a substantial tile manufacturer, rose to be mayor of his native town

[1] H. Mendras, *Les Paysans et la modernisation de l'agriculture* (1958), 84.

throughout the consulate and empire, while his father became its leading barrister and married the judge's daughter. Jules Ferry was a man of independent means. He married into the republicans' Alsatian industrial plutocracy. Hanotaux remembered him above all as a 'bourgeois, son of a bourgeois, brought up correctly in the bourgeois manner, wearing the bourgeois top hat and frock-coat, with a pale complexion between his mutton-chop whiskers, his fingers in his mouth, biting his nails, withdrawn, cold when he listened and cold when he spoke, intimidating anyone who addressed him by his straight and penetrating look, always certain of himself, affirmative and peremptory, lacking, above all else, any hold on the crowds'.[1] Ferry's mother had died when he was four years old; his conscientious and serious father supervised his education. One suspects—though no one has ever penetrated the psychology of his youth—that his intellectual approach to life was rooted in firmly repressed emotions. He saw the world as moved by large forces and an inexorable evolution, before which individual human passions were powerless. He found a refuge for his own individuality in the private pursuit of painting, which he studied for four years, at the same time as he prepared for the bar; at one stage he even thought of devoting himself completely to art. However, he was far too ambitious, determined, self-willed to be content with that. He had planned to enter the Conseil d'État, but he reached manhood just as the Second Empire was established and his family had no influence with it. He became a barrister instead, and was a moderately successful one, though he lacked any special gifts in this direction. His real talents, for clear, logical argument and vigorous exposition, emerged more forcefully in his work as a journalist. He joined Le Temps (a liberal–conservative paper), where he wrote commentaries on contemporary events, which showed exceptional powers of lucid analysis, penetration and detachment. He became famous for his articles attacking the financial irregularities in the rebuilding of Paris, which he republished under the clever title of Les Comptes fantastiques d'Haussmann; and in September 1870, when the Bonapartist regime fell, he was appointed to Haussmann's job.

Ferry was always intensely serious, and determined to be

[1] G. Hanotaux, Mon temps, 2 (1938), 178.

clear sighted. He considered the establishment of fraternity to be the great need of the time because he was profoundly conscious of the tensions which were straining and paralysing France. He saw the peasants 'avid for gain, isolated, mistrustful, spending their lives on the defensive', regarding everything as dangerous to them—the weather, the neighbours, strangers, and above all the police. He dismissed as a schoolboy dream the notion of them 'loving the parliamentary regime, developing a taste for the Paris press, following the details of diplomacy and being ready to die for some charter. Politics for the men of the fields will for long remain local, narrow, self-interested, timid. It is for this reason that universal suffrage, which is revolutionary only in the passport it carries, is at bottom nothing but a conservative instrument.'[1] Things, however, could not be left as they were. The problem of the relations between rich and poor was becoming more acute with the passing of time, because the separation of capital and labour was increasing. Wealth was becoming more and more concentrated in the hands of a few, and a powerful class of entrepreneurs was emerging. It was no use trying to prevent these developments: they were inevitable, and they could not be fought. They had their good side to them, because they were reducing the costs of production and so were contributing to a necessary improvement in the lot of the masses, enabling the workers to satisfy their just demands for increasing prosperity. However, the power of the capitalists had to be held 'wisely in check, with counterweights'. He saw two ways in which this could be done. First by the use of 'opinion, as the agent of social morality, upon the capitalists', and secondly by the collective organisation of the workers in trade unions—with increasing education to make this possible. Ferry thus accepted capitalism as 'a natural law' but condemned *laissez-faire* as 'immoral'. Pure individualism was antisocial. It was valuable as a weapon to fight against oppression, to secure independence, to destroy the restrictions of the *ancien régime*, but it was powerless to create anything; it led only to conflicts of egoism and was the negation of social life. The great problem of this period, he considered, was national unity, spiritual unity, harmony between the disparate elements in France, divided by alien traditions and torn by a

[1] *Discours et opinions de Jules Ferry*, ed. Paul Robiquet (1893–8), 1. 50.

century of political strife. He saw France as faced with almost
the same kind of problem as the U.S.A., which was likewise
attempting to build up a national identity.[1]

The Second Republic had attempted to achieve unity in a
spontaneous emotional outburst of fellow feeling, led by poets,
but Ferry dismissed this sentimentality of 1848 with contempt
as a miserable failure. He preferred therefore to talk not of
fraternity, but of sociability—a more scientific concept—as
his aim. The two great enemies of modern free thought, he
said, were mysticism and intellectual frivolity.[2] Religion could
no longer perform the function it once had; it was 'irremediably
decadent', and its 'theological illusions' could not stand up
to criticism. Its morals 'rest on an egoistic calculation which
places it in contradiction to the most imperious manifestations
of modern life. Its preoccupation with personal salvation is, in
itself, antisocial. It leads to the monastic ideal, that is to say, to
the condemnation of liberty and the desire for prosperity . . .
For the masses for whom life means liberty and who aspire to
prosperity, it can now offer only vague counsels of resignation.'
Religion had 'an incontestable social value' in the Middle
Ages, for resignation was highly appropriate when slavery and
oppression ruled—but it was no longer adequate.

Ferry's thinking was deeply influenced by that of Auguste
Comte, far more decisively than Gambetta's. Ferry was one of
the republican leaders who both read and absorbed Comte,
being introduced to positivism by one of Comte's disciples,
Deroisin. Ferry said he belonged 'to the religion of the Feasts
of Humanity'. Comte came to be one of the main philosophers
of the republican regime, compulsory studied in schools,
but mediated by many different interpretations. Ferry was
not a devotee of any one Comtist sect—neither that of Laffitte,
to whom he gave a chair at the Collège de France, nor that of
Littré, who set himself up as philosophical adviser to the
republicans. He drew his inspiration from his own reading and
understood Comte through the bias of his own personality.

The religion of humanity meant liberty for Ferry because it

[1] Article by Ferry, reprinted from *La Philosophie positive* (Sept.–Oct. 1867) in
Discours, 1. 581–8; two unpublished articles by him on industrialism, written for
the *Revue des Deux Mondes* in 1862, and published in *Discours*, 7. 447–535; cf. also
Discours, 3. 69.

[2] *Discours*, 2. 194–5.

encouraged the development of 'sociability', which he saw as a
growing force in modern society. He meant that the egoism he
attributed to Christianity was being replaced by a new outlook
with the right of the strongest giving way to the duty of the
strongest. Humanity was now emerging as 'no longer a fallen
race, doomed by original sin, dragging itself painfully in a
valley of tears, but as a ceaseless cavalcade marching forward
towards the light'. He felt himself 'an integral part of this great
Being which cannot perish, of this Humanity which is ceaselessly
improving' and he believed he 'had conquered his liberty
completely, because he was free from the fear of death'. The
next stage was to effect 'that fusion of classes which is the aim
of democracy'. Ferry wanted to make men equal, not to the
extent of 'the absolute levelling of social conditions which will
suppress relations of command and obedience', but in their
rights and in their dignity. Mutual respect must replace
animosity and contempt. Contracts, which gave both sides
rights and obligations, must replace the oppression of castes.
He saw the change as a moral much more than as an economic
one. Equality of this kind would not be possible so long as some
people were educated and others were not. 'I defy you ever to
make out of two such classes an egalitarian nation, a nation
animated by that spirit of unity and that confraternity of ideas
that makes the strength of true democracies, if, between these
two classes, there has not been the first *rapprochement*, the first
fusion which results from the mixing of the rich and the poor as
children on the benches of a school.' He wanted education to be
directed to creating a common morality. He wanted it placed
therefore in the hands of a united body of teachers. The influence of the Church must be removed. The teachers must
concern themselves with the inculcation of altruism, for human
nature had two fundamental and contradictory dimensions—
altruism and egoism—and education was the way to make the
former preponderant. Women must be educated as well as men.
Ferry read and quoted J. S. Mill on their emancipation. The
two great prejudices that needed to be eradicated in order to
achieve equality were, he said, class prejudice and sexual prejudice. Democracy was impossible so long as the Church kept
women in subjection. 'He who controls women controls everything, first because he controls the child and secondly because

he controls the husband.' Women must be given an education in harmony with that of men. The family must be united, so that society would be also. 'Modern anarchy' must be ended in the home as well as at work. He praised the plans of Condorcet, in the first Revolution, for a national educational system and in many ways implemented them, but whereas Condorcet aimed for happiness, Ferry more precisely wanted unity as the end product. When asked by Jaurès to summarise his ambitions, he replied decisively, 'My aim is to organise humanity without God and without King.' The word organise was significant.[1]

Whereas Gambetta concentrated on foreign affairs and electoral reform, Ferry preferred to be minister of education and he held that office for fifty months in all.[2] He inaugurated the regime's concentration on education and his work touched every branch of it. Primary education was made both free and compulsory; the teaching of the catechism in schools was abolished and replaced by 'civic and moral education', given by teachers, who were made lay state employees; every department was required to establish a training college for women primary teachers to replace the nuns; and state help was provided for the building of new schools. At the secondary level, state schools were established for girls, the classical syllabus was reformed to allow more individual thinking and less memorisation, gymnastics were made compulsory and military training introduced. The Catholic universities were suppressed. The details of these reforms and their social consequences will be discussed in separate chapters, devoted to the development of education. But from the political point of view, their effect was to introduce a great deal of confusion.

Far from establishing unity, the insistence on lay education, and the elimination of God from the civic manuals, divided the country profoundly, and exacerbated the clash of Church and republic. Ferry antagonised not only the Catholics, but the moderate republicans too, led by Jules Simon, and the radicals, led by Clemenceau, the former because they thought he was going too far, and the latter because he was not doing enough.

[1] Louis Legrand, *L'Influence du positivisme dans l'œuvre scolaire de Jules Ferry* (1961), 103–94.
[2] Feb. 1879–Nov. 1881, Jan.–Aug. 1882, Feb.–Nov. 1883.

Opinions were divided on this very delicate issue in infinite gradations. Ferry himself had no desire to destroy religion, because he believed it was going to die of its own accord; but the radicals were unwilling to wait patiently in this way; and Ferry, because of the balance of parliamentary forces, was obliged to use their support. His hopes of appeasement were dashed. The Catholics, for their part, could not conceive that a school could be neutral. Both sides in fact attributed far more influence to it than, in the long run, it proved to have. In the twentieth century it emerged that good Catholics could survive in the lay schools, obtaining their spiritual inspiration from their parents and priests; but it took a very long time for this to be seen and accepted. The battle was all the more misleading because Ferry, though he talked of a new moral code to be instilled into the young, meant by it nothing different from 'the good old morals of our fathers', and it was in effect barely distinguishable from the traditional one. What resulted, therefore, was a battle over principles much more that a real struggle of conflicting interests, but the subsequent history of the next fifty years was profoundly embittered as a result. The expulsion of the congregations was largely symbolic: it affected only some 5,000 men, who were soon allowed to return in any case; the establishment of free education (which some Catholics objected to, because they thought education should be a moral duty that fell on parents, rather than a right for children) was not a complete innovation, because primary education was largely free in most parts of the country; compulsory attendance was for long only partially implemented, and the physical training programmes—if they had any significance—were a farce in practice. The reforms of Ferry illustrate how ministers hovered, as it were, over the peaks of volcanoes, interpreting the omens and not infrequently spreading alarm. Several of the laws associated with him were in fact initiated by deputies, remodelled over and over again by the two houses, and often did more than the minister intended.

Just as Gambettism could be seen as the protest of the parvenus, so Ferryism has sometimes been described as the revenge of the Reformation, because a large number of the people around him were Protestants: Freycinet, Waddington, Léon Say, Le Royer, Jauréguiberry, Buisson, Pécaut, Cazot, Steeg,

Scheurer-Kestner, not to mention the fact that both he and Paul
Bert married Protestants. It will be seen, in another chapter,
how men like Renouvier, one of the philosophers of republicanism, preached Protestantism as the solution to France's problem
—a way of combining modernity and religion, order and freedom—and how the anticlerical movement was influenced by
Protestant thought. The Protestants in France as a whole were
not predominantly republicans, but belonged to every party.
The republican leaders who were Protestants were nearly all of
them non-practising renegades, men who had despaired of the
conservatism of their own sect and were seeking other solutions,
keeping only the severe morals of their upbringing. This whole
question of religion, anticlericalism and education is, however,
a very large one, which cannot be understood simply in terms of
the ideas of Ferry, of a few politicians or indeed of parliamentary
legislation. One can offer many other clever explanations of
anticlericalism, as a substitute, for example, for military revenge
against Germany, as a method of holding the republicans
together, as a way of diverting the attention of the workers from
their grievances against their employers. But anticlericalism
became intermeshed with so many aspects of life that its significance must be unravelled in a broader framework. The
struggle of republic against the Church becomes more complicated, and less straightforward, the closer one looks at it.

Ferry need not have alarmed the traditionalists as much as
he did. Polemic obscured his intentions, even though his
exceptional clarity of exposition enabled him to formulate the
guidelines of his actions far more precisely than Gambetta was
able to do. He accepted the inheritance of the old monarchy,
in that he believed in the maintenance of a strong centralised
state. In his liberal days under the Second Empire, he had
supported decentralisation, but he later retracted and said he
had learnt better. He insisted that the republic's government
should be one that really governed, denying that there was a
contradiction between the ideas of authority and progress. He
condemned the desire to diminish the government's power as
being 'in complete opposition to the state of our civilisation
and our customs, and all our traditions'. He considered that
'because of our historical antecedents, which cannot be
suppressed with a stroke of the pen', because the people 'were

accustomed to look above, through habits acquired over centuries, to seek supreme direction', a republican government, based on the popular will, had to provide leadership. The government must not be shackled by the chambers, but left free to carry out the demands of the people. The first of these, he claimed, was that order should be maintained: the people had no desire for radical transformations, and neither had he. He declared that he stood half-way between complacent fatalism on the one hand and irrational utopianism on the other. Progress was not achieved in quick changes nor by force: 'It is a slow development, an evolution, a phenomenon of social growth, of transformation, which starts first in men's ideas, and then descends into habits, and only finally passes into laws.' Governments had to provide protection and stability for this slow evolution to take place. The intransigent determination of the radicals to destroy the past, to refuse all compromise, was futile. The fact had to be accepted that democracy in France had to be based on the peasants. He considered it an achievement to have won them over to it. A peasant republic was 'not gay, not Athenian' but it was the only kind possible; and he was aware that, as he put it, the peasants had become republican because they were conservative.[2]

Ferry believed in a careful balance between state intervention and free enterprise. He accepted the capitalist system. 'Every legitimate profit,' he wrote, 'and in our system of unlimited free competition it is not possible to say that there are illegitimate profits—every profit corresponds either to an invention, or to an improvement or to better commercial or administrative organisation . . . To abolish the element of profit in the economic field is to suppress the essential stimulant of progress.' In his youth he had been a free trader, but he came to modify this view and helped to start the move back to protection. He thought that political liberty was one essential counterweight to the industrial oligarchy that capitalism produced, but he thought also that the government ought to encourage, and to a certain extent subsidise, mutual benefit societies, savings banks, insurance schemes with which the poor could improve their material lot. A government's duties, he said, 'certainly do not include finding immediate remedies' to social problems; but

<hr>

[1] *Discours*, 7. 53–6.   [2] *Discours*, 6. 170–3, 280; 1. 284–8; 7. 40–2.

though its 'functions were not therapeutic', it did have duties of 'social hygiene'.[1] One of the most characteristic of his reforms was to make the new lay university a corporation run by the professors themselves, independent, to a certain degree, both of the state and also of other influences. This may recall Comte's 'spiritual power', but it was also a half-way house between two extremes.

Ferry was a nationalist, in the tradition of the old monarchs perhaps even more than of the Revolution. He insisted that France could not be simply free, like Belgium or Switzerland; it must also be great, 'exercising on the destinies of Europe all the influence that it has, it must spread this influence over the world and carry everywhere its language, its customs, its flag, its arms, its genius'.[2] Apart from his educational work, he is associated also with the development of the French colonial empire. He was not originally responsible for the colonial expansion which took place in these years. It was civil servants, explorers, soldiers and sailors, acting under their own initiative, who carried the French flag to new lands. But Ferry supported them, once they had involved themselves, in order to save its honour. It was Baron de Courcel, director of political affairs at the Quai d'Orsay, who persuaded Gambetta to take Tunis. Ferry had never been interested in colonies and was the last of the ministers to be converted to taking action in this case. He did not intend it to be a precedent, and he has with some justification been accused of playing the whole episode down in such a manner that French colonialism never recovered: as a result of his tergiversation, Tunis appeared to be another Mexico expedition and the French became as divided about their colonies as about so many other things. It was Brazza who gave France its opportunities in Central Africa, but Ferry supported his expeditions and then won European sanction for his annexations at the Berlin Conference. In Madagascar Ferry was persuaded to act by the colonists of near-by Réunion, who were seeking trading advantages and who misled Ferry on the difficulties and the issues. He rather recklessly moved into war in Indo-China in order to consolidate the gains his predecessors had made. Only afterwards did Ferry develop a neo-mercantilist doctrine to justify his actions and to argue that

[1] *Discours*, 6. 236.   [2] *Discours*, 5. 220.

France needed colonies for its economic growth and its political prestige. In fact just as Britain acquired much of its empire at the very time when colonies were considered to be useless, so France acquired its when its population was falling, its colonial trade minute and its people had no interest in over-seas expansion. Ferry argued that France needed markets. It was only twenty years later that the economists realised that France could really use its colonies, but as a source of raw materials, not as markets.[1]

It was Ferry's patriotism that turned him into an imperialist but at the same time his imperialism alienated French patriots and caused his downfall. He achieved what he did thanks to the encouragement of Bismarck, who was glad to turn France's energies away from Alsace, but Ferry's realism in seeing that revenge had to be postponed for the time being won him accusations of treachery. He became one of the most unpopular men in France. No politician had been reviled so mercilessly since Émile Ollivier (whom he had admired in his youth and whose first wife he worshipped) had been publicly declared worthy of lynching. Twice assassinations were attempted on him and the radical press regretfully attributed his escapes to the fact that he had no heart to shoot. A temporary setback in Tonkin was the immediate source of his downfall but only because hate of him had become a 'sort of paroxysm'. During the Commune when he had organised rationing, he had won the opprobrious title of Ferry Famine: he was then Ferry the persecutor of the Church and now he was Ferry Tonkin, Ferry the valet of Bismarck, who was ruining his country in foreign adventures. He was particularly unpopular in Paris, which harboured so many extremists, so that he could not show his face in the streets without being insulted. All his efforts to defend himself in newspapers, which he bought up with the help of an impressive collection of capitalists, but which he ran with incompetent journalists, were in vain.[2]

His failure was the product of his manner as much as of his policy. As the wilier Freycinet wrote: 'He was too confident in

[1] F. Pisani-Ferry, *Ferry et le partage du monde* (1962); C. A. Julien, 'Jules Ferry', in *Les Politiques d'expansion impérialiste* (1949), 11–72.

[2] René Bastien, '*L'Estafette*, le journal de Jules Ferry 1889–93' (unpublished D.E.S. mémoire, Nancy, 1963).

his own intelligence and wisdom, and had adopted an air of
disdain towards the moderates which recalled Guizot. The
parliamentary successes he had won brought about in him that
phenomenon frequent in men who have been in power long—
the evil of infallibility. The disciples of Gambetta around him
who formed the most solid core of his majority suffered from
this manner which was so little in harmony with their own
tendencies. The anathemas he cast upon reforms made them
uneasy. Several of them got into the habit of voting with the
radicals.' The hostility to him was partly personal, partly the
result of his very competence of which he was the victim just as
Gambetta had been the victim of his own popularity. Ferry
himself admitted that he could not be considered representative
of the masses. He had long thought that once he had passed his
reforms, he could then follow a policy of moderation. By 1885
he had concluded that he had no option at all. He regretted the
sectarianism which had introduced such bitterness into politics.
It was necessary to mark time, for at least four years. His
reforms, he said, had not been 'digested' by the masses, there
was a noticeable movement of reaction amongst them and it
was not possible to pursue 'great innovations'.[1] This was not
quite a confession of failure, but an acknowledgement of the
barriers that separated the different levels of republicanism.[2]

The republican system required ambition to be kept in check.
Ministers who threatened to become dictators were invariably
eliminated, though they might be briefly rescued from retirement to deal with serious crises. The kind of minister who was
most acceptable to parliament was a person like Freycinet,
who made it his rule to serve it, and who had no ambition to
dominate it. His long tenure of office shows how power rested
ultimately with the deputies and the civil servants. Freycinet
was prime minister four times, and a member of nine other
ministries. He was senator for Paris for forty-three years.
Originally he was a civil servant on whom Gambetta picked,
simply on the grounds of ability, to assist him in technical and

[1] J. Ferry, *Lettres, 1846–1893* (1914), 388.
[2] The fullest biography is by Maurice Reclus, *Jules Ferry 1832–1893* (1947); cf.
G. Froment–Guieysse, *Jules Ferry* (1937), the memorial volume, *Jules Ferry* (1894),
and P. Sorlin, *Waldeck-Rousseau* (1966), which is the best guide to the politics of
this period.

administrative matters; he had no oratorical gifts, no popular appeal, no political standing or even allegiances but he became one of the most powerful men of the republic because he carried to perfection his role as an intermediary, a conciliator and a manager. He was a Protestant engineer, and a graduate of the Polytechnic. He managed the Midi Railway for several years under the Second Empire, and was Gambetta's administrative assistant at the ministry of war in 1871. His political views can only be defined as 'moderate'. Though he published two volumes of memoirs, they are written in such carefully guarded style, with no offence given to anyone, and studied compliments to everyone, that it is difficult to conclude anything positive about him. Self-effacing modesty ensured that he made no enemies: his aim, he said, was simply to be an organiser and administrator of the great ideas which great men had, to be a scientist in the service of the republic. The extraordinary effect this had was seen on the occasion of his first election to the senate. Gambetta put him up and vouched for him, against the objections of those who doubted his republicanism. Victor Hugo was considered the master of this election, as the leading republican luminary of the senate, and his approval was essential to every candidate. Freycinet cultivated him with fawning flattery. But Hugo considered himself free to advocate radical policies—like an amnesty for the Communards—which was not to the taste of the staid local councillors who formed the bulk of the electorate for the senatorial seats. Hugo was elected last but one. Freycinet, though completely unknown to them, was elected top of the list. They wanted a man who had no dreams of grandeur, but would make the system work in the way they wanted it to work. This is the explanation of the dominance of safe mediocrities in the republic.

Gambetta admired Freycinet's skill at giving clear summaries of technical questions: he called him 'un filtre'. Freycinet certainly excelled at producing formulae to solve difficult problems, which had the appearance of clarity or even firmness, but he knew also how to skirt round difficult issues at the same time. Until he established himself in politics, he remained in the civil service, obtaining repeated periods of leave while he carried out political or industrial jobs. He was an exceptional example of the way business, bureaucracy and politics avoided conflict by mutual penetration. The result of this was an approach to problems which Freycinet summarised in two words—opportunism and union. This was what guided his whole political career. Opportunism meant that though one should be bold in one's ideas, one should be prudent in executing them. He was too wily to make the mistake Ferry made, of pushing his reforms through quickly, because he thought they were right. He saw danger in the multiplicity of innovations and in excessive haste in bringing them forward. Priorities should be established and the more controversial measures postponed. For, correcting Ferry's other mistake, he saw the greatest danger of all to be the disintegration of the republican party. Controversy and haste would kill it. 'Concentration' was his watchword, which meant that the ideal government was a coalition of all factions. He devoted much of his career to trying to get the radicals—Ferry's great enemies—to join with the moderate republicans in holding office: together, they would have an impregnable monopoly. He advocated conciliation towards the enemies of the republic, but insisted that it should be offered from a position of strength. He was in favour of purging the administration of hostile elements, of building up a self-conscious republican party, and then of admitting outsiders who were willing to accept this system. Thus though Freycinet entered politics as a protégé of Gambetta, and always spoke of him with profound reverence, he soon developed an independent line. He refused to serve in Gambetta's great ministry, knowing that it would not last long, and he was careful not to join the right-wing republicans—with whom he had much in common—because they had only limited chances of getting power. The reward of this discretion was that he was the middle-of-the-road choice on whom everybody could agree. Freycinet's kind of government meant papering over divisions, excluding men of energy, and sacrificing all to stability. Freycinet believed that the divisions of France were superficial, that what it needed was conscientious and gradual reform, and that political stability was the essential basis for progress. He had above all a keen sense of material interests. These are what Freycinet represented. He reflected a vital part of the republican mentality, as opposed to its ideology.

The consequences of this kind of attitude were revealed in

Freycinet's public works programme. He drew this up in the late 1870s and obtained final parliamentary approval for it in 1883. It was an enormously expensive plan to extend the railway network of France on a scale even greater than Napoleon III had attempted. It was in due course carried out, and France's railways were doubled in length over the next twenty years. This steady transformation of the country was something that deserves as much attention as the Parisian political debates, because it was one of the most important local preoccupations, one of the most impressive economic achievements and one of the greatest financial scandals of the period. The contradiction or conjuring trick contained in the type of republicanism Freycinet represented was that it attempted to reform the country without any increase in taxation. Instead the republic promised and indeed gave reductions in taxations to various sectional interests, particularly the peasants, balancing equality and privilege with exceptional skill. This meant that within a few years of their gaining office, the republicans had plunged France into recurrent deficits. They nevertheless wanted to embark on this grandiose public works programme.

They did it by means of a remarkable deal with the railway companies. Out of office they had looked on these companies as a resurrection of feudalism, bastions of reaction run by monarchist directors, and they had preached the nationalisation of railways. France had since the very beginning been divided between those who had wanted the state to build the railways and those who had favoured private enterprise. Fear that the state would become too powerful if it entered this new industry, and fear of the heavy taxes which the vast capital expenditure necessary would involve, had resulted in a characteristic compromise solution evolved by the July Monarchy and the Second Empire and completed, without fundamental change, by the Third Republic. The accusations made against the first two of these regimes, of being run for the benefit of the speculators, seemed to become even truer under the last of them. The principle adopted was that the freehold property of the railways remained with the state, which gave concessions to private companies for up to ninety-nine years. Ultimately, the state expected to get all this property back, worth as much as the whole national debt. Meanwhile it was saved any large outlay of state funds. Under the Second Empire, when profits were considerable, the railway companies did well and the state did not lose anything. But in 1865 a new situation arose. The major intercity lines had been built, and the problem of dealing with less profitable local railways presented itself. The state refused to subsidise these, but offered a guarantee on the loans which the companies raised to build them with. In return the state was to receive a share of any profits. The local railways, of course, failed to make any profits, and quite a few of them were threatened with bankruptcy.

In 1871 the first thought of the republicans was to nationalise everything. But the six large companies were far too expensive to buy out. So attention was turned to the ailing local companies; and in 1878 the state bought up a number of them in the Charentes and the Centre. This was thought of as being a trial run, to see how state ownership could improve things; but since the lines bought had not been commercially viable in any case, it was not a successful experiment and greatly weakened the case of the partisans of nationalisation. The Second Empire had already started what the Third Republic took to greater extremes, the habit of yielding to local pressure to authorise railways in every constituency, for largely electoral reasons. The question then was, who would foot the bill? In the Charentes experiment, the state had tried to build railways itself, but it did not have enough engineers to pursue this policy, nor was it willing to borrow the capital necessary. When the era of deficits began in 1882, the conservative financiers of the republic, led by Léon Say, insisted that the state must stop borrowing. The republicans, after having threatened nationalisation, therefore capitulated to the companies.

A deal was made by which the six main companies would agree to build the vast new network of secondary railways. They would raise the money themselves, so that the national debt would not be burdened and taxation could remain steady. They agreed to pay the state two-thirds of any profits made. But in return they exacted very favourable conditions. The state would subsidise the construction of these lines to the extent of seven-eighths, from funds which the companies raised on its behalf, and which the state would then pay back to them in annuities. The state would guarantee the dividends and the interest on loans of the companies. The companies therefore could not lose. The politicians made out that the state would thus get a railway network built without endangering the credit of the state and without further taxation, and that it was unlikely that it would ever have to fulfil its promise in guaranteeing the companies' finances. This, however, proved too optimistic a forecast. All but one of the companies failed to make adequate profits. The deal of 1883 was made at the end of a period of boom and at the beginning of a long-drawn-out depression. Railway revenue failed to progress as fast as the state had calculated. So the bargain turned out to be all in favour of the companies. Thus in the eleven years following it, 7,016 kilometres of railway were built, at a cost to the companies of 1,200 million francs. But the state was called upon to pay out 926 million francs in guarantees on interests. The person who had actually signed the conventions with the railway companies was a Jewish merchant, Raynal, minister of public works at the appropriate time. In 1895 the radicals attempted to impeach him for damaging the interests of the state. The six-day debate in parliament brought out a lot of interesting information about this complicated negotiation. The radicals sought to unmask it as a gigantic hoax or swindle at the expense of the country. But nothing was done about it, because there were too many beneficiaries from it.

Thus railway shares had become a gilt-edged investment, even though the railways were not making a profit, and even though the state was having to bolster them, subsidising a small section of the community at the expense of the rest. Electoral pressures were successfully met. Freycinet's original estimate for the whole cost of his programme had been four milliard francs: parliament had doubled it, so that nearly every constituency got a share of the spoils. The railways, in any case, were built, so that whereas in 1870 there were 17,400 kilometres, by 1910 there were 39,000. Outwardly, there was consistent progress; chaotic competition was avoided. The state was able to keep a supervisory control over the railways and to enjoy the illusion that it was their ultimate proprietor: the principles of centralisation were safeguarded. But at the same time the railway companies increasingly became the great capitalist bogy-men of the republic, draining its blood. This was one of the legacies of opportunism. It will be seen in due course that when the radicals won power and dealt with the problem, their policy was just as equivocal.[1]

Another example of the way reform had to be dropped or postponed is national military service. Freycinet's experience in the Franco-Prussian war had convinced him of the serious inadequacy of his country's military organisation. He rejected the conservative complacency of Thiers. He believed universal short-term service was essential. However, the forces of inertia were so powerful, and his own system of pleasing everyone so irreconcilable with drastic reform, that he succeeded in obtaining a minor modification to the professional army's five-year service only in 1889. What he achieved then was only a feeble compromise (reducing the period of service to three years): it made little real difference, because the bulk of the conscripts served only one year, and were not to be used for front-line fighting. France still did not have a properly trained fighting force. Only in 1905 were the exemptions and inequalities ended. Freycinet's inability to do more is particularly significant because he placed great store on military reform and expected important political results from it. He thought that if everybody served in the army they would learn the need to obey in civil life also, 'to understand and to accept everywhere the principle of authority and the hierarchy without which there is no stable organisation. As a result, the military establishment, instead of being in opposition to civil society, will become its foundation and best support.' His failure to bring this about, like his failure to end the formalism of bureaucracy, which in his youth he had seen as a major evil, was, however, an inevitable consequence of the policy of conciliation he adopted.[2]

[1] Henry Peyret, *Histoire des chemins de fer* (1949), is the best brief general history; Richard de Kaufmann, *La Politique française en matière de chemins de fer* (1900), is a massive study with excellent summaries of the parliamentary debates; cf. C. Colson, *Les Chemins de fer et le budget* (1896); Henry Ferrette, *Étude historique sur l'intervention financière de l'État dans l'établissement des lignes de chemins de fer* (1896).

[2] C. de Freycinet, *Souvenirs* (1912), 1. 90, 96, 160, 254-5, 287; 2. 79-83 and *passim*; Noël de Clazan, 'M. de Freycinet', *Le Correspondant*, 291 (1923), 693-712; Hector Depasse, *De Freycinet* (1883); André Beauvier, *Visages d'hier et d'aujourd'hui* (1911), 241-7; Capt. W. Zaniewicki, 'L'Œuvre de Freycinet au ministère de la guerre 1888-1893', *Revue historique de l'armée*, 19, no. 2 (1963), 55-72; review of his scientific work in *Journal des savants* (Mar. 1896), 125-32.

One can thus see three different ways in which republicanism produced stalemate and immobility. First, the hostility shown to powerful ministers by the deputies meant that those who wanted to change things drastically were kept out of office. Secondly, the ministers who did get into power adopted in varying degrees the traditions of the ancient monarchy and upheld the rights of the state to a degree which was incompatible with the attainment of the reforms they had preached in opposition. Thirdly, those ministers whom the deputies allowed to hold office could survive only by making compromises to uphold unity and by respecting vested interests. The republic, which originally had been viewed as the instrument for a thorough transformation of the country, had become strangely conservative. This had become clear within a dozen years of its foundation. The problem now is why it could not be got out of its rut.

8. Solidarism

AFTER the establishment of the republic, its victory over monarchism and its inauguration of a lay educational system and a colonial empire, one is generally given the impression that, by the 1890s, the regime represented a spent force, with nothing new to offer. Jacques Chastenet, in his six-volume history of the Third Republic, claimed each decade in it had a special character. The 1870s were marked by a determination to recover from the humiliating defeat of the Franco-Prussian war and the Paris exhibition of 1878 was a gesture to show that France was itself again. Eleven years later, the exhibition of 1889 demonstrated that the republic was securely established, and preaching its dedication to science. But after that the exhibition of 1900 'lacked a soul': France had no new ideal. The Panama scandal (1892–3) and the Dreyfus affair (1894–9) gave the impression that internal bickering, corruption and an ageing oligarchy had brought reform to a halt. Stagnation appears to be the mark of the nineties. There is a traditional view that only in 1905, when the clerical question was more or less solved, did the republic at last free itself from its old preoccupations and henceforth it was the social question which dominated politics. The *fin de siècle* is thus an interlude.

This kind of generalisation is the result of regarding French history as a chronicle, in which laws and crises follow each other in blundering succession. To concentrate on the scandals is to give excessive importance to symptoms and to lose sight of continuities and breaks of deeper significance. It is wrong, first of all, to imagine that interest in social questions became predominant only after 1905. The opportunists are usually criticised for not having a social policy, but the previous chapter has shown that though they may not have passed many laws on the subject, social questions were very much in the forefront of their minds. They believed in political and educational solutions to them, and those which they offered did seem to win much support. They were not blind to the threat of socialism, even though that was then attracting only a tiny minority. And moreover, in the nineties a new social doctrine— solidarism—was virtually adopted by the republican government to meet the increasing challenges of industrialisation.

It is wrong, secondly, to assume that after 1905 religious disagreements ceased to be a major divisive force, even though Church and state were separated. The problems facing the French did not change drastically at the turn of the century: the unequal distribution of wealth, education and religious belief was a permanent feature, and successive regimes and governments had policies on each of them. These are the acknowledged continuities in French history. The question that remains unresolved is why so little headway was made in tackling them. The nineties are particularly illuminating in providing the answer, for they were a period when original efforts were made to adopt new approaches, in institutional, religious, social and diplomatic ways. This chapter will describe these efforts—some less well known than others—and will try to explain why they were largely unsuccessful. The failure is very important, because it meant that France could not get out of its rut. The purpose of this group of chapters is to indicate what this rut was, what ways of thinking and what inherited institutions were so firmly entrenched that they cast off reforms like water off a duck's back.

In politics, a situation of deadlock had been reached through the triangular conflict of state, ministers and parliament. This could only be ended by revolution or a *coup d'état*. That is what Boulangism attempted. Boulangism has a very colourful side to it, with the result that it is usually studied in a largely personal way. The vanity and ambition of General Boulanger with his blond beard, on his white horse, turning discipline in the army upside-down, trying to win popularity with the junior officers against his fellow generals, collecting votes in election after election, negotiating with every opposition party, accepting vast sums from the royalists, consorting with shady political adventurers, placing all his bets on being able to capture power, but lacking the nerve to be a new Saint-Arnaud or the character to be another Mahdi, so finally running away to Belgium and committing suicide on the grave of his mistress, provides an entertaining contrast to the boring speeches of the grey-beard politicians.[1] This comic-opera approach has led a recent historian of the Third Republic, Guy Chapman, to call Boulangism 'a trivial and tedious episode, which should never have happened and almost certainly never would have but for the absence of men of character and courage. It is surprising that after so much fret so little resulted from it.'[2] This judgement, however, is precisely the opposite of that which this chapter will put forward. The Boulangist crisis deserves to be compared with that of 1848 rather than with some adventurer's intrigue. It had a similar social background, and it was similarly a challenge to a whole system of government. For twenty years the politicians were absorbed in getting a sufficient measure of agreement in the country to consolidate the republic. They thought they had found it. Ferry was proud of having got the peasants behind him. 'We must seek nothing further beyond this for a long time to come,' he said. Boulangism questioned this. The country's judgement, as between Ferry and Boulanger, was a vital one, pregnant with implications.

By 1885 republicanism had shown its limitations as well as its merits. It could be accused of being, like the July Monarchy, a joint stock company to exploit the country for a small group of shareholders. The opportunists who held power ceased to command a majority in the country. Ferry was unable to hold his policy of marking time for a decade. Just as Louis-Philippe was abandoned by some of his supporters, so Ferry found radicalism undermining his system. The deputies discovered the electoral advantages of criticising the government. The policy of conciliation, preached by the ministers, was unworkable in the constituencies, which were seething with a new generation of ambition. In 1885 the opportunists lost almost half their seats, falling to about 200 and the radicals returned with 170. The conservatives, profiting from this division, doubled their numbers (from 90 to 180). Parliament was thus faced with a stalemate of three almost equal and irreconcilable parties. The reformers made a survey of the opinions of the deputies and found that there was not a single policy for which a majority could be found. Out of 543 deputies, the most who could be

---

[1] Saint-Arnaud, general in charge of the *coup d'état* of 1851; it was Ferry who made the comparison with the Mahdi.

[2] Guy Chapman, *The Third Republic: The First Phase* (1962), 291.

got to agree on anything were 240 who were in favour of a reduction in the period of military service, 184 who wanted the separation of Church and state, and 159 who favoured income tax. The opportunists could not stand still, since alliance with the right would mean abandoning their anticlericalism and favouritism, and alliance with the left would lead them to reforms they did not want.

The only way out of the impasse was a revision of the constitution. Different parties viewed this each in their own way, but they were agreed on the destruction of the system Gambetta and Ferry had established. Numerous grievances were ready to hand to justify and support the agitation. The most important was economic. Opportunism was failing to give prosperity. The peasants were suffering from the import of foreign wheat and from the phylloxera crisis; the fall in the value of their land began ironically with the establishment of 'the republic of peasants'. The building, metallurgic and mining industries suffered a serious slump after 1885, with around a quarter of a million workers being thrown out of work. The impact of this was all the more noticeable in that it was concentrated in certain areas and in Paris worst of all. Import duties were now levied to save the peasant, so the price of bread rose in 1887, and increased further because of the bad harvest of that year. A general slackening of economic activity plunged the state's budget into greater deficits: receipts from taxation between 1883 and 1887 were repeatedly inferior to the estimates. The Wilson scandal (the president's son-in-law selling decorations) revealed corruption in high places, barely concealed behind a front of moral rectitude.[1]

The massive support that united behind General Boulanger showed how powerful were the forces which rejected the opportunist republic. The royalists are said to have put between 6 and 8 million francs in the campaign in his favour. Even the U.S.A. joined in, with the publisher of the *New York Herald* and an American cable magnate contributing enormous cheques.[2] Radicals and Bonapartists and socialists, Jews and anti-Semites, nationalists, mobsters and intriguers, combined

---

[1] For the wider significance of the Wilson scandal, which was the climax of a fascinating career as a press magnate, see vol. 2.

[2] Frederic H. Seager, *The Boulanger Affair* (Ithaca, New York, 1969), 258, 186.

strangely in the hope that he would overthrow the system. But the system survived, because it too had great strength behind it. First, it tried to meet the challenge by carrying out reforms, to dish the radicals. Floquet, a radical, but much mellowed as president of the chamber of deputies, was made prime minister. When he failed to stem the tide, force was used. Constans was appointed minister of the interior. This bankrupt manufacturer of lavatory cisterns who had then become a professor of law, deputy and governor-general of Indo-China, had survived accusations of corruption, and won fame as a master of election management. He threatened Boulanger with arrest, but cleverly allowed him time to escape, which Boulanger obligingly did. The agitation was quickly snuffed out. The radicals, terrified by the monster they had created, agreed to co-operate with the opportunists in the election of 1889. The republic was saved.[1]

The importance of Boulangism was twofold. On the one hand it showed the limits of opportunism. Ferry did not fully understand the Boulangist movement and dismissed it as the work of extremists manœuvred by monarchists. He failed to appreciate the social discontents which had given Boulanger much of his popular support. But so too did the radicals. The result was that the republic lost the chance of keeping the support of the industrial workers. These had rallied to Boulanger in the hope of getting a government which would do something to alleviate their distress. The crisis was a double disillusionment for them: not only the opportunists, but even the radicals revealed themselves as being incapable of really understanding the workers. As a result it was the socialists who became the backbone of Boulangism when the radicals deserted it. They defined it clearly as a movement for social reform, for action to meet the economic crisis, with constitutional revision as the means. Boulangism survived after the flight of the general, to become one of the elements in a reinvigorated socialism. It turned Jaurès, hitherto an opportunist, into a socialist. It was thus an important catalyst in the development of a new social conscience. But secondly the apparent defeat of Boulangism confirmed the conservative tendencies of the regime. Ferry failed

[1] The result was 363 united republicans, 167 conservatives, 38 Boulangists (18 of these being in Paris).

to become president of the republic, because too many people hated him, but he was elected president of the senate, and his system was thus entrenched in that bastion of moderation. The long-term significance of Boulangism is that it confirmed that, in a crisis, the republic would show itself to be conservative rather than attempt innovation, and that though its oratory was all about justice, its instincts rated stability more highly. The ultimate meaning of republicanism is to be found in the values which it thus tried to preserve, and from which it could not escape.[1]

By the 1890s, the time seemed to have come for a new classification of political divisions, on the basis of the changed realities of the time. Monarchy was no longer a practical possibility. The nobles and notables who had attached themselves to it needed to find a new outlet for their ambitions. The question was whether the republicans could be flexible enough to provide this, to give them some stake in the regime, democratically accepting the fact of their surviving influence and growing economic power. The position of the Church also had to be reconsidered. The battle against its influence had become somewhat confused, as was shown by the contradiction between the polemical rhetoric and the moderation of what was actually done. The republicans were not as totally at war with the Church as appeared, and, for their part, many Church leaders were conscious that the war had got out of hand and that they could not profit from its continuation. The problem of how to deal with industrialisation, with socialism and with increased expectations among the masses in general demanded new thinking. There were good reasons therefore for the 'new spirit', which Spuller, Gambetta's faithful disciple, demanded and for the *ralliement*, by which the former enemies of the republic were invited into its fold.

[1] Jacques Néré, 'La Crise industrielle de 1882 et le mouvement boulangiste' (Paris doctorat d'État, 1959, unpublished, in the Sorbonne library), is the fullest study of the social and economic basis of the movement; also his complementary thesis, 'Les Élections de Boulanger dans le département du Nord' (unpublished, 1959). A. Dansette, *Le Boulangisme* (1938), and F. H. Seager, *The Boulanger Affair* (New York, 1969), are also very able accounts, from different viewpoints. For contemporary views see Mermeix, *Les Coulisses du boulangisme* (1890), and Maurice Barrès, *L'Appel au soldat* (1900).

As early as 1880 the Church had tried to make a deal with
Freycinet for mutual concessions. The very news of it had caused
parliament to force his resignation, but in 1890–2 Freycinet
was back in office as prime minister, and once more open to
offers. Several attempts had already been made in the 1880s to
reach some agreement. In 1886 Raoul Duval, an energetic
Bonapartist industrialist, had attempted to start a conservative
alliance against socialism and radicalism, which would have
cut across the old alignments and created a *Droite républicaine*;
his death a year later destroyed what small chances it had of
success. In 1887 Baron Mackau, leader of the monarchists in
parliament, had offered the opportunist Rouvier his support,
to save the republic from the radicals, but Mackau then went
on to back Boulanger, with the hope of overthrowing the republic, so it is not surprising that these monarchist overtures were
treated with great suspicion. In 1888 Albert de Mun had tried
to found a Catholic Party, free of dynastic attachments,
modelled on the Centre Party in Germany, but his social ideas
worried the conservatives and the pope, fearing that he would
be unable to control it, ordered its dissolution. A basic difficulty of any *ralliement* was that in order to benefit from it, the
Catholics needed to be united in a party; but their leaders,
having royalist backgrounds, could never be trusted by the
republicans and so could never obtain office, however many
concessions they made. The more concessions they made to the
republicans, the more they lost their royalist supporters.

This was the dilemma that ruined the efforts of Jacques
Piou. In 1890 he founded another 'Constitutional Right', consisting of Catholic and royalist deputies who, after the Boulangist débâcle, were willing to make a deal. They would abandon
their support of a royalist restoration in return for religious and
economic concessions: that religious instruction should be
allowed in primary schools which wished to give it, that the
laws exiling the pretenders should be repealed, that public
expenditure and taxation should be reduced, and that decentralisation, social legislation and tariff protection should be
introduced. Piou's idea was to collect support on the right
to enable opportunists (who now usually called themselves
progressists) to do without radical votes and so to end the
anticlerical campaign. In February 1893 he agreed to be

satisfied if the government merely enforced the school laws in a 'neutral' way, abandoning the demand for their repeal. He declared that he accepted the republic *with its laws* and he changed the name of his party from 'Constitutional Right' to 'Republican Right'. But in the election of that year only thirty-six of his ninety-four candidates were elected. He himself, de Mun and Lamy, the three leaders, were defeated. The royalists as a whole refused to accept the bankruptcy of their movement and fifty-eight intransigent ones were elected as such. The dying cause of the monarchy refused to die. The confusion of the monarchist and clerical issues led to a stalemate.

It is true the advocates of a *ralliement* had mixed motives. A new pope, Leo XIII, brought a new willingness to negotiate and to compromise, based on a realism and an awareness of social change which marked an important modification in the Church's attitudes. But the republicans were, not surprisingly, suspicious of the fact that he hoped to widen the appeal of the Church by this modernisation, that his attack on Gallicanism would strengthen his own power, and that, from the diplomatic point of view, he sought in France an ally to help him recover the papal states from Italy. Cardinal Lavigerie, whose famous toast to the republic in 1890 publicly launched the idea of the *ralliement*, believed that a modification of the Church's attitude to the republic was essential, because the Church's very existence was at stake: he feared that the ending of the concordat would ruin its finances. He did not expect the republic to last very long, at least in its present anticlerical form; he urged co-operation with it simply to reduce its hostility to the Church, and to keep the Church going until the inevitable collapse. Nevertheless, Étienne Lamy, whom Leo commissioned to found a republican Catholic party, was one of 363 deputies who had followed Gambetta in 1876, and he was willing to accept that the majority of Frenchmen were not active Catholics. He wanted the Church to work not for a purely Catholic programme, but for the end of anticlericalism in the name of liberty, to unite, that is, liberals and Catholics. In the election of 1898, he put up Catholic candidates wherever they had some chance of success, and, when they were defeated on the first ballot, he arranged for them to desist in favour of the opportunist-progressists in return for promises of a relaxation of the anticlerical campaign. However, he could find few men who were both republican and Catholic, able and willing to stand as candidates. He was unable to impose a central control over local politics, and his plans for a united party collapsed. The pope's hope of a *ralliement* was sabotaged above all by the parish priests, who, since they were the people who suffered most from the republic's anticlericalism, had little sympathy for the idea of reconciliation. The Assumptionist Order, important for the newspapers it controlled, waged a vociferous campaign against the republic, oblivious of the papal commands.

On the other side, the republican government was half-hearted in welcoming these overtures from the Church. It paid lip-service to religion as a great moral and social force which, provided it was freed from the domination of the royalists, could be an invaluable weapon against socialism. It allowed unauthorised religious congregations—even the Jesuits—to go about their work unmolested. It took local circumstances into consideration in its enforcement of the laicisation programme, and did not force the clergy out of primary schools when there were no ready replacements. But it was worried by the accusation that it depended on the aid of the reactionary Right, on the obscurantist Catholics, for its survival, that it had sold out the traditions of the republic. The fear of progressing beyond these traditions paralysed it; and in any case it could not carry its supporters in a new policy. The local republican notables, even the prefects, could not abandon the habits of a generation, and continued their anticlerical struggles, just as the parish clergy did. The national leaders were powerless. They would not offer the Catholics any share of power. They were willing to accept Catholic votes only with reservations. They said their republic was an open one, but it was not to be handed over to the Catholics, *ouverte* but not *livrée*. The *ralliement* was a failure. The attempt to achieve it had shown that some people had a vision of politics organised on new lines. But the clerical obsession could not be exorcised.[1]

[1] Alexander Sedgwick, *The Ralliement in French Politics* (Cambridge, Mass., 1965), using the papers of Étienne Lamy; Maxime Lecomte, *Les Ralliés. Histoire d'un parti 1886–1898* (1898); Denys Cochin, *L'Esprit nouveau: origine et décadence* (n.d., about 1912); David Shapiro, 'The Ralliement in the Politics of the 1890s', in *The Right in France 1890–1919*, St. Antony's Papers, no. 13 (1962); Emmanuel Barbier, *Histoire du catholicisme libéral*, vol. 2 (1924); id., 'Du royalisme à la république ou

In the economic field, there was a similar inability to meet the challenge of international competition, or to adopt new attitudes in industrial planning. The failure can be illustrated in the career of Jules Méline, who as minister of agriculture under Ferry and who as prime minister in 1896–8, gave clearest expression to this policy of resistance to change. Méline is known to history as the principal creator of the far-reaching system of protection established in the 1880s and 1890s, and called the Méline tariff.[1] Some historians have tended to dismiss him as a mere tool in the hands of the industrialists; others have it the other way round and believe he represented the agricultural interest, using the industrialist for its benefit. His skill as a middleman is certainly revealed in this double reputation. He won fame as the saviour of both industry and agriculture.

He was himself neither a manufacturer nor a farmer and he knew very little about either occupation. His daughter said that he could never tell the difference between a sheaf of wheat and one of barley. He came of modest, lower middle-class stock. His father had owned some land but had also been *greffier de la justice de paix* of Remiremont, a very junior civil servant. His mother was the daughter of a provincial notary of peasant origin. Méline's ambitions always remained modest, circumscribed within his own small world. He dreamt of a career in the *Bureau de l'enregistrement* (which registered documents and levied stamp duties). He became a barrister, but did not achieve any particular success. He lived most of his life on his salary as a deputy, in the same humble apartment in the rue de Commaille.[2] He made no pretence of being other than what he was, though he was very proud of his wife who came of a family of small calico manufacturers, representing a marriage above his station and setting a seal on his rise in the social hierarchy, minimal though that was. He entered politics, moved neither by enthusiasm, nor by passion nor by a vivid imagination, but as an essentially practical, common-sensical,

le ralliement du marquis de Solages', *Annales du Midi* (Jan. 1959), 59–70. For provincial opinion see Gaston Routier, *La Question sociale et l'opinion du pays. Enquête du Figaro* (1894).

[1] E. O. Golob, *The Méline Tariff* (New York, 1944); cf. Marcel Dijol, *Situation économique de la France sous le régime protectioniste de 1892* (n.d., about 1910).

[2] No. 4, Paris 7ᵉ.

stubborn party worker, with a smiling and somewhat sly equanimity. Small, thin, with slight gestures and a discreet bearing, he gave the impression of being an obscure provincial notary. As a student in Paris he had been an admirer of Proudhon, whose ideal of a society of satisfied petty proprietors reflected his own exactly. He had joined the Freemasons in 1865 but by 1870 he had left them. He was too *sage* for their increasing bellicosity. He had reservations about Ferry's anticlerical programme. He believed in a lay state, but also in tolerance. He was a deist who thought that religion was inextinguishable. His wife was a fervent Catholic and he approved of his daughters being brought up to practise that religion. He had worked for Thiers in the electoral campaign of 1869 and he ever retained a genuine admiration for this incarnation of the self-made provincial. He spoke with reverence of Jules Ferry as a great statesman but he was never on intimate terms with him. Ferry was too aristocratic for him. His patron in politics was Claude, senator and president of the *conseil général* of Vosges, who had been a foreman in a textile factory, rose to be its director, and then its owner. 'I am only the pupil of M. Claude', he said, and if he had gone further than his master, 'it was only the force of circumstance.' Méline typified the petty bourgeois in a static society, whose mentality the Méline tariff helped to save and perpetuate.[1]

Méline was not an economist nor a theorist, nor had he studied the controversy between free trade and protection in any serious way. He had certain elementary beliefs. 'The best economic regime for a country', he said, 'is that which produces the greatest amount of employment.' He stated plainly that he was an opportunist not a doctrinaire, and 'if I were an Englishman, I should be a free trader'. But he had no wish that the French should become like the English. His tariffs have been criticised for slowing down the pace of industrial development, but then that was precisely what Méline wanted. He was against industrialisation, and here the continuity of attitudes between Proudhon, Thiers and himself is evident. He admitted industry had produced some material benefits, but on the other hand it was draining the countryside of labourers, it was

[1] A. M. Heber-Suffrin, 'Les Débuts politiques de Jules Méline 1870–1885' (unpublished D.E.S. mémoire, Nancy, 1963).

always having crises of overproduction, and in the future increased mechanisation would produce even more unemployment. The socialist remedy of reduced hours of work would only raise costs and prices. His own solution was the revival of agriculture, which should be made efficient and prosperous once more by protective legislation, modernisation, co-operative marketing, less taxation, more liberal credit, the revival of rural industries. He published a book entitled *The Return to the Land and Industrial Overproduction*.[1] He compared his ideas rather vaguely to those of Chamberlain in England and the Centre Party in Germany, but the parallels were misleading. The arguments he used to justify protection reveal a different attitude, distinctive of France in this period. He did not offer industry protection so that it could afford to modernise and produce more. He had a deep fear of producing too much. French taste, he thought, conflicted with mass production: it was suited to making varied but individual goods. France should therefore keep its 'multitude of small workshops' and from the moral and social point of view 'nothing is more desirable than a sensible distribution of work and of profits, to allow thousands of small employers to win a modest competence'. Protection was the only way to avoid a reduction of wages, which would be forced by foreign competition, since he ruled out the possibility of modernisation. He frankly admitted French employers were timid, inefficient and failed to use enough capital, but he accepted this as an inevitable counterpart of the pursuit of the golden mean and the virtue of moderation. He did not spurn the progress of science. He looked to it and to education to make agriculture profitable once more, but he always put aside any notion of structural change among the peasantry. Transport costs were a major cause of the uncompetitive price of both agricultural and industrial products in France, as well as high taxation. His remedy was not to remove these impediments, which with peasant resignation he accepted as inevitable, but to offer compensating protection. He believed that the duties he imposed, after elaborate calculations, were mathematically the exact compensation needed to offset these disadvantages.

It was the economic crisis of the 1880s which gave him the

[1] J. Méline, *Le Retour à la terre et la surproduction industrielle* (1905).

idea by which he reconciled protection of both industry and agriculture. The poverty of the peasants was making it impossible for them to buy the produce of the manufacturers. Since the republic was above all a government based on public opinion, it was only fair that the peasants should get some advantages from the state like everybody else. Steeped in the old centralising tradition, he did much to confirm the peasantry in their habit of looking to the state for their salvation. The widespread sympathy Méline won was recognised in his election as president of the chamber of deputies (in preference to Clemenceau). His assumption of Ferry's mantle was seen in his tenure, from 1893 to 1902, of the editorship of *La République française*, the paper which Gambetta had established as the principal organ of the republicans.

When Méline became prime minister in 1896, he made an attempt to reorganise the political parties on the basis of the issues which he considered were the real ones. He believed that there was an urgent need to end the meaningless republican coalitions, repeatedly abortive of legislation. Méline formed a cabinet composed entirely of moderates. He wanted to redefine the divisions in politics, to show that the major difference among politicians was over socialism. The republicans were no longer divided simply in degree, over questions of method. The socialists were no longer simply their left wing, just advanced reformers, as they might have been in Gambetta's day, for they wished to subvert the whole social order of which Méline was the champion. The groups of the right were no longer a threat to the republic, because they had virtually abandoned their royalism. They were obvious allies in the struggle against socialism. The radicals, on the other hand, needed to be split: they embraced too many incompatible tendencies. A section of the radical party had, under the leadership of Goblet, made common cause with the socialists. No alliance was possible with it. By contrast, there were only two questions on which the moderate republicans differed from the right—the army and the Church. On these Méline advocated the implementation of Walpole's famous maxim, 'Let sleeping dogs lie.' The army, he insisted, must not be provoked: the Dreyfus case must be silently buried. Attacks on the army by the left were only producing a reaction in the form of a dangerous nationalist movement. For the same reason, the progress of socialism must be halted or it would produce a demand for a new saviour of society, a new Napoleon. The monarchists should therefore be welcomed into the republic, instead of being forced into opposition by persecution. Anticlericalism should in the same way be abandoned, to cement this alliance with the right: and in any case it was a dead issue, which profited only the radicals. The republic had built up enough defences against the Church. It would be an enormous source of strength if, by a policy of appeasement, the Church could be induced to accept Ferry's legislation and a limited role in the new order. In this way there could be a genuine political confrontation of the defenders of private property against those who wished to abolish it, of those who believed in the conciliation of the classes against those who advocated the class struggle, between those who saw trade unions as instruments of a new co-operative society and those who regarded them as a revolutionary means of paralysing capitalism, between those who looked on taxation as a contribution to public expenses and those who hoped to use it to produce greater economic equality, between those who saw in the senate a rampart of order and those who wished to weaken or abolish it, between those who respected religion and would allow freedom to the Church provided it respected the concordat and abstained from politics, and those who, denying that this was possible, demanded the separation of Church and state.[1]

Méline's ministry lasted longer than any previous one under the republic, but he was unable to achieve the political reorganisation or religious appeasement with which he hoped to complete his economic work. It required more than the skill of an individual. Méline never succeeded in building up a party to present his ideas to the electorate; his followers were poor attenders in the chamber; they never dominated the parliamentary commissions; some of them objected to his hostility to the radicals.[2] But Méline deserves to be remembered not just as the author of protection, but also as the person who carried

[1] J. Méline, 'Les Partis dans la république', *Revue politique et parlementaire*, 23 (Jan. 1900), 5–16; see also Edmond Demolins, 'La Nécessité d'un programme social et d'un nouveau classement des partis', *La Science sociale* (Feb. 1895), 105–16.

[2] 'Le Parti progressiste, par un député', *Revue politique et parlementaire* (10 June 1897), 485–507.

through the law of 1898 on friendly societies (*sociétés de secours mutuel*). The significance of this has seldom been noticed. It was part of the solidarist movement which characterised the 1890s. The period cannot be understood without going further into this product of a philosophy, by which the Third Republic attempted, again unsuccessfully, to break away from the past.[1]

Solidarity was the most talked about ideal of the nineties and the first decade of the twentieth century. The president of the republic, Loubet, opening the great Exhibition of 1900, declared that all governments paid homage to 'this higher law', and acknowledged it as 'the great common inspiration' of the day. His socialist minister of commerce Millerand hailed solidarity as a new scientific revelation containing 'the secret for the material and moral grandeur of societies'. The monarchist comte d'Haussonville remarked, 'Today, anyone who wishes to receive a sympathetic hearing or even to obtain professional advancement must speak of solidarity.' It was claimed that solidarity was exciting people as passionately as Cartesianism had once done, and that its formula 'Every man his neighbour's debtor' caused as much stir as Proudhon's 'Property is theft.' People started writing theses about it, conferences were held, and the Academy of Moral and Political Sciences devoted four sessions to debating it.[2]

The first significant feature of solidarism was that it represented a new attitude to the French Revolution. Worship of the principles of the Revolution had always been an essential mark of a republican. Lip-service to these principles still continued to be paid, but now, coinciding almost exactly with the

[1] *L'Œuvre économique et sociale de M. Jules Méline* (pamphlet published by the Association nationale républicaine, 1902, copy in Remiremont Municipal Library); *L'Œuvre agricole de M. Jules Méline* (n.d., Assoc. nat. répub.); Georges Lachapelle, *Le Ministère Méline* (1928); Gabriel Hanotaux, 'Jules Méline', *Revue des Deux Mondes* (15 Jan. 1926), 440–53.

[2] The fullest account is in J. E. S. Hayward, 'The Idea of Solidarity in French Social and Political Thought in the Nineteenth and Early Twentieth Centuries' (unpublished Ph.D. thesis, London, 1958). See also his article, 'The Official Philosophy of the French Third Republic: Léon Bourgeois and Solidarism', *International Review of Social History*, 6 (1961), 22–5. John A. Scott, *Republican Ideas and the Liberal Tradition in France 1870–1914* (New York, 1951), 157–86; Charles Gide, *La Solidarité*, cours au Collège de France 1927–8 (1932); C. Bouglé, *Le Solidarisme* (1907); Louis Deuve, *Étude sur le solidarisme et ses applications économiques* (Paris thesis, 1906).

centenary of 1789, a more critical and even hostile reaction emerged among men with impeccable radical antecedents. There had been vague talk about implementing the promises of the Revolution more fully, but now people suggested that they were inadequate. Léon Bourgeois, leader of the radical ministry in 1895, said that the Declaration of the Rights of Man needed to be supplemented by a declaration of his duties. The individualism which the Revolution had consecrated was an evil and a delusion. The liberty it proclaimed was only force under another name, which allowed the rich to oppress the poor. The individual it tried to liberate was an abstraction, for men were not independent beings capable of being considered apart from their obligations and ties to other men. The sociologist Durkheim wrote that the Revolution must be studied in its historical context, and only when this had been done would it be possible to say whether it was a 'pathological phenomenon' or not. The Revolution was seen as the product of metaphysical confusion, which the new positivism rejected. It was described in the schoolbooks as the dawn of a new era, but it was becoming clearer all the time that it did not break with the past all that completely. Tocqueville's dictum was recalled, that the *ancien régime* was still alive, and that the repeated attempts to kill absolute power had only placed new heads of liberty on the same servile body. As the problems involved by implementation of the Revolution's ideas became increasingly complicated, protests were raised against persisting in 'a tradition that was exhausted, and a political method that was out of date and sterile'.[1]

Laissez-faire, which the Revolution had adopted as a principle, had in the course of the century been rejected by the republicans in varying degrees, but they had been equivocal about it when they gained power. Charles Gide's *Principles of Political Economy*, published in 1883, demanded that it should be openly and officially abandoned. He declared that orthodox liberal economics were discredited and 'a thaw' of its harsh doctrines had set in.[2] Henri Marion's thesis on *Moral Solidarity* ('an essay in applied psychology') argued that morality could no longer be considered simply a question of individual virtue,

---

[1] Th. Ferneuil, *Les Principes de 1789 et la science sociale* (1889); review of this by Durkheim in *Revue internationale de l'enseignement* (1890).

[2] C. Gide, *Principes d'économie politique* (1883).

that the ideal of the noble savage was a false one, that reliance on divine providence or exhortation were inadequate, because human character was deeply influenced by the environment in which it developed. Man's liberty was really very restricted, and moral progress therefore required active organisation: it could not be expected to happen naturally.[1]

The new discoveries of science were held to require new attitudes in politics. Hitherto Darwin's teachings about the struggle for life had been seen as justifying *laissez-faire*, for it led to evolutionary progress. But now Milne-Edwards (a French zoologist) argued that living organisms were made up of large numbers of cells working together. The 'law of nature' was therefore co-operation, not hostility, solidarity not individualism. Works on the *Fauna of the Normandy Coast* and *Comparative Physiology* were quoted by politicians to support the view that man should no longer be considered as being born perfect, invested with rights against his fellow citizens, but rather as part of a larger organic whole, from which he had much to gain and on which he was necessarily dependent. Durkheim's thesis on the *Division of Labour* (1896) condemned the society of the day as crumbling from 'anomie'. The weakening of the old bonds of religion and the family had created moral chaos, and economic specialisation had completed the disruption. The Revolution had believed in effecting reform by state action or by leaving it to the individual. Neither was adequate. Durkheim argued that a new morality was needed to hold the country together and a new social organisation, based on professional associations—precisely the bodies the Revolution had tried to destroy.[2] Every branch of knowledge was reinterpreted, to show man's interdependence and the need for co-operative action, rather than unrestricted liberty, to enable him to flourish.

It was Léon Bourgeois who brought together all these hints from the scientists to make solidarism a political doctrine. Born in 1851, the son of a watchmaker, he had made his own way out of the lower middle class, through the civil service, to become prefect of police at the age of thirty-six. He was a man of great

[1] Henri Marion, *De la solidarité morale. Essai de psychologie appliquée* (1880, 3rd edition revised 1890).
[2] E. Durkheim, *De la division du travail social* (1896).

charm, animated by a constant desire to please, but it was a sign of the new times that, though brought up as a servant of the state, he did not continue to worship it when he became a politician. Bourgeois's contribution was to give solidarism a theoretical basis, with his doctrine of the 'social debt' and the 'quasi-contract'. Men were not born free, he said. Even a child was a debtor to society, first to his mother for his food, then to his teachers for his education, then to a far wider group for his economic opportunities, and he incurred new debts all his life. This idea was not a new one, but Bourgeois transformed it from a moral one into a legal one. He claimed that men had not simply a moral duty to repay their debt, but a positive obligation, enforceable with sanctions, because they had made a 'quasi-contract' with society. He found an obscure section of the Civil Code which showed that individual agreement was not essential to create a binding contract. Rousseau's notion of the social contract for mutual benefit was overthrown. Rights were replaced by obligations. However much one contributed to society, one also had debts to repay. In this way the rich owed something to the poor, who were part of society. Charity, which was optional, should be replaced by solidarity, which was compulsory. The state could legitimately force people to pay their debts.

This gave a new justification for a programme of social welfare, founded on an income tax, but one poised carefully half-way between liberalism and socialism. On the one hand solidarism accepted that men were unequal in ability, and that they should continue to derive benefits from their different natural endowments; but justice required that these inequalities should not be increased by inequalities of social origin, like education and inherited wealth. All who enjoyed special advantages of this kind should be required to pay larger taxes to compensate. However, Bourgeois firmly rejected socialism. Its ideal, he said, was a collective one, whereas he started with collective obligations as a fact of life, and his aim was to free men from them, by getting them to pay their debts to society. His ideal was the free individual, and he believed that private property was the 'prolongation and guarantee of liberty'. 'My social ideal is one in which every man will have reached, within the limits of justice, individual proprietorship.'

Solidarism required men to co-operate not in production or in the division of wealth, but in insuring themselves against the risks of life. Equal wages were neither possible nor desirable, but a minimum wage was necessary, in the name of justice, and illness, accident and unemployment insurance were a social duty. Taxation should exist not for the purpose of levelling incomes but to support common services, though each should contribute in proportion to his income. Education should be free. The important thing was that the only limit to a man's ascent should be his natural abilities. Bourgeois thus saw society as a giant mutual insurance company, which helped the disadvantaged, but left each man free to make his own way once he had paid his premiums. There was no need to hope optimistically that men would behave altruistically. As Alfred Croiset, one of his supporters, said, 'Once the machine is set up, it works automatically, and the well-being of all is the necessary result of the operation, if it is conducted intelligently. This gives it a sort of scientific character which is pleasing to the spirit of our time.' Charity was condescending. Justice was too dry and narrow. Fraternity, as was seen in 1848, was too sentimental. Solidarity, based on biology, was scientific. It would transform the blind and unfair but inevitable interdependence of humans, which had created so many social evils, into a voluntary and rational relationship based on equal respect for the equal rights of all. It would socialise not property, but men's minds and give them a new conscience. France would then be, in Michelet's phrase, *une grande amitié*.[1]

Though solidarism was supported by arguments drawn from the natural and social sciences, which made it appear topical and new, its doctrines were of course composed of much older elements. The word itself had been invented by Pierre Leroux, as the opposite of individualism. Auguste Comte had written about it, though largely confining himself to solidarity between generations. Renouvier had attacked the ideals of the eighteenth century and had urged that solidarity should be added to liberty. The revolution of 1848 had expressed the same

---

[1] Léon Bourgeois, *La Solidarité* (1896); Maurice Hamburger, *Léon Bourgeois 1851–1925* (1932); Alfred Croiset and Léon Bourgeois, *Essai d'une philosophie de la solidarité* (1902); Léon Bourgeois, *La Politique de la prévoyance sociale* (1914–19, 2 vols.); Émile Ferré, *Un Ministère radical* (1897).

longings in a more emotional manner. Solidarism could not escape the accusation that it was fraternity dressed up in scientific clothes. However, it was popular because many aspirations—socialist, aesthetic and Christian—found some echo in its teachings. It was to the Third Republic what Cousin's eclecticism had been to the July Monarchy. It was, almost inevitably, equally confused, if not hypocritical. It had more than a suggestion of being designed to steal the thunder of the socialists. It was more or less contemporaneous with William II's new course in German politics, in which Christian socialism was aimed at winning the workers away from revolution: it could be called a lay version of it. Though the solidarists claimed that the peculiar feature of their movement was that it was totally French, this international context was not irrelevant. They were, to a certain extent, inspired by fear or remorse, as much as by a constructive idealism. Hanotaux said that the bourgeoisie 'has sinned by its laziness, its imprudence, its egoism'. It had treated the government as its enemy and it had therefore not used it to help the people. It had failed to bridge the gap between the classes. Poincaré, in a famous speech, asked in the same vein, that the bourgeoisie should make 'necessary concessions'. Renouvier—the profoundly religious inspirer of so many republican ideas—declared on his death-bed, 'The bourgeoisie has not kept its promises: it has worked only for itself.' Solidarism was a kind of retribution.

Its theoretical paraphernalia was probably more cumbersome than helpful. To suggest to those who possessed nothing that they were in fact debtors to society, and to add that they could never repay their debt because they were always contracting new ones, to inform them if they succeeded that their achievements were not their own, was hardly a way to win enthusiastic support. Though solidarism contained idealistic elements, it was also, in important ways, conservative. It appeared to be a new justification of unequal private property. Its sociological arguments took what existed as the norm and condemned forces that disrupted society as pathological. Durkheim's professional groups seemed too like the corporations of the *ancien régime*. Izoulet, professor of philosophy at the Lycée Condorcet, whose book on the modern state was quoted approvingly by the solidarists, defined the problem they were

trying to solve as how to prevent the crowd from overthrowing
the élite, while yet admitting the crowd 'loyally and cordially
into the state'.[1] The solidarists were divided among themselves
as to exactly what they meant, and as to what language they
ought to use. Those with religious (usually Protestant) backgrounds disliked the word debt and wanted to talk of duty or
sacrifice. Liberals objected to the use of sanctions, which, they
said, made solidarism no different from socialism; but the
socialists ridiculed it as a half-way house, which ignored
the problem of the exploitation of labour. It was pointed out
that though microbes might indeed be mutually dependent,
there was no evidence that they loved one another. Gabriel
Tarde, whose book on *Imitation* had argued that this was the
main principle determining human conduct, claimed that
solidarism was based on a contradiction and would therefore
inevitably lead to socialism: it aimed at harmony, but the idea
of debt was bound to lead to quarrels about the extent of
each individual's debts and either the debtors or the creditors
would seize power. This showed that the doctrine was not
properly understood, and that was certainly one of its weaknesses.[2]

The solidarists placed their main hopes on the development
of voluntary mutual benefit societies. They hoped that these
would provide the whole range of social services—employment
exchanges, loans, medical attention, pharmacies, pensions and
insurance—all without much cost to the state. 'The French
Republic', said Paul Deschanel, 'must become a vast mutual
benefit society.'[3] Now mutualism already had a long history in
France. Though forbidden by the Revolution, societies had
started up soon after. They received encouragement from the
July Monarchy, which in 1837 allowed their formation provided
official permission was obtained. By 1845 there were 262 in
Paris alone. The revolution of 1848 gave them a new stimulus,
so that in 1852 there were 2,488 societies with 239,500 members.
Then Napoleon III found a new use for them. Fearing that they

---

[1] J. Izoulet, *La Cité moderne: métaphysique de la sociologie* (1894).

[2] 'Étude sur la solidarité sociale comme principe des lois', *Séances et Travaux de
l'Académie des sciences morales et politiques* (June 1903), 305–434. C. Bouglé, pro-
fesseur de philosophie sociale à l'université de Toulouse, 'L'Évolution du solidarisme', *Revue politique et parlementaire*, 35 (10 Mar. 1903), 480–505.

[3] G. Weill, *Le Mouvement social en France* (1924), 452.

might develop into subversive organisations, he transformed
their character. He exempted them from the general prohibition of clubs, provided they did not have members from more
than one commune, and kept their numbers to a maximum of
500 (if 'approved' or 2,000 if declared of 'public utility'). He
reserved to himself the right to appoint the president of every
society, and to dissolve them with the minimum of formality.
They had to admit as 'honorary members' the village notables
who would preserve them from revolutionary tendencies; prefects, *curés* and mayors were required to help establish societies
in as many communes as possible. Ten million francs, from the
confiscated Orleanist estates, were set aside to provide encouraging subsidies. Napoleon thus made these societies the
stimulants of thrift and prudence, nuclei for a new self-reliance,
but also political and electoral organisations, disunited so that
they could not develop any independence against him. By
1870 half a million people had been enrolled.

The solidarists gave this movement an enormous boost. A
law of 1898 gave the societies the same freedom as the law of
1884 had given trade unions, but adding financial privileges
and the promise of state subsidies on an elaborately calculated
scale, proportionate to their achievements. By 1902 over a
million more people had joined, to which should be added
half a million school children enrolled in a junior branch.[1] In
1910 it was claimed that there were 15,832 societies with
3,170,000 active members and 400,000 honorary members.

Mutualism was the practical and popular aspect of solidarism. There was a National League of Mutuality (launched
with a gift of 10,000 francs from the millionaire owner of the
Magasins du Louvre, Chauchard, and the blessing of Sadi
Carnot, president of the republic). Six national congresses were
held by it, from 1883, and in 1900 the first international
congress, in Paris, was an impressive affair. Newspapers and
journals entitled *L'Avenir de l'Épargne*, *L'Écho de la mutualité*, *La
France prévoyante*, *Le Mutualiste*, *La Mutualité*, *La Revue des
institutions de prévoyance*, etc. appeared in large numbers. It is
curious that no historian has ever done research on these papers

---

[1] This junior branch was known as the *petit Cavé* after its founder. The children
paid very small subscriptions, but considerable insurance benefits were promised,
down even to funeral expenses.

or these congresses, in contrast to the large number who have investigated the activities of the far less numerous socialists.[1]

Being a member of a mutual society came to be looked on almost as a public service. Organisers were rewarded with medals. The Second Empire had instituted a special medal— black ribbon with a blue selvage—for the most successful of them, but it was a decoration which could not be worn on its own and in any case only at society meetings. Between 1898 and 1903 the restrictions on its use were abolished, and the holders of the gold medal were allowed to wear it publicly as a rosette (instead of as a mere ribbon). In 1875 only 579 such medals had been awarded. In 1895 no fewer than 3,281 were given. In 1900 the figure rose to 8,175 and in 1907 no fewer than 17,000. It was almost as though the societies were formed to obtain medals, and it was asked what kind of medals these were, which were awarded for extorting subsidies from the state. If left to their own devices, the societies would have made a loss of about 10 million francs a year. Subscriptions accounted for only two-thirds of their income; the rest was obtained from public subsidies and even more from honorary members. It was not surprising therefore that many people looked askance at the societies, as organisations for legalised begging, subject to the domination of the rich. The presence of honorary members, like the state subsidies, made these societies very different from the English friendly societies (which had far more members— over 5 million in 1898—and were three times as rich as the French societies). They never had any of the *friendly* character of the English ones. In England, social activities played as important a part as the insurance, with the annual feast or outing, the hearty drinking at the monthly meetings—the expenses of which were put down as 'room rent'—the initiation ceremonies and mystic rituals of such bodies as the Oddfellows and the Free Foresters. The English, by excluding the upper classes, made it possible for these societies to form a part of working-class culture. The French societies, by contrast, were absorbed into the tradition of state intervention, employers' paternalism and political manœuvring.

[1] *Premier Congrès international de la mutualité 1900*, (president M. V. Lourtiès, sénateur), report ed. Jules Arboux (1901), contains a lot of information. Cf. the criticism of the national organisation by Eugène Joly, president of a society in St. Étienne, *Le Passé, le présent, l'avenir de la mutualité* (St. Étienne, 1893).

Subscriptions were very low—on average 13 francs a year
(about 50 pence). The benefits were therefore equally low. The
average pension paid at the turn of the century was less than
71 francs (£3) per annum. The societies sought to offer as many
benefits as possible, in order to qualify for the maximum number
of subsidies which each kind of service attracted. They therefore
performed none satisfactorily. Running expenses absorbed on
average 27 per cent of their income. The societies were far too
small to provide a proper insurance service. In 1902 71 per
cent had fewer than 100 members and 39 per cent had fewer
than 50. Ignorance of the principles governing insurance was
common, methods of administration amateur in the extreme.
The government did not really help, even though innumerable
guides on how to practise mutualism were issued. The most
serious omission was that the whole movement was never
established on a proper actuarial basis. The tables of sickness
and mortality promised in a decree of 1852, promised again in
the law of 1898, were still unpublished in 1907, when the
minister of labour, Viviani, declared that they were so difficult
to prepare that they could not be expected for some time.
France was in this respect over fifty years behind England,
where more or less reliable tables had been produced in
1845.

Unlike Napoleon III, the solidarist politicians urged the
mutual societies to unite. They had visions of a great moral
upsurge, in which the egoism of the small societies would
be replaced by a solidarity spread throughout the land:
the union of friendly societies would be the basis of a new
reconciliation of all Frenchmen. But the old habits were too
firmly ingrained. A national council was formed, but it had no
authority over the societies and merely acted as an organ of
propaganda. It was accused of being unrepresentative and its
policies were disputed. Some federations were established on
the departmental level, and these were sometimes effective:
they were able to provide, between them, pharmacies, clinics
and baths. The contrast between the idealism and what
was achieved can be seen in the matter of baths. Baths, it was
said, were extremely important. Fernand Faure declared:
'When Frenchmen come to have two baths a week, the moral,
intellectual and political condition of our country will be trans-

formed.'[1] The researches of Russian and Japanese professors on the value of baths were carefully studied. The number of microbes removed by baths of various kinds were counted, from which it emerged that all baths increased the microbes, while showers reduced them. This was fortunate, for showers were much cheaper to build and used less water, and the hygienists had intended to build showers in any case. But then came the question of money, and far less was done than was promised. Similar frustrations arose in the medical services provided by the societies, which moreover were often used more by the well-to-do than by the poor. Relations with the doctors and pharmacists always remained difficult. So the effect of mutualism was to create a great new vested interest, which did not provide the social services demanded of it, but stoutly resisted their development by the state. In 1900 only 30,000 peasants had joined and only half a million manual workers out of 11 million.[2] The politicians inflated the membership figures (just as the trade unions did theirs) and talked of a 'mutualist élite', comprising one-fifth of the working class, infused with a respect for the established order, and a pillar against 'the rising champions of collectivism and anarchy'.[3]

Mutualism made far more rapid progress than the co-operative movement. A bill to encourage the latter was discussed and amended for eight years, only to be finally rejected by the senate. This was largely due to the opposition of the small shopkeepers. Only about half a million people showed an interest in co-operation before the war. The movement was split in 1890 between socialists and independents, with the result that small local societies tended to avoid joining either federation. Reunion was finally negotiated in 1912, with victory going to the independents under Professor Charles Gide, one of the earliest solidarists, but he admitted that its progress was halted by more than these doctrinal divisions: 'Frenchmen', he said, 'and especially French workers, do not like to be governed by their equals.' The movement for profit sharing, on which a

[1] Michel Heim, *Contribution à l'étude de quelques services supérieurs de la mutualité dans le département de l'Hérault* (Montpellier thesis, 1913), 99.

[2] Léon Bourgeois's figures in *La Politique de la prévoyance sociale* (1914–19), I. 149.

[3] A. Weber, *A Travers la mutualité: étude critique sur les sociétés de secours mutuels* (1908), 262; Armand Alavoine, *L'Action économique et sociale des sociétés de secours mutuels* (Paris thesis 1914); Georges Assanis, *La Mutualité pratique: guide . . .* (1914).

great deal was also written, and which also held national and international congresses, converted only a tiny minority and involved only about 500 firms. The appeal to private enterprise was not successful.[1]

One of the common misconceptions about the Third Republic, before the 1914 war, is that it passed very little social legislation. On the contrary, there was a great deal of it. It is worth examining because it shows, on the one hand the solidarist ideas being put into practice, and on the other the limitations, inadequacies and failures of the doctrine. To supplement the work of the mutual societies, several important social services were set up. The largest problem that needed to be tackled was that of the poor. If private charity was to be replaced by solidarist assistance, a major redeployment of resources would be needed. There was already an institution for dealing with the poor in the *bureaux de bienfaisance*, which in theory were supposed to distribute aid in each commune, under the direction of the mayor; but in 1871 only 13,367 out of France's 35,989 communes had one, catering for only 60 per cent of the population; and on average they distributed only 28·6 francs in a whole year to each person they helped in Paris and 14·9 francs in the provinces. The commission appointed to inquire into them in 1872 made no recommendations for any radical change, since it accepted the traditional attitude to charity.[2]

However, in 1886 a special office to deal with public assistance was set up at the ministry of the interior and Henri Monod, a Protestant solidarist, took charge of it until 1905. He soon realised that the implementation of the solidarist ideals could not be achieved in one general reform. Opposition to helping able-bodied men out of work was strong. So he started by agitating for help for the sick, the infirm, children and the aged. Several societies were started and five national congresses were held between 1894 and 1911. In 1893, 'in the name of the great principle of solidarity', a law was passed by which 'every Frenchman without financial resources should receive without charge . . . medical aid at home, or, if he cannot be effectively

[1] J. Gaumont, *Histoire générale de la coopération en France* (1924); Albert Trombert, *Charles Robert, sa vie, son œuvre* (1927–31), and the publications of the *Société pour l'étude pratique de la participation du personnel aux bénéfices*, founded 1879.

[2] Ministry of Interior, *Enquête sur les bureaux de bienfaisance* (1874), report by Paul Bucquet.

cared for there, in a hospital'. Every commune was required to establish a *bureau d'assistance*, to draw up lists of those entitled to such aid and the state promised 80 per cent subsidies. At that date the communes were aiding less than half a million people. By 1897 the list of those entitled to aid contained 1·9 million persons and 13 million francs were in fact distributed to 701,000 people in medical aid. This, however, represented only 19·5 francs a head per year. The incurable, moreover, were excluded from this law, so though a hospital would take in a poor man free of charge, it would send him home as soon as it declared him incurable. An attempt was made in 1897 to remedy this serious defect by offering a state subsidy to local authorities, to enable them to pay pensions to the incurable old; but again this failed because local authorities refused to spend money for this purpose: five-sixths of the sum voted by parliament was never used. The situation therefore was that in order to get an old man free medical treatment it was necessary to prosecute and convict him for begging. Even so free hospital treatment did not carry with it payments to compensate for loss of wages, or to care for dependants. A bill was therefore moved to create in the words of its title 'a public service of social solidarity', in the form of obligatory assistance to the old, infirm and incurable and in 1905 it finally became law. It provided for the relief of the sick aged over seventy. In its implementation it revealed widespread distress. Over half a million people were to benefit from it each year: the state's subsidy was 49 million francs in 1907 and by 1914 it had been increased to 100 million.[1] But the poor still received on average only 34·9 francs each annually, compared to 180 francs (£7·20) distributed to almost twice as many in England. In 1914 there were still 8·6 million Frenchmen living in communes without *bureaux d'assistance*. The bureaucracy created to manage all this became filled with political nominees, so the standard of efficiency was exceptionally low.

In 1901 the government introduced, as 'an act of solidarity', a bill to give about 10 million workers the right to a pension,

---

[1] C. W. Pipkin, *Social Politics and Modern Democracies* (1931), 2. 190. This is a good study of the social legislation of this period: volume 2 deals with France. L. Mirman, 'Une Loi de solidarité sociale', *Revue politique et parlementaire* (July 1903), 49–73; J. H. Weiss, 'The Third Republic's War on Poverty' (unpublished paper, Harvard, 1966); Henry Joly, *De la corruption de nos institutions* (1903), 196–7.

but it was only in 1910, after much protestation by the senate at the expense involved, that it became law, in modified form. The delay was encouraged by the opposition of employers and workers alike. An inquiry into the opinion of trade unions in 1901 revealed that a great number of them were hostile to all contributory pension schemes because they believed it would diminish what they had to offer and would make the collection of their own subscriptions more difficult. The chambers of commerce declared they preferred mutuality to a compulsory state scheme. But mutuality had clearly not been successful, for in 1900 only 10 per cent of the working class were insured for their old age.[1] Under this new law, some 10 million workers were to receive pensions at the age of sixty-five, from a fund of which half was to be subscribed equally by employers and workers and half by the state. Some 6 million independent workers and peasant proprietors were given the chance to insure voluntarily. In 1912 the pensionable age was reduced to sixty. France took a long time to reach this result, and appeared all the more dilatory because the principle of compulsory insurance against illness and old age had been admitted as far back as 1894 in a law confined to miners.

A law of 1898 provided that workers who sustained accidents would be compensated on a generous scale, whoever was to blame. (Previously the victim had to prove that the employer had been negligent.) Three further laws had to be quickly passed between 1898 and 1902 to remedy serious defects produced by excessive caution. Employees were encouraged but still not compelled to insure themselves against accidents. The insurance companies, over-anxious to profit from the new business, began forming a consortium to raise their premiums. The state therefore offered an alternative official insurance scheme (1899) but most of the insurance continued to be done by the companies. Mutual schemes were disappointingly inactive. In any case, the laws applied only to industries using machines, and they excluded illnesses contracted at work.

The *prud'hommes* had long provided a court of arbitration for the settlement of disputes between masters and individual men.

[1] Maurice Bellom, 'Les Retraites ouvrières en France, Le Referendum de 1901', *Revue politique et parlementaire* (Jan. 1902), 119–39; M. Duboin, *La Législation sociale à la fin du dix-neuvième siècle* (1900).

The new solidarist hopes of social peace, together with the
emotion caused by the great miners' strike at Carmaux, gave
birth to the law of 27 December 1892, setting up similar
machinery for arbitration in collective disputes. Appeal to
arbitration, however, remained entirely voluntary and little
use was made of it. In November 1900 Millerand moved a bill
to make arbitration compulsory, but this received such opposition from both employers and trade unions that it was never
even discussed by parliament. Instead masters and men were
brought together in a series of consultative institutions. In 1891
a *Conseil supérieur du travail* was created to advise the minister on
social problems; at first it was nominated by the minister, but
after 1899 one-third of the members were elected by trade
unions and one-third by employers' organisations. It was an
important body, for all its tribulations, because it did a lot of
work on most laws proposed in this period, virtually taking over
the functions of the legislative section of the Conseil d'État, as
far as labour questions were concerned. In 1891, likewise, an
Office du travail was set up in the ministry of commerce, with
the function of collecting information on labour conditions. It
issued some fifty volumes in its first ten years of more or less
imaginary statistics, for it had no power or staff to undertake
direct inquiry, and it had to rely on others for its sources.
Local *conseils du travail* were set up in theory by a decree in 1901,
elected by employers' and workers' organisations, but this
meant that the majority of French workers, not being members
of unions, had no vote: the idea was to encourage them to join.
In practice only five were set up in the main cities.

The first law controlling the employment and working hours
of children in factories had been passed in 1841 (eight years
after the English Factory Act of 1833), but in the absence of
governmental interest or any effective inspectorate, it had been
ignored.[1] The census of 1851 showed that half of the employees
in factories were women and children, but only in 1874 was
a new law passed providing for the appointment of fifteen
inspectors and forbidding factory work under the age of twelve
(or, with government permission, ten). This law again was
only partly effective, so in 1881 and in 1885 the chamber of
deputies passed further bills, which were, however, rejected by

---

[1] A decree of 1813 had forbidden the employment of children under ten in mines.

the senate. Only in 1892 had the spirit of solidarity spread
sufficiently for a law to get through, limiting women and children
aged sixteen to eighteen to eleven hours a day, children of
thirteen to sixteen to ten hours, and forbidding children under
thirteen to work at all, unless they had a certificate of primary
studies, in which case they could work at twelve. This law also
required one day's rest a week. There were thus several different
legal working days. The result was that enforcement proved to be
almost impossible, and the government closed its eyes to the
flouting of the law. A new law of 1900 limited all factories in
which women and children were employed to a uniform ten
hours a day (including men). The employers again ignored this,
or else paid the small fines for breaking it; some dismissed the
children in order to be free from inspection. Exceptions were
moreover officially sanctioned by a law of 28 March 1902 and a
decree of 30 April 1909. Nevertheless the importance of the law
of 1900 was that, in certain cases, i.e. in model factories, the
hours of adult men were limited and this was the thin end of the
wedge that led to the eight-hour day. But workers in shops and
in the food trade remained unprotected. In 1905 the eight-hour
day was introduced for miners—but only in 1919 was it extended
to all workers.

The fixing of a minimum wage, though promised, was
postponed. Millerand in 1899 asked state public works to pay
the 'normal wages in the region', but this requirement was not
binding on local authorities who (except for a few large ones)
ignored it. A truck bill introduced in 1892 was held up by the
senate. A wages law, passed in 1895, protected workers against
creditors receiving over one-tenth of their wages, but the main
beneficiaries seem to have been the legal officials who drew
large fees from the complicated machinery established to
enforce it. The *livret*, which every worker, like a suspect
criminal, had to carry since Napoleon instituted it, and whose
abolition had been promised as far back as 1870, was finally
abolished in 1890, at last making employer and worker equals
in law. That was as far as the solidarists could get.[1]

If carried to its logical conclusion, solidarism would have

[1] E. Levasseur, *Questions ouvrières et industrielles en France sous la Troisième République*
(1907); Astier, Godart *et al.*, *L'Œuvre sociale de la Troisième République*, leçons pro-
fessés au collège libre des sciences sociales (1912).

involved a very drastic transformation not only of social relations but also of the state. Some of its advocates adopted an entirely fresh outlook on the traditional character of the state. Until the end of the nineteenth century, French jurists had been content to comment on laws and decrees, to describe the judicial system as it worked, but they did not attempt to explain or to question its bases. The cult of the law was too powerful and jurists considered themselves as its priests. This attitude was shown by the publication in 1886 of a version of the Civil Code in verse: it had become a classic. Sieyès had said: 'The end of every public institution is individual liberty', and Esmein, a leading law professor at the turn of the century, approved this in his standard work on public law. Now, however, the question of where the state derived its authority, and what it could use it for, was reconsidered by a new school of legal theorists, led by Léon Duguit. Because the purpose of the state was considered to be the safeguarding of liberty, and because after the establishment of universal suffrage it was held to derive its authority from the people, the conclusion had been drawn that—apart from administrative errors—the state could do no wrong. Duguit protested against this, pointing out that in effect this meant that the *ancien régime* state had been preserved in a new guise. He argued that the rule of law and justice was independent of the state and of the government, which should be subject to it as much as the individual. The civil servants should be regarded as performing a public service, not as exercising sovereignty, 'a myth whose efficacy is exhausted'; and power should be considered as legitimate only when properly used. Governments had obligations, more than rights; they were not the embodiment of the nation, as they claimed; and the individual should be able to sue them if they did not carry out their duties. The Conseil d'État went some way to accepting this new doctrine and to allowing appeals by individuals against official mismanagement. A new kind of jurisprudence developed. But the courts could not force the civil service to act, they could only issue injunctions to them. The omnipotence of the state was therefore not undermined.[1] Solidarism did not produce the radical change it could have

[1] Michel Halbecq, *L'État, son autorité, son pouvoir 1880–1962* (1965), discusses the new legal theories; Léon Duguit, *Law in the Modern State* (1919).

done. This, rather than the lack of social legislation, was the
great failure of the nineties.

One explanation of the stability which underlay the polemic
can be found in the career of Waldeck-Rousseau. It spans two
generations: he was minister under Gambetta (1881) and also
prime minister at the time of the Dreyfus Affair twenty years
later (1898–1901). His career is particularly instructive because
he was associated with some striking, though unsuccessful,
attempts to bring about change. In it one can see why the grand
paper reforms were so often less than what they appeared to
be, and one can get a clearer understanding of the limitations
both of the politicians and of the environment in which they
worked.

Waldeck-Rousseau was the son of a barrister of moderate
means (with an income of 5,000 to 6,000 francs—£200 to
£240—rising to 12,000 in the best years). His origins were thus
distinctly modest; he inherited little; he was brought up to
economise; and he had to support his father in his old age.
By the end of his life, however, he was one of France's most
successful barristers, able to save 136,000 francs in the three
years 1885–8. He married at the age of forty-two the widow
of an even richer colleague and lived in great style in a grand
house filled with impressive *objets d'art*.[1] He kept a yacht and
mixed with the rich. His friends, he said proudly, were 'great
industrialists'. He was set on his feet by the Société Dreyfus,
exporters, whose legal consultant he became and who paid him
a retainer during most of his career. He specialised as a barrister
in commercial cases bringing in large fees. His admiration was
increasingly for the rich. He criticised the men of 1848 for being
too emotional about the lot of the poor. He once asked himself
why he was so little moved by their misery, and he never
seems to have had any particular sympathy for them.

Like so many of the followers of Gambetta, he had been an
unsuccessful student; he had failed his *licence* at the first try, he
had abandoned his doctorate, and at the age of twenty-two he
was already filled with a profound bitterness towards life which
never left him. He concealed his timidity and disillusionment
with a coldness and a reserve which made everyone compare

[1] 35 rue de l'Université, Paris 7e.

him to a fish. Success turned his brusqueness only into arrogance. He never had a personal following. His best friends were his animals—dogs, cats and birds. As a student he had not mixed with his contemporaries; he had lived on the right bank in Paris. As a barrister establishing himself in a town where he had no ties, he had shunned society and could be seen daily at the same café, alone: he was famous for his public silences. He was barely influenced by the intellectual movements of his day. He knew virtually nothing of positivism; he read little; he despised politicians, theoreticians and doctrinaires. When he did go into politics—which he never looked on as a career but to which a strong ambition drove him—his disappointments exacerbated his animosity and added a hate of parliaments and deputies, whom he called 'pygmies' and 'larvae'. As an adolescent he had been a practising Catholic, a fervent defender of the pope's temporal power and even a member of the Society of St. Vincent de Paul. In 1868 he lost his faith not from conversion to science, but in a revulsion produced by a sense of having wasted his youth, and possibly as a result of separation from and disagreement with his father. He never dreamt of replacing faith by science. He did not share the republicans' passionate interest in education; he never asked for a school for his constituency. He had been educated in a church school in Nantes and had no complaints about its teachers: it had taught him, he said, that Catholicism need not necessarily be militant. He was uninterested by Gambetta's anticlericalism, as he was by his patriotic fervour: he hated the nationalism of Deroulède. He travelled all over Europe in his holidays, but went mainly to beaches and museums. One month by the English seaside was enough to make him conclude that the English were a nation of hypocrites. He appears to have had little knowledge of foreign affairs and to have taken little interest in them. He was almost blind in one eye. His main hobby was painting. Hunting, riding, canoeing, gymnastics, boxing, 'all sports, even violent ones, attracted him'. He accepted with resignation that life was inevitably boring and happiness impossible to achieve. 'Puisqu'il faut s'ennuyer, ennuyons nous.'[1] Waldeck-Rousseau is worth studying because he was so different from the standard

---

[1] Henry Leyret, *Waldeck-Rousseau et la Troisième République (1869–89)*, 54, 56. See the excellent, stimulating biography by Pierre Sorlin, *Waldeck-Rousseau* (1966).

image of the optimistic republican militant, an idealised mythical creation if there ever was one.

It was this man, however, who was chosen by Gambetta to be his expert on the social question. Waldeck's ideas on the subject were pretty vague. His principal interest hitherto had been the reform of the magistracy, which he believed to be crucial to the development of the republic: this was something barristers (and even more republican ones who had been fined or imprisoned by judges) felt strongly. The social programme he developed was one aimed at establishing social peace. He considered that industrialisation had given the capitalists an excessive and therefore dangerous preponderance. The workers would not put up with this indefinitely. They had to be given greater equality, and this could be achieved through association: united they could face their employers on a fair basis. 'I consider', he said, 'association as the regulator of social forces and the way to bring about equilibrium in them.' They would enable the educated and moderate workers to teach the ignorant and impulsive ones, and the responsibility of managing these organisations would show them that strikes were not the answer to their problems. Improved moral and material conditions would make the workers bastions of order. Waldeck preached to them what he had done himself—that they should rise in the world, save, make money, and lead a sober bourgeois existence—and he did so sincerely, for he had no prejudice against the lower classes. He harboured something of the fraternal utopianism of 1848, inherited from his father. It should not be forgotten that before becoming a republican, he had been an admirer of the naïve romantic Émile Ollivier (whom he had described in 1869 as the only statesman who had studied politics 'scientifically') and that his favourite in literature was Lamartine. Waldeck's ideal was a fraternal society, without any of the paternalism or hierarchy of the Christian socialists. Bills he introduced into parliament in 1882 included many of the proposals the solidarists were to adopt on pensions, insurance, *prud'hommes* and *sociétés de secours mutuels*. The trade union law of 1884, with which his name is linked, was not his own, and he only helped it pass its final stages. He wanted a much broader treatment of the question of associations, and thought unions— which were only one form—should not receive special treatment.

This reveals how much his proposals were developed in isolation from the working-class movement. The socialist Malon said his ideas were admirable but utopian, out of touch with reality. Waldeck in fact met only moderate worker's leaders, and mainly artisan ones; he seems not to have appreciated what the miners told him, that in the mines workers' associations would never be strong or rich enough to free them from capitalist domination. He saw a minority of extremists as misleading the large mass of sober, honest workers. This meant that his social policy, when he became prime minister, was one of hostility to the vigorous, organised, politically oriented unions, while he tried to raise a new kind of workers' association against them. His bills on pensions and compulsory arbitration were opposed by the unions. In social questions, he hovered between two positions. On the one hand he felt uncomfortable in crowds, he did not wish to be led by the masses and thought that men like him had a duty to establish a new order of justice, to help transform the wage earner into a property-owning partner, even if the masses in their ignorance could not properly understand what he was doing. But on the other hand he believed that, in his resistance to extremism and socialism, he represented the silent majority, 'the true country, the hard-working country, which is not heard often enough because it does not speak enough, and whose opinion needs to be found in its very intimate manifestations'. Increasingly he looked to the provinces against Paris, to the peasants against the extremist towns. He saw the radicals as the great menace. His situation in 1900 was thus not all that different from Louis Napoleon's in 1848. He continued to preach the ideals of that revolution. He wished to win the workers away from their leaders. He appointed a renegade socialist, Millerand, to his ministry: he looked on left-wing politicians as simply men with strong ambitions. But he was also firm with the employers, whose paternalistic attitudes he criticised as being equally serious obstacles to social peace. Arbitrating in a strike at Le Creusot, he laid it down as a principle that employers must not discriminate against trade unionists and must not oppose the election of shop stewards.[1]

[1] R. Waldeck-Rousseau, *Questions sociales* (1900), contains his main speeches on this subject; cf. Henry Leyret, *De Waldeck-Rousseau à la C.G.T.* (1921).

Waldeck had a reputation for firmness, which he established with his authoritarian, antiparliamentary attitudes as Gambetta's minister of the interior. He was opposed to decentralisation. He opposed the granting of more freedom to the city of Paris, and its emancipation from the control of the prefect of police. He condemned the city councillors as unrepresentative and he urged businessmen to replace the professional politicians among them, so that the 'economic élite' could run its administration in the most efficient manner. He had temporarily retired from politics in 1889 'in disgust' with the parliamentary system. He returned as a senator, but seldom attended debates, and never spoke much in parliament even when he held office. His most interesting political experiment was an attempt in the 1890s to start a new kind of party. He wanted to 'close the era of politicians'. 'Purely speculative politics has lost its importance and its interest.' Practical questions should replace it. Businessmen and industrialists should get elected to parliament instead of the lawyers, doctors and journalists.[1] He wanted to introduce his image of English parliamentary government into France: to unite the scattered moderate groups in the chambers and what political associations existed into a cohesive party, to hold elections on issues, and to reduce the power of the individual deputy to obstruct government by interpellation. He had, as minister of the interior, been interpellated about dustbins and his government could have fallen on this issue. The country needed strong and long-lasting ministries. He attributed the slowing down of the economy to political instability: the important effect of his reforms would be to stimulate prosperity, and so make it unnecessary to introduce an income tax, for the old taxes would, if properly reorganised, yield enough revenue once more. He looked upon income tax as subverting the principle of the French Revolution that there should be equality of rights and burdens. The tax would, he claimed, create a new privileged class, dividing the nation between those who paid taxes and those who did not. His great aim therefore was to split the radicals, to win over the moderate antisocialists among them, and so create a great centre party. This would, he hoped, not be simply a new coalition, and certainly

---

[1] Speech of 3 July 1896 to the Société d'économie industrielle et commerciale, quoted Sorlin, 382.

not the old 'concentration'. It would be based on a common programme, not on a compromise. He dreamt of putting up 500 candidates with one platform.

In June 1897 Waldeck-Rousseau launched the *Grand Cercle républicain*, modelled on the English Carlton and Reform Clubs, and a sort of counterpart to the aristocratic Jockey Club. The subscription was high: 200 francs for Parisians and 100 for provincials. He sent young men out to canvass the rich businessmen and industrialists throughout the country. His club would be quite different from the other similar associations (and to some of which he himself belonged). The *Association nationale républicaine* (presided over by Audiffred), the *Association gambettiste* (whose president was Cazot) were primarily concerned with spreading republican propaganda from Paris into the provinces. Waldeck-Rousseau's new organisation was designed to recruit a new kind of leadership for the nation. But by March 1898 he had managed to persuade only about 1,000 people to join. His club never really got under way. The politicians had no wish to destroy the system they were running or to submit to Waldeck's yoke. He got the support only of a few fence-sitters like Poincaré and Deschanel, who were without any personal following. The local notables were unwilling to sacrifice their independence. The defeat of Méline gave the club a serious set-back: the Dreyfus case completed its disintegration. Waldeck-Rousseau himself destroyed his own creation when he took office with a socialist in his government, and accepted socialist and radical votes, abjuring the very policy for which he had founded his club. In any case he lacked the demagogic talents necessary to create a popular party. The *Revue politique et parlementaire*, founded in 1894 to further Mélinisme, and which became the principal organ of the new club, was the only relic that survived of Waldeck-Rousseau's plans; but it was too serious, running to 240 pages each month, with only a narrow intellectual appeal. The businessmen refused to stand for parliament, though a few, including a regent of the Bank of France, gave him sizeable donations. The *Comité républicain du commerce et de l'industrie*, which he helped to found and of which Mascuraud, a jewellery manufacturer, became president, preferred to work behind the scenes, representing the interests of employers, trafficking in decorations—and discreetly subsidising the professional politicians. Waldeck thus failed to change the system. It is not clear that he would have got much further even if he had had more suppleness and guile.[1]

Waldeck-Rousseau sought not the separation of Church and state but the very opposite, the strengthening of governmental control over the clergy and particularly over the religious orders. These latter had not been mentioned in the concordat of 1801 and so by implication they continued to be excluded from France, but they gradually infiltrated back and they enjoyed a freedom from state supervision quite unknown to the secular priests. Waldeck-Rousseau wished to remedy this lacuna in the law, to be 'the Bonaparte of the monks', to bring the concordat into line with the realities of the new situation, to republicanise (not to abolish) the Church. In 1900 there were about 162,000 regulars, almost 60 per cent more than in 1789; they appeared to be the richest single group within the state; it was estimated (rather wildly) that they had doubled their wealth in the last fifty years and that they now possessed at least a milliard francs (£40 million). They had openly taken a part in politics, culminating with their violent campaign in the elections of 1898; the Assumptionists in particular had developed an antirepublican organisation to rival the state. They had refused to pay the admittedly heavy taxes imposed upon them and had been an obstacle to the *ralliement*. With the years the republic had succeeded in filling the bishoprics perhaps not with docile prelates but at least with conciliatory ones, and Waldeck-Rousseau revelled in the power to treat them in the same way as he treated his prefects, to send them stern letters of rebuke when they made the wrong political pronouncements and to withhold their salaries if they were obstinate. Waldeck-Rousseau believed (too optimistically) that the rivalry which had developed between bishops and regulars would enable him to win assistance from the former in making the latter submit to them. For the regulars had usurped many secular

[1] Léopold Marcellin, 'Waldeck-Rousseau et le Waldeckisme', *Revue universelle* (1 Aug. 1923), 306–29; Boris Blick, 'Waldeck-Rousseau 1894–1904' (Ph.D. Wisconsin, unpublished, 1958); *Revue politique et parlementaire* (1894 ff.), and in particular the issue of Apr. 1900 (vol. 24) which contains a history of the journal and the club; Victor Meric, 'Mascuraud', in *Les Hommes du Jour* (12 Mar. 1910), no. 112; Paul Reynaud, *Waldeck-Rousseau* (1913), for his authoritarian reputation.

functions: in Paris alone they had 511 chapels as against 76 parish churches; in France they ran 49 of the 87 grand seminaries which were training the new parochial clergy.[1] Waldeck-Rousseau's aim then was not to abolish all congregations, but to bring them as far as possible within the fold of the episcopal hierarchy, virtually to secularise them. Waldeck-Rousseau brought forward a bill on associations requiring congregations to be authorised by the Conseil d'État, and laying it down as a condition that they should accept the jurisdiction of the bishop. Certain orders would of course never do this, and Waldeck-Rousseau definitely intended to evict the particularly intransigent ones, like the Assumptionists and the Jesuits with whom no compromise was possible. (One of his first acts indeed had been to prosecute the Assumptionists as an illegal association and the courts had declared them dissolved in January 1900.) Altogether 215 congregations, out of 830, preferred not to seek authorisation and formally dissolved themselves in order to escape the law. Waldeck-Rousseau, persevering as ever, issued instructions that secularisations would not be recognised unless the former monks placed themselves under the authority of their bishops.

Nothing worked out as Waldeck-Rousseau planned. The deputies added a clause to his bill forbidding members of unauthorised congregations to teach at all. This attack on the Catholic schools precipitated matters and made quite impossible any compromise with the bishops. Another addition required the congregations to be authorised by parliament, not by the Conseil d'État, and so Waldeck-Rousseau lost control over his schemes.

Waldeck-Rousseau had come to power at the head of a government of republican defence but he never succeeded in turning it into one of republican union. The republican leaders refused to join it, in the same way as they had refused to join Gambetta's great ministry of 1881: Waldeck-Rousseau's ambition to be a 'real' prime minister was incompatible with his having over-powerful colleagues. In consequence two of his ministers (Caillaux, finances, and Baudin, public works) had been deputies for only one year; another (Decrais, colonies) was a former prefect and ambassador of Orleanist origins, who

[1] Lecanuet, 3. 262.

had only been elected to parliament in 1897. His main adviser
was the minister of war, General de Gallifet, famous for his
repression of the Commune.

So, far from uniting all moderates, Waldeck-Rousseau split
them. When voted into office in 1899 he was opposed by the
right, the nationalists, most of the progressists and some 30
radicals. He had the support of only 61 moderates, and survived
thanks to 173 radicals and 21 socialist votes. Waldeck-Rousseau
had little skill in the management of men, and for all his
dominating personality, found himself carried away by the
left, whom he disliked but on whom he depended. It was he,
not the left, who was duped. He virtually admitted as much
when he resigned after increasing his majority in 1902, saying
it was too large. He advised the formation of a radical government. Perhaps he hoped to give the radicals a chance of discrediting themselves, in the expectation that he might then
return to power at the head of a moderate party of which he
could be the real leader. He suggested that Combes should
succeed him. Combes at once proceeded to destroy his work.
Waldeck-Rousseau died in 1904 protesting against the consequences of his own political career.[1]

It is against this background of deadlock and stalemate that
one should judge the significance of the Dreyfus Affair. It
is frequently said that the case of the obscure Jewish army staff
captain who was wrongly convicted of handing military secrets
to the Germans, and who, because of the opposition of the
army, the nationalists and the clericals, was never able to get
the verdict reversed, split the country into two. On the one
hand, the Dreyfusards are seen as standing for justice and for
the individual, demanding his acquittal whatever reasons of
state or military prestige stood in the way. They appear as
heirs of the eighteenth-century movement of individualism and
liberty. Against them were the army, devoted to order, hierarchy, obedience, possessing a different set of values from the
republicans, with Catholic officers perpetuating the ideals of
the *ancien régime*. Against them also were the anti-Semites, who

---

[1] Sorlin, op. cit., gives a full bibliography. For a more laudatory view of Waldeck
see Henry Leyret, *Waldeck-Rousseau et la Troisième République 1869–1889* (1908).

saw in the Dreyfus case an enormous Jewish conspiracy, backed by Protestants—for the Dreyfusards included a lot of both—undermining the integrity of the nation. The clergy took up this cry and the hierarchy refrained from condemning them. However, the matter is far more complicated. The truth about this case has not been fully established, and almost every year a new theory is produced to explain its mysteries. Dreyfus was not guilty but it is not known who was, and the discovery that a forgery to help convict him was concocted by an over-zealous officer, who later committed suicide, does not solve the question of who the traitor was. The suggestion that the government and the army tried to suppress further investigations, in the name of the national interest, is only partly true: repeated inquiries and new trials were ordered, but the truth was so complicated that no obvious course of action emerged. The refusal to release Dreyfus, even when it became clear that his conviction was debatable, to say the least, shows not a reactionary conspiracy, for those in power were far from united, but rather two more fundamental factors.

It was difficult to be rational when all the facts were not known and nearly everybody knew only some of the facts; the conviction was upheld on the general circumstances of the case, and people were variously affected by these. Once they had formed their opinion, they found it difficult to change it, because the proofs were never conclusive; passions and prejudices repeatedly clouded the issues. It was thus a human, psychological failure more than a political one. Secondly, it was a legal failure. The case showed the limitations of the French legal system, in which the odds are loaded against the accused, and Dreyfus, who was a poor witness, could never refute the circumstantial evidence which made him a more or less plausible culprit, particularly in the atmosphere of the time, when spies were seen on every side.

The defence of Dreyfus was taken up by a number of distinguished intellectuals, who presented his case as the same one for which the French Revolution had been fought, and themselves as defenders of truth against expediency. Certainly, it was due to their insistence and sometimes courageous agitation that an innocent man was released. But one cannot accept completely their version of the matter. The Dreyfusards were not all inspired simply by a passion for justice. There were a large number, Boulangists among them, happy to seize this new occasion to fight the established system. They, for their part, made accusations almost as wild as their opponents did, without adequate proof, even if they did present them in the name of 'science'. Their *esprit de corps* was probably stronger than that in the army they attacked, which was much more socially diverse than they imagined. As experts trying to identify the criminal through examination of different hand-writings, they showed the limitations and divisions of science. The battle for Dreyfus was part of a battle against clericalism for many people, as much if not more than for individual liberty; the claim of the Dreyfusards that they were the representatives of liberalism was hardly borne out by their willingness to persecute Catholics.

The Dreyfus affair was important, perhaps above all else, in giving the intellectuals a sense of their mission, and in confirming their importance. The politics of the nineties, as has been seen, were dominated by a desire to escape from the traditions and divisions of the past. The intellectuals claimed that they were clarifying issues when they insisted that the French could not escape, that they were inexorably divided by the Revolution, between those who accepted and those who rejected its principles. It may be claimed that they set France back thirty years by this, refusing to let it go forward to the solution of the problems of the day. One result of the Dreyfus case was the resurrection of the question of Church and state and the persecution of the congregations. It is curious that socialist historians have continued to accept and transmit so much of the mythology of this period. The mass of the people were not interested by Dreyfus.[1] He was hardly mentioned at all in the election of 1898, which was fought, if anything, on the issue of the price of bread, which had just rocketed because of a bad harvest, despite the temporary duty-free importation of wheat allowed by 'Méline Pain-cher'. The case did indeed serve the purpose of freeing the socialists of their anti-Semitism, and turning this into an exclusively right-wing phenomenon;

[1] On the election of 1902, see Claude Levy, 'La Presse de province et les élections de 1902: l'exemple de la Haute-Saône', *Revue d'histoire moderne et contemporaine* (1961), 169–98.

but it also exacerbated anti-Semitism and chauvinism into far larger proportions. It was one of the great failures of the republic, precisely because it impeded advance beyond the disputes of the nineteenth century.[1]

[1] Joseph Reinach, *Histoire de l'affaire Dreyfus* (1901, 7 vols), the fullest Dreyfusard account; Douglas Johnson, *France and the Dreyfus case* (1966), the most judicious and perceptive study; Roderick Kedward, *The Dreyfus Affair* (1965), contains selected documents, which very effectively bring the passions back to life, with penetrating comments by the editor. The bibliography on this subject is enormous: good guides will be found in these last two books and in L. Lipschutz, *Une Bibliothèque Dreyfusienne* (1970). For general deflation, see Georges Sorel, *La Révolution Dreyfusienne* (1911, 2nd edition); for the intellectual view, the lively account by Léon Blum, *Souvenirs sur l'Affaire* (1935). Modern French studies include M. Baumont, *Aux sources de l'Affaire* (1959), F. Miquel, *L'Affaire Dreyfus* (1961), M. Thomas, *L'Affaire sans Dreyfus* (1961).

9. Radicalism

RADICALISM was one of the main pillars of the Third Republic. It was, however, an extremely contradictory, many-sided and complicated force. Its partisans preached doctrines they did not implement. They claimed to speak in the name of reason, logic and principle; they divided the country clearly into those who stood for progress and those who were against it, but they were constantly allying with their supposed enemies, temporising, compromising and muddling through. They incarnated so many of the ambivalences to be found in French society that they are exceptionally difficult to characterise precisely. It might be best, therefore, to examine them not through their vague political programmes but through two of their leaders—Combes and Clemenceau. This will make possible an investigation, in concrete terms, of two essential aspects of their work: the separation of Church and state and their treatment of the social problem.

Émile Combes (1835–1921), radical prime minister from 1902 to 1905, described himself as 'short in stature, with a common face and a common appearance. I looked a perfectly ordinary man and indeed I was a perfectly ordinary man for the crowds.' His father had been a peasant who had also engaged in tailoring and kept a small wine shop. Through the patronage of an ecclesiastical relation, he was admitted into the local church seminary. His Superior decided that he did not have the vocation to be a monk, so he was instead appointed a teacher in a Church secondary school. In later years, when he became a leading enemy of the Catholics, and was denounced for turning against his benefactors, he replied that as the son of a poor man, he had had to obtain his education where he could find it. He had worked without salary for his first year as a teacher and so, he said, he had paid his debt—a common enough attitude towards Church education, perhaps, for the majority of the Church's pupils never took holy orders. This early background certainly made Combes cynical about why

men of his own class entered the Church. Most religious vocations, he claimed, resulted from a very practical view of life:
young peasants saw in the congregations an easier, more agree-
able life than any to be found in their own world. He had no
fear that in attacking their privileges he was attacking anything
holy. But though he was a renegade, the imprint of his early
education was firmly stamped upon his political work. His
doctoral thesis on Thomas Aquinas had attacked the saint for
his liberalism; his Latin thesis on St. Bernard and Abelard had
severely criticised modernistic ideas. Both revealed him as a
firm ultramontane, a militant, it was even said, who would not
hesitate to re-establish the Inquisition. He was equally extreme
when he changed sides. He was always intolerant and saw
issues in clear-cut terms. He transferred to politics something of
that obsessive passion first kindled by the Albigensian heretics
of his native Tarn and not totally extinct.

He was also determined to get on in life. While a teacher in
the Catholic school at Pons (Charente), receiving a salary of
3,000 francs (£120) per annum, he made a judicious marriage
with the daughter of the local novelty merchant, who brought
him a dowry of 70,000 francs (£2,800). Her mother insisted,
however, that as a teacher he was not quite worthy of his bride.
He therefore went to Paris and, keeping his family by giving
private lessons, he studied medicine. Six years later, having
qualified as a doctor, he returned to Pons. For his first ten years
he earned much the same as he had done as a schoolmaster,
but as rivals died off and he built up his practice, his income
rose to £400–480 per annum.

Combes quickly entered republican politics in Pons. He
became a municipal councillor in 1869 and mayor in 1874,
retaining this office (apart from a temporary dismissal by the
conservative government of 1876) till his death. He acquired
considerable popularity for the improvements he carried out in
the town and he developed electioneering skills to rival the
Bonapartist Jolibois, the Grand Elector of Charente. He knew
every one of his electors in Pons and memorised a great deal of
personal details about the inhabitants of the whole parliamentary
constituency. Twenty years later he could still recite, without
hesitation, the exact numerical results of every local contest in
the region. In 1885 he was elected a senator. He organised

a group, the *gauche démocratique*. In recognition of his acumen at political manœuvring and his zeal in the service of the radical cause, he was elected a vice-president of the senate; and in 1895 he was briefly minister of education under Bourgeois. He was the senate's *rapporteur* of Waldeck-Rousseau's law on associations and this suggested that he might be a suitable successor to carry out Waldeck's unfinished work. He was expected to be a docile tool, but he carried out the ideas of those who prudently remained behind the scenes with such fanatical zeal that he became the symbol of the anticlerical movement, wildly popular and bitterly hated.

He was not quite what he appeared to be. He was a spiritualist and believed in immortality, but he was far more old-fashioned than Ferry who had also been a spiritualist, for Combes had no faith in the positivism with which Ferry had sought to replace Christianity. He dismissed the teaching of the state primary schools as superficial and narrow and insisted on the continued need for the Church's moral doctrines. Though he rejected the hierarchy and many of the dogmas of Catholicism, he still felt a need for its consolations. The abstract principles and uncertain conclusions of positivism left him uncomfortable and dissatisfied; and he could not do without faith. He found one in a muddled mystical belief in progress as a great force ruling the world according to settled laws, not far different from Voltaire's Great Watchmaker: the legacy of his past revealed itself when he quoted Bossuet to make the point that in such a scheme of things, there was no room for chance. He saw himself, a poor man raised to the heights of power, as the instrument of Progress, chosen to destroy the menace of the congregation. He was not the leader of new forces or of new ideas. He picked up his principal beliefs from Michelet, whom he worshipped as the prophet who had 'lifted a corner of the veil' covering 'the great Secret'. He vaguely hoped science would one day complete the revelation. His great hero in politics was Lamartine, whose speech on taking office on 24 February 1848 he used to declaim repeatedly for the edification of his friends.[1]

He was a model of bourgeois domestic virtue. He adored his family and wrote poems to celebrate its anniversaries. He handed

[1] Émile Combes, *Mon Ministère: mémoires 1902–5* (1956), 33–5; cf. Léopold Marcellin, 'Émile Combes et le combisme', *Revue universelle* (1 Oct. 1923), 65.

over his earnings to his wife, who paid all the bills and gave him
35 francs a month (£1·40) as pocket money, which he would
partly use to buy books on the stalls on the *quais*. Before setting
out on a journey, he would arm himself with small coins to
enable him to avoid giving excessive tips. He liked to economise on paper, and wrote so small as to get 3,600 words on to
a single page. He seldom entertained, and never went to the
theatre or the café, saying he had not been able to afford these
as a young man and was too old to learn to enjoy them. He was
a teetotaller, though at public banquets he drank reddened
water so as to offend no one. In the evening he studied languages; having got through Spanish, Italian, English and
German, he was learning Russian when he was prime minister.
At sixty he learned to ride a bicycle, regretting that he had not
done so earlier, and so been spared the expense of a carriage.
His son, however, did not inherit these characteristics: he
married an American heiress, Miss Cutler, and lived in great
style.[1]

Combes began as a figure-head prime minister. In 1902 it was
in fact the *Délégation des Gauches* which took power. His name
was only used to characterise the new situation. 'Combisme'
came to mean political partisanship carried to extremes, but it
was the rise of new organisations that made this possible. In
1901 an Action Committee for Republican Reform had been
created, to fight the coming election. The republican, radical
and radical-socialist groups, while keeping their individual
labels, agreed to co-operate in the elections, and so between them
won thirty-five more seats. Whereas Waldeck-Rousseau could
never be certain of getting a majority, Combes, after 1902,
could, and this majority was held together for him by hidden
party managers. The origin of the *Délégation des Gauches* goes
back to 1893, when it had begun as a loose combination of
groups, but now it took over the leadership of parliament, and
it organised the majority for Combes, so that, freed from the
need to bargain for votes, he could concentrate on carrying out
its legislative programme. Each member of the *Délégation*
represented about ten deputies: seven were moderates, eight
radicals, six radical-socialists, and five socialists. The astute, if
somewhat pompous, radical Sarrien was its president, but the

[1] Yvon Lapaguellerie, *Émile Combes* (1929).

real direction came from that master of compromise, the socialist leader Jaurès, who time and again saved the majority from disintegration and the ministry from collapse. The function of the *Délégation* was to find acceptable formulae on which all four groups could agree—no easy task, in view of the diametrically opposed views of moderates and socialists. Anticlericalism was one thing they could agree on. The socialists realised they could not hope to achieve their reforms until the Church question had been got out of the way. Just as Waldeck-Rousseau was a moderate carrying out a radical programme, so Combes was a radical egged on by the socialists. Jaurès, significantly elected one of the vice-presidents of the chamber, became in fact the secret 'leader of the house'. He frequently drafted motions to satisfy all sides, and then had them recopied by someone else, lest his writing should be recognised and his too frequent direction resented. Combes, however, readily accepted the leadership of the *Délégation*. He tried even to establish one in the senate, but Waldeck-Rousseau, with his fondness for authoritarian rule, defeated him, denouncing it as a 'dangerous method, which tends to place government not in the hands of ministries but in that of political groups.'[1]

Combes's aim was to 'republicanise' the administration, the army and the Church. He issued a circular urging the prefects to reserve 'the favours of the republic' for the friends of the parliamentary majority. A 'delegate' was appointed for each canton to watch over the distribution of these favours. The partisanship of the civil service was accentuated. Combes's son Edgar, as secretary-general of the ministry of the interior, declared that he was determined to expel the reactionary prefects and that he would reserve decorations for political services. Combes surrounded himself with the largest retinue of political acolytes any ministry had seen: fifteen *chefs de bureau* and eighteen *attachés*.[2] The Freemasons supplied the ministry of war with information about the political and religious beliefs of officers, to ensure that only republican ones should be promoted.

Combism has been called 'Bonapartism, minus the glory'. The foundations for such extremism did not exist. Combism

[1] R. A. Winnacker, 'The Délégation des Gauches', *Journal of Modern History* (1937), 449–70.
[2] Abel Combarieu, *Sept Ans à l'Élysée avec le président Émile Loubet* (1932), 206–7.

was based on compromises, and these could not survive the strain. Combes's increasing popularity among the anticlericals in the country, his unrealistic sense of mission, and his increasing lack of tact, alienated more and more of the political leaders. The moderates became worried at the excessive influence of the socialists in the framing of policy; the *affaire des fiches* (the revelation of the army's use of Freemasons' notes on the political and religious views of officers) gave them the opportunity to break away. In 1905 the decision of the International at Amsterdam to forbid socialist participation in bourgeois governments compelled Jaurès to withdraw from the *Délégation* and thus the temporary union of the centre and left was ended. It lasted long enough, however, to make possible the carrying out of the separation of the Church and state.

The separation is remarkable for the very great difference between what it was intended to do and what it in fact achieved. Most republicans—from the time when Gambetta issued his Belleville programme in 1869—had demanded the separation but they had never found it convenient to carry this out when they won power, because they found they could exert more control over the Church through the concordat. The separation was now passed in something like a fit of temper after the Dreyfus Case, in retaliation against the Catholics' violence.[1]

Whereas Waldeck-Rousseau had planned to bring the religious congregations under state control, Combes transformed his 1901 law on associations so as to effect the complete dissolution of the monasteries. He spared only five orders, politically useful because they engaged in missionary work in the colonies, or harmless like the silent Trappists. All the others were declared illegal. Their property, estimated to be worth 1,071 million francs, was confiscated, to be used to finance the workers' pensions scheme. Their numerous chapels were ordered to be closed, on the ground that the 38,000 secular churches in the country were enough for their needs. Above all, an attempt was made to shut down all their schools, and to forbid them to teach in other schools: their threat to the moral unity of the

[1] Dr. M. J. M. Larkin is writing a book on the separation. See meanwhile his articles in the *Journal of Modern History*, 36 (1964), 298–317, *Historical Journal*, 4 (1961), 97–103, *English Historical Review*, 81 (1966), 717–40.

nation would thus be ended. Jules Ferry's Article Seven rejected in 1879 was at last passed by Combes.

In practice the dissolution was far less effective than was
intended. Though a large number of the regulars went abroad,
particularly to Belgium, most of them simply turned themselves
into secular priests and continued their old work in a new
costume. The Church secondary schools were closed down
easily enough but the primary ones frequently could not be,
because in a great many villages there was no alternative
school. Enormous funds and vast numbers of new state teachers
would have been needed to replace them. The state therefore
decided to close them only gradually over a period of ten years;
so in practice the majority survived. Again, the congregations'
'milliard' somehow evaporated. This sum was probably a gross
overestimate, because it ignored debts and mortgages: the
congregations were not all as prosperous as was believed; but
in any case the state obtained little of whatever wealth they
did possess. In order to make the liquidation appear impartial,
it was carried out by the courts, instead of by the administration. The result was that much of the money was swallowed up
in lawyers' fees and expenses. (Millerand is said to have made
a lot as legal representative of various congregations.) The
sale of their property was inefficiently and frequently dishonestly
carried out. The Chartreuse, the source of the well-known
liqueur, valued at 10 million francs, for tax purposes, and paying
270,000 francs a year in taxes, was sold for 629,100 to Cusenier,
a rival maker of liqueur, who had, it was said, bribed the liquida-
tor. One of these liquidators, Duez, was arrested and condemned,
confessing to having extracted at least 6 million francs from the
congregations. Whereas in the first Revolution the property of
the Church was bought by people with money, the dissolution
in 1902–5 seems to have benefited people who could make
friends in the right places. The whole operation is shrouded in
obscurity. The dissolution has had many books written about
it, but all from the political and legal point of view. Its economic
history and its practical consequences have still to be studied.[1]

The same is true, to a lesser extent, of the separation of

[1] A. Latreille, J. R. Palanque, E. Delaruelle and R. Remond, *Histoire du catholicisme en France* (1962), Book 4, contains a good summary of research to that date;
J. M. Mayeur, *La Séparation de l'Église et de l'État* (1965), for extracts from the debates.

Church and state. Here again Combes did not achieve all he
set out to do. His main work was to start a quarrel with the
papacy, break off diplomatic relations and start legislation for
ending the concordat. However, he fell from power before this
was carried out and the separation as finally arranged was far
more liberal than he had intended. Combes's own bill—which
was not passed—would not have effected a real separation at
all. The Church would have lost its privileges, but the state
would have kept the right to interfere in its affairs; it would
have leased the churches to each parish on renewable ten-year
leases, 'according to its needs'. Combes would also have used
the separation to destroy the unity of the Church, for he would
have forbidden parishes to form unions extending beyond one
department. Supporting Combes there were some men of
Protestant origin who saw in the separation an opportunity to
effect a second reformation, to encourage the growth of schis-
matic sects, so that the power of popes and bishops would dis-
integrate. Méjan, the permanent head of the *ministère des
cultes*, was the son and brother of Protestant pastors and hoped
that the separation would produce an internal spiritual revival
or reformation of the churches. But he wanted a liberal law
allowing freedom to worship, for he believed the French nation
was, like himself, a nation of believers.[1] The extremists who
wanted to destroy religion as such were a minority. The radical
Allard declared: 'We are fighting religion and all religions,
religious feeling and all religious dogmas . . . Offspring of
Judaism, the Christian religion is a scourge which has wrought
such havoc on humanity that it can be compared only to
alcoholism.' But the men with views like his never won power.
Ferdinand Buisson, president of the chamber's commission on
separation, and one of the radical leaders, made it clear that
he was in favour of liberty for the Church.[2]

A settlement designed to be widely acceptable was provided
by Aristide Briand, a young socialist who had only just entered
parliament. After having advocated revolution and the general

[1] L. V. Méjan, *La Séparation des églises et de l'État* (1959), an important thesis based
on Méjan's private papers. On the Protestants, see the attacks by Ernest Renauld,
Le Péril protestant (1899), and *La Conquête protestante* (1900), which gives names.
[2] F. Buisson, 'La Crise de l'anticléricalisme', *Revue politique et parlementaire*, 38
(Oct. 1903), 5–32. Louis Capéran, *Histoire contemporaine de la laïcité française* (1957–
61), and *L'Invasion laïque* (1935).

strike, he now suddenly emerged as the apostle of conciliation towards the Church. It needed a man from outside to sense the changing atmosphere. The radical majority which had only recently applauded the violence of Combes, now approved of Briand's moderation. One of the characteristics of radicalism was that it seldom implemented its doctrines, when it came to deeds rather than words. Clemenceau had already led the way when he had supported the dissolution of the monasteries but had opposed the persecution of the monks and the prohibition against their continuing as teachers. The violence of the polemic was producing a reaction. An interesting inquiry into the 'social, political and religious tendencies of French youth', carried out in June 1901, concluded that a new tolerance was entering French life. This was made up partly of indifference to religion and partly of exhaustion at the perpetual struggles in France. The negative animosities of the anticlericals were ceasing to arouse enthusiasm among many of the young, who were seeking more generous emotional outlets for their energies. They felt they were being burdened with out-of-date quarrels, too old to be of interest or to be capable of solution, and still fomented only by ambitious politicians for whom they felt no respect. A more constructive approach was needed to deal with the divisions of the country, since the moral unity Ferry had sought to establish had so clearly failed.[1]

Combes was thus not representative of the country in 1905 (nor even of his own party for that matter, as his 1848 spiritualism shows). The clash with the Church was brought to a head ten whole years after Dreyfus's conviction, when the paroxysms had already begun to die down. They had not died down enough, however, to allow negotiations with the Church, still less with the papacy. This produced the great snag in Briand's bill, that it was unilateral, was rejected by the pope, and could not be carried out as planned. The interest of the separation is thus twofold: how Briand modified the idea of separation and secondly how Briand's law was, because of the Church's refusal to accept it, itself modified by the force of circumstances in the course of its execution.[2]

[1] Eugène Montfort, 'Les Tendances sociales, politiques et religieuses de la jeunesse française au vingtième siècle', La Revue, 37 (15 June 1901), 581–609.
[2] For Briand, see A. Briand, La Séparation (1904–5), and La Séparation, application

The law of separation ended the state's support of the Church and the 40 million odd francs it had been paying annually to it. Church buildings (which since the Revolution belonged by law to the nation) would continue to be available to the faithful, but provided that in each parish a religious association was formed, consisting of at least seven resident adults, to take over the responsibilities of their upkeep. This was a key provision in the law. Its effect would have been to give laymen a majority in the running of the local churches, for small communes had only one *curé*. It would have been fatal to the hierarchic Catholic organisation. Briand publicly admitted that in freeing the Catholics from the control of the state, he did not wish to 'leave them bound by the discipline of Rome'. The democratic transformation of the Church was his ultimate aim. The associations were forbidden to receive bequests, on the ground that 'religion must not be maintained by the heritage of the dead, but by the voluntary liberalities of the living'. The accumulation of mortmain was forbidden, and the amount of capital each parish association could possess was limited to five times its annual budget. Property left to the Church for purposes not strictly religious—particularly for charitable purposes—was given to the communes to assist the poor in the state's institutions. Priests were forbidden to attack the government or the civil service on pain of fine or imprisonment. The Church was thus disarmed politically. Otherwise, however, every effort was made for the actual act of worship and the administration of the sacraments to continue without difficulty. Pensions would be paid to priests for four years— starting at full salary and gradually falling to half—to enable the faithful to worship in the transitional period until they could finance their priests from their own contributions. In small rural communes, where this would be more difficult, the pensions were extended over eight years. Though the church buildings remained state property, they could be leased to the associations at nominal rents where the municipal council was well disposed. For the first ten years the rent payable for the

du nouveau régime (1909); also L. Crouzil, *Quarante ans de séparation* (Toulouse, 1946).

buildings was in any case limited so as to save Catholicism from immediate extinction in hostile villages.[1]

The liberalism of the Briand law was offered at a price. Most of the bishops of France (and many leading laymen) were willing to pay some of that price, for they had had long experience of making compromises with the state. They argued that the Catholics in Germany had managed to turn an even more rigorous system of associations to their advantage. They accordingly devised a form of association which was inoffensive from the hierarchic point of view, but acceptable to the state and able to benefit from the Separation Law. It would simply manage the property but would not involve lay interference in church government. Pope Pius X, however, embittered by the government's unilateral actions, wished to put an end to the tradition of Gallican compromise and indeed to the independence of the Gallican Church. He believed that firm resistance could destroy the law and that ultimately a restoration similar to that of 1815 would follow these persecutions in the style of 1793. In two encyclicals he condemned both the government's associations and those devised by the bishops. The Catholics, though many of them did so reluctantly, accepted his decision. The law was thus effectively checked at the very outset.

Briand, however, as minister for religions from 1906 to 1910, was able to save much of his policy by preventing the Church from being martyred. 'If the adepts of a religion, whether clergy or laymen, do not wish to form religious associations' he announced, 'they are not, because of that, deprived of the right to practise their religion.' He passed a law (2 January 1907) giving Catholic priests the right to use the churches, and a circular (1 December 1906) pointing out that services could be held in accordance with the law of 1881, which permitted meetings of all kinds, provided only the police were given notice in advance. Briand specially exempted churches from the rule that meetings could not be held after 11 p.m. (so as to allow midnight masses) and he dispensed them from the requirement that the 'meeting' should begin with the election of a chairman and secretary. When the Catholics refused to give notice of their

---

[1] Gustave de Lamarzelle and Henry Taudière, *La Séparation de l'Église et de l'État. Commentaire théorique et pratique de la loi du 9 décembre 1905* (1906); Charles Gide, *La Séparation des églises et de l'État* (Toulouse, 1905).

services to the police, Briand passed another law (28 March 1907) abolishing this requirement. It was this careful avoidance of persecution, this consistent refusal to make matters intolerable to the Catholics, that ensured the relative success for the separation.

The obscure complications of Briand's law, however, required the Catholics to wait and see what would happen, since they could not know how things would change. The law needed interpretation by the courts for its detailed application, and the courts, in a long series of judgements, consistently interpreted it in the Church's favour. They extended the definition of 'place of worship' so widely as even to include the building of a gymnastic society sponsored by the Church. Instead of being narrowly confined to their altars, the priests were enabled to enjoy possession of all the buildings they needed for a full religious life. Indeed, they soon obtained more than just possession. Briand had declared that the *curés* had the right to occupy churches but 'without legal title' (for only associations could have a title). The courts, however, ruled that their right to use churches was a legal one, for it involved legal responsibilities and therefore legal rights. Whereas at first Catholics appeared to have the right to go to church only in the same way as they had the right to go to market, now they were able to sue others for disturbing their use of the churches. The courts even forced recalcitrant mayors to assist the churches. The law of 1905 left the upkeep of the church buildings to the associations, but since these were not founded, the law of 1908 allowed the state, departments and the communes (which legally owned these buildings) to repair them, though it did not compel them to do so. The Conseil d'État in its decisions extended this law so as to allow partial rebuilding, and in 1914 it even compelled a commune whose church had been burnt down to use the insurance money to rebuild it. Communes which granted their churches hidden subsidies, part-time jobs or cheap accommodation for the *curé*, were supported by the courts, and those which tried to interfere in the celebration of services, by requiring the churches to be open or shut at certain hours, had their decrees annulled. The *curé* emerged master of his church, free to organise its worship and access to its services as he pleased. All idea of fomenting schism disappeared: the courts supported only the *curé* approved by the bishop. This attitude of the courts was partly an implementation of the spirit of the separation laws of 1905 and 1907, but it needs some further explanation, for the Conseil d'État under Combes had been violently radical in its treatment of the congregations. The variation in the opinions of the judiciary needs further study. The new moderation, however, was not universal, and men like Doumergue and Viviani protested against it. Anticlericalism was far from dead. In 1912 Chaumié, as minister of education, decreed that priests could not compete in the *agrégation*. Only in 1939 did the Conseil d'État lay it down that a woman could not be refused a job as a primary school teacher on the ground that she had been educated in a religious school.[1]

These legal decisions were made to settle particular disputes. They indicate the triumph of the spirit of conciliation, but they also show the survival of the traditional feud of the mayor and the *curé*. There were very many villages where persistent attempts were made to obstruct and annoy the clergy. Ingenious mayors prosecuted *curés* for habitual mendicancy when they sought gifts from the faithful, for obstruction when they processed through the streets, for disturbing public tranquillity when they rang church bells, and they played innumerable tricks with the keys to the church. But though the feud continued, the law now repeatedly came in to protect the clergy and not the mayor. Such was the paradoxical consequence of the separation. The only real danger that threatened the Catholics was the law that if a church was not used for six months, it could be turned by the village to other purposes. Though the Catholics were able to continue to worship, their refusal to form associations meant that they had no legal method of inheriting the property of the Concordat Church, which was instead 'resumed' by the state. Some 30 to 35 million francs were involved—but once again unknown profiteers must have been the principal beneficiaries. As soon as the state obtained possession, it began

[1] Gabriel Le Bras, 'Trente Ans de séparation' in *Chiesa e Stato*, 2 (Milan, 1939), 435–62; René Fontenelle, *L'Échec pratique de la loi du 9 décembre 1905 au regard du culte catholique et les efforts d'adaptation au fait cultuel* (Lille thesis, 1921); Pierre Prugnard, *Les Églises publiques depuis la Séparation* (Paris thesis, 1923); Paul Bureau, 'La Séparation de l'Église et de l'État devant le parlement et les tribunaux', *La Science sociale* (Jan. and Feb. 1912), fascicules 89 and 90.

selling, but it seldom sold at the full value and it seems to have realised only some 10 million francs. It is interesting that there was no property at all to sell in nineteen departments and virtually none in twenty others.[1]

The Church after 1905 reflected this unequal distribution of piety and its clergy became much more unequal when they lost their uniform salaries. The priests in the large towns were frequently better off as a result of the separation. Mgr Delamaire was given two palaces by benefactors, one at Cambrai and one at Lille. The Archbishop of Toulouse built himself a very sumptuous one. On the other hand, the Bishop of Tarentaise moved into a very humble cottage. The rich clergy became richer, the poor ones poorer. Paris, Lyon and Lille soon found they could collect adequate incomes from their parishioners. Twenty-four new churches were built in Paris between 1906 and 1914. The diocese of Le Puy, however, could raise only one-third of the sums it needed for current expenditure. Much depended on the financial acumen of each bishop, for they were left to their own devices. Many placed their funds in Russian bonds, fearing a second confiscation if they bought French ones. Cardinal Richard in Paris abolished luxurious funerals and marriages, urging those who would have paid the high charges to donate these savings instead directly to the Church. This proved to be based on a misjudgement of human nature; the order was soon rescinded and the Church began encouraging elaborate ceremonies, so as to profit from the increased fees. The state's salaries were replaced by the 'denier du culte', a form of ecclesiastical taxation backed by religious sanctions, sanctions which were used also to urge parents to send their children to church schools. Little information, however, is available about the new Church's finances.[2]

One important consequence of the separation was the increase in the power of the pope and the destruction of the independence of the Gallican Church. The pope could now choose his bishops freely and he chose them for some time afterwards— as the French government had long done—for their docility. He forbade them to meet, just as Napoleon had done. While

[1] Joseph Filatre, *Étude du droit de retour crée par la loi du 9 décembre 1905. Les biens repris par l' État dans le département du Pas-de-Calais* (Lille thesis, Arras, 1914), 132.
[2] J. de Narfon, *La Séparation des églises et de l' État* (1912), 218–97.

strengthening his hold over them, he reduced their omnipotence over their clergy: after 1910, the ordinary *curé* ceased to be liable to be dismissed at will by his bishop. The lower clergy certainly needed to have their position improved, for the separation produced an accentuation in the fall in recruitment. The Church could no longer offer an assured salary and a pension. On the other hand, the clergy gained greatly in vitality when they ceased to be part of the state and associated with its bureaucratic complacency. Catholicism was certainly not annihilated.

The separation was completed in 1921 when diplomatic relations between France and the Holy See were resumed from obvious political convenience. Rome now accepted a new form of association, diocesan in form, controlled by the bishops, with power and legal right to own property, collect subscriptions and donations (but unable, until 1940, to receive bequests). The roundabout subterfuges of forming private companies to build new churches could thus be abandoned. The clergy were allowed to form ecclesiastical unions to manage the religious affairs of the Church, and the education and pensions of priests. The agreement between the pope and the government was reached despite vigorous opposition from the rank and file, radicals and priests alike, for whom compromise was anathema. A new place for the Church in society now became possible. But the anticlerical war did not therefore end. There were still grievances: in particular the Church demanded state subsidies for its schools, resented the limitations on its wealth and regretted the considerable sums it had forfeited in 1905. The battles of the past could thus continue, even though most of the issues had been settled. Men could not change their habits so quickly. It would take some years for the pope to bring in bishops with a new outlook; and even longer for a new generation of radicals to emerge.[1]

The separation of Church and state is usually regarded as marking the victory of the anticlerical, lay republic, but an analysis of the way it was carried out, and the results which followed from it suggest that this is too simple a view. On the

---

[1] A very good guide to this period is Harry W. Paul, *The Second Ralliement: The Rapprochement between Church and State in France in the Twentieth Century* (Washington, D.C., 1967).

surface, the struggle of radicals against clericals was the dominant theme, and that struggle continued in party programmes.
But beneath the surface, it was conciliation which triumphed.
The relation between these two levels of consciousness is what
provides the key to the apparent contradictions. French politics
can become clearer if one investigates not simply what the
parties demanded, but also the seemingly incoherent, colourless,
compromising realities which followed from their demands,
and which won general approval even though they were universally attacked. Politics in many ways was a protest against the
facts of life. Historians need to study not just the protests but
also the acceptance of them and how people got by while protesting. In volume 2, an attempt will be made to investigate
further the origins and functions of the activity of protesting.

Clemenceau

The elections of 1906 were a triumph for the radicals who won
247 seats—42 per cent of the total—and who were thus easily
the majority party. The radicals had a long programme of
social legislation which held out the promise of a new era. But
in the next few years it became clear that they had no intention
of implementing it. They proclaimed their belief in progress,
but no longer represented it. They appeared increasingly to
look on reform now as a concession, not as a conquest. Justice
began to interest them less than power; and foreign policy—
revenge for 1870—increasingly preoccupied them. Already
before 1914 radicalism had the makings of an ageing valetu-
dinarian who knew how to look after himself. The interesting
question is why it remained alive till 1940.

Clemenceau's ministry (1906–9) can be taken as a turning-
point. He came to power with a programme of no fewer than
seventeen reforms which suggested that at last, now that the
monarchist and clerical obstacles had been eliminated,
Gambetta's radical administrative and social reforms, proclaimed at Belleville in 1869, would be implemented. But
though his ministry lasted two and three-quarters years,
Clemenceau achieved virtually nothing, and on the contrary
distinguished himself for the violence of his repression of all
opposition. The reasons for this are all the more worth dis-

covering because Clemenceau had for long been the principal
advocate of radical reform, against opportunism. What made
him change? He took good care to see that posterity should not
know. During his retirement, he systematically destroyed his
papers. No full biography of him exists and it will never be
possible to write one. Enough is known, however, to make one
guess that there was no real change in him in 1906. His ministry
revealed the latent sterility of his life, as it did that of the radicals; it showed up the contradictions in both.

Georges Clemenceau (1841–1929), who for so long had made
himself the partisan of justice for the people, was of noble stock.
His father was the Chevalier Clemenceau de la Clemencière
and lived in a moated medieval château in the Vendée. But the
family were rebels against their class and were leaders of the
small minority which opposed the royalists for which the west
was famous. One of them voted in the Convention for Louis
XVI's death. For at least three generations they practised as
doctors as well as being country gentlemen: this marked their
link with the bourgeoisie and the people, but they remained at
war with their own society. There seems to have been some deep
resentment in the family, which suggests that part of Clemenceau's hostility to the world has a hereditary explanation. His
father, at any rate, is known to have been a dour misanthrope
with vigorous hatreds and a mocking, revengeful irony, who
led a lone and brooding existence among the Vendée woods;[1]
he too was a republican (a friend of Michelet and Blanqui)
and arrested as such by Napoleon III. The violent hatreds
of his father and the romantic destructiveness of Blanqui—
whom Clemenceau also greatly admired—were the principal
inheritance of his youth.[2] His own training as a doctor—he
never practised—gave him an interest in science and particularly in the theory of evolution which provided a doctrinal
basis for this bitter view of life. The struggle for survival,
violence, carnage was the law of nature, applicable equally to
man as to all living things. Wisdom consisted in accepting this
and realising that peace was unlikely. Whereas Léon Bourgeois

---

[1] Gustave Geffroy, *Clemenceau* (1918), 27–9. This book is by one of Clemenceau's
best friends—the biographer and friend of Blanqui too.

[2] Fernand Neuray, *Entretiens avec Clemenceau* (1930), 43–4; General H. Mordacq,
Clemenceau (1939), an interesting study of his character by an admiring but not
uncritical subordinate.

and the solidarists drew an optimistic conclusion from the discoveries of science, Clemenceau declared that he, as a pessimist, saw in nature not co-operation but conflict.[1] He did not therefore reject solidarism. Selfishness produced in men 'the need to be called and later the need to feel good, generous, helpful'. Altruism thus develops, but in perpetual conflict with egoism; from this conflict comes all progress. The function of politicians was to stimulate this altruism and develop justice from it, but politics was essentially a struggle against the laws of nature, to light up an ideal in 'the sombre cosmos where everything is linked by an iron law'. 'To contain conquering [nature], to raise up the conquered, appears to be the first duty of him who understands the supreme law. Let us preach peace, since there is only battle; justice, since iniquity surrounds us; goodness, since hate flourishes. Above all, let us act, for merit lies in protesting by action against the fatal law of the fall of the weak.'[2]

Clemenceau felt alone in the world. An unhappy marriage— significantly with an American—soon ended in separation. He gave himself up entirely to politics, which enabled him to fight the world. He made a virtue out of his loneliness. He became a champion of radical individualism, but with this difference, that he sought to protect his independence by a vigorous aggressiveness. His unhappy experience of the Commune, when as mayor of the eighteenth *arrondissement* he had in vain sought to avert the conflict, left terrible memories and the consciousness that he had a greater gift for making enemies than friends.[3] He devoted his long parliamentary career (he was first elected a deputy in 1871) to attacking the republicans for their in-adequacies: he broke with Gambetta and became the leading figure in the radical opposition. He carried radicalism to extremes, into radical socialism. In a vague way he claimed he was a socialist, though he believed neither in revolution, nor in general nationalisation nor in Marxism. When asked by Jaurès what his programme was, he replied; 'You have it in your pocket: you stole it from me.' The only difference was, he claimed, that he wished to achieve it more gradually. His

[1] G. Clemenceau, 'Sur la démocratie', *Neuf Conférences rapportées par Maurice Ségard* (1930) [Lectures given in 1910], 128.

[2] Id., *La Mêlée sociale* (1895), preface, xlii, and *passim*.

[3] Id., *Sur la démocratie* (1930), 17.

programme can be summarised more accurately in the words
justice and *patrie*. It was in their name that he demanded social
reform, that he opposed colonial expeditions which frittered
away the national resources, that he attacked Ferry so bitterly
and that he prevented him from being elected president of the
republic. But if examined with care, his ideas are seen to be
full of contradictions, for he could not resist attacking even
them. Though he claimed to be the great defender of the
French Revolution, he despised the Convention as 'an assembly
of cowards who killed each other from fear'.[1] Though he
championed democracy, he spoke contemptuously of the
masses and insisted on the importance of élites (open ones, it is
true) to lead them.[2] He argued that parties were essential, but
he devoted himself to attacking their corruption and bankruptcy.[3] He was the most passionate partisan of a single
chamber, but he ended up a satisfied senator. His view of himself as the representative of modernity contrasted strangely
with his belief that political problems had not changed much
since the Greeks. Demosthenes, if anybody, was his hero.[4] The
real key to his career is to be found in his temperament rather
than in a doctrine. He was essentially a fighter. He took up the
case of Dreyfus, partly, it is true, because he believed in his
innocence but much more because it was just the kind of battle
that he loved, against everybody. When he urged Anatole
France to join him in 1897 in support of Dreyfus he said, 'We
shall be alone. We shall have all the world against us', and he
complacently enumerated all the forces which were hostile
to Dreyfus. 'But we shall win', and he repeated the phrase with
pleasure, 'we shall be alone, but we shall win.' 'How many
intellectuals', commented Anatole France, 'has Clemenceau
won by filling them for an instant with his frenzy of courage
and pride?'[5] Clemenceau admitted that he enjoyed fighting;
peace, he said, would never exist among men. Men were inevitably selfish, biased, unfaithful, ambitious, passionate.[6] His
only novel, called *The Strongest*, about the struggle for power and

---

[1] Georges Wormser, *La République de Clemenceau* (1961), 84.

[2] Georges Clemenceau, *Sur la démocratie* (1930), 60–2.

[3] Id., *Dans les champs du pouvoir* (1913), 400.

[4] Id., *Démosthène* (1926).   [5] J. Caillaux, *Mes Mémoires*, 1 (1942), 301.

[6] A. G. Gola, préfet honoraire, *Clemenceau et son sous-préfet* (Fontenay-le-Comte,
1937), 35, 54. (Reports of conversations with him.)

a frustrated affection, showed his preoccupation with human conflict and the little hope he placed in harmony or in love.[1] That is why he was the right man to lead France to victory in 1917. He knew how to fight, not how to yield. But his choice as prime minister in 1906 was less happy.

Clemenceau's nickname was The Tiger. This conveyed his wild destructiveness but it should not mislead into suggesting that he was a mass of strength. He was a small man and after middle age fat as well as short, undistinguished. He was extremely nervous and given to the most profound depression, which he relieved by violent outbursts of rage. Like Bismarck (another mythical man of iron, who spoke with a squeaky voice) Clemenceau was no thunderer. He suffered from an asthmatic condition which compelled him to avoid forcing his tone, so as to prevent fits of coughing. His speech was sharp, short, jerky; Anatole France called him 'the most nervous orator of his time'. He made few gestures, and indeed often spoke with his hands in his pockets. He was more at home in the Vendée than in Paris. He loved the solitary sports of riding and shooting. In old age he started doing gymnastics, for he took great care of his health. He consumed a lot of medicine, frequently consulted doctors and went regularly to Vichy and Carlsbad. In 1906 he was already an old man—sixty-five and out of date, for he stood on the left from cussedness rather than conviction. He was impulsive, impatient, obstinate; he could not do things by halves; he was more a bull than a tiger. Jaurès called him an 'evil man'.[2] They were certainly exact opposites.

Clemenceau derived his influence from his energy. He was an unsuppressable, eternal duellist (in deed, as well as in speech). He had few friends in parliament but he was a deadly opponent. His biting invective seldom missed its mark. He could manipulate his anger with precision. He could display 'now an aggressive and contemptuous ill temper, now an easy manner at once bantering, familiar and abrupt. He spoke like a man who would brook no restraint.'[3] His enmities were fiery and implac-

[1] G. Clemenceau, *Les Plus Forts* (1898). Cf. Edmond Gosse, 'The Writings of M. Clemenceau', *Edinburgh Review*, 229 (Apr. 1919), 253–70.
[2] Daniel Ligon, 'Jaurès au Parlement', in *Jean Jaurès présenté par V. Auriol* (1962), 144, and L. Blum, *Jean Jaurès* (1937), 18.
[3] A French contributor, 'M. Jaurès and M. Clemenceau', in *The Dublin Review* (Apr. 1906), 311–17.

able. He was a man not of steel, but of fire. In the country he aroused extreme opinions. He had some difficulty in keeping his seat, lost it twice and in the end retired to the safer senate. His constituents, though proud of his notoriety, complained that he seldom visited them and never got them jobs or favours. When he came, his speeches were great oratorical successes. His opponents aimed not at refuting him, but only at stopping him from speaking. Ernest Judet, editor of *Le Petit Journal* (with a circulation of a million), one of his bitterest enemies, vowed in 1893 that he would lose him his seat. He spent considerable sums hiring Piedmontese hecklers from Marseille to follow him around on his electoral campaign, shouting 'Aoh yes', meaning he was sold to England. A forgery was published showing he was an English spy. Thousands of free copies of *Le Petit Journal* were distributed with a cartoon of him juggling with sacks of sterling. A league of his enemies was formed against him. He was narrowly defeated. This shows the nature of the feelings he roused.[1]

His private life, as recently revealed by his grandson, helps to explain the bitterness of his politics.[2] He had a gay time with women, he was fond of actresses, but he would not tolerate any liberty in his wife. He obtained his divorce from her by taking a policeman with him to catch her in a compromising situation. He had her convicted to fifteen days imprisonment for adultery, and then expelled from the country like a common criminal. He destroyed the bust, the photographs and drawings he and his three children had of her. All the children had marriages as unhappy as his own, with a quite exceptional record of divorces. His son, Michel, after being expelled from various schools, finally completed his education in Zurich, and was then discreetly sent to work in Hungary. In 1905, he returned to France and prospered as a businessman on government contracts—which ended in a scandal. He was exiled to the Vendée; Clemenceau refused to speak to him for several years, but relented when he joined up in the war. Later he prospered again as the agent in France for Vickers-Armstrong armaments.

[1] Yves Malartie, 'Comment Clemenceau fut battu aux élections législatives à Draguignan en 1893', in *Provence historique* (1962), 112–38.
[2] Georges Gatineau-Clemenceau, *Des pattes du tigre aux griffes du destin* (1961).

He divorced his Hungarian wife to marry a secretary thirty
years younger than himself; after another divorce he married
the widow of a Californian oil magnate. Both of Michel's
sons became millionaires: one married the daughter of a
Jewish diamond merchant and the other (after a divorce
with a descendant of Sarah Bernhardt) the heiress of the New
Orleans Grunewald fortune. His direct descendants are Americans. Clemenceau's two daughters had unhappy lives. The
husband of one shot himself after finding her committing
adultery and, to the fury of Clemenceau, he left a will appointing
Poincaré, the latter's rival, as guardian of his son (whose
marriage also ended in divorce). The second daughter was
deserted by her husband. Clemenceau was severe and tyrannical
towards his family. Though he was capable of joviality and
kindness, these moods alternated rapidly and inexplicably with
ones which inspired terror. He took good care to see his comfort
was not spoilt by anyone. He lived in some style, like the petty
aristocrat he was. He was looked after in his fashionable Passy
flat by two servants cowed into obedience. He wore English
clothes and bought his furniture from Maples. He was very
definitely a member of the upper class. His brother Paul, an
engineer, made such a considerable fortune from dynamite as to
become one of the 'Two Hundred' wealthiest men in France.
His brother Albert was a successful barrister—and counsel for
Stavisky.[1]

Clemenceau passed only one of the seventeen reforms he
promised—the nationalisation of the Western Railway[2]—
and this he carried through the senate by only three votes,
after posing a vote of confidence. Some suggested that the
measure was allowed through not from any reforming zeal but
in the hope that the inevitably discouraging results of buying
a railway in deficit would save the other companies from
nationalisation. It smelt of corruption because the shareholders were grossly over-compensated, after having allowed
the track to fall into serious disrepair. There was a definite
political gain for the radicals, nevertheless, for they acquired

[1] David Watson of the University of Dundee is writing a biography of Clemenceau. Meanwhile see his articles in *The News Letter*, 6, part 1 (1970), 13–19, and
The Historical Journal (1971), 201–4.
[2] For the list of promised reforms and Clemenceau's 'ministerial declaration' on
taking office, see *Revue politique et parlementaire* (Dec. 1906), 604–8.

a very considerable amount of new patronage in the west, where their influence was weakest.[1]

Clemenceau turned out to be so stern an upholder of the rights of the state that his social policy consisted principally in the savage repression of strikes; and in him the state revealed itself an even greater enemy of the workers than the employers. He became minister of the interior a few days after a terrible explosion in the mines at Courrières when over 1,100 men were killed. In the strike which followed Clemenceau quickly showed how tactless and brutal he was. He went to Lens to address the miners, but he spoke to the Broutchoux extreme union—thus discrediting the more moderate union of Basly. He promised not to send troops, but soon after filled the area with no fewer than 20,000 soldiers—one for every two strikers. A month later, he arrested Griffuelhes and Monatte on the eve of the 1 May demonstrations of the C.G.T. and concentrated 40,000 soldiers in Paris, as though in preparation for a siege. He openly declared war on the C.G.T. 'You are behind a barricade, I am in front of it. Your method is disorder. My duty is to preserve order. My role is to oppose your efforts.'[2] Opposition, rather than negotiation or compromise was indeed his tactic. His use of troops inevitably led to bloodshed. In at least five strikes there was loss of life and on one occasion, at Villeneuve-Saint-Georges, the troops apparently charged the strikers without provocation, killing several in the process. In July 1908, the C.G.T. leaders were again arrested. Labour unrest reached unprecedented heights not because there was so much more of it in total, but because a political issue was made of it and it became a struggle against the government. It even seems that Clemenceau or his subordinates used *agents provocateurs* to stimulate some of this violence. It was argued that he was glad to have enemies on the left to keep the support of the right. In any case, the old days when the republic knew no enemies on the left were clearly over.

When the post-office workers went on strike, Clemenceau at once dismissed 300 of them; when the primary teachers

[1] André Dejean, 'La crise de transports et le matériel roulant des chemins de fer', *Revue politique et parlementaire* (Mar. 1907), 542–64.

[2] Jacques Julliard, *Clemenceau, briseur de grèves* (1965), 23. Deals mainly with the affair of Draveil Villeneuve-Saint-Georges (1908), but generally very instructive on Clemenceau's social policy.

protested their right to form a union, they were treated in the same way. To the objections in parliament, Clemenceau replied that these men were civil servants who had 'put themselves in a state of revolt against the French republic'. The restiveness of the civil servants was indeed a sign that the traditional view of their role, which Clemenceau held, was no longer acceptable to them. They were refusing to be considered any longer as simply instruments of the government, required to be politically loyal, subject to favouritism, nepotism and arbitrary dismissal. Their numbers had increased enormously over the last fifty years; and they claimed, with a flourish of exaggeration, that they formed 10 per cent of the electorate.[1] They were demanding to give up their role of election agents, to be admitted and promoted on merit only, by examination, to have a statute guaranteeing their careers. The radicals had placed in their programme the passing of such a statute, but they were disagreed on its details; they argued inconclusively and were unable to undertake any constructive reform. Clemenceau's policy of obstinacy and repression was clearly a failure: he merely made the C.G.T. revolutionaries into martyrs and won for them the sympathy of more moderate workers who normally did not accept their leadership. Briand and Viviani, the two former socialists in his government, lamented Clemenceau's ruthlessness and shortly before his fall began a new policy of using greater tact. Griffuelhes was released. The election of the more moderate Jouhaux to the leadership of the C.G.T. was the reward of their patience.

Although these dramatic strikes by revolutionary workers created an atmosphere of social crisis, the rebellion of the winegrowers in the south in 1907 was perhaps even more serious. It involved larger numbers and it showed that another pillar of the old 'republic of peasants' was tottering. As has been seen, after the replanting of the south with American roots to replace the vines destroyed by phylloxera, there had been a great expansion of the area devoted to vines. The new plant could be grown on the plains as well as the slopes; it spread further north and it produced higher yields. The land planted with vines in the Aude, for example, increased almost threefold between 1863 and 1900. In the latter year, so great was the over-production of *vin ordinaire* that prices tumbled to a fifth of the normal.

[1] Georges Deherme, *La Crise sociale* (1910), 149.

In a dozen years, land values in Béziers fell by between 30 and 60 per cent. In some villages of Roussillon, such was the poverty that men put on masks and went begging. It was impossible to borrow or sell; labourers were dismissed, tradesmen ruined. The blame was put on the merchants who falsified wine, and on the government which allowed them. Marcelin Albert, a small owner who had been agitating for some years in protest against this crisis, suddenly acquired a tremendous popularity. His mass meetings on Sundays attracted, it is said, a quarter and even half a million people. He was compared to the Biblical Apostles, to the Mahdi. Committees to support him sprang up in every village. Placards declared: 'Death to Clemenceau'. Royalists and socialists secretly fanned the agitation. *Curés* announced the movement would bring the end of the republic. The pressure of the agitators stopped people paying taxes, for fear of mob violence if they did. There were mass resignations of municipalities: one-third of the communes of the Aude, Hérault and Pyrénées-Orientales were left without an administration. Crowds besieged the sub-prefecture of Narbonne and the prefecture of Perpignan, and attempted to burn them down. Troops sent to disperse the crowds mutinied. Clemenceau is usually given credit for his handling of Albert. Albert, terrified by a movement he could no longer control, and by the prospect of arrest, fled to Paris and surrendered to Clemenceau personally. Clemenceau chided him paternally, contemptuously gave him his fare home and told him to make amends by restoring peace. The movement suddenly collapsed. It was not just the train fare, however, that destroyed Albert's popularity overnight. He had lost his nerve before that. His followers were tired of the revolt and the interruption of ordinary life was becoming inconvenient. Parliament rapidly passed a law on falsification to assuage the insurgents (it was soon revealed to be inadequate). Clemenceau sent the mutinous soldiers to a distant outpost in Tunisia. But no fundamental reform was undertaken to remedy the economic problems raised by monoculture in this region; nothing was done to reconcile the interests of the growers and the merchants. Was solidarity just talk?[1]

[1] Maurice Le Blond, *La Crise du Midi* (1907), the fullest study; Paul Hamelle, 'La crise viticole', in *Annales des sciences politiques* (1908), 625–61; André Avignon, 'Marcelin Albert et la presse régionale' (Montpellier D.E.S. mémoire, unpublished, 1964).

The measures avowedly designed to put it into practice were so watered down by reservations and by considerations of economy that they had very little practical effect. Clemenceau's minister of labour, Viviani, tried at first to apply the law of 1906 establishing a six-day week, but yielding to pressure, he soon issued so many circulars granting exceptions as to greatly reduce its value.[1] The workers themselves were hostile to it, because they were not paid for their day off. The application of the law of 14 July 1905, providing assistance to the old and incurable, was likewise, as has been seen, a disappointment. This had been inadequate to begin with: the senate had passed it on condition that aid should be given only to those over seventy who could prove that they were incapable of working, and in order not to discourage thrift, savings should be taken into account before the feeble allocation—of a maximum of 20 francs a month—was given. Few people knew how to claim or how much was due to them: such was the chaos that in 1907 the government abolished the means test. Briand in 1909 tried to clarify the procedure for applying but it still remained complicated and the distribution of aid arbitrary.[2]

Again, the minister of labour, Viviani, got a workers' pensions bill through the chamber, but it was only in 1910, in the ministry of Briand, that he passed it through the senate; and it was even less successful. Its *rapporteur* said it represented 'not only the greatest financial effort but the greatest and finest reform of the Third Republic'.[3] But there once again the senate had limited its scope, raising the pension age from 60 to 65, and reducing the benefits: those at present aged between 60 and 70 (after which they had a right to assistance under the 1905 law) would get a pension straightaway, even though they had paid no contributions, but the maximum they could receive was only

[1] René Wallier, *Le Vingtième Siècle politique: année 1907* (1908), 260–1.

[2] *Recueil des lois, décrets, circulaires etc.* (1908), 42–52 gives the text of the law; p. 32 gives the modifying article 36 of the budget for 1908; ibid. (1909), 258–61, circular of 3 August 1909 on its application. Henri Ripert, 'L'assistance aux vieillards infirmes et incurables et la loi du 14 juillet 1905', *Annales des sciences politiques* (15 May 1906), 289–316, gives a history of the law's passage; Léon de Seilhac, *Revue politique et parlementaire* (Feb. 1907), has some interesting comments on it; L. Bonnevay in P. Astier *et al.*, *L'Œuvre sociale de la Troisième République* (1912), 153–72, has a good chapter on insurance and pensions.

[3] René Samuel and Georges Bonnet-Maury, *Annuaire du Parlement* (for 1910–11), 9 (1911), 114.

100 francs. Amendments became necessary almost at once and an additional law of 1912 reduced the pension age to 60. This could be done because it soon became clear that the scheme would not be fully implemented and its financial implications need not be taken too seriously. The workers objected to paying contributions at all. Ignorance and suspicion of the law resulted in only one-third of those eligible actually paying anything, and they paid less than they were supposed to. The administrative machinery for the law was inadequate and there were long delays before small sums trickled out to pay some of the pensions due.[1]

The first volume of a new *Code du Travail* (first suggested in 1896) was promulgated in 1910, a second in 1912, but this turned out to be a mere compilation of the existing legislation, and contained nothing new. It showed how inadequate the law on labour was, how much of the influence of the *ancien régime*'s compendium of law, Pothier, remained and how the rights of man, propounded in the Civil Code, ignored the rights of workers. A bill for a minimum wage was spurned; the inspection of factories remained a farce; the problem of accidents at work produced only a long parliamentary report but no action.[2]

The most urgently needed reform was that of taxation. Without it, no social programme could be undertaken. Between 1899 and 1909 government expenditure had increased by 18 per cent, but this was only partially met by the increased yield of existing taxation from economic expansion. In 1907 the budget was just balanced, but in the two following years there were deficits. Parliament, dominated by a fear of offending the electorate, voted only one-third of the new taxes that were needed.[3] Increasing use was made of loans. The achievement of the Third Republic was to give France the largest national debt in the world.[4] Now, quite apart from social reform, increased military expenditure on an unprecedented scale

[1] Louis Béjard, *L'Application de la loi sur les retraites ouvrières et paysannes* (Lyon, 1914)—one of the few studies of the practical application of a law, rather than a theoretical juridical thesis.

[2] Georges Renard, *Le Parlement et la législation du travail* (1913), 28.

[3] E. Pelleray, *L'Œuvre financière du parlement de 1906 à 1910* (1910), viii and 8.

[4] Raphaël-Georges Lévy, 'Comparaison des budgets anglais, allemand, russe, ottoman avec le budget français' in *La Politique budgétaire en Europe*, lectures at the École Libre des Sciences Politiques (1910), 257–307; A. Landry and B. Nogaro, *La Crise des finances publiques en France, en Angleterre et en Allemagne* (1914), 121, 241.

made drastic changes in the financial system essential. French taxes were still basically those of the *ancien régime*: the Revolution had done little more than give them new names. The *taille* became the *impôt foncier*, the *capitation* became the *personnelle-mobilière*, the *droits de jurande* were transformed into the *patente*. The stamp duties of the Years III and VII re-established those of 1671. Finally, a law of 1816, reproducing Colbert's ordinances of 1681, revived most of the old indirect taxes. The only innovation with which the Revolution could be credited was the tax on doors and windows, borrowed from England or possibly from Ancient Rome.

The principal reason for the survival of the old taxation system was that it affected things and not men: the freedom of the individual from the inquisitions of the administration was safeguarded, his style of living, not his income, determined what taxes he paid; and these taxes, being clear and definite, gave rise to very little litigation. But they had two overridingly serious defects: they were very unequally distributed and they were inelastic. The amount of land tax paid depended on where one lived, since the amount to be raised was divided among the departments, partly on an estimate of their prosperity made at the time of the Revolution and partly on surviving privileges of the *ancien régime*: the old *pays d'élection* and the *pays d'état* still paid different rates. Corsica, favoured by Napoleon, paid a derisively small amount in land tax; so did the Landes, once poor but far richer since the Second Empire. The whole system survived because periodically adjustments were made to render it tolerable—usually by reducing the taxes of decaying rural departments. But it was a system incapable of meeting sudden emergencies. In 1848, the imposition of 45 *centimes additionnels*—a small increase—was impossible to apply. The war of 1870 produced another crisis, but once again serious reform was avoided. Loans were used to deal with the immediate problem, but when this was seen to be inadequate, a tax of 3 per cent (increased to 4 per cent in 1890) was imposed on stocks and shares. But state bonds were exempted, preferential treatment was given for foreign bonds and no one was required to declare his income. Later, protection was used to raise further revenue. This, however, was the only reform carried out in the nineteenth century, despite the transformation of the country by industrialisation. New sources of wealth remained virtually untapped.

Between 1872 and 1907 no fewer than sixty-five bills were moved to introduce some form of income tax.[1] They had all come to nothing. Clemenceau had promised that the income tax would be the great achievement of his period in office. He appointed Caillaux, a former inspector of finance and the most authoritative advocate of the income tax, to be his finance minister. But he took little interest in the matter himself and the chamber dealt with it very slowly. It was not until 1913, when military service was increased to three years and vast expenditure on armaments made it inevitable, that Caillaux got a section of his proposals through the senate; it was only in 1917, through the inescapable pressure of war, that the income tax as a whole was passed and then it was passed only with numerous limitations. The long struggle to achieve this reform showed how vested interests had come to dominate the republic and how the radicals, far from representing justice, were in fact the greatest coalition of these vested interests. The details of the debates are interesting because they cast light upon archaic prejudice and privilege, hidden fears and profound conservatism over which the self-advertising political programmes glossed quietly. Different sections of the community thought they had a special claim to a lower rate of tax. This was particularly the case of the peasantry, which because of its massive vote, had long been given tax rebates; now, because the senate was its special representative, it was altogether exempted. Caillaux proposed taxation on different types of income (at different rates), for example, income from property (land, houses, shares) at 4 per cent, on profits from industry, commerce and agriculture which involved reward both for work and interest on capital, $3\frac{1}{2}$ per cent, wages and salaries 3 per cent.[2] This simple arrangement, however, hit too many people. Profits from agriculture had until then been untouched by the land tax (in compensation the new income tax on land was in fact lower than the old land tax). Wages had been

[1] J. Caillaux, *Les Impôts en France* (1896–1904), preface; cf. id., *Mes Mémoires* (1942–7).

[2] Marcel Rouffie, 'Le nouveau projet d'impôt sur le revenu', *Revue politique et parlementaire* (Mar. 1907), 495–532.

untaxed too. State bonds (the *rente*) had been exempt and it was claimed that to tax them was the equivalent of declaring national bankruptcy. The great problem was how to discover people's incomes. It was immediately assumed that nobody, if left to himself, would declare his income honestly. The idea that the profits of industry should be made public was attacked as spelling immediate ruin for it: secrecy was its tradition. The bourgeoisie were horrified by the prospect of having their affairs and their fortunes placed at the mercy of petty civil servants who owed their jobs to political intrigue. They were even more incensed by the second part of Caillaux's scheme. In addition to these taxes, levied at a standard rate whatever a man's income, he also proposed a super tax at a progressive rate payable by those with total incomes exceeding 5,000 francs, reaching a maximum of 4 per cent on incomes over 25,000 francs. Statistics were produced claiming that two-fifths of French wealth was owned by 124,000 people, and that about 539,000 people had over 50,000 francs capital each.[1] These would be the victims. The super tax was denounced for dividing the nation, as a tax of the class struggle. The threat to the bourgeoisie brought to light a large number of organisations formed by them: twenty-seven committees and associations of industrialists and merchants (and including the 'association for the defence of the middle classes') now combined to form a Central Committee for Fiscal Study and Defence (Comité central d'études et de défense fiscal) which was a powerful pressure group in parliament.[2] When the chamber of deputies eventually passed the bill, many members did so knowing that it had little chance of getting through the senate.

Even if the tax system had been reformed more rapidly, it is not certain that this would have been enough. An inquiry into a succession of serious naval accidents revealed a staggering amount of waste and inefficiency in the naval department, inadequate supplies of artillery, munitions of bad quality, mistakes in the construction of new vessels, long delays in the

[1] Bernard Vandeginste, 'Le Sénat et l'impôt sur le revenu 1909–1917' (unpublished Sorbonne thesis, 1966), 1. 68, 168. Very informative, and broader than the title suggests.

[2] Pierre Callet, 'La bataille de l'impôt sur le revenu: fiscalité moderne et réactions bourgeoises (1906–1917)', *Cahiers d'histoire*, 7 (Grenoble, 1962), 465–92. Interesting especially on the bourgeoisie of Lyon.

arsenals.[1] Large credits were needed to bring the navy even
up to the standard at which it stood on paper. This issue
provided the occasion for the overthrow of Clemenceau, but
his position had long been weak. His long tenure of power did
not mean that the radicals had a stable majority. The sterility
of this period was the result of a deep malaise, so that men
began talking of the crisis of radicalism and indeed of the crisis
of the parliamentary regime.[2] A very interesting inquiry was
organised by *La Revue* in 1908, taking as its text a phrase from
Waldeck-Rousseau's *Testament politique* (1905) to the effect that
the pace of reform had slowed down greatly in the last ten
years. 'Public opinion', it said, 'is tired of the increasingly false
promises of the demagogues. General dissatisfaction is extreme.
All faith in parliament has been lost.' So it asked famous men
to explain why. Some, including Poincaré, placed the blame
on the domination of deputies by electoral considerations, by
local committees of politicians and local issues, the remedy was
to replace the *scrutin d'arrondissement* by a *scrutin de liste* and proportional representation. This became one of the major con-
troversies of this period and a lot of time was spent discussing it;
but it would be a reform at the expense of the radicals; so
nothing was done till 1919.[3] Others blamed the indecisiveness
of the government. Paul Leroy-Beaulieu, the conservative
economist, rightly pointed out that the trouble with parliament
was not that it did not pass enough laws but that it passed too
many which were incoherent and inapplicable. (Certainly it
should not be thought that Clemenceau's period in office was
barren of legislation simply because he did not fulfil his programme of reforms. Numerous laws were passed but not ones
of fundamental importance, and they were seldom effective.
For example, one established special houses of correction for
prostitutes under eighteen, but in the following year another

---

[1] Achille Viallate, *La Vie politique dans les deux mondes*, vol. 3 (1908–9): a useful
annual.

[2] Camille Pelletan, 'La crise du parti radical', *La Revue*, 80 (15 May 1909),
145–64; Georges Deherme, *La Crise sociale* (1910); 'L'impuissance parlementaire,
enquête', *La Revue*, 73 (15 April 1908); Henri Chantavoine, *En province: lettres au
directeur du Journal des Débats* (1910); André Cheradame, *La Crise française* (1912);
J. L. de Lanessan, *La Crise de la République* (1914).

[3] Cf. P. G. La Chesnais, 'Les radicaux et la représentation proportionnelle',
Revue politique et parlementaire (Oct. 1906), 50–78; Armand Charpentier, *Le Parti
radical et radical socialiste à travers ses congrès 1901–1911* (1913), 118–88.

postponed its application for two years. There were a large
number of laws amending laws which, despite the long time
they took to get through parliament, turned out to be inadequate. The law of 1909 establishing the inalienable family home
appeared to be a belated triumph for the ideas of Le Play, but
it turned out to be too complicated for many to bother to
make use of it.)[1] Anatole France complained that the members
of the government were too bound up with the institutions they
were supposed to be reforming: the minister of war was a
soldier, the minister of finance was a company director, the
minister of the navy had connections with Le Creusot, the armaments factory. Victor Margueritte thought that only the
abandonment of widespread attitudes could improve matters:
the love of bureaucracy, the fear of risks, the enslavement to
routine and petty interests which was characterising French
life. Durkheim, the sociologist, thought there was no hope at all.
'The evil . . . is profound. It derives above all from the disarray
of consciences and the extreme confusion of ideas. The most
diverse and the most contradictory conceptions clash in men's
minds and hold each other in check. How should the legislature
not be powerless when the country is so uncertain as not to
know what it wants?'[2]

The radical party was much divided within itself, to the
point of finding positive action very difficult, and yet it was to
be the largest single party from 1902 to 1936. Its weakness was
that it was essentially negative. Herriot once said that if they
wanted to know what to do, they had only to see what the right
was doing and follow the opposite course. The radicals who
summoned the congress of 1901 at which the party was founded
had no wish to create anything new. They wrote: 'The deliberations will not be concerned with the establishment of a new
programme. Our programme is known. It was fixed by our
fathers.' The radicals indeed looked back to the Revolution (and
perhaps far forward to a philosophical utopia) rather than to
the present. They had a profound sense of history. They wished
to implement the principles of the Great Revolution. But their
ideas on it were deliberately vague. Clemenceau declared 'the

[1] *Recueil des lois, décrets, circulaires etc.* (1908), 335; (1909), 241, 209.
[2] *La Revue*, 73 (15 Apr. 1908), 397.

Revolution is a bloc' and this denial of the variety and contradictions of its ideals showed how imprecise these worshippers of reason were. They remained loyal to the programmes of their historical heroes with almost the same devotion as their Catholic enemies upheld their ancient dogmas. Gambetta's manifesto of 1869, issued at Belleville, summarised most of what they wanted. They had frequently repeated it and could still do so forty years later because they implemented very little of it. It was in fact difficult for them to assume the reins of power and carry out reforms because they were essentially the enemies of power and of authority. Their devotion to reason came from a critical rather than a constructive temperament. They knew who the enemies of the people were. They found it easier to be *against* things than for them. The very first conclusion of their inaugural congress in 1901 was 'the need for union *against* the common enemy'. Alain, the principal philosopher of radicalism[1] held that all power was evil, with an inevitable tendency to tyranny. Freedom was to be found only in individuals; 'thought is revolutionary'; the duty of the citizen was to hold his government in check. 'What matters is not the origin of power, but the continual and efficacious control of the government by the governed.'[2] This was a democratic principle with prophetic importance for the coming age of fascism, but it made a radical government almost self-contradictory. The gradual withering away of the state was a radical principle;[3] and one of the characteristics of the radical party was the consistent hostility and suspicion of the party members towards the *élus*, deputies and councillors.

The conclusion of radicalism was not so much to carry out a programme as to fill the administration with loyal supporters, to evict and destroy the enemy. The radicals ruled for their friends, against their enemies.[4] It is not surprising therefore that they were keener on obtaining ministries which carried patronage and the gift of practical advantages for their clientele rather than the mere show of power. Between 1900 and 1939 no radical was ever president of the republic, and there was a

[1] Émile Chartier, alias Alain, *Éléments d'une doctrine radicale* (1925).

[2] Claude Nicolet, *Le Radicalisme* (1957), 39.

[3] Jules Simon, *La Politique radicale* (1869).

[4] Armand Charpentier, *Le Parti radical et radical socialiste à travers ses congrès, 1901–1911* (1913), 366–70.

radical prime minister for only a quarter of this period. But the ministries of the interior, of education and of agriculture were held by the radicals for 23, 21 and 23 years respectively; indeed the ministry of the interior was theirs for 31 out of 39 years if one also counts periods when a politician favourable to them held it. In 1896 the radicals in parliament vigorously demanded a purge of the civil service when they formed their own ministry for the first time, saying, 'It is above all by the attitude of the civil servants that the country perceives the tendencies of the government.'[1]

The radicals could never work up a fighting enthusiasm for social reform. In 1908 and 1909 three major reports were presented to the party, one on *laissez-faire*, one on property and the class struggle and above all one by Debierre on the social ideas and programme of radicalism; and in 1909 a long social programme was adopted by their congress, involving national-isation of mines and railways, municipalisation of public services of local importance, death-duties, income tax, pen-sions, insurance assistance, equal pay. But this programme was passed quickly and unanimously and the congress showed quite clearly it did not find it very interesting. Speakers on social questions in the congress were frequently urged to finish, so that in 1911, in the debate on the cost of living, the president protested: 'You would not wish it said that the radical party concerns itself with purely political issues and that economic ones do not interest it.'

The debates which aroused real passion were those on religion and this was still the predominant obsession of the party. It should not be forgotten that Combes remained the party's president until 1913. The party bulletin which published the proceedings of local radical committees had very little on social matters, and far more on religion and education. A volume describing the party congresses between 1901 and 1911 devoted the first 200 of its 450 pages to education, the Church and electoral reform, in that order; it then dealt with finance, the army and the law; and this traditional hierarchy accurately

---

[1] Jacques Kayser, 'Le radicalisme des radicaux', in *Tendences politiques dans la vie française depuis 1789*, edited by Guy Michaud (1960), 75–6. Jacques Kayser's book, *Les Grandes Batailles du radicalisme des origines aux portes du pouvoir 1820–1901* (1962), was unfortunately never continued.

reflected their priorities. Certainly, in education they remained pioneers: they placed more emphasis on it than anybody else; and their leading expert Buisson (once Ferry's director of primary education) got them to adopt resolutions in favour of absolute equality of opportunity, scholarships for those who could not afford secondary education, more technical and vocational training, syllabuses drawn up by the teachers themselves. But though he argued that the *lycées* must stop forming an élite, he still placed great emphasis on examinations which ensured, he thought, 'the democratic rule which makes the winning of social advantages dependent on merit'.[1]

They were not levellers. They represented, said Buisson, 'at least a part of the middle classes animated by a spirit which hitherto they have never had'. Formerly these middle classes had been conservative. 'Today—one cannot say how, or why, or since when—the middle classes no longer think as before; and they do not vote as before. Have they become less egoist or more clear sighted? Have they understood their duties or their interests or the force of circumstances better? In any case, henceforth, instead of taking up a position against the masses, they are tending to make common cause with them . . . So there has entered into the mechanism of our government a vital part which has hitherto been missing: a majority which is perfectly sensible, balanced, reasonable and prudent but which nevertheless decidedly wants reforms.' They had taken up the 'programme of their fathers, the democratic and social republic . . . The petty bourgeois, small employers, small tradesmen, small landowners, small employees, small civil servants have discovered that they are nearer the working class than the great bankers, the great capitalists and the great ones privileged by wealth.' They have therefore adopted the doctrine of solidarity —though there was still need to stimulate the feeling of solidarity. The radicals, Buisson concluded, 'are a bourgeois party which has the soul of a people's party. They paradoxically reconcile in themselves the two opposites of the social antinomy. They are, a rare thing in the history of democracies, a class which aspires to confound itself with the nation. They are a class of proprietors who work and of workers who have property, a group of small men who are not parvenus, a sort of family

[1] A. Charpentier, 53.

founded on a marriage of reason, uniting good-will coming
from different sources but heading in the same direction.'[1]
This pregnant definition of radicalism shows clearly enough
why social reform was not its prime aim. The party's frail unity
had been achieved in 1901 in the heat of the Dreyfus affair,
based on a desire to win victory in the religious struggle. Its
immediate and natural result had been the separation of
Church and state: after this victory the radicals were somewhat
at a loss. They could not voluntarily weaken themselves now
by expelling the moderates whose interests were not in social
reform. They had originally won their successes in large cities,
but their main support now came from small towns and above
all rural districts. They gave more attention therefore to the
reform of taxation (always the peasants' principal concern)
than to the improvement of the conditions of the factory worker.
Having achieved power, they were already on the defensive,
they could not throw off the idea that they were somehow
oppressed. The idea that they were building a new society fell
into the background and was taken over by the socialists. Their
social conscience degenerated into a defence of the *small man*,
of whose virtues they now made a myth.[2]

There was a great deal of variety within the party. The
religious issue, which still excited them more than anything,
was interpreted in different ways. The separation of Church and
state, at the level of legislation, was made as moderate as
possible and dissociated from any idea of religious persecution.
But the laws were applied in different ways at a local level.
Many ardent municipalities now fought 'the war of the priest's
house', pulling it down, or turning it into a post-office or other
public use. The executive committee of the party published
a pamphlet to guide radical municipalities in this matter,
which provided the main excitement of local politics in these
years. The question of church schools continued to be debated
ardently too—and the party was divided on the question of
whether education should be a complete state monopoly or not.

[1] F. Buisson, 'La politique radicale socialiste', in *Revue hebdomadaire* (12 Feb.
1910), 159-81.
[2] For an interesting study of radicalism on a local scale, see R. Vandenbusche,
'Aspects de l'histoire politique du radicalisme dans le département du Nord,
1870-1905', *Revue du Nord* (Apr.-June 1965), 223-68. But the problems of this
department were rather special.

It found itself at war with the primary-school masters and the junior civil servants—hitherto its most important representatives in the village. These now wanted to form trade unions, with the right to strike against the state—even the radical state. Could the radicals refuse this elementary right of all men to a single section of the community? They were aghast that the *instituteurs* could turn against their makers. In 1912 they thought of a compromise: the civil servants would be allowed to form unions but these would be forbidden to join the revolutionary C.G.T. They were in a cleft stick and inevitably they lost many of these civil servants to the socialists. Having captured the jobs, these local politicians still wished to remain *against* the state even though it now fed them. Pelletan begged the radical congress not to 'reject [these] small men who were and are still the pioneers of the republic' but there was nothing to be done. The business of reconciling divergent interests (and justice at the same time) presented many difficulties. The radicals solved some of the problems with clever verbal compromises, as in foreign policy, where they declared themselves ardently patriotic but also resolutely in favour of peace and international arbitration, honouring military service but also wishing to transform its character. This was harder to do with electoral reform, since they got 42 per cent of the seats with only 33 per cent of the votes; in 1910 it took an average of 14,000 votes to elect a socialist deputy but only 11,200 to elect a radical. The *scrutin de liste* disagreed with their love of independence; but such was the pressure of public opinion against the 'stagnant pools', as Briand described the single-member constituencies, that they adopted resolutions to reform the system, though without any real intention of doing so.

The radical party was not organised for action. Though founded in 1901, until 1928 it could barely be called a party, and as one of its leaders said, its formation 'preceded what some have defined as the invasion of the masses'.[1] As a party, it did not accept individual enrolments (unlike the S.F.I.O.). Joining it was essentially a local matter, and the only real unit was the local committee. All committees which had a minimum of ten members were considered equal, paying the same subscription (13 francs p.a.) to the central fund and sending the same

[1] Daniel Bardonnet, *L'Évolution de la structure du parti radical* (1960), 9.

number of delegates to the congresses. Such was the looseness of the movement, however, that there were also many radical committees which did not join the party, so as to avoid paying the subscription, minute though it was. In 1910 there were 836 committees adhering to the party and perhaps 600 to 800 outside it: altogether this meant there were probably between about 80,000 and 150,000 members of radical committees. (Compare the socialists' 54,000 members in 1910, and 90,000 in 1914.) The local committees met between six and twelve times a year, and concerned themselves mainly with elections. Attempts were made to organise them into federations, but by 1910 only twenty-three departments had a federation, and in any case these had very little life of their own. The main exception was the Federation of the Seine, run by J. L. Bonnet, the principal advocate of a centralised party. There were also a few regional federations, the most active of which was that of the south-east, run by Estier, but though these held congresses, and helped with propaganda, they had no powers. The sovereign body in the party was the national congress, which met annually in October, and which was attended by all radical deputies, *conseillers généraux*, delegates of municipal councils, delegates of committees, leagues, unions, clubs, Freemason lodges and newspapers which accepted the party programme. Local committees could send as many delegates as they pleased provided they paid the appropriate fee (10 francs for the first, and 5 for every other). Some 800 people usually attended these congresses. For about four days they had a very enjoyable time in passionate debate and wild outbursts of enthusiasm: they interrupted unpopular orators mercilessly, sometimes invaded the tribune, and sessions not infrequently had to be suspended. The congress elected an executive committee of no fewer than 680 members (including all members of parliament) which met once a month (though no more than 100 ever attended any one meeting). It also elected a *bureau* of 33 (half of them members of parliament) which met once a week. But neither of these had any real power; and all efforts to strengthen the central organisation were rejected by the congresses, which spurned the interference of Parisians who, as one member said, 'could not speak the local dialect' and would meddle with matters 'which did not concern them'.

The result of this was that there was very little discipline in elections and no control of the candidates who stood as radicals. A single constituency could have more than one radical candidate—this was particularly noticeable in 1910. The label itself meant very little. Royalists who thought their chances would be improved by calling themselves radical did so, especially in the south. The radical party in parliament therefore consisted of real members of the party paying their subscriptions, and giving up 200 francs of their salary to the party funds, but also of deputies who had been elected under the radical label but who had not accepted its programme, or who had not paid their subscriptions (in 1910 there were about 80 out of 250 of these). The situation was further confused by there being two radical parties in parliament—the radicals and the radical-socialists—despite the unification of 1901. The radicals had been kept in being partly in order to recruit more deputies to support Combes's religious policy. But the division between these two groups did not coincide with the division between 'true' and 'false' radicals. Moreover, the party had no control over the behaviour of its deputies. These could vote as they pleased, and when they were ministers they could follow what policy they pleased. In 1913 Barthou's ministry, based on the right, was condemned by the radical party, but the vice-president of its executive committee, Dumont, nevertheless became a member of it.

Clemenceau's position as prime minister can now be better understood. He was not the leader of the party—there was no such person, or at least the president was purely honorific. Clemenceau seemed the right man because he had adopted a liberal attitude towards the separation—saying that it was not worth losing lives in order to inventory a few chandeliers—and so he was acceptable to the moderate radicals who held a key position. These moderates, however, were hostile to social reform; strikes and social unrest increased their conservatism. In 1908 when the government demanded the prolongation of the parliamentary session in order to get the income tax bill through, 140 radicals voted with the right to defeat it. On the other hand, Clemenceau's policy of repression alienated the left wing of the party. His harsh treatment of the civil servants led over 100 radicals to vote against him in 1909. The extreme

right-wing radicals were virtually indistinguishable from the
conservatives: the extreme left often voted with the socialists. It
is surprising Clemenceau lasted so long. Already in 1907 Pelletan
complained bitterly against his government: 'It must be told
that it is time to return to the path of radical policy.' Clemenceau defiantly replied: 'I do not wish to be strangled by the
silent seraglio . . . Messieurs les radicaux, je vous attends!' The
struggle over the income tax and fear of the social agitation
held party and government together for a while but in May
1909, three months before he fell, the executive committee of the
party passed a resolution regretting 'that by its improvidence
as much as by its successive and contradictory policies the
government of M. Clemenceau has deceived the hopes of
republican democracy and aggravated the misunderstandings
between the various parts; the radical and radical-socialist
party rejects all solidarity with a cabinet whose methods of
government are contrary to the traditions of the party.'

So, despite their parliamentary majority, the radicals were
unable to control the conduct of the ministers. The election of
1910 increased the confusion. On paper the results were more
or less the same for them as in 1906, but the radical deputies
now included a considerably larger number of men elected
with the support of the right and not 'genuine' radicals. Beneath
the surface there was a change in the nature of the majority,
which was given more and more to outbursts of indignation at
the government for not giving it what it wanted, though it did
not quite know what it did want. It thus lost the initiative in
politics. Clemenceau was succeeded by Briand, an independent
socialist favouring appeasement and symbolising the union of
the extremes against the radical centre. The radicals complained
of his 'reactionary compromises' and overthrew him. But they
had no leader with whom to replace him. Pelletan, a radical
of the old generation and formerly Clemenceau's lieutenant,
was the idol of the constituencies: he believed in favouritism
and patronage but his application of these principles when he
was minister of the navy created such administrative chaos
that it was generally agreed he was too whimsical and demagogic for office. Berteaux, a wealthy stockbroker, was very
popular among the radicals in parliament, partly because of
his affability and good humour, partly because he lent money

freely, so that it was said no less than 100 deputies were his debtors. But he was killed in an accident in 1912. Monis, whom the radicals put in to succeed Briand, was a figurehead; and he was injured in this same accident. Caillaux who succeeded him, though not a radical, pleased them because his policy was at once authoritarian and advanced. But his foreign policy, too conciliatory towards Germany, led to his fall. The radicals could provide no alternative and the chief posts of the republic went to moderates. Poincaré became prime minister and then president; Deschanel, even more moderate, became president of the chamber of deputies. Briand followed as premier once again, and then finally Barthou with a ministry avowedly relying on right-wing support and with only three lone radicals in it. The decline of their influence was seen when the navy was ordered to fly its flags at half mast on Good Friday; when pupils of a public school were forbidden to attend a celebration of the bicentenary of Diderot, on the ground that neutrality should be observed in these matters. Social reforms, the income tax, anticlericalism were forgotten; the only bill of importance brought forward was to increase military service to three years.

In the face of this continued and frightening advance by their opponents, the radicals attempted to rally in 1913. They adopted, first, a programme more practical and up to date than their traditional utopia. They stopped talking, for example, about the election of judges and ceased to add the farcical comment that 'if this cannot be achieved soon', less radical reforms of the judiciary should be undertaken.[1] They produced something much shorter than the Belleville programme and Clemenceau's seventeen points. Two-year military service, a progressive income tax, anticlericalism in education and social insurance became their policy. Church questions no longer occupied first place. Cutting down the army and taxing the rich was a popular cry and in addition could win them support from the socialists. Secondly, an attempt was made to form a single radical group in parliament. This failed in the senate and was only partially successful in the chamber, where splinter groups persisted on both right and left. Despite the party's policy on the army, thirty-eight radicals voted for

[1] F. Buisson, *La Politique radicale, études sur les doctrines du parti radical et radical-socialiste* (1908), 167.

three-year military service. Nevertheless a little more discipline was introduced; some 'false radicals' were unmasked; those who had served in Barthou's ministry were expelled from the party. The executive committee became more active and undertook more propaganda. The subscription was increased to 25 centimes per member. Efforts were made to reduce multiple radical candidatures in the same constituency, again not always successfully—in two constituencies of Creuse, for example, there were nine radical candidates in 1914—but on the whole there was progress. As a result the party emerged from this election a little more disciplined—smaller but less amorphous. Thirdly, they found themselves a new leader, brought in from outside. Caillaux, having broken with the moderates from whom he originated but whom he frightened with his income tax, was in bitter rivalry against all other parliamentary leaders. So he joined the radicals in 1913 and was at once elected president. Though cold and distant, he seemed to be the only man capable of reviving them. Certainly he led them successfully for a while, and a ministry under him and Jaurès should have followed. But once again the radicals had bad luck. Caillaux was the victim of a scandal occasioned by his divorced wife. She shot dead the editor of the *Figaro* who had published letters between her and her husband. His complacency towards Germany made him unacceptable in the new patriotic atmosphere occasioned by the war. So in 1914 the radicals were still a party without a clear sense of direction, unable to take advantage of their popular support.[1]

[1] The best guide to this subject is M. Fournier, 'Le parti radical de 1906 à 1914' (unpublished thesis, Fondation Nationale des Sciences Politiques, 1960). For further details on party structure see G. Fabius de Champville, *Le Comité exécutif du parti républicain radical et radical-socialiste de 1897 à 1907* (1908), and Pierre Andréani, 'La formation du parti radical-socialiste', *Revue politique et parlementaire*, 206 (1952), 33–41.

10. Socialism

HISTORIES of socialism in France normally begin in 1870, and have as their principal thread the spread of Marxist doctrine. It is perfectly true that an organised socialist party developed only in the late nineteenth century and that its Marxism had little in common with the socialism of the early utopians. It is impossible, however, to understand the rapid success of the socialist party without going back to 1848. During the Second Republic, the vagueness and moderation of early socialist thought meant that a very large number of people could sympathise with it, and the severe economic crisis made many look to it for the solution of their difficulties. It was in the years 1849–51 that substantial sections of the peasantry were won to socialism, principally in the backward regions of the centre and south-east. It took some forty years for the profound consequences of this event to be appreciated. The socialist party of 1900 could become a major force in politics while France was still hardly industrialised and while there was still only a small minority of industrial workers—the obvious subjects of their propaganda—because these rural areas gave it mass support. By going back to 1848 one sees why the majority of the socialist vote in the early twentieth century came from certain backward rural areas. One sees also why its programme could not be a clear-cut Marxist one. Its peasant backers had been won over to a brand of socialism current in 1848, and to a large extent this is what they still voted for in 1900. The mark of the Second Republic was thus powerfully imprinted upon the movement.

In 1848 the socialists were diverse, individualistic, dispersed, organised at most into tiny societies but without links between each other. The followers of the utopian thinkers did not form active political groups with mass support, let alone one party. The secret societies of revolutionaries in Paris involved only a couple of thousand men; those in the provinces—usually not revolutionary but rather expressing traditional animosities and the relics of old antagonisms, such as the White Terror of 1815 —were isolated and parochial in outlook. This situation did not change in the early months of the republic. The socialists could not stand as a party in the elections of 1848. Only in Paris were they sufficiently numerous or self-conscious to act independently. Louis Blanc, in co-operation with socialist clubs, put up a list of candidates which included twenty workers. All but one were defeated. The leading socialist celebrities indeed were generally defeated in Paris, except when supported by the moderates. They had better luck in the provinces; and altogether some 55 out of the 880 deputies to the constituent assembly were in some way socialist, or at least partisans of a 'democratic and social republic'. Already socialism revealed itself as having an appeal beyond the hothouse of the capital, but the lines between parties were still too undefined to make it possible to distinguish at all clearly between them. Men were often elected on this occasion as individuals, or as expressing peculiar local conditions, more than for the precise nature of their opinions. So the socialist deputies included both Blanquists like Martin Bernard, a compositor with long experience of conspiracy, who criticised the workers for wanting to become bourgeois, but also the mason Totain who, while seeking the improvement of the lot of the masses, wished to 'lengthen the jackets without shortening the frock-coats'.[1] They were at first isolated. They formed a separate group in the Assembly—the Société des représentants républicains. Ledru-Rollin and his followers (essentially Jacobins, looking back to the revolution of 1793) went to some pains to dissociate themselves from them. Their impetuous involvement in demonstrations and insurrections led to numerous arrests among them. One famous trial, at Bourges, was even more damaging because it revealed their divisions, mutual hostilities and even treachery.

However, in the course of the Second Republic, the socialists grew into something like a national movement, for three reasons. First, the indiscriminate persecuting of the left-wing republicans which became increasingly intense after the June days, led the party of Ledru-Rollin and the socialists to unite.

[1] *Biographie des 900 représentants à la Constituante*, published by Victor Lecou (1849), 406; G. Weill, *Histoire du parti républicain en France* (1928), 129 n.

The national leadership remained in the hands of the Jacobins, but they took up a large part of the programme of their new allies. The socialist following thus suddenly swelled. Secondly, vigorous propaganda on a regional or a national scale, in which the Jacobins had grown adept, was now put to the service of socialism, and was directed with unprecedented effectiveness at the poor peasantry. Innumerable pamphlets, almanacs, engravings, songs—all written with the rural constituencies in mind—flooded the countryside despite the censorship, often being recopied by hand over and over again as they were passed around. Banquets, at which political leaders spoke and started a local organisation, became very frequent. In certain areas almost every commune came to have a left-wing secret society. The Solidarité républicaine, a national society founded in Paris to assist Ledru-Rollin's presidential campaign with the Blanquist Martin Bernard as president and the Jacobin Charles Delescluze as secretary, and modelled on the Société des Droits de l'Homme (which had done so much to organise the revolution of 1830), spread branches everywhere.[1] Active leaders got small secret societies to correspond with each other; Alphonse Gent, for example, in this way established a formidable regional organisation in the south-east. Thirdly, the movement spread rapidly not only because its propaganda was highly relevant to the peasantry's immediate needs, but because its methods were grafted on to traditional peasant institutions. The secret societies cannot be explained as a sudden birth. They were a transformation and adaptation of the old *chambrées*, drinking clubs, Freemason lodges, *carbonari* groups, workers' unions and friendly societies; they revived traditional hates against royalists, landlords, enclosers and money-lenders. In certain parts of the country the number of these societies was astonishingly large. In some communes almost every inhabitant was enlisted. In the department of Vaucluse, with 80,000 electors, there were about 12,000 members of left-wing societies, and 6,000 of legitimist ones. In the presidential election of 1848, Ledru-Rollin polled only 370,119 votes, while Raspail standing as a pure socialist won 36,920. After their union, in the legislative elections of 1849, the left made very substantial gains and obtained 40–50 per cent of the votes in

[1] Marcel Dessal, *Charles Delescluze 1809–71* (1952), 93–120.

twenty-three departments. Socialism was in this stage a branch of republicanism and appeared all the more formidable because it could not be readily differentiated from it.[1]

It is no wonder that the bourgeoisie were terrified by the 'Red Menace',[2] and all the more so because the Reds were purposely lying low until the election of 1852. It is true the divisions among the Reds were so great that they would not have known what to do with power if they won it. Some preached the union of classes, but some a revolt of the *petits* against the *gros*. This did not imply a class struggle, however. There was no bitter animosity among the peasantry against large landowners or rich men as such. Their principal enemies were their creditors—who were men of all classes. Socialist propaganda was particularly successful among indebted peasants. It used the economic distress effectively to win them—whether small proprietors, farmers or daily labourers—from traditional attitudes of respect, but it did not go beyond preaching fraternity, credit, a reform of taxes, the ending of poverty. The real leaders of the left-wing societies were principally bourgeois themselves—barristers, notaries, doctors, schoolmasters, landowners, with artisans usually taking the lead only at village level.

The *coup d'état* of 1851 showed the strength of the movement and also destroyed it. In the Drôme 15,000 to 20,000 men took up arms (nearly a quarter of the electorate), in the Basses-Alpes 15,000 out of 45,000 electors. Thirty-two departments were placed in a state of siege.[3] In a few small towns the rebels were able to seize power until troops arrived: their first decree was to 'abolish usury', and debts, and indirect taxation, to proclaim free education and promise the division of common lands among the masses.[4] The large number involved points to the effectiveness of the secret societies; but the almost total absence of pillage or murder shows that it was not total revolution that they planned. 26,000 men were arrested, out of whom about 10,000 were transported out of France. The more prominent leaders who escaped took refuge in exile. More than a dozen

---

[1] Jacques Bouillon, 'Les démocrates-socialistes aux élections de 1849', *Revue française de science politique*, 6 (Jan.–Mar. 1956), 70–95.

[2] A. Romieu, *Le Spectre rouge en 1852* (1851).

[3] Eugène Tenot, *Étude historique sur le coup d'État* (1877–80).

[4] Philippe Vigier, *La Seconde République dans la région alpine* (1963), 2. 332.

years elapsed before the socialists recovered from this repression. The early successes of Louis Napoleon, it might be added, turned many of them into Bonapartists—for the two parties, to a certain extent, *promised* much the same.

The failure of the Second Republic discredited the utopian socialists. It produced a profound intellectual crisis of depression and self-doubt among their followers. 'After the hammer-blow of 2 December', wrote Vallès, 'some went mad, some died . . . Some see and hear still, but their misfortune has withered, wrinkled and emptied them. . . . Still these men were less unhappy than we were. Those who in 1845 were around twenty years old, discovered what it was like to live. We have hardly known it, we who left school in 1850. In 1851 we were already beaten.'[1] However, socialist ideals were not fundamentally modified. Apart from Proudhon (whose ideas did change, as has been seen, on a number of points), there was little new socialist thought during the Second Empire.[2] The socialist movement as such virtually disappeared. The majority adhered to the republican party, which was wide enough to absorb as great a variety of opinion as the party of 1849. In the eyes of the general public socialism, often appearing to be dead for a dozen years, came to be identified with the First International. Socialism in the 1860s is thus very different from that of the 1840s. It was almost entirely an urban and working-class movement.

The French section of the workers' International owes its origin to a rebellion by a small group of workers against the domination of the republican movement by the bourgeoisie, in the belief that the workers could effectively win their emancipation only by their own efforts. The Manifesto of Sixty Workers in 1864 was the first expression of this view and as such is a landmark in French history. But the bronze worker Tolain who, in pursuance of this manifesto, stood for parliament in 1864, obtained only 395 votes.[3] His party, and the International which he helped to found in London, was at first suspect to the socialists because of Tolain's friendly relations with the radical Prince Napoleon. Certainly the government

[1] Jules Vallès, 'Un chapitre de l'histoire du 2 décembre', in *Courrier de l'Intérieur* (8 Sept. 1868), quoted by J. Tchernof, *Le Parti républicain au coup d'État* (1906), 166.

[2] T. N. Bernard, *Le Socialisme d'hier et celui d'aujourd'hui* (1870), 274.

[3] Against 14,444 votes for Garnier-Pagès, the republican candidate, and 6,530 for Frédéric Lévy, the conservative.

tolerated the International, and made no protest when it deposited its statutes. Its working-class character did not prevent a number of bourgeois politicians from joining it, like Jules Simon, Ferdinand Buisson, Henri Martin, which shows how moderate it was. Its founders were keen that it should be a *société d'étude* not a new version of the Carbonari; they were anxious to avoid falling into the old errors of the secret *compagnonnage*, and refused to be a secret society. They were hostile to strikes and at first used their energies to prevent them (as with the builders in 1865–7). Their hostility to revolutionary methods won them the fervent enmity of the Blanquists. They concerned themselves mainly with discussing how workers' societies, co-operatives for production, consumption and credit could be organised. They feared that if they won higher wages, their employers would import foreign labour, so international solidarity was important to them. But they aimed only at reforming capitalist society and obtaining equality for the worker in it, not at overthrowing it. Tolain's purpose was to enable men to exercise their individual initiative; his dream was to 'make every man a property owner'; it was only frustration, through inability to exercise their initiative, that made workers communists which, he said, 'they are neither by belief nor by instinct'.[1]

The International obtained a small office in the rue des Gravilliers which for a year contained only a broken stove, a white wood table and two stools (in the day time Fribourg, one of the founders, used it for his job as a decorator). Only later were four chairs added. The International sent out 20,000 copies of its programme; this was paid for by Edouard Blot, a printer, for they had no money themselves. After seven months they still had recruited only 500 members. Their plans to establish Proudhonian exchange and credit centres could not be put into effect; the practical advantages they offered their members in return for their subscription of 10 centimes a week, in the form of insurance and mutual assurance, were illusory, because their funds were inadequate. They contented themselves with planning to enable workers to buy their own tools and to support them against capitalist competition until they were established. The International began as little more than a friendly society;

[1] *Enquête parlementaire sur l'insurrection du 18 mars 1871* (1872), Tolain's evidence, 425.

SOCIALISM 367

it became revolutionary under the pressure of events in the space of a few years.[1]

There was a take-over bid first of all from the republicans.[2] Henri Lefort (whose father, a legitimist convert to Orleanism, had died in 1832 defending the monarchy of Louis-Philippe against a republican rising) was a bourgeois journalist who had himself taken up the ideas of Proudhon, Victor Hugo and the Rochdale pioneers. He tried to effect a union between the A.I.T. and 'republican radicalism'. He claimed he would swell the A.I.T.'s ranks with 10,000 men loyal to him in the co-operative societies he had formed. But the A.I.T. leaders wished neither to be absorbed in this way, nor to involve themselves with the political opposition to Napoleon III, which would only make their existence even more precarious. As a result they expelled Lefort and laid it down that they would admit manual workers only. This was the first of a series of disagreements between the French and other nations in the International (which had non-worker members like Marx). The International at first accepted the moderate mutualism of the French, and their hope of improving existing society rather than destroying it. But in 1868 widespread nationalisation was adopted as the A.I.T.'s programme and in 1869 Proudhonian doctrines were finally defeated in it. The character of the French section changed rapidly. The hostility to strikes disappeared. In February 1867 the strike of bronze workers was supported by the A.I.T. (in which they were strongly represented), and a few thousand francs aid was even obtained from the English section. Rumours spread that millions were being sent across the Channel. The employers gave way in panic. The prestige of the A.I.T. rocketed. Trade unions all over the country began joining it in hope of receiving similar aid. The industrial agitation of the years 1868–70 added an unexpected fillip to its growth. It was widely believed that the A.I.T. was fomenting the numerous strikes: in fact it was the strikes which brought it recruits: joining it became a symbol of the strikers' determination to fight to the end. Notions of the A.I.T.'s power became grossly inflated. The government believed in 1870 that it had 250,000

[1] E. E. Fribourg, *L'Association internationale des travailleurs* (1871), 92–8.
[2] Cf. Charles M. Limousin, 'Coup d'œil historique sur l'Internationale', *Journal des économistes*, 38 (1875), 68–87.

members; the public talked of a million. In fact it probably
had only between 20,000 and 40,000 and most of these were
affiliated through their unions in a very loose way, for the purpose of benefiting temporarily during a strike.[1] 'People join the
A.I.T.', it was said, 'in the same way as they offer and accept
a glass of wine.' It had branches in the principal industrial
areas of France (it was entirely urban) but these branches
were often the creations of a few individuals and rather precarious.[2] Where traditions of political opposition were strong,
as in Lyon, the A.I.T. made slow headway.[3]

Involvement in strikes changed the character of the A.I.T.
It was no longer able, as its founders had intended, to study
economic problems and leave politics aside. It found itself
forced to retaliate every time troops were used to suppress
strikes, by attacking the government and the bourgeoisie. 'It
is impossible for us to live', they wrote in 1869, 'under a social
regime in which capital replies with fusillades to demonstrations which are sometimes turbulent but always just.'[4] Arrests
and persecution completed the transformation. In the first
trial of the leaders of the A.I.T. in 1868 they were very moderate
during the defence, and with no hint of any revolutionary
intentions. Later, in their appeal against conviction, they were
far more independent and further trials accentuated their
hostility. The arrest of these moderate leaders led to the election of new leaders to replace them, who marked a further step
to the left. By 1869 the original French section of the A.I.T.
had virtually disintegrated.

A new leadership now transformed it.[5] It concentrated its
efforts on organising the workers into unions, and became
avowedly socialist and revolutionary. Varlin in Paris formed
a vigorously aggressive federation of workers' societies in
December 1869, which was scarcely distinguishable from the
A.I.T. In Lyon Richard, in Marseille Bastelica showed the

[1] J. Rougerie, 'Sur l'histoire de la Première Internationale', Le Mouvement
social, 51 (1965), 31 and n.
[2] J. Maitron and G. M. Thomas, 'L'Internationale et la Commune à Brest',
Le Mouvement social, 41 (1962), 48–53.
[3] J. Rougerie, 'La Première Internationale à Lyon', Annali dell'Istituto G.
Feltrinelli (1961), 126–93, esp. 145.
[4] Jacques Freymond, La Première Internationale (1962), 1. xiv.
[5] Jeannine Verdès, 'Les délégués français aux conférences et congrès de l'A.I.T.',
Cahiers de I.S.E.A. (Aug. 1964), 83–176.

flirtation with the ideas of Bakunin. The A.I.T. became the
new 'red spectre' haunting France and indeed Europe. But
the menace was of course superficial, far more so than in 1851.
Repression was easy, as soon as it was resolutely decided on.
The arrests and trial of its leaders in June 1870, followed by
efficient repression in the provinces, destroyed it as effectively
as the *coup* of 1851 had destroyed the first socialist party. The
war completed its disarray. By the time of the Commune it had
virtually ceased to exist.

In England, the A.I.T. was principally backed by artisan
unions in declining or traditional industries.[1] In France this
was true to a certain extent, but they were far from being its
only supporters. France differed from England in having fewer
members of the A.I.T. but dispersed over a wider range of
occupations and social types. The doctrinal beliefs of the French
were also more varied. The view that they were basically
Proudhonists is too simple. They may have begun as such but in
practice the force of circumstances soon made them give up
their hostility to political action, to strikes or to violence. They
ignored the precepts of Proudhon in standing for parliament
in 1863 and in 1869 (agitating in favour of Poland and Italy).
Later the new leaders, even if they were influenced by Bakunin,
insisted on political action for all his opposition to it. They
were perhaps Marxists without knowing it—but not by any
influence. The A.I.T. was composed essentially of practical
men, not of theorists.[2]

The history of a couple of workers' leaders, reputed to be leading Proudhonists, is interesting in this connection. Henri Tolain
(1828–97) holds a place in working-class history comparable to
that of Pelloutier. He was the engraver who did most to organise
the workers' delegation to the London Exhibition of 1862, the
first workers' parliamentary candidatures in 1863 and the
Workers' International in 1864. He was regarded as the leader
of the Proudhonist section of the International. But, like
Griffuelhes, Tolain was essentially a practical organiser, not
a theorist. 'The people', he wrote of Proudhon's abstentionist

[1] H. Collins and C. Abramsky, *K. Marx and the British Labour Movement. Years of the First International* (1965), 70.
[2] J. Rougerie, 'Sur l'histoire de la Première Internationale', *Le Mouvement social*, 51 (1965), 40–3.

programme in 1863, 'do not often let themselves be led by a theory, whatever its value may be. The abstract deductions of metaphysics have little hold on them. Almost always at decisive times, they follow the impulse of sentiment much more readily than pure reason.'[1] Their aim, he believed, was above all to obtain 'a liberty equivalent to that which 1789 gave the capitalist and agricultural proprietor'. In 1848 they had been unable to formulate their aspirations clearly, and 'it was more by intuition than by reasoning that the workers adopted this or that social doctrine'. Gradually, in the silence of the early years of the Second Empire, their leaders put aside exaggerated views and impracticable utopias, and sought feasible reforms. Tolain was no revolutionary; and he was even hostile to strikes (not because he was a Proudhonist, but because he saw their practical inconveniences). He quoted with approval from Louis Napoleon's *Extinction of Pauperism*: 'The working class is like a people of helots in the midst of a people of sybarites . . . Poverty will cease to be seditious when opulence ceases to be oppressive.' He hoped for the emancipation of the workers through education, through trade unions (of both workers and employers), 'the mother institution of all future progress', and through the conscious limitation of industrialisation. The snag, to him, about the development of machines was that 'without capital, it was impossible to show one's individual initiative'. So he thought France should not try to compete with England, but concentrate on producing high-class goods, so that 'French taste and artistic sentiment [should not be] extinguished by the discipline of the factory hierarchy'. Tolain soon left the International and he did not support the Commune. Just as the mass of the workers had not followed Proudhon in 1863, so they did not accept the extremism of the International. Tolain, accurately reflecting their moderation, expected to obtain more from within the bourgeois system than by trying to topple it over. He became a deputy in 1871 and a senator in 1876. He spoke with some contempt of workers who accepted communism because it was the simplest idea, 'being as it were self-explanatory'.

The limitations of Proudhon's influence can be seen in a different way in the case of Eugène Varlin (1839–71) who is

[1] H. Tolain, *Quelques Vérités sur les élections de Paris* (1863), 23.

the second great figure in working-class politics of this period. The son of an agricultural labourer (who also owned a tiny plot of land) he was apprenticed to an uncle as a bookbinder in Paris at the age of 13. At 18 he was a founder member of the Bookbinders' Friendly Society; he helped to organise their strikes in 1864 and 1865, in which latter year he joined the International. He placed faith for the emancipation of the workers in trade unions and co-operatives which led him, as his biographer puts it, 'to work in keeping with the theories of Proudhon before he really knew the works of the philosopher of Besançon . . . His own observations have guided him and not any philosophical system.'[1] His independence was shown in his rejection of Proudhon's advocacy of keeping women in the home and leaving education to the control of parents. He decried the 'Proudhoniens enragés', who preached abstention in the election of 1869: he was anxious to have workers opposing candidates of all parties to mark 'the break of the masses with the bourgeoisie'.[2] Though he soon broke away from the mutualists in the International, he did not become a Marxist, for he retained a profound dislike of the state and of authoritarianism. Though he had much in common with Bakunin, he drew his ideas essentially from his own experience as a union organiser, in which he showed exceptional talent. Unlike Tolain, he was not personally ambitious, but dedicated, ascetic, seldom laughing, always active; it was symbolic that one of his last acts was to disallow the expenses incurred by a general of the Commune who sent in a bill for a new uniform, of the finest cloth, made for him by the deposed emperor's tailor. But for his early death, he might have played a major role in the social history of his country.[3]

The Commune

The Commune was not a socialist government. It has a place in the history of socialism, however, because many contemporaries believed it to be socialist. Marx misinterpreted it completely.

[1] Maurice Foulon, *Eugène Varlin, relieur et membre de la Commune* (Clermont-Ferrand, 1934), 45.   [2] Ibid., 108.
[3] On Benoist Malon in these years see Gerald Hoeffel, 'Some Aspects of Reformist Socialism in France' (Oxford D.Phil. thesis, 1973), which is the first part of what will be a major study of this influential figure; see also below, pp. 774-5.

He celebrated it as 'the glorious harbinger of a new society', believing, quite wrongly, that it was 'essentially a working-class government, the result of the struggle of the producing against the appropriating class', establishing the dictatorship of the proletariat, intending to abolish property, so popular with the masses that if it had 'three months free communication with the provinces', it would have brought about 'a general rising of the peasants'.[1] Marx's mythical views had an important influence on Lenin, but in French history the Commune has a totally different significance.

It was first of all not the result of any revolution. Two attempts to start an insurrection by the revolutionaries in the city—chiefly Blanquists—on 31 October 1870 and 22 January 1871, were complete fiascos, raising virtually no support.

The Commune was the product of more subtle causes, some of long standing and some more immediately connected with the Franco-Prussian war. Paris had since 1789 been the principal asylum of advanced republican ideas in France and a faithful source of strength for every opposition. It had made and overthrown governments time and again. Its whims had had to be accepted as commands by the provinces. But though it had mastered the country, it was not free itself. The state had had its revenge by depriving it of self-governing institutions. It was administratively the most backward commune in France. It had no mayor and no municipal independence. The prefect of police watched over it with an army of spies and hated Corsican *agents*. The hostility between town and country reached its highest pitch here. As a rapidly growing city full of recent immigrants, of *arrivistes*, of many lost illusions and few successes, it was immeasurably attractive, hateful and competitive. It contained the strongest contrasts of wealth in the country. The animal degradation of its poor, on the border-lines of starvation and crime, appeared as a constant menace to bourgeois society. Comparing them to savages and barbarians, Buret in his *De la misère et des classes laborieuses en Angleterre et en France* (1840) wondered already whether 'they are perhaps meditating an invasion'.[2]

[1] K. Marx, *Civil War in France* (first published 1871; London 1933 edition with an introduction by Engels), 19, 43, 47, 63.
[2] L. Chevalier, *Classes laborieuses et classes dangereuses* (1958), 452–3.

The June days of 1848 and the rising after the *coup d'état* in December 1851, showed just how dangerous Paris could be. The war of 1870–1 exacerbated these old antagonisms: the siege of Paris accentuated the separation of the capital from the rest of the country and filled the inhabitants with an almost hysterical hate of the incompetent government which had lost the war. The National Assembly of 1871, with a monarchist majority, showed the completeness of their isolation, and even more so when it symbolically moved its meetings to Versailles. Paris wanted to preserve the republic and to pursue the war. The overthrow of the conservative government became vital to it when the war-time moratorium on commercial debts was ended, so threatening many small artisans and shopkeepers with bankruptcy. It was not an upsurge of socialism or of any new force that produced the Commune. Paris did not rebel. Rather the Commune was brought about by the conservatives wishing to end the old problem of Parisian insubordination. Thiers had an old score to settle with the city which had overthrown him in 1848. When the Parisians refused to surrender their artillery, he withdrew all troops from the city, and made military preparations to retake it by force, as he believed Louis-Philippe should have done twenty-three years before. He determined not only to obtain the submission of the Parisians but to exterminate once and for all their intransigent radical opposition, the perpetual threat to all stability. It was this withdrawal of the government that created the Commune and made Paris autonomous for 73 days (18 March–28 May 1871).

Suddenly the ministries, the barracks, the police stations, town halls, courts and post-offices were empty. All signs of bourgeois government disappeared. There was no revolution of joy, as in 1848. Gloom, uncertainty, surprise at Thiers's extreme action and his refusal to parley, indignation and hate of the state created a sombre, anxious atmosphere. On the other hand, Paris could now 'live its own life' in conformity with its temperament and its ideas.[1] As a result—and this is perhaps what makes the Commune so fascinating and important to the historian—it is possible now to see Paris naked, for its conventional clothes were suddenly removed. One can see

[1] Arthur Arnould, *Histoire populaire et parlementaire de la Commune de Paris* (Brussels, 1878), 1. 114, 3. 45. (By a participant, very good for atmosphere.)

just where the government and the economic system were repressive—where the clothes had been too tight—but also where masses would continue to behave as they had always done even when official obligations and sanctions were withdrawn. The extent to which popular ideas had changed or remained static since 1848 or indeed since 1789, is revealed first by what the Commune did and secondly by the records of the criminal proceedings which followed it. Almost 40,000 people were arrested after March and files for 15,000 of these survive, in which ordinary men speak in their own words. This is a unique source for making contact with those who normally leave no written trace in history.[1]

In 1871 Paris was not to any great extent socialist or revolutionary. In the elections of that year only four of the forty-three candidates supported by the International were elected; and these were successful partly because they received support from other parties; Blanqui obtained only 50,000 votes. The first thing Paris did on finding itself independent was to hold elections for a municipal council—which then assumed the name of Commune. Twenty-five manual workers (artisans) were returned, and this gave the Commune a uniquely proletarian flavour—but the sixty-five other members were bourgeois—doctors, teachers, lawyers, journalists.[2] About one-third of the population of Paris had left during the war or after the siege, including most of the upper classes: the leadership of the city significantly devolved to the petty bourgeoisie, when the top layer—social and governmental—was removed. Two-thirds of these ninety members of the Commune were Jacobins, inspired not by a vision of a socialist future, but by memories of the Revolution of 1789, seeing the Commune as a continuation of that of 1793, capturing power in the interests of the people and using the authority of the state to destroy its enemies. Only one-third were in some way socialists and these were divided between Proudhonists, seeking the abolition of the state, and Blanquist revolutionaries. The acts of the Commune were generally the work of the Jacobins, but the manifestos and justifications of these actions were written by the more theoreti-

[1] J. Rougerie, *Le Procès des communards* (1964); id., *Paris Libre* (1971).
[2] H. P. O. Lissagaray, *Histoire de la Commune de 1871* (first published 1876, new ed. with an introduction by Amédée Dunois 1947), 135-6.

cal Proudhonists. So the aims of the Commune are, not surprisingly difficult to discover, and all the more so because even
this division between Jacobins, Proudhonists and Blanquists is
too simple. The Jacobins were not necessarily antisocialist for
some were members of the International. Most social reforms
were voted unanimously. The Blanquists had much in common
with the Jacobins. There was no coherent socialist minority
group, which only existed, if at all, at the very end of the
Commune, when they had got to know each other. In any
case very few acted consistently according to any one doctrine.
Within the parties there were representatives of several
generations with very different outlooks. Beslay had begun as
a Bonapartist under the Restoration, and had been in turn
a liberal and a republican before becoming a Proudhonian
socialist. He was a well-to-do manufacturer, who had unsuccessfully experimented with schemes for sharing profits with his
workmen.[1] Delescluze was a journalist, a prefect in 1848, one
of Ledru-Rollin's principal supporters. He was a passionate
admirer of the men of the great Revolution and particularly
of the 'martyrs of Thermidor', whom he regarded as 'infallible
oracles'. He had attacked the socialism of both Louis Blanc and
Proudhon, as likely to turn France into a 'convent or a barracks';
Robespierre's Declaration of Rights and a revival of the Committee of Public Safety were his programme. But during the
Second Empire he had shown much sympathy for the efforts of
the workers to establish the International and for practical
attempts to win their emancipation by association; though
leader of the Jacobins, and accused of being ignorant of social
questions, he retained the respect and even won the admiration
of the socialists.[2]
The bookbinder Varlin (aged only 32) talked of class
struggles; but Vermorel, who also called himself a socialist,
spoke of social harmony: already well known as a journalist at
30, he was highly eclectic, as influenced by Delescluze as by
Proudhon.[3] Tridon, the wealthy son of a speculator in national
lands, was a Blanquist: he devoted himself to restoring the

[1] Charles Beslay, *Mes Souvenirs* (Neuchâtel and Brussels, 1874).
[2] Marcel Dessal, *Charles Delescluze 1809–1871* (1952), 421–6 and *passim*; B. Malon,
La Troisième Défaite du prolétariat français (Neuchâtel, 1871), 141; A. Arnould, 2. 89.
[3] A. Vermorel, *Le Parti socialiste* (1870), v and *passim*; Jean Vermorel, *Un
Enfant du Beaujolais: Auguste Vermorel, 1841–1871* (Lyon and Paris, 1911), 131.

reputation of the revolutionary Hébert, but, though a Blanquist, he sided with the socialists during the Commune. Gustave
Flourens, son of an Academician and professor at the Collège de
France, himself a professor of some reputation and of brilliant
promise, heir to an income of 30,000 francs, had an overwhelming longing for swashbuckling romance and he gave everything
up to be a mob leader. Babick, a perfumer, was a religious mystic
(a 'fusionist'); and Régère, a veterinary surgeon, was actually
a clerical. Allix had invented a lunatic telegraph system using
'sympathetic snails' and as mayor of the eighth *arrondissement*
organised gymnasia for women. Assi was a mechanic who had
served under Garibaldi and organised strikes at Le Creusot,
but Rigault, the youngest member of the Commune (only 24)
was the son of a sub-prefect of the Second Empire. He had
made himself an expert about the secret service of that regime:
he got to know the police spies of Paris by following them after
their appearances in court; he compiled a long list of them,
just as they had a list of the opposition.[1] These examples are
enough to show how varied the composition of the Commune
was and how complex the motives of its members were. One of
them once said to another: 'The best day of my life will be that
on which I shall arrest you.'[2]

The Commune's main preoccupation was to feed and defend
itself against the government of Versailles. It had no time to
institute, let alone to try out, any far-reaching reforms. The
atmosphere of war and siege was not conducive to careful
planning: one member recorded that he undressed and went
to bed fewer than ten times in these two months. However,
the decrees which the Commune passed are highly significant.
There was very little in them that was anti-capitalist. The
Commune did indeed attempt to establish a few workers'
production associations and to give some large firms this form
of organisation, but only after promising compensation to the
owners. A few trade unions did run factories established in this
way, though they were deeply disappointing, inefficient and
a prey to endless squabbling. But these experiments represented

[1] Jules Clère, *Les Hommes de la Commune. Biographie complète de tous ses membres*
(1871), 16–17, 146; Jean Allemane, *Mémoires d'un communard* (n.d.), 72–3; Charles
Rihs, *La Commune de Paris, sa structure et ses doctrines* (Geneva, 1955), 76–94, 143–78.
[2] A. Arnould, 3. 31.

a return to the ideals of 1848, not an implementation of Proudhon's theories. A demand for state intervention continued, which was very much against the ideas of Proudhon. When the Commune abolished night work in bakeries, the Proudhonists objected that though the reform was desirable it was the bakers themselves, not the government, who should have effected it. The Commune indeed failed to become the anarchist non-state: it ended by instituting a Jacobin Committee of Public Safety, to the protests of a sizeable minority. Though it contained so many journalists, it instituted censorship of the press. Rigault, its head of police, was even more arbitrary than the Napoleonic police he had once attacked.

The Commune's most interesting reforms were relatively minor practical ones.[1] The abolition of fines in workshops clearly reflected a popular demand. The granting of pensions to widows of men killed in the fighting—whether legally married or not—was a striking recognition that many workers were not married, and a great blow for the emancipation of women, who, with the wage-earner, were considered the most oppressed sections of the community. Dr. Vaillant, at the head of the Education Committee, ordered the establishment of two experimental technical schools, one for boys and one for girls, in which Fourierist 'integral education, the true basis of social equality' would be given. He also attempted to laicize church schools, but here again the actual changes were very slight. At the Lycée St. Louis, prayers still continued to be said twice a day: all that was different was that the two almoners put on civilian clothing and bowler hats and let their beards grow, to the considerable puzzlement of the children.[2] It was difficult to transform the educational system quickly; but even in the sphere of justice, where this might have been possible, little that was radical was attempted. Protot, who was placed in charge of Justice, was the son of a peasant; he had risen to be a barrister, become an admirer of Blanqui, participated in politics and defended prosecuted socialists. He decreed the election of magistrates, but, fearing the results, in fact appointed

---

[1] *Procès-verbaux de la Commune de 1871*, edited by Georges Bourgin and Gabriel Herriot (1924 and 1945, 2 vols.), I. 159, 187, 282–4.

[2] Maurice Dommanget, *L'Enseignement, l'enfance et la culture sous la Commune* (1964), 54, 57.

new ones himself, most of them bourgeois. He abolished the venality of the offices of notary and court officials, but kept those offices in being, merely bringing them into the civil service. No fundamental reform of the law was undertaken or envisaged.[1] The finances of the Commune, placed in the hands of a methodical and honest book-keeper from a department store, Jourde, were scrupulously conservative. The Bank of France was left unmolested, and money only borrowed from it; there was no mention even of the idea of nationalising it. The traditional taxes continued to be levied, no attempt to reform them—a particularly surprising fact. Church and state were declared separated, the property of religious houses confiscated, but in fact—apart from numerous arrests of priests, and the holding of public meetings in churches, transformed into club-houses—little was done to put these decrees into practice. The Commune's hesitation in social reform was shown by the appointment of a procrastinating commission, to which the public were invited to make suggestions. The very idea of social legislation was suspect to some, who preferred to leave it to the workers to make their own arrangements with their employers, on the grounds that they were now powerful enough to get satisfactory terms. Minimum wages were fixed for public workers, but competition was fully accepted provided it was not at the expense of wages or quality. In its manifesto to the peasantry appealing for support, the Commune offered them not nationalisation of land, but ownership of a house and plot for each one and no taxation for any but the rich.[2]

The Commune would have gone much further had it paid attention to the numerous proposals and delegations sent to it by the political clubs. These multiplied quickly after 18 March, aspiring to a new role, as participants in the construction of a new order rather than as organs of opposition. For their meetings they frequently took over churches, and their debates were published in the equally numerous newspapers. A central club attempted to act as a link between the clubs, to serve as 'a thermometer of public opinion', without imposing its

[1] Georges Laronze, *Histoire de la Commune de 1871 d'après des documents et des souvenirs médits: la justice* (1928), 197, 673-9.
[2] Malon, 169-71; Jean Bruhat, Jean Dautry, and Émile Tersen, *La Commune de 1871* (1960), 191-217; cf. E. Schulkind (ed.), *The Paris Commune of 1871* (1972), for a good analysis of left-wing interpretations.

own views. Popular interest in public affairs reached a degree unprecedented since 1848. The wild and extreme views advocated in these clubs had, however, little practical effect and represented the views of a minority. The majority, as revealed by the files of those arrested after May, was much more conservative. The average man in the street wanted self-government for the capital: the abolition of the prefecture of police, the right to elect its municipal council and the officers of its national guard. He wanted popular sovereignty: the theory of direct government of the people, involving representatives elected for short periods and constantly revocable, was particularly favoured. Some looked on this as giving them an opportunity to hold public office, to obtain state jobs. To more, however, it was just a persistence in the ideal of 1793. Social antagonisms were distinctly vague. Though most of those arrested were wage-earners, and though they spoke vaguely against the rich, the bourgeoisie and the idle, they were not rebels against their employers, and there are practically no instances of class hostility against these. On the contrary, many got their employers to testify in their favour at their trials: the employer was an enemy only when he had fled from Paris. On the whole, the people seemed to hate the clergy more than any other class; after that, their landlord, and then their *concierge*. The only capitalist against whom they aired a particularly strong grievance was the forestaller who raised prices—a traditional pre-revolutionary enemy. All this should not be surprising. Paris in 1871 was economically nearer 1789 than 1940. Most men still spent their lives either in small workshops or on their own, rather than in factories; and even when they had moved into factories, they largely retained the undisciplined traditions of the old artisan. They were not even townsmen: three-quarters of those arrested had been born in the provinces. Nor should the Commune be considered a sudden, unexpected rising against the law: 21 per cent of those arrested, and 29 per cent of those found guilty, had previous convictions.[1]

Historically, the suppression of the Commune was perhaps more important than the regime itself. The army from Versailles, when it finally invaded the city, took a week of bloodshed

[1] Jacques Rougerie, *Le Procès des communards* (1964), based on the archives of the ministry of war, which contain the court-martial files.

to capture it. The resistance by the people was spontaneous, unorganised, based on a 'chauvinisme de quartier', for as soon as the Versailles army penetrated, the Communards rushed back pell-mell each to defend his own street, instead of trying to halt the enemy at the gates. The slaughter by the army, 130,000 strong, was without parallel in the century, far outstripping the June days of 1848. Between 20,000 and 25,000 people were summarily executed or killed. 38,578 were arrested, after almost ten times as many denunciations had been received. It took two years to try their cases, during which they rotted in atrocious prisons. 10,137 were convicted and nearly half of these deported to New Caledonia. Paris after the Commune was a different city. Bereavement, hunger, empty workshops, gloom, exile. 'The soldiers themselves are silent. Victorious, they are sad; they do not drink or sing. Paris has the atmosphere of a city taken by dumb men.'[1] Outside, the myth spread that the Communards had behaved like savages: the press demanded they should be slaughtered like beasts; at the very mention of an amnesty the peasants outside were terrified and clamoured for merciless punishment.[2] This myth caused a breach between the bourgeoisie and the masses, much more profound than that created in June 1848. It made numerous writers speak with contempt and horror of the poor. The lesson Renan drew from it was that democracy was the cause of all France's ills.[3] It made Taine write his antirevolutionary *Origin of Contemporary France*. It stimulated Albert de Mun to found his Catholic Workers' Clubs in an attempt to cure the masses of their dangerous ideas: had not the pope himself talked of the Communards as 'men escaped from Hell who spread fire through Paris'?[4] The Commune made many bourgeois more conservative, and less sympathetic to the workers than they would otherwise have been. At the same time it made the workers more extremist. 'Since [the bourgeoisie] does not wish to receive us fraternally into the human city', concluded Malon, a member of the Commune and one of its best historians, 'we

[1] Catulle Mendès, *Les 73 Jours de la Commune* (1871), 326.
[2] Georges Tersen, 'L'opinion publique et la Commune de Paris (1871–79)', in *Bulletin de la Société d'études historiques, géographiques et scientifiques de la région parisienne* (1960 and 1962, 4 articles).
[3] E. Renan, *La Réforme intellectuelle et morale de la France* (1871).
[4] A. Dansette, *Histoire religieuse de la France contemporaine* (1948), 144.

shall get into it through the breaches.'[1] After all the slaughter, it was difficult for the socialists to be moderate, or more particularly to compromise with their executioners, on pain of seeming to deny their dead. The growth of the moderate trade union movement of the 1860s, was cut short, and the opportunity was given for more violent elements to come to the fore. Old socialist leaders like Louis Blanc and Tolain opposed the Commune from Versailles, and the Commune shot as a hostage Gustave Chaudey, Proudhon's testamentary executor: it thus created a breach among the socialists themselves. After the amnesty of 1879, the leaders who returned from exile brought back a heavy load of bitterness with their memories.[2]

The Guesdists

Marxism was introduced into the socialist movement principally by the efforts of Jules Guesde, who is important also for creating the first centralised and organised political party in France. His name means little to most people today, for he was a far less magnificent or attractive figure than either Jaurès or Blum; but in his own day he incarnated those aspects of socialism which terrified the bourgeoisie most. He was very tall and very thin: he had often nearly starved from sheer poverty. His hair grew to his shoulders; his face had a sickly pallor (from almost constant illness) accentuated by the blackness of his flowing beard. Fiery eyes shone from behind metal-framed glasses. When he spoke, even about ordinary things, his lips seemed to quiver with rage. He talked fast, with passion; his voice was grating, sharp, bitter; his irony was always acrid, his insults violent. He was appropriately nicknamed Pope Guesde or the Red Jesuit. He had a dour, authoritarian temperament and was quite ruthless in his methods; he was not loved and his personal following was always small, so that it is not surprising that he has been forgotten. But he was an outstandingly persuasive, enthusiastic and impressive orator, a vigorous, unsuppressible journalist, a tireless organiser. He exerted enormous influence and left a profound mark on the country.

[1] B. Malon, 532.
[2] For the parliamentary debates leading to the amnesty see J. T. Joughin, *The Paris Commune in French Politics 1871–1880* (Baltimore, Md., 1955).

Born in 1845, the son of a schoolmaster, he had to abandon his studies for lack of money. At nineteen he became a translator in Baron Haussmann's prefecture in Paris, but soon gave up the job to become a journalist. Victor Hugo's *Châtiments* (from which he could still recite long passages in old age) made him a republican as a boy; the eighteenth-century philosophers made him an atheist. He was first a follower of Gambetta, then a sympathiser with the Commune; in 1871 he was sentenced to five years' imprisonment for this. He escaped to Italy where he came under the influence of the anarchists. In 1876 he read Marx, was converted, and henceforth he was the principal populariser of Marxism in France.[1] It was his newspaper, *l'Égalité* (1877), with a circulation of about 5,000, which spread the new vocabulary. It was he who determined to capture the trade union movement for Marxism and turn it into a political party. In collaboration with Marx he prepared a programme and passed it through the Marseille Third Trade Union Congress of 1879 which he filled with his rapidly won supporters. Thus was founded the Parti des Travailleurs Socialistes, later the Parti Ouvrier français, which, standing at once in the elections of 1881, won about 50,000 votes. But Guesde never really captured the trade union movement, for this first victory was due to his swamping its congress with unrepresentative delegates. The trade unions soon expelled him and although he tried to form a rival National Federation of Unions, this failed to win much support. From an early stage he was thus beset by a dilemma which worried the socialists ever after. His aim was to establish a working-class party, in conformity with Marxist dogma, but the party created turned out to be something different. His preoccupation with politics alienated the workers: he took little part in strikes and gave little attention to the organisation of unions; he never participated in industrial life. He simply wished to use the workers for political purposes.

Only the textile workers of the Nord and Pas-de-Calais,

[1] For his youth see Jules Guesde, *Textes choisis 1867–1882*, ed. by Claude Willard (1959), introduction. For a contemporary portrait, Mermeix, *La France socialiste* (1886), 60. A. Compère-Morel, *Jules Guesde, le socialisme fait homme 1845–1922* (1937), is dull but useful. Marx's *Capital* was first translated into French by Jules Roy and published in instalments 1872–5. Gabriel Deville published an abridged version in 1876, which was more influential.

were genuinely won over by him. They soon gave him massive
support and made him a power to be reckoned with. The
reason for this was that his party penetrated the local life of the
textile towns to an extraordinary degree, and used traditional
festivals and recreational societies for the service of the party.
It organised balls, concerts, country fêtes, competitions, billiard
and card-games, dramatic societies and shooting clubs, and in
this way gave a new revolutionary content to traditional social
activities. It was not just poverty that made men join Guesde's
party. The textile weavers of eastern France gave him few
votes; the wretched conditions of their employment were not
by themselves enough to turn them into extremists. Likewise
the miners of the north found that their particular corporate
interests were better served by other, more moderate leaders,
and Guesde made little headway among them: in this sector
he obtained support only from workers in small mines and
small ironworks, as at Commentry and Montluçon. From the
beginning therefore socialism did not appeal automatically to
all industrial workers and Guesde made recruits not where
certain economic conditions prevailed, but where a combination of many circumstances, and particularly the activities of
an able disciple, organised support for him.

A wide variety of social types entered the party; artisans as
well as factory workers, even small shopkeepers (17 per cent of
the party, nearly half of them publicans) and peasants (7 per
cent of the party, one-third of them proprietors). Guesde's
success was confined to three regions, which were very different:
the north, the east centre (particularly Allier) and the Medi
terranean west. The north was the most solid basis of his power,
providing him with one-third of his votes. He was successful
here partly because the textile workers had no strong political
traditions which clashed with his theories (as they did in Paris
for example, where he had few followers), and partly because of
the indefatigable propaganda of Gustave Delory (1857–1925).
A textile worker, sacked for his union activities, Delory set up
as a perambulating newspaper merchant, walking twenty-
five miles a day to spread the party teaching; he next opened
a wine-shop, and then a printing works, both essential political
tools. He became mayor of Lille in 1896 and its deputy in 1902.
Likewise a watchmaker, Pedron (1849–1931) was principally

responsible for the party's success in the Aube, where his news-paper, his speeches, and his practical organisations of trade unions for the bonnet makers of Troyes and Romilly, no less than the lively *soirées familiales* arranged by them, made many converts.[1] In the centre of France, the Guesdist party grew out of the secret society, *La Marianne*, active in 1850-1 and 1872-7, and itself continuing the traditions of the Charbonnerie. The first socialist mayor of France, Christophe Thivrier (1841-95) of Commentry and Jean Dormoy (1851-98), mayor of Mont-luçon, who between them led the party in the Allier, were both originally members of this society. Thivrier had gone down the mines at the age of ten; he had refused to become a foreman, saying 'he did not want to boss his friends'; seeking indepen-dence, he set up on his own as a baker and later as a brick maker, wine merchant and builder; with his savings he built his own house. In 1872 the *Marianne* secret society first met in his attic; when it outgrew it, it met in fields at night, in a different place each time. Its members had an elaborate secret language: on entering a café they would say 'it is a fine day' in a special way; they clinked their glasses first by the stem and then by the lip; they had a special handshake, and sent out their summonses to meetings concealed in handkerchiefs in the form of a letter from a girl summoning her lover to a rendez-vous. These practices appealed to the miners, so that when Guesde visited Commentry and converted Thivrier to his cause, the party that was built up developed as much as a sort of club as an ideological movement. Thivrier's popularity was due above all to his being a very likeable man. 'He was not proud.' He became nationally famous for wearing a worker's blouse (over his frock-coat) when he got into parliament, a gesture, like Keir Hardie's cap, which signified that he was not abandoning his class origins. On one occasion he was expelled from the chamber and carried out bodily for shouting 'Vive la Commune' and refusing to withdraw. But his socialism was far from being that of an orthodox Marxist. His municipality, for example, demanded the abolition of the mine-workers' co-operative because this was ruining the small shopkeepers. His party absorbed some of the radical leaders—like Deslinières,

---

[1] Henri Millet (1865-1902, bonnet maker, later mayor of Romilly), *L'Évolution socialiste à Romilly-sur-Seine* (Troyes, 1896), 25.

the founder of a Freemason lodge—but not without being somewhat diluted.[1] He himself indeed ended by leaving the Guesdist party. His seat in parliament, it is interesting, was inherited by his son.

His rivalry with the other principal Guesdist leader of the region, Jean Dormoy, stresses the diversity of the party even within a small area. Jean Dormoy had been a metalworker since the age of thirteen. Active in republican politics after 1870, he organised an invitation to Guesde to lecture in Montluçon in 1880 and this converted him to Marxism. In consequence, he lost his job, and instead became a perambulating pedlar. He improved his knowledge of Marxism by spending six months in jail together with Guesde and Lafargue (Marx's son-in-law), after a conviction for incitement to the murder of employers and to pillage. He specialised in union organisation, and introduced the 1 May demonstrations into France. When he died at forty-seven such was his personal popularity that 30,000 people are said to have marched in his funeral procession. However, he was never able to establish anything like the disciplined and organised party structure characteristic of the Guesdists in the Nord and in the Aube.

In the Allier, Guesdism recalled much more the Montagne of 1849.[2] In the south of France, Guesdism was taken up by dissatisfied radicals who saw in it a new form of extremism, but who were not at all interested in its Marxism. Its leaders here were largely of the petty or middle bourgeoisie. The most famous, Dr. Ferroul, mayor of Narbonne from 1892 till his death in 1921, had been in turn a Freemason, a radical, and Boulangist: his popularity came from his genius at defending local interests.

The Guesdist party, therefore, turned out very different from what its founder had intended. Karl Marx was exasperated by it. It became the largest single socialist party in France in the late nineteenth century. By 1898 it had 16,000 members; in the elections of that year it had put up 96 candidates, and won 13 seats with 294,000 votes (2·7 per cent of the electorate). It

[1] Ernest Montusès [1880–1927, editor of *Le Socialiste*, later *Le Combat* of Allier], 'Le député en blouse' [a biography of Thivrier], in *Les Cahiers du Centre*, 52 and 53 (Moulins, May–June, 1913).

[2] Georges Rougeron, *Le Mouvement socialiste en Bourbonnais 1875–1944* (Moulins, 1946).

captured control of many municipalities.[1] But in the process it quite ceased to be the vigilant guardian of Marxist orthodoxy, or indeed a party with a coherent policy at all. It won its success frequently by alliances which diluted its doctrines with a variety of the socialisms as well as with radicalism and nationalism. After 1892, it rallied to the defence of the republic, it supported Bourgeois's radical ministry in 1895 and, abandoning its view that capitalism was not worth improving, it adopted reformism. It now said that the municipalities it won could not only serve as a useful preparation for the socialist future but also improve immediately the lot of the masses. Guesde expected to gain power very soon. 'We are on the eve of victory', he said in 1893. 'The new century will be the beginning of the new era', he said in 1897. 'The Revolution is at hand', he repeated again and again. He was determined therefore to win all the seats he could (he hoped to have 115 or 120 deputies in 1898); and he was willing to seek votes by all means. The party's agrarian programme wooed the peasantry with the promise of less taxation and the nationalisation of only the very large properties, leaving the small owner 'in quiet possession of the plot he cultivates with his sweat'. They talked less and less of class struggles and revolution. To get rid of their nickname of 'Prussians' (after Marx), they became patriots, indeed chauvinists. However, these changes did not benefit them. The elections of 1898 were a profound disappointment and after them the Guesdists reverted to their old revolutionary policy. One might speculate that had they been more successful at the polls, they would have become increasingly moderate, and developed into mild radicals, in the tradition of Gambetta. In fact neither moderate nor revolutionary tactics availed them much. They appear to have reached the limit of their expansion by the turn of the century. Their Marxism was somewhat irrelevant to French conditions and they made little effort to adapt it to the changing times. They preached that wages were bound to fall even though in France they were quite clearly rising. They made no study of French capitalism or industry though they claimed their doctrines were scientific. Their stress on theory

[1] Claude Willard, *Le Mouvement socialiste en France 1893–1905: les guesdistes* (1965), 316, 348. This very detailed and informative thesis is the basis for any study of Guesdism and a model of its kind.

degenerated into a facile repetition of inert dogmas. Refusing to be utopians, they did not paint any picture of the society for which they were working—and indeed they had no clear view of the future. The regimented, centralised party Guesde tried to establish was unique at a time when other political groups were extremely loose, but it alienated much support. There seemed to be little room in it for able men who aspired to more than local eminence: when Guesde talked of unity to other socialists, they understood by unity only his dictatorship. Guesde's control of his party was in fact deceptive. The hierarchic organisation of sections and federations was only effectively established in the north; elsewhere there was much more variety and informality. The attempt at national centralisation was inefficient; it only stimulated conflicts, especially when Guesde was ill, as he frequently was. Local parties, particularly in the south, were able to pursue an independent policy of alliances regardless. The Guesdists had little money, and only one paid propagandist (Zévaès). Their newspapers were inadequate: they had 130 between 1890 and 1905, mainly weeklies, but over half of these lasted less than a year and only a fifth more than two years. Only six of them had a circulation of over 5,000; most of them were mediocre and uninspiring. The lack of daily newspapers (except in the north) was a considerable handicap. The party, at the same time, became something of a racket, specialising in finding jobs for its members. 22 out of 36 municipal councillors of Roubaix were licensed tavern keepers. Only two of the party deputies in 1898 were in any case real workers.[1]

Guesde did not have the qualities either to create a truly national party or to unite the various sects behind him. He was too tactless, impatient, authoritarian. He was over-anxious for immediate results in his own lifetime and failed to understand the gradual evolution of political opinion in the Third Republic. His opportunism was unsuccessful. He did not give enough emphasis to the immediate improvement of the lot of the poor and he was unable to win the leadership of the trade unions. He attacked both Boulanger and the bourgeois republicans, and so failed to profit from the crisis. He did

[1] Claude Willard, 'Contribution au portrait du militant guesdiste dans les dix dernières années du xixᵉ siècle', in *Le Mouvement social* (Oct. 1960 and Mar. 1961).

not take part in the Dreyfus affair, unlike Jaurès and Clemenceau who both profited greatly from doing so. He too puris-
tically ignored anticlericalism, even though it was the most
potent prejudice of his time. By the turn of the century he had
reached the limit of his achievement.[1] His contribution to the
socialist movement was, however, of lasting importance. He
continued to be influential in the united party congresses till
the war; but, even more, he left behind him a strong tradition
of Marxist socialism which is one of the major strands in the
party's history after that. The conflict between it and the more
humane tradition linked with the name of Jaurès and Blum is
one of the principal problems of French socialism. Guesde's
tradition lives on to this day, strongest in the north, where he
had won most adepts. The triumph of Guy Mollet after the
Liberation of 1944 marked the revival and the revenge of
Guesdism. The idea that the party should be exclusively the
representative of the workers, engaged in a class struggle
against the rest of society, once again became the official doctrine, in opposition to Blum's desire to broaden the party's
appeal, and to rethink its role in French society. Mollet's
defeat in 1965 of Defferre's candidature for the presidential
election showed how Guesdism still held sway.[2]

The Possibilists

Guesde's authoritarianism soon brought divisions among the
socialists. Dr. Paul Brousse, as early as 1881–2, created a rival
party which advocated a very different kind of socialism.
Brousse blamed the failure of the socialists at elections on
Guesde's rigid dogmatism and he demanded that each constituency party should have the right to decide its own programme, appropriate to local conditions. He argued that
Guesde's programme—so esteemed by its supporters for its
precision and clarity—was impractical and utopian: it sought
to obtain everything at the same time, with the result that it
obtained nothing at all. In a phrase that (unconsciously no

[1] See the interesting assessments of Guesde by Marcel Cachin, 'Le centenaire
de Guesde', in *La Pensée, revue du rationalisme moderne* (11 Nov. 1945), 5. 19–28, and
Samuel Bernstein, 'Jules Guesde, Pioneer of Marxism in France' in *Science and
Society* (1940), 29–56.
[2] On neo-Guesdism see B. D. Graham, *The French Socialists and Tripartism
1944–47* (Canberra, 1965), and Club Jean Moulin, *Un Parti pour la gauche* (1965).

doubt) echoed Gambetta, Brousse wrote: 'The ideal should be divided into several practical stages; our aims should, as it were, be *immediatised* so as to render them *possible*.' Guesde contemptuously labelled Brousse and his followers *possibilists*, a new type of opportunist. They accepted the name gladly, saying the alternative was to be, like the Guesdists, *impossibilists*. Thus there occurred within the socialist party much the same development as only a short while before had taken place among the republicans and radicals.

The Broussists differed from the Guesdists in three ways. First, they allowed a great deal of autonomy to local groups: they did not seek doctrinal uniformity but a union of all exploited workers, in which there would be room for different opinions in tactics and doctrines. They called themselves the Federation of Socialist Workers, but each local group had the right to add a sub-title, indicating its special views. Secondly, they abandoned the idea of revolution as a means of achieving their ends. They insisted that experience was needed to run a state; the Commune had failed because it lacked it. 'One cannot suddenly turn oneself into a director of a great public service, simply with the qualification of having made a good speech.' So, thirdly, they concentrated on winning power on a municipal scale, for which Brousse (basing himself on the Belgian socialist César de Paepe) developed an alternative to Marxism, the 'theory of public services'. He argued that there was no problem about whether the bourgeoisie ought or ought not to be expropriated. Economic forces would determine their fate. The inevitable development of capitalism was towards the formation of monopolies. It was logical that these should then be transformed into public corporations or services. Socialism would thus be achieved gradually, at different speeds in different sectors, as economic growth led up to it. Finally, when public services were used to their utmost extent, the cost of administration would be greater than it was worth, and they would become free. This might happen first of all in the post-office. When all services became free, communism would be established. Meanwhile Brousse wished to work for a practical municipal socialism.[1] This political programme was in some ways almost

---

[1] Paul Brousse, *La Propriété collective et les services publics* (first published 1883, reprinted with a preface 1910).

indistinguishable from that of the radicals; the tone of his social programme, in its attitude to the class struggle, recalled the moderation of 1848. He was quite willing to support bourgeois governments if they gave practical benefits to the poor. But the bulk of his programme was concerned with local affairs and the municipalisation of transport, water, gas, etc.—which would be either free or sold at cost price. He obviously met a need—parallel to that which Gambetta had satisfied—for he won considerable popularity and in the 1880s it was his party which made the most rapid progress. One of his supporters was the first socialist to be elected to the municipal council of Paris; by 1887 they had nine members of it; in 1889 they won two seats in parliament and about 50,000 votes. They had two daily newspapers, three provincial weeklies, one monthly journal. Their strength was largely confined to Paris, but they also had some thirty odd groups in the west.[1]

There was never much chance, however, that this would lead to any large movement. Brousse was quite incapable of organising on a national scale. He was a fairly rich doctor (with, it is said, an income of 60,000 francs—£2,800). His grandfather had been a well-to-do grain merchant; his father was a professor of medicine, and he was related to a bishop. It is not clear how far he got away from this respectable world, or indeed whether he tried to at all after his youthful escapades, and little is known about his strange marriage with Natalie Landsberg who, for her part, was the rebel daughter of a Russian prefect of police. Brousse represented a form of bourgeois nonconformity. He had got to know Guesde in Montpellier when he was a student; he had been sentenced to three months' imprisonment for a press offence, had fled to Spain, and joined the International. He then deserted Marx for Bakunin, less for doctrinal reasons than because he objected to any strict orthodoxy.[2] When he eventually settled down in Paris, he built up a very influential position for himself in the seventeenth *arrondissement*, particularly in the quartier des Épinettes, of which he was for long a municipal councillor. He organised a socialist club there and a general trade union of small tradesmen, workers and clerks.

[1] Sylvain Humbert, *Les Possibilistes* (1911), 48 ff.
[2] Paul Brousse, *Le Suffrage universel et le problème de la souveraineté du peuple* (Geneva, 1874), shows him in this phase.

He took great trouble to help his electors in their practical
concerns, holding what was perhaps the first political 'surgery'
twice a week, and showing himself always very friendly and
obliging.[1]

The paradoxical aspect of Brousse's life was that he spent
some ten years of it arguing about anarchist and socialist
theory, engaging in vituperative disputations in international
congresses, when he had a deep distrust of all theory. Because
of these early activities, he earned something of a reputation as
a dangerous agitator: he had been exiled by France and
Switzerland in turn. But he was not made to be a sectary. Both
as an anarchist in the Jura Federation and later as one of the
founders of the French Socialist Party, he had urged the
abandonment of metaphysical debates about doctrine. As an
anarchist, he had urged 'propaganda by deed', by which he
had meant not assassination and terrorism, whose failure had
been conclusively demonstrated, but simply municipal socialism.

The starting-point of Brousse's thinking was that in France
there was no chance of a general strike. It was totally unrealistic
to expect one when the workers had barely begun to organise
and when their political activity was in a pitifully embryonic
and chaotic state. The masses did not read books and it was no
use trying to convert them with turgid works of theory, or even
with newspapers. The only way to make an impact on their
ignorance and their prejudices was to show them that socialism
worked, in a practical, visible form. Rather, therefore, than try
to overthrow the whole bourgeois state, it would be more
sensible to obtain control of a few municipalities and reorganise
them on socialist lines. This would fit into the tradition of the
Paris Commune. But each commune should be allowed to
go its own way. Anyone who knew French conditions had to
accept the fact that large areas of the country were thoroughly
under the influence of the nobles, the clergy or the bourgeoisie.
France was an extremely varied amalgam of regions with very
different historical traditions. No party had succeeded in
winning an outright majority in parliament. The socialists
should not therefore expect all communes to be socialist. They
must wait until, in due course, the contrast between the happiness of the socialist ones and the misery of the clerical ones

[1] Léon de Seilhac, *Le Monde socialiste* (1904), 37.

became so great that the masses would voluntarily renounce the domination of their traditional rulers.

Brousse did not propose to destroy the state immediately he obtained municipal office. He planned only to transform the commune gradually, so that *public service* should replace government. This meant the elimination of the authoritarianism and the hierarchical character which government inevitably possessed. He attacked the Marxists with vigour, dismissing them as 'revolutionaries by taste, neurotics, fanatics, romantics of insurrection'.

Brousse's aim was to start a Labour Party in France. This was the title he wished to give his organisation, implying a broad, undoctrinaire appeal. He was keen on maintaining contacts with the English trade unions, in contrast with other French socialists who condemned them as reactionary. Brousse co-operated with the radicals in defending the republic when General Boulanger appeared to threaten its existence, and he was a founder member of the Society of the Rights of Man, though his followers soon forced him to withdraw from it. This society was a predecessor of the league which was to be a force in French politics for a generation. Brousse's work survived also, without his name being generally associated with it, in the ministerial socialism of men like Millerand, for whose newspaper, *La Petite République*, Brousse frequently wrote. His absorption into the republic may be seen in the way, when he lost his parliamentary seat in 1910, he was pensioned off with a directorship of a state mental hospital, one of the republic's favourite sinecures.[1]

Just as the socialists had split into Broussists and Guesdists in 1882, so in 1890 the Broussists split in their turn. The leader of the revolt was Jean Allemane (1843-1935), a typographer, trade unionist and member of the Commune sentenced to hard labour in New Caledonia for his participation in it. Allemane represented the protest against the increasing opportunism of Brousse, against association with the radicals, to the extent of becoming scarcely distinguishable from them in the common pursuit of office. Allemane had got involved in a personal rivalry with Brousse, each of them having a daily newspaper of his own. In 1890 he broke away and founded his own group,

[1] David Stafford, *From Anarchism to Reformism* (1971).

the Allemanists. He wanted his party to be genuinely a workers' party, which would unite the merits of Guesdism and Broussism. He was interested in municipalism and immediate reforms but made it clear that they represented the first stage only. He supported the idea of a general strike, but insisted that the workers should first be organised in unions and that the strike should be international. He objected to all hero worship within the party—of which he declared Brousse and Guesde equally guilty—and was indeed hostile to all politicians, because they too easily lost contact with their electors. The Allemanist candidates in elections were strictly subordinate to the local constituency parties, they had to sign an undated letter of resignation, which the party could use if it ever wished to, and they were required to pay their salaries to the party funds, from which they drew a smaller allowance. Allemanism represented a reiteration of the determination of the workers to win their own emancipation by their own efforts; its stress was on egalitarianism, and a distrust of the bourgeoisie. But at the same time it was revolutionary only in principle and it was unable to discover a method of bringing about practical reforms without polluting itself in the mire of the existing system. Allemane himself had been able to do this. His popularity came precisely from his having through the vicissitudes of his career remained always a worker in his habits and his hopes; he never gave the impression that he was a leader on the make. His anarchist ideal of politics without politicians could not, however, work. His party secured five seats in parliament in 1893, outdoing the Broussists and spreading their influence outside Paris. But these deputies soon found their subordination to their constituency parties intolerable, they refused to give up their salaries; in 1896 they resigned from the party and joined the Blanquists. The Allemanists thus in their turn were split; the surviving remnant later joined the independent socialists (showing how the party stood uncertainly between reformism and revolution). This movement too was thus abortive.[1]

Jaurès

Jaurès is, with Gambetta, perhaps the most venerated politician of the Third Republic. He may not be admired by such a broad

[1] Maurice Charnay, *Les Allemanistes* (1912).

variety of parties, but he is admired for a greater variety of qualities, as something more than a politician. Romain Rolland wrote of him: 'Jaurès is a model, almost unique in modern times, of a great political orator who is at the same time a great thinker, uniting enormous culture with penetrating observation, moral elevation with energy for action. One needs to go back to Antiquity to find anything similar. He could raise the masses and enchant the élite at the same time.'[1] Blum said, 'I have never met any man—except perhaps Albert Einstein—on whom the seal of genius was so obviously and so evidently imprinted.'[2] The English socialist, Max Beer, who knew most of the politicians of this generation, wrote that of all the men he had met Lenin and Jaurès impressed him most.[3] More biographies have probably been written of him than of any other French politician of this period; but the materials for a proper assessment of his achievements are still lacking. His complete works comprise only about a tenth of his writings; their publication was abandoned after volume 9; it was estimated that 90 tomes of 400 pages would have been needed to make them comprehensive. Fewer than a hundred of his letters have been published, so that one has to rely almost entirely on his public pronouncements. Only recently have a few researchers embarked on a really detailed examination of his life and in 1960 a Society of Jaurès Studies was founded.[4] The historian must be very conscious of the many questions about Jaurès which remain unanswered. His problem is to see his way through the legend, to assess and explain the unstinted praise Jaurès received, which seems at first sight too exaggerated to obtain credence outside the charmed circle.

Jaurès's political importance is that he created a unified socialist party out of the numerous sects, that he saved it both from the dogmatism and utopianism which had characterised them, and gave it a wide appeal within the framework of the republic and of French life. He came on to the scene at an opportune moment, when the socialists were longing for unity,

[1] *Journal de Genève* (2 Aug. 1915), quoted in *Europe* (Oct.–Nov. 1958), 3.
[2] L. Blum, *Jean Jaurès* (1937), 8.
[3] J. Hampden Jackson, *Jean Jaurès* (1943), 11.
[4] See its *Bulletin de la Société d'études jaurésiennes*. The leading and most thorough biography is by Harvey Goldberg, *The Life of Jean Jaurès* (Madison, Wis., 1962).

but this does not diminish his achievement, for Millerand failed to do what Jaurès did. Jaurès was particularly well suited for his task by his origins, his education and his temperament. He was a bourgeois by birth, from a fairly well-off clan of Castres (Tarn), which had included merchants and barristers, two admirals and a bishop, but his father, though he married the daughter of a cloth manufacturer, was the poorest and least successful of the family; he failed in business several times and ended up with a small farm of fifteen acres. Jaurès thus grew up quite poor. He owed his early education to the generosity of an uncle; but he won all the first prizes at school, and so obtained a scholarship to Paris and to the École Normale Supérieure. He did brilliantly there and passed out third in merit (Bergson was second and a forgotten schoolmaster first). After a period as a sixth-form master at Albi, he became a lecturer and soon after a professor of philosophy at Toulouse University. But as a philosopher he was not the advocate of any particular doctrine: he sought to reconcile logic and common sense, to produce a synthesis of realism and idealism. As a teacher, he treated his pupils as personal friends. For Jaurès was not a typical professor, nor indeed typical of anything.

On first acquaintance he gave a rather uncertain impression. Eulogies of him are so common that it is perhaps worth balancing them by the pretty realistic description given of him by Jules Renard: 'Jaurès looks like a junior secondary schoolmaster who will never get his higher degree (*agrégation*) and who will not take enough exercise, or he looks like a fat merchant who eats well. He is of medium height and square. His head is fairly regular, neither ugly, nor beautiful, neither unusual nor common. Hirsute . . . A nervous tic of the right eyelid . . . A very cultivated intelligence. He does not even allow me to finish my quotations. He is perpetually referring to history or cosmogony. An orator's memory, very full, astonishing. Frequently spits into his handkerchief. I do not sense a strong personality. He gives me the impression rather of a man whose file could say: good health in every respect. At one of his jokes, he laughed too much, with a laugh that climbed down the stairs and didn't stop till the ground. His speech is slow, thick, slightly hesitating, without nuances. In religious matters he appears rather timid. He is embarrassed when this subject is raised. He gets out of it by "I assure you it is more complicated than you think." [1]

Jaurès was a bourgeois but also a peasant—he called himself 'a cultured peasant'.[2] He belonged to the intellectual élite, he was a small proprietor, but in appearance he could be mistaken for a worker on holiday. He wore the bourgeois uniform of a black frock-coat, but so untidily, dirtily and inelegantly—with his trousers always too short, revealing socks falling over his shoes, his pockets crammed full of papers and books—that he did not clearly belong to any class. This was the secret of his charm. He was 'essentially a human—not a professional man, not a member of a class or of a party, or the supporter of an idea, but a complete, harmonious, free man'. He had an extraordinary gift for sympathising with every type of person. He was neither proud, nor competitive, nor self-assertive. He combined his undoubted intellectual gifts with a childish *naïveté* and perfect plainness. He was thus readily acceptable as a leader, all the more because he had a dislike of deliberately offending anybody. 'He was by nature a pacificator' and his affability was honest.[3]

He was, and this clinched his success as a politician, a spell-binding orator. His technique was not impressive: he could not compare for fluency and perfection of style with Viviani, who had taken lessons at the Comédie Française and who used to re-enact the great speeches of the past for practice. His gestures were banal and repetitive: he used to raise a half-clenched fist and bring it down rapidly to his waist, he would point at the sky or at the audience, occasionally he would raise both arms high above his head in a manner which the experts judged 'heavy'. Yet he was considered to be the equal of Bossuet.[4] He was allowed to go on in parliament for two or three hours in ordinary debates and in important ones for two whole days. He was captivating because his speeches reflected his character but he had an uncanny feeling for the reactions of his audience. He always began hesitatingly until he could sense his way. What

[1] M. Auclair, *La Vie de Jean Jaurès* (1954), 258.
[2] To Vincent Auriol, *Jean Jaurès* (1962).
[3] Augustin Hamon, 'Souvenirs sur Jaurès', *La Grande Revue*, 88 (July 1915), 107–12.
[4] By Bracke, p. 26, in Michel Lannay, 'L'éloquence de Jaurès', *Europe* (Oct.–Nov. 1958), 23–39.

distinguished him from other speakers was his gift for expressing the feelings of a crowd, for making himself the interpreter of a mass, even though the link between them disintegrated when he had stopped. As soon as he had found the metaphor which combined the ideas he wished to express, he was off, on dazzling verbal flights, whose poetic phrasing and rich imagery were as intoxicating to the audience as to himself. Something said by him or by an interrupter would evoke a whole series of ideas. Blum used to speak as a Parisian intellectual, carefully giving all the arguments for and against, using his speech to satisfy an inner demand of conscience; but Jaurès always reflected the feeling of the moment—'He would then take all those who were listening pell-mell by the hair and unite them round an idea, whether they wished it or not.' His genius, said the Guesdist Bracke (at first an opponent and later an admirer) was 'to formulate the ideas which were common to those who were around him . . . to seek to unite them . . . to draw together bits of ideas and fragments of humanity'.[1] As an orator, he was not just a great tenor, but an attractive personality. Trotsky wrote of him: 'For Jaurès, oratory had no intrinsic value . . . Though the most powerful speaker of his time and perhaps of all times, he was beyond oratory; he was always superior to his speeches, as the artisan is to his tools.'[2]

Jaurès took to politics naturally. He made a brilliant impromptu speech in a public meeting held by a Bonapartist, at which he defended the educational reforms of Jules Ferry. His oratory was compared to that of the youthful Gambetta. He was invited to stand for parliament on the republican opportunist (Ferry) list and was triumphantly elected. He was then only twenty-five and the youngest deputy in parliament. But in Paris he was disappointing. He spoke hardly at all; he felt ill at ease; it took him some time to find his way. In later years he claimed he had always been a socialist, even though he sat in the centre in this parliament, but his consistency was in fact of a different kind. The characteristic of his political opinions was that they were always evolving. Though he made so many speeches, he never said the same thing twice. However, he differed from most other politicians of the Third Republic, who

[1] Bracke, ibid.
[2] Harvey Goldberg, *The Life of Jean Jaurès* (Madison, Wis., 1962), 188.

gradually became more conservative. Jaurès on the contrary came to appreciate the left-wing and also a large number of other points of view. His horizons were constantly widening. It has been well said that he was not converted to socialism: he understood it. He did so because he had an exceptionally open mind. 'The idea that needs to be safeguarded above all', he said in 1895, 'is the idea that no power, no dogma should limit the perpetual effort, the perpetual search of the human race—humanity sits like a great commission of inquiry with unlimited powers. It is the idea that every truth that does not come from us is a lie; it is the idea that in every agreement our critical spirit must nevertheless remain awake.'[1] He respected opposite opinions and abhorred only intolerance. Though forward looking, he also as he himself said, 'worshipped the past. It is not in vain that all the hearths of human generations have burned.'[2] He combined his liberalism with a passion for unity. When he read Cardinal Newman describing how men were being divided by the gulf of damnation, he had nightmares. He applied himself more than anything to bridging this abyss of incomprehension between men. 'The need for unity', he believed, 'is the most profound and the most noble of human needs.'[3] He had a passion for the reconciliation of apparently contradictory ideas. In his philosophical thesis on *The Reality of the Perceptible World* (1891) he expressed the hope of 'bringing about, on the basis of metaphysics and science, the great dream of union.'[4] Now when Jaurès entered politics the very idea of a separate socialist party displeased him. He believed in the union of all republicans. He was a supporter of Jules Ferry, whose colonial policy he thought was helping Frenchmen to forget their petty differences in the accomplishment of national expansion: he talked even of the 'touching union of the family of France'.[5] He was horrified by class antagonisms, by the

[1] Speech of 11 Feb. 1895, quoted in M. Jaurès and M. Clemenceau, by a French Contributor, in *The Dublin Review* (Apr. 1906), 310 n.

[2] Romain Rolland, op. cit.

[3] Quoted by Charles Rappoport, *Jean Jaurès, l'homme, le penseur, le socialiste* (1915), 104. A still useful book, particularly for Jaurès's ideas.

[4] Quoted by Félicien Challaye, *Jaurès* (n.d.), 115. This valuable study of Jaurès's philosophy is part of a series in which the other subjects are Socrates, Plato, Descartes, Kant, etc., showing the esteem Frenchmen had for him.

[5] Jean Jaurès, *Textes choisis*, vol. 1, *Contre la guerre et la politique coloniale*, ed. by Madeleine Rebérioux (1959), 13. A good introduction.

bitterness of labour disputes. He wrote in 1889: 'It is not by the
violent and exclusive agitation of this or that social faction, but
from a sort of national movement that justice must emerge . . .
The masses and the working bourgeoisie must unite to abolish
capitalist privileges and abuses.'[1] He hoped that the republicans
would see the need for bringing about social justice; he himself
introduced a bill on workers' pensions, in a premature anticipa-
tion of solidarism. But Ferry was not interested in the social
question in the same way and failed to provide enough scope
for Jaurès's idealism. After Jaurès lost his seat in 1889, therefore, his political method changed. Contact with trade union
leaders in Toulouse and in the mining town of Carmaux gave
him a new respect for the socialists, whom he no longer considered factious. He began borrowing books from the public
library on socialism, and wrote a subsidiary thesis on *The Origins
of German Socialism* (1891).[2] His work on the Toulouse municipal
council made him take a more practical view of the possibilities of obtaining reforms. So when in 1892 the miners of Carmaux invited him to stand as their socialist candidate for
parliament, believing he was specially suited to rallying the
peasants in the rural part of the constituency as well, he agreed,
and he accepted their condition that he should declare his
approval of the P.O.F. programme.[3]

He did not, however, join the party and he sat as an independent socialist. Jaurès was not a Marxist. He accepted some Marxist doctrines but, like Malon, he combined them with other—
contradictory—ones. He paid homage to Marx and seldom
criticised him openly, but he liked to reconcile idealism with
materialism, and he had much in common with Bernstein's
revisionism. Just as Bernstein believed that economic forces
cease to be supreme in capitalism, so Jaurès argued that when
capitalism reaches the stage of monopoly, its great magnates
realise the need to satisfy the workers. It is their conscience

[1] Rolande Trempé, 'Jaurès, député de Carmaux' in *Jaurès présenté par V.
Auriol* (1962), 86–119, quoted p. 90.
[2] For the influence of the librarian of the École Normale Supérieure see Charles
Andler, *La Vie de Lucien Herr* (1932).
[3] Madeleine Rebérioux, 'Jaurès et Toulouse 1890–1892', in *Annales du Midi*
(1963), 295–310; Rolande Trempé, 'Jaurès et Carmaux', in *Europe* (Oct.–Nov.
1958), 64–73; J. Jaurès, *Discours parlementaires* (1904), introduction by him on
'Le socialisme et le radicalisme en 1885', an important piece of autobiography.

which will change their attitude; a system of morals common to both bourgeoisie and the workers was thus possible and in consequence so was the collaboration of classes. Jaurès believed that capitalism could be penetrated gradually by socialism, and that its violent overthrow was unnecessary. He held that taxation and the development of companies with increasing numbers of shareholders was introducing socialism into the bourgeois state. Capitalism was not worsening the lot of the poor. It was not moving towards crisis, for it had passed the stage of anarchy into one of regulated cartels. It had the elements of progress in it. Jaurès complained that 'Marx had not sufficiently recognised the part of human good faith, of sincere moral and social enthusiasm which at certain times sustained and roused the bourgeoisie'; he praised the bourgeoisie's 'fanaticism for human progress' and in particular he admired 'those great individuals who by their brains, their technical ability, their genius, their courage, create new sources of wealth'. With a Saint-Simonian faith in the great international industrialists and financiers Jaurès believed they could prevent economic crises. The class struggle he considered to be unnecessary in a democracy like France where it was replaced by a political struggle. Parliament represented the general will for him; and socialism would eventually be established by the vote of legislature.[1] He did not accept the Guesdist hostility to colonies as such, but simply demanded a more humane and liberal colonial policy. In the first years of the twentieth century he saw the formation of the Ententes and Alliances as pacific developments, the beginnings of a European federation. He did not wish to destroy the idea of *Patrie*, but to socialise it. Though one kind of capitalism was chauvinist, another was capable of organising peace, under the leadership of the great banks: he could thus remain optimistically pacifist.[2] Like the Saint-Simonians too, he was hostile to the clergy and the military, but not to religion itself. He believed in immortality, and in God, though probably of a pantheistic rather than a personal kind; he laid stress on the importance of ideas and of religion in men's

[1] J. Klément, *Jaurès réformiste* (1931), and J. Jaurès, *L'Armée nouvelle* (1910), especially chapter 10, and *Études socialistes* (reprinted in vol. 1 of his *Complete Works*); Edward Claris, 'Du capitalisme au socialisme d'après Jaurès', in *L'Actualité de l'histoire* (Apr.–June 1959), 22–3.

[2] Madeleine Rebérioux, Introduction to *Jean Jaurès, textes choisis* (1959).

lives.[1] Socialism was thus for him, as Blum said, 'the point of
convergence, the inheritance of all that humanity, since the
obscure beginnings of civilisation, had produced in wealth,
virtue and beauty'.[2] And his view of civilisation was constantly
broadening. In his last years, he regretted having read too much
German and not enough of the English writers: he began
reading Newman and Shakespeare. Hume's *Dialogues on Natural
Religion* was one of the last books he read and it gave him 'one
of his greatest intellectual joys'.[3]

Jaurès's theoretical passion for unity was matched by exceptional skill as a practical politician in achieving it. He was
brilliant at drafting resolutions which all sides could accept, at
the very moment when their disagreements seemed to have
reached a deadlock. His combined gifts as a parliamentarian,
a journalist, an intellectual and a speaker at party congresses
and at public meetings made him highly influential; and his
amiability and self-effacement rendered this influence widely
acceptable, so that he ultimately emerged as the leader of the
party. His contribution to the growth of the party was very
considerable. He was, after Millerand, a prime influence in
urging socialist support of bourgeois governments whenever
they showed themselves willing to carry out reforms. He backed
the radical ministry of Bourgeois in 1895 (which proposed to
introduce an income tax), the Waldeck-Rousseau ministry of
republican defence (1899–1902), and he was the organiser of
the Bloc des Gauches which enabled Combes to separate
Church and state. In electoral terms this policy produced very
large rewards. Alliances with the radicals made possible most
of the socialist victories at the polls, which they could never
have achieved if they had remained an isolated, anti-republican
party. In the short term, Jaurès's determined desire to collaborate with other republicans accentuated the breach between his
followers and those of Guesde, so that in 1900, when an attempt
was made to unite the various socialist factions, agreement was
impossible, and two separate parties were formed, one under
Jaurès and one under Guesde. Guesde sought the help of the

[1] J. Jaurès, *La Question religieuse et le socialisme* (1959); Claude Tresmontant, 'La
religion de Jaurès', in *Esprit* (1960), 2038–51.
[2] L. Blum, *J. Jaurès* (1937), 37.
[3] J. Jaurès, *La Question religieuse et le socialisme* (1959), 17.

International, and in 1904 obtained from its Congress of Amsterdam a condemnation of Jaurès's policy of collaboration. It was now that Jaurès showed his magnanimity and his acumen. He accepted this decision; he withdrew from the Bloc des Gauches, he acquiesced in the socialists becoming a revolutionary party. It was in this way that in 1905 a united socialist party was at last formed, as the S.F.I.O. (French Section of the Workers' International).[1] But once unity was achieved, Jaurès gradually influenced it back to his own reformist policy, while at the same time satisfying the revolutionaries. He drafted the declaration of principles issued by the party's congress at Toulouse in 1908, which ingeniously reconciled the conflicting aims by arranging them into a chronological order. The *ultimate* aim of the party was, to please the Guesdists, declared to be the total conquest of power by the revolutionary establishment of collectivism. To please the Blanquists and Allemanists, the party declared that it would, *when opportunity arose*, use insurrection and the general strike. But its *immediate* method was to be electoral campaigning, parliamentary and municipal action, the spread of trade unions, co-operatives and education.[2]

The limitations of Jaurès's achievement must not, however, be overlooked. A unitary, as opposed to a federal, structure was adopted for the S.F.I.O., which issued its own cards to members in return for a subscription paid direct to central funds. The congress was made the sovereign body of the party; it was based on the numerical representation of members; the deputies and federations were kept firmly subordinated to it. Between 1905 and 1914 party membership doubled, to reach 90,725 by the war. But this was trifling compared to the German Social Democrats, who in 1912 had over a million members. The rule of the congress, moreover, was unacceptable to many of the socialist deputies. Twenty-four independents remained outside the party in 1906, and though the S.F.I.O. forbade its supporters to vote for them in elections, even when there was no other socialist candidate, about thirty independents were elected in 1910, forming the *Parti socialiste républicain*. This was

[1] A. Noland, *The Founding of the French Socialist Party 1893–1905* (Cambridge, Mass., 1956).
[2] The text of the Motion de Toulouse is in Georges Lefranc, *Le Mouvement socialiste sous la Troisième République* (1963), 397–8.

numerous enough not to be eclipsed by Jaurès's S.F.I.O., and
its able members—notably Briand, Viviani and Millerand—
repeatedly held ministerial office uncontrolled by him. It was
small consolation to argue that their ambition made them
unsuitable for collective action and that they were best outside,
for Jaurès would certainly have liked more influence on governments. His nostalgia for the Bloc des Gauches remained; it was
only in 1914, when it was too late, that he was able to revive it,
finding at last in Caillaux a continuator of Combes. Jaurès was
not a man of the opposition. 'The only real and pure joy of
public life', he said, 'is to be associated, in all independence,
without chicanery, in substantial works of political organisation
and of democratic and social progress. All the joys of criticism
and combat are noble, no doubt, but they are bitter.'[1] The
question of whether he would have accepted power had he not
been assassinated just before the outbreak of the war must
remain unanswered; but it might well be asked whether he
used his talents fully in the years 1905–14.

The unification of the socialists was very far from bringing
to an end their doctrinal disputes: on the contrary, it increased
them, because all the old battles, which had been settled by
separation, now had to be fought again. The duel of Jaurès and
Guesde was one of the major events of the congresses. The
leaders of the old factions continued to advocate their viewpoint, and in addition new attitudes also emerged. Alexandre
Varenne, following Bernstein, demanded that the party should
become openly reformist, and bring its proclamations of doctrine into line with its acts. At the other extreme Gustave
Hervé led a highly embarrassing campaign for insurrection and
total antimilitarism. On the one hand Albert Thomas strongly
urged co-operation with the radicals, while on the other Charles
Andler expressed contempt for the parliamentary system, and,
opposing Jaurès's view that socialism was the logical conclusion
of democracy, argued that it was something essentially different.[2]
Divisions persisted on the party's attitude to war, on its precise
view of nationalisation and municipal socialism. Its newspaper,

[1] Quoted by Marcel Prélot, *L'Évolution politique du socialisme français 1789–1934*
(1939), 201.
[2] A. Thomas, *La Politique socialiste* (1913); B. W. Schaper, *Albert Thomas* (Assen,
Netherlands, 1959); Charles Andler, *Le Civilisation socialiste* (1912).

L'Humanité, founded by Jaurès in 1904 with no fewer than
seventeen *agrégés* on its staff, at last became a daily in 1913, but
it never enjoyed a mass circulation. The party's finances made
really active propaganda impossible; there were only six paid
officials; one half of its income came from contributions by the
deputies who had to surrender part of their parliamentary
salaries.[1]

Above all the party failed to win either the trade unions or
the peasantry. The Guesdists were anxious to maintain the
primacy of political over economic action. Jaurès succeeded in
carrying an acceptance of trade unions and co-operatives as
legitimate forms of preparation for socialism, and personally he
established good relations with some of the C.G.T.'s leaders.
Jouhaux declared at his funeral that Jaurès had 'by the justice
and clarity of his mind, succeeded in reducing the disagreements between' their two doctrines; 'he was the link between
our two factions',[2] but all the same the trade union movement
remained separate. On the question of the peasantry, Jaurès had
from an early stage been regarded as an expert, both in parliament and in his party. He continued the policy, which even
the Guesdists had adopted, of promising to exempt small
peasant proprietors from nationalisation. 'Your property is
sacred', he wrote; 'if you are in debt, I shall help you out of
your mortgage . . . I shall supply you with machines. To non-
owning peasants I say: I shall help you to become proprietors,
taking precautions only that you do not become in your turn
exploiters of labour.'[3] The Marxist idea that the socialists
should appeal only to agricultural labourers was clearly worthless, since the countryside was rapidly being drained of them
as they migrated to the towns. There was a strong temptation
to become in rural areas a peasant party, rather than a socialist
party. In 1906 the Limoges congress decided to 'pursue the
realisation of the demands of the peasantry'. It appointed
a commission to discover what these were: 20,000 questionnaires were sent out, but very few returned. The report in 1908
showed that these demands were essentially practical, like help

[1] Hubert Rouger, *La France socialiste* (1912), 149–52.
[2] Georges Guy-Grand, 'Jaurès, ou le Conciliateur', in *La Grande Revue*, 97
(July 1918), 1–20, quoted p. 10.
[3] G. E. Prévot, *Le Socialisme aux champs* (Toulouse, 1905), preface by Jaurès, 6–8.

with mortgages, reduction in the price of fertilisers, and higher prices for their products. After inconclusive attempts to reconcile this with Marxism—for Compère-Morel, the most active proselytiser of the peasantry, was a Guesdist—and a further inquiry, the party adopted, in 1910, a programme which differed very little from that of the radicals and which remained on the socialist platform till 1919. The conversion of the peasantry to socialism was thus in practice abandoned: and this failure to win the peasants over—as opposed to merely securing some of their votes from reasons of expediency—was to produce a major weakness in the party.[1]

The Independent Socialists

There were still other types of men whom these various forms of socialism did not suit and whose socialism was of a different kind: those who were interested in practical achievement rather than precise doctrine and those who, like the politicians of all other parties, could not accept the idea of being a member of an organised and regimented sect. In 1885 a group of independent socialists was formed in the chamber of deputies by socialists who were not members of any socialist party. They were an anti-party and they long remained simply a group of deputies without any organization in the country. Only a few of them were elected as socialists; the majority were radicals especially interested in social reform. Their programme, though it talked of gradual nationalisation, was couched in very vague terms. Jaurès, elected as a republican in this same year and in search of more definite ideas, thought of joining, and asked one of them what they would do if they got power; he got a very noncommittal answer, that it would depend on the circumstances. The group included some interesting men, whose careers illustrate the changes taking place in the left wing within the republican system. Antide Boyer, who was one of the principal organisers of the group, was the son of an earthenware dealer: he began life as a tiler, became a railway worker, then a

[1] Maurice Lait, *Le Socialisme et l'agriculture française* (1922), 35–41; J. Bourdeau, 'Revue du mouvement socialiste' in *Revue politique et parlementaire* (Sept. 1910), 569–78; A. Compère-Morel, *La Question agraire en France* (1908); id., *La Question agraire et le socialisme en France* (1912); Michel Angé-Laribé, *Grande ou petite propriété* (Montpellier, 1902); Ernest Tarbouriech, 'La propagande agraire du parti socialiste', in *Revue socialiste* (Mar. 1910), 252–76.

book-keeper and finally a socialist journalist and politician. He
was one of the leaders of the socialist party in Marseille and entered the chamber in 1885 with radical support. Brialou was first
a weaver, then a gas-fitter at Lyon: he was elected on Clemenceau's list. Camelinat, originally a vine labourer, then a factory
worker, had been a member of the First International and of
the Commune: he too was supported by both radicals and
socialists. Numa Gilly, a cooper who after a time had set up on
his own, had been elected mayor of Nîmes by a coalition of the
extreme left and right, anxious to overthrow the opportunist:
he called himself a radical-socialist. Planteau was a porcelain
painter of Limoges who had migrated to Paris, learnt foreign
languages and become a professional translator: at forty-three
he started studying law, in which he got a degree. He had been
active in radical, not socialist, politics. A few were old republicans like Daumas, a mechanic who had been imprisoned for
his politics for eight years by the Second Empire and had then
set up as a brewer in Toulon: he had been a deputy since 1871
and was to end up as a radical senator. There was the Provençal
poet Clovis Hugues, who had been elected as a radical in 1881,
had joined the Guesdists in the following year, then quarrelled
with them because he insisted on attending Louis Blanc's
funeral, and so he had returned to the radical benches. He was
a colourful character, who had killed a Bonapartist in a duel
over his wife, who in turn a few years later shot another man
dead for pestering her: both of them had stood trial for these
murders and been acquitted. By no means all the independents
were workers: there were also doctors and barristers among
them. But they called themselves the Socialist Workers' Group.
They were really a wing of the radical party, to which some of
them continued to belong at the same time. Quite a few of them
became Boulangists: their division on this issue destroyed their
cohesion, which was slight enough.[1]

After the crisis, Alexandre Millerand (1859–1943), one of
the few men to remain neutral over Boulanger, attempted to
recreate the group and develop it into a broad-based 'reformist
socialist' party. His efforts are highly instructive because they
make it possible to understand more easily the relationship of
the socialists to the radicals and to appreciate more accurately

[1] Albert Orry, *Les Socialistes indépendants* (1911).

the nature of the achievement of Jaurès, who was to succeed where Millerand failed. Millerand ended his career as a right-wing president of the republic (1920–4) and for this reason he has seldom received his due in histories of socialism, but he should not be dismissed as an ambitious unprincipled renegade. He was certainly very keen on winning office and he became the first socialist minister of the Third Republic. He was an extremely hard and methodical worker, who enjoyed administration. He was uncultured, cold, bovine, with a 'square face, square shoulders, square obstinacy', myopic to the point of being unable to recognise his own family in the street. Born the son of a modest draper, he was a barrister but interested in politics from early youth, he began writing for Clemenceau's *Justice* almost as soon as he had qualified. When still only twenty-five he was elected, on the latter's radical list, to the Paris municipal council and, a year later, to parliament. He was the youngest deputy after Jaurès. He showed considerable independence as a radical, joined the Socialist Workers' Group, and broke with Clemenceau, whom he regarded as being too obsessed by anticlerical questions. In November 1891 he joined René Goblet, the founder of the radical-socialist party, and some other radicals, in issuing an appeal for a new policy, with the stress on economic rather than political reform, to be backed by republicans and socialists alike. A year later, he succeeded Goblet as editor of *La Petite République* and used it to lead a vigorous 'independent socialist' campaign in the elections of 1893. Nine of the men he supported were elected in Paris and a dozen radical deputies from the provinces soon joined them, making the 'Independents' the most numerous socialists in parliament. Millerand tried hard to widen the appeal of this group, to attract as many more radicals as he could, while at the same time drawing in the socialist sects. In a celebrated speech at Saint-Mandé (30 May 1896)[1] he defined his socialism as the gradual substitution of social property for capitalist property (i.e. the nationalisation of monopolies, and the municipalisation of public services, but leaving small proprietors alone). His method was political action directed towards winning a parliamentary majority. He favoured international co-operation with other socialists, though remaining

[1] Printed in A. Millerand, *Le Socialisme réformiste français* (1903), 19–35.

in the tradition of the French Revolution, patriotic at the same
time as internationalist. This threefold 'minimum programme'
of Saint-Mandé, as it came to be called, provided the basis for
unified action by the socialists in parliament, though significantly its approval by the deputies was combined with a proviso
that this approval would in no way limit their independence.
In the legislature of 1893–8 Millerand was the effective leader
of a campaign for practical reforms for the working class. The
logical conclusion of his work was that he should accept office
as minister of commerce and industry when offered it by
Waldeck-Rousseau in 1899. Here he saw the chance to carry
through the legislation they had been pressing for, as well as
to defend the republic against the reactionary challenge of the
anti-Dreyfusards. Unfortunately for him, the minister of war
in this cabinet was Gallifet—remembered all too bitterly by the
socialists for his repression of the Commune. This was carrying
reconciliation too far. The issue of participation in bourgeois
governments was thus confused. Millerand was disowned,
Jaurès almost alone speaking for him. His career as a socialist
leader was cut short. In 1904 he was expelled. In the same year
the Guesdists obtained from the International Congress at
Amsterdam a condemnation of the policy of co-operating with
bourgeois governments. In revulsion against his too rapid
triumphs, for which he had failed to prepare them, the socialists
rejected his policy.[1]

Millerand shows socialism developing out of radicalism and
his career illustrates the attitudes which caused so many radical
constituencies to elect socialist deputies. It should not be forgotten that it was on this radical foundation that socialism was
largely built, from the point of view of parliamentary representation. Millerand's socialism was a development of the doctrine
of solidarity. He had apparently never read Marx, at least not
properly. If he talked of the class struggle it was only to regret it
and to look forward to its rapid disappearance. He accepted
the republic and had no use for talk of violence or revolution.
He soon found his ideal in the 'great reformist republican party'
which Waldeck-Rousseau's ministry sought to create, and in
the practical social reforms it introduced. He saw it in contrast
to the mere radicals who only talked of reform; but he placed

[1] L. Derfler, 'Le cas Millerand', *Revue d'histoire moderne et contemporaine* (1965).

himself in the tradition of Gambetta, who had laid down the principle that reform should be divided up into manageable stages and carried through gradually 'treating with tact not only old habits but even prejudices'.[1] Like Gambetta, he was concerned above all with obtaining national support: but what he lacked was Gambetta's skill at keeping his friends happy at the same time. He insisted he did not wish to 'build a church for a sect'.[2] 'One should concern oneself less with one's friends and one's partisans', he said, 'than with one's adversaries, and above all one should consider that indifferent mass which is nearly always the majority. One must know how to draw it to one little by little; above all one should never, by imprudence or by exaggeration—which is both dangerous and useless—turn it away from one or against one.'[3]

He said of himself: 'I was and I remain a timid man.'[4] At this period the country found this timidity more congenial than the wildness of the socialist party. Millerand, however, possessed considerable abilities as an administrator which were not allowed to go to waste. His achievements as minister of commerce in 1899–1902 and as minister of public works in 1909–10 were substantial: his new label for his ideas was 'la politique de réalisations'. He cut down red tape in the post-office, for which he planned a forward looking modernization. He instituted the Office du Tourisme. Above all he advocated—and introduced in the public services under his control—consultation between management and workers. He hoped this would at the same time reduce the influence of the revolutionary trade unions (as would compulsory arbitration, his other pet scheme). It is not surprising that he dropped out of the socialist movement. His departure set the pattern for other important defections, of which Briand's and Viviani's were the most famous. As a result of the Millerand case and of its condemnation by the Congress of Amsterdam, ambitious socialists who had parliamentary and administrative gifts could not find scope for their talents within the party and left it. It was in the tradition of Millerand, and

---

[1] Speech on 'La politique sociale de la République', 28 Feb. 1909, printed in A. Millerand, *Politique de réalisations* (1911), 6.

[2] A. Millerand, *Le Socialisme réformiste français* (1908), 8.

[3] Speech to the Société d'Histoire de la Révolution de 1848, ibid., 348.

[4] Quoted from his unpublished memoirs by J. Magnien, 'Alexandre Millerand' (D.E.S., 1962), 4.

of the radical traditions he continued, that the independent
socialists survived as a separate group—as will be seen—after
the unification of 1905 had brought all the other socialists
together under Jaurès.[1]

The variety and vagueness shown by the independent socialists
was given a theoretical justification by a rather remarkable
man, who can in some ways be regarded as a second Proudhon.
Benoist Malon (1841–93), the son of agricultural labourers in
the Forez, grew up in the almost incredible poverty which he
later described in an extremely moving fragment of memoirs.[2]
Working at first as a shepherd, he learnt to read only at the
age of twenty, during a long convalescence spent at the house
of his elder brother, a primary-school master. For the rest of his
life he was a voracious reader, so that there was scarcely any
important book on politics or economics he did not know. He
found virtues in practically all of them, for his ideal was as
broad as could be. Malon was essentially an amiable, warm-
hearted and generous man and he showed this equally in his
attitude to ideas and in his relations with men. He spotted a fore-
bear of socialism in almost every author he read, starting with
Plato and going on to Cardinal Manning.[3] In Paris, where he
took a humble job in a dye works, he quickly became a leading
organiser of unions, co-operatives and the First International;
he was elected a deputy in 1871, resigned to take part in the
Commune, spent his subsequent exile in Italy organising the
workers there and then returned to help Guesde found the Parti
Ouvrier Français.[4] But Guesde's narrow sectarianism was alien
to him, and in 1885 Malon founded *La Revue socialiste*, a journal
to which he invited socialists of every variety and radical
fellow-travellers to contribute with a view to bringing about

---

[1] Raoul Persil, *Alexandre Millerand* (1949), 11–13; Jean Magnien, 'Alexandre
Millerand' (unpublished D.E.S. mémoire, Paris Faculty of Law, 1962), very useful
using Millerand's unpublished memoirs; A. Lavy, *L'Œuvre de Millerand: un ministre
socialiste* (1902), for Millerand's work 1899–1902; A. Millerand, *Politique de
réalisations* (1911), introduction of 92 pages, signed P. L. G. on his work 1909–10;
A. Millerand, *Travail et travailleurs* (1908), his speeches as minister, 1899–1902;
A. Millerand, *Le Socialisme réformiste français* (1908), speeches 1896–1902, with an
important preface defining reformism; Vincent Badie, *M. Alexandre Millerand,
socialiste réformiste. Son œuvre social* (Montpellier, 1931), an interesting apology.

[2] B. Malon, 'Fragment de mémoires', *Revue socialiste* (Jan.–July 1907) (five
articles).   [3] B. Malon, *Histoire du socialisme* (1879).

[4] B. Malon, *Le Nouveau Parti* (1881): François Simon, *Une Belle Figure du peuple,
Benoît Malon, sa vie, son œuvre* (Courbevoie, 1926).

mutual understanding. This became the organ of a new non-sectarian kind of socialism, of which the independents were the parliamentary representatives. Malon had a passion for reconciliation, and a gift for seeing the common links between apparently different men and theories; his critical abilities were as limited as his sympathies were wide, and so he developed what he called integral socialism. Socialism, he argued, should be the synthesis of 'all the progressive activities of humanity'; Marx, though he paid him due homage, saw things only from one viewpoint. Progress could not be explained simply in economic terms: political, religious and economic factors all contribute to it: 'Innovators should not content themselves with appealing to the class interests of the proletariat, they should also voice all the sentimental and moral forces to be found in the human soul.' So they must seek not only economic change but all types of reform—educational, social, political, civil, the emancipation of women and the 'softening of manners'. He agreed there was a struggle of classes, but regarded this as a tragedy. There was no need to wait till capitalism pauperised the proletariat and proletarianised the bourgeoisie. A start could be made at once, and preferably by peaceful means. Malon is important for drawing into the socialist movement the traditional French concern for humanity, the respect for individuality, the wide idealism. 'No struggle simply concerned with material interests', he wrote, 'has ever drawn the masses.' He provides the link between the ideas of 1848 and those of Jaurès, who was considerably influenced by him.[1]

The Anarchists

The anarchists were important rivals of the socialists. For some time, particularly in the 1890s, they retarded the recruitment of the socialists by providing an alternative revolutionary

[1] B. Malon, *Le Socialisme intégral* (1890–1), 1, 13, 16, 178, 190, 212–14, 443 and *passim*; A. Veber, 'La mort de Benoît Malon', *Revue socialiste*, no. 106, vol. 18 (Oct. 1893), 386–443; Eugène Fournière, 'Benoît Malon et le marxisme', ibid. (Nov. 1893), 541–3; Eugène Spuller, *Figures disparues*, 3rd series (1894), 233–51. Malon's successors as editor were Georges Renard, Gustave Rouanet, and then Eugène Fournière. The last of these is particularly interesting—a self-educated jeweller, he wrote about fifty books. See Justinien Raymond, 'Eugène Fournière', in *L'Actualité de l'histoire*, 25 (Oct.–Dec. 1958). Renard and Rouanet would also repay study.

movement which appealed to many who disliked the regimenta-
tion and dogmatism of the socialists. In the following decade,
they were influential in many trade unions, with the result that
these remained independent of the socialists. Socialism would
thus no doubt have been far more successful but for them. There
was competition between the two because they were not entirely
different. The ultimate ideal of both was a classless communism, in which the state would have withered away.
Proudhon, who was the founding father of French anarchism,
also inspired some sections of the socialists. Both movements
wished to destroy the bourgeois order. But there were fundamental differences between them. The anarchists placed much
more emphasis on liberty than on equality. Unlike the Marxists
who were willing to use the state for a long time before its ultimate abolition, they considered it to be an instrument of oppression at all times. They wished to abolish it immediately, not to
capture it. The principal evil of existing society, according to
the socialists, came from the abuses of private property, but the
anarchists saw authority as the greatest enemy and they hoped
to end it simultaneously in its triple manifestation of the state,
the Church and capital. The methods they envisaged were also
different. They had no use for electoral agitation and they did
not try to get into parliament. They believed in direct action,
'propaganda by deed', 'permanent revolt', living freely,
individually, ignoring the legal order, rather than setting up
organisations to replace it. By definition they could hardly
be a party. There were probably never more than 1,000 active
anarchist militants, distributed in about fifty groups, most of
them in Paris and Lyon. None of their newspapers ever sold
more than about 7,000 copies. But they may well have had
100,000 people sympathetic to them and some of their attitudes
infiltrated, often unacknowledged, into the minds of a far
larger proportion of the country.[1]

Anarchism passed through several stages in France. In its
Proudhonist variety, it was influential in the First Inter-

---

[1] Figures in Jean Maitron, *Histoire du mouvement anarchiste en France 1880–1914*
(1951), 114–15, 128, 432. This is the standard history, with a comprehensive
bibliography. For more recent works see the supplementary bibliography in
J. Maitron, 'L'anarchisme français 1945–1965', in *Le Mouvement social*, 150 (Jan.–
Mar. 1965), 97–110. But there has been far less research on the anarchists than
on the socialists.

national, until about 1873, when Bakunin's influence replaced
mutualism by anti-state collectivism. Bakunin came to Lyon
in September 1870 and on the 28th proclaimed the abolition
of the state. The state replied by sending two companies of
national guardsmen; and he at once fled to Geneva. This
failure turned his interests to other countries, and his expulsion
also meant that Switzerland became the headquarters of the
movement. There several victims of the repression of the Commune, like Élisée Reclus (the author of the nineteen volumes of
the *Nouvelle Géographie universelle*) and Paul Brousse (later the
leader of the possibilists) were converted to it. As a result,
because of its proximity to Switzerland, it was principally in
Lyon that anarchism flourished at first, but in 1883 sixty-six
anarchists were arrested and put on trial there. After that
the leadership passed to Paris, where several newspapers won
some success. Their first paper, *La Révolution Sociale* (1880),
started with funds provided by the prefect of police through
an *agent provocateur*, was perhaps too serious and dull to attract
recruits.[1] (Much later Grave used the fortune of the English-
woman he married in 1909, Miss Mabel Holland Thomas, to
keep his *Temps Nouveaux* going.)[2] Emile Pouget (who has been
mentioned in the chapter on trade unions) ran a very lively
Père Peinard, scurrilous, witty and slangy, which won some
success. Other newspapers caused a stir by raising funds through
lotteries in which pistols and daggers were offered as prizes.

After the early optimism, a realisation arose that the struggle
for freedom would be a long one. Anarchism now entered a new
phase, in which direct acts of violence were its principal method.
This phase reached its climax in 1892-4, when terrorism,
explosions, robberies and murders, culminating in the assassination of Carnot, president of the republic, turned anarchism into
a major threat to bourgeois order. This violence with which
anarchism is usually identified in the popular mind, was, however, the work of only a few individuals, acting on their own
initiative, and it did not have wide support in the movement,
even though the leaders seldom condemned it. Its effect nevertheless was to produce drastic repression by the *lois scélérates*
(1894). The anarchists therefore moved on to trying other

[1] L. Andrieux, *Souvenirs d'un préfet de police* (1885), I. 339.
[2] Maitron, *Histoire*, 434.

methods. They attempted to win the workers through the trade unions, in which they soon obtained highly influential positions. Pelloutier, Yvetot, Delassalle and Pouget made revolutionary syndicalism—anarchism acting through unions rather than individual efforts—a considerable force in French politics. It provided the workers with a doctrine which enabled them to do without the bourgeois state—though too much should not be made of the doctrinal aspect. The workers could call themselves revolutionary syndicalists or anarchists because it justified to them what some of them had long wanted—independence. It was only in 1913, finally, that a party was formed: the Fédération Communiste Révolutionnaire Anarchiste, with anti-parliamentarianism, antimilitarism and trade union action as its creed. It condemned individualist violence and terrorism, but it also declared its respect for the independence of individuals within the groups of the party and of the groups within the Fédération. Twenty-five groups from widely dispersed provincial towns joined it; but it did nothing to stimulate any growth of a political movement, and after the war organised anarchism was only a small sect.

The most famous names of anarchism are perhaps found in art. Courbet—friend of Proudhon and member of the Commune—probably applied its ideas to painting most directly.[1] The two Pissarros, Paul Signac and Steinlen contributed illustrations to the anarchist newspapers; Vlaminck regularly supported the cause with the proceeds from the sale of a painting every year from about 1900 to 1939.[2] Grave's paper, *La Révolte*, was read by Anatole France, Stéphane Mallarmé, Leconte de Lisle, J. K. Huysmans. André Gide's *L'Immoraliste* and *Les Caves du Vatican* perpetuate the memory of individual anarchism. The educational experiments of Sébastien Faure and others were pioneering examples of progressive schooling and active methods. Paul Robin, director of the orphanage at Cempuis and a leading advocate of eugenics, published a monthly journal from 1890 to 1905 significantly called *L'Éducation intégrale*; Armand advocated co-education to the extent of not objecting to sexual intercourse between children.[3]

---

[1] See James Joll's excellent study, *The Anarchists* (1964), 164-70.
[2] J. P. Crespelle, *The Fauves* (English translation by Anita Brookner, 1962), 23.
[3] Maitron, 324-35.

In 1905 *La Science sociale*, the journal of the Le Play school of sociology, published a study of an anarchist, based on a long series of interviews. The man concerned was of no importance at all, an ordinary rank-and-file adherent, and this makes the detailed account of his life all the more illuminating and valuable. The interviewer first met Lebrun in 1897. Lebrun had been working in a cardboard-making factory for twenty-two years, without ever having been unemployed; his wife had worked there for the same period. They had never had a strike, and no dismissals when work was slack; only occasionally had they had a shorter working week. Lebrun expressed esteem and friendship for his boss, who treated them well, insured them against accidents and gave three weeks' maternity benefit. He worked eleven hours a day, earning 5 francs 25 on piece rates. His wife worked ten hours; as a mother she was allowed to arrive half an hour late and to stay away during school holidays. She only earned 3 francs 90 a day. But together their income totalled 70 francs 20 a week. He had a rented flat of three rooms, with no running water. 'I am only an anarchist theoretician', he said. 'I know that society as it exists at present is bad, but personally I have not too much to complain about, since I and my family have pretty well all we need.' It was true his work was no longer skilled, as it had been before machines were introduced, but in compensation, as he philosophically observed, 'it leaves the mind free'.

Lebrun's father had been a practising Catholic, but he read the republican *Siècle* newspaper (which he bought second-hand from a subscriber the day after it was published) and he supported the revolutions of 1830 and 1848. He was also a cardboard maker—he made cartons for porcelain and his hope had been that his son should become a commercial traveller in porcelain. Lebrun's mother had inherited 40,000 francs [£1,600] from her father—a former Chouan—but had lost it all in unsuccessful trade and had become a cardboard maker too. She sent him to a seminary in the hope that he would become a priest, but he was expelled for biting a monk. He then tried his hand at various jobs—as a sculptor of umbrella handles, a maker of artificial flowers (or rather, since this last industry was highly specialised, he made only the leaves while others made the flowers and others still the fruit), and a gas-fitter. He had then settled down to his present job. Thanks to his wife's earnings, he was living quite comfortably. They could afford to send their babies to nurses in the country, at 27 francs a month.

Lebrun had originally been a Gambettist, until 1879 when he had read some pamphlets published by the Guesdists, which said that the introduction of machines would produce unemployment: soon after eighteen workers were dismissed for this very reason. He was greatly impressed and became interested in socialism. A workmate took him to a group called L'Union Socialiste and so he became a member of the P.O.F. He read Jules Vallès's paper *Le Cri du Peuple*. Then one day he read in a conservative paper *La France* an attack by the liberal Francisque Sarcey on Kropotkin's *Paroles d'un révolté*, giving extracts and expressing surprise that such an advanced revolutionary could be an honest man. These extracts made Lebrun want to read the book. He bought it, read it—being particularly struck by the chapter entitled 'Aux jeunes gens'. He became an anarchist. He left the P.O.F., stopped participating in electoral agitation and ceased to vote; but he did not join any anarchist group, though he contributed funds to one of which he approved. The trouble with it was that it did not have a library. So instead he formed a club with some anarchist friends to create a library. They all bought books themselves and used their subscriptions to buy more; they met weekly for discussion; and they once published a pamphlet, entitled 'The Workers of the towns to the workers of the countryside', which was revised by Malato, who, though not a member, frequently came to their meetings. But the police dissolved them. So Lebrun joined the socialist library of the 19th *arrondissement*, where, for 50 centimes a month, he had access to a thousand volumes. On Sundays he used to go to anarchist meetings but less often now that he was getting older. He spent 20 sous a month on anarchist newspapers and pamphlets; he particularly liked the *Temps Nouveaux* because it was a serious paper discussing social theories; but he also read S. Faure and Pouget. He had a passion for reading. His great aim was to become more educated, though there was no one subject he specially wished to study. Before he had become a socialist, he had read Rousseau: the *Social Contract*, he said, had made him very discontented and had shown him many defects in society. Voltaire had made him sceptical about God. Darwin, Spencer and Lanessan's *Le Transformisme* had made him an atheist. He had a large collection of books.[1] But he had no savings: the expense of bringing up his family left him little to spare. Still, he led a full life. His wife's great interest was the theatre, and for the first ten or twelve years of their married life they had gone to the theatre twice a week (her brother made shoes for actors and got them tickets at reduced prices); now they were going only once in two months. They ate well—meat every day—buying their food from the co-operative. They had begun their married life with a single bed and one trunk but their flat was now reasonably well furnished. The only outward sign that Lebrun was an anarchist was—apart perhaps from his books—his dress. Fifteen years before he had been a member of a choral society and had bought a frock-coat and top hat for 70 francs, which he had worn on Sundays. 'I was growing into a bourgeois', he recalled laughing. But when he became an anarchist, he found his dress 'insufficiently simple', so he had not worn it since, and instead had an ordinary suit costing 21 francs. He then decided an overcoat was also not sufficiently simple, and he now wore a long hooded cloak, costing only 10 francs 75.

Eight years later, the sociologist interviewer paid him another visit. As a result of Millerand's law, Lebrun was working only 10 hours a day, and his wages were therefore lower, but his wife, now that the children had grown up, was also working 10 hours, so that together their earnings were a little higher, 75 francs a

[1] Henri Martin, *Histoire de France*, 7 vols.; L. Blanc on the Revolution and *Histoire de dix ans*, Regnault on 1840–8, Lavetelle on the eighteenth century, Gordon de Grenouillac, *Paris à travers les siècles*, 5 vols., Challamel, *La France à travers les siècles*, 4 vols.; A. Guilbert, *Histoire des villes de France*; Augustin Thierry, *Histoire de la conquête de l'Angleterre, Récits du temps mérovingien, Histoire du tiers état*; Malte-Brun, *La France illustrée* (bought for 100 francs, and then bound), Alex de Laborde, *Itinéraire de l'Espagne*, 5 vols.; *Histoire pittoresque des grands voyages*. Fourteen volumes of popular science by Camille Flammarion, L. Huard, *La Science pratique, Le Monde industriel*; Alexis Clerc, five volumes on physics, chemistry and medicine. Littré's Dictionary. Homer, Plato's *Republic*. Eight volumes of Greek and Roman classics. The complete works of Racine, Molière, Boileau, Mme de Sévigné, Goethe; almost all of V. Hugo, D. Defoe's *Crusoe*, six volumes of Lamartine, Musset, E. Augier, G. Sand, E. Sue, Maupassant. Scott's *Midlothian*, Turgenev, F. Cooper, 5 vols., J. Verne. 200 volumes of La Bibliothèque nationale; twenty volumes of Flammarion's Petite Bibliothèque universelle. Renan's *Jésus*; the Koran; Lamennais's Rousseau, 3 vols., Montesquieu, 3 vols., J. Simon, Dupanloup, Cabet, Mazzini, Blanqui, Kropotkin, H. Spencer. Many pamphlets. But no Proudhon.

week. His son was doing well as a locksmith, and his daughter as a corset maker, though their second daughter had died. He could now save. Despite his anarchist theories, he was growing into a petty bourgeois. In 1899 he had founded a workers' club which invested subscriptions of 1 franc a week in premium bonds—but it never won anything. In 1900 he founded another aiming at the purchase of land for its members. Two years later he found a piece of land—400 square metres—for 1,200 francs. He bought it, paying in instalments. In 1903 he bought another plot, again on instalments. On the one plot he grew vegetables in accordance with the principles of Georges Ville, a writer on intensive agriculture frequently cited by the anarchists; the other he lent to a friend to cultivate, free of charge. He had built himself a shack on his plot, but a storm had destroyed it; he was now building something more solid. His repayments came to 10 francs a week (one-seventh of his income); he was economising to such an extent that he hardly bought books any more. In four years' time, he calculated, his house would be built and both plots paid for. His wife would then give up work to rear chickens and rabbits. He would take a season ticket to his job in Paris. He had lost his faith in his local co-op, where dividends had fallen. He had resigned from his friendly society. He had just joined a trade union of labourers (this is what he called himself, without illusions) but it was only in order to be able to use the library of the Bourse du Travail which had 8,000 volumes. Though still an anarchist, he seemed to hope less from the natural goodness of man. In his own life, certainly, he was turning himself into a petty capitalist. His life story illustrates the triumph of the ideal of property and thrift.[1]

The Progress of Socialism

In the elections of 1906 the united socialists obtained 54 seats in the chamber, in 1910 they got 76 seats and in 1914 103 seats.[2] The regional distribution of these was very unequal. The

[1] Dr. J. Bailhache, 'Un type d'ouvrier anarchiste. Monographie d'une famille d'ouvriers parisiens', *La Science sociale*, 14 (May 1905).

[2] These figures are approximate, because of some individual desertions etc. See E. Fournière, 'Les socialistes à la Chambre', *Revue socialiste*, 44 (Aug. 1906), 205–12. They exclude the independent socialists.

party was particularly successful in the Mediterranean south, in the east and centre, and in the Nord and in Paris. It did not even try to put up candidates in certain departments of the west. In 1910 it obtained, in the first ballot, 1,125,877 votes, i.e. 13 per cent of votes cast, but in the Var it won 42 per cent, in Nord 31 per cent, in Seine 27 per cent; in 23 other departments it won more than 13 per cent but in 7 departments it obtained less than 1 per cent of the votes cast.[1] These regional contrasts make it easier to understand the nature of the support it received, though this is a subject on which a great deal of research is still needed.

Enough has been said of the particular circumstances of Paris and the Guesdist Nord. Most of the other socialist constituencies were rural. But this did not necessarily mean that the peasants there voted socialist. First, many of these deputies got in as a result of an alliance with the radicals. The example of Draguignan (Var) in 1898 shows how a mere third of the votes was enough to secure victory. In the first ballot the conservative candidate obtained 5,821 votes, the socialist 4,554 and the radical 4,131. The radical withdrew in favour of the socialist, who therefore won in the second ballot.[2] Alliance with the radicals sometimes meant that the socialist victor was not really free to press his socialist opinions in practice. In Isère, the alliance was formed in 1906 to expel the opportunists who had been dominant for a long time. In that year Vienne got a socialist mayor, thanks to this alliance. Joseph Brenier had been a weaver in a factory and had risen to be its principal foreman, but having been dismissed for his political activities, he set up a small workshop of his own, which prospered, so that he became an employer though 'loyal to the class of his origins'. His socialism was very mild, for he was more interested really in anticlericalism; and even on this question he was not above bargaining with the Catholics for their votes, in return for which he showed himself benevolent to their Eucharistic Congress in 1912.[3] Such arrangements were by no means unusual

[1] Charles Duffart, 'La poussée socialiste en France d'après les élections générales de 1910', in *Revue socialiste*, 52 (July–Dec. 1910), 37–51, 147–54.

[2] H. Rouger, *Les Fédérations socialistes* (1913), 3. 25–48, has a useful article on Var.

[3] P. Barral, *Le Département de l'Isère sous la Troisième République 1870–1940* (1962), 526–32.

and it was not only with the radicals that the socialists allied. Compère-Morel, the Guesdist, won his seat in Gard thanks to the support of the extreme right wing. Electoral considerations were certainly one factor in keeping the socialists moderate and behind Jaurès. Secondly, in rural constituencies, it was frequently the artisans rather than the peasants who were the chief propagators of socialism. The main nuclei of socialism in rural Var turn out to be very sizeable villages like Flayosc (population 2,500) which had numerous small factories producing shoes, oil, tiles, and Vidauban (population 2,650) which had cork, brick and even machine factories.[1] Often too, peasants were part-time artisans, who migrated to neighbouring towns or to Paris, sometimes for part of the year and sometimes for a considerable portion of their working lives: they returned bringing urban ideas into the countryside.[2] Thus one of the first constituencies to go socialist in the isolated Creuse was Bourganeuf, which exported large numbers of masons and which in 1849 had elected a mason, Martin Nadaud, to parliament.[3] Likewise Ussel in Corrèze was an exporter of coachmen and taxi-drivers; Saint-Sulpice-les-Feuilles in Haute-Vienne exported navvies. Though surrounded by conservative country, they were early converts to socialism. The influence of a socialist town like Limoges, which drew its workers from the surrounding area, was also important, for these workers kept their links with their native villages and the ideas they acquired there travelled home eventually.[4] Once again, however, the nature of this socialism varied. The woodcutters of Allier, Cher and Nièvre, who started one of the most vigorous rural agitations in the 1900s, gave a false impression of socialism, for though they elected socialist deputies, they were principally

[1] Yves Malartic, 'Comment Clemenceau fut battu aux élections législatives à Draguignan en 1893', in *Provence historique* (1962), 112–38, especially 115; Paul Joanne, *Dictionnaire géographique et administratif de la France* (1894–1905), 1498, 5258.

[2] Paul Bois, *Paysans de l'ouest* (1960), is the most brilliant study of this subject.

[3] Gérard Walter, *Histoire des paysans de France* (1963), 409–10, 417; Martin Nadaud, *Mémoires*.

[4] A. Perrier, 'Esquisse d'une sociologie du mouvement socialiste dans la Haute-Vienne et en Limousin', *Actes du 87ème Congrès national des sociétés savantes, Poitiers 1962, section d'histoire moderne et contemporaine* (1963), 377–98. Cf. R. Baubirot, 'Remarques sur la condition au 18 et 19 siècles des communautés des paysans du nord de l'actuel département de la Haute-Vienne', ibid., 905–33.

concerned with the redress of their immediate grievances about
methods of payment for their work. The sharecroppers of
Allier likewise elected a socialist but all he demanded was
detailed reforms of the particular abuses to which sharecroppers were subject in this region.[1] The revolts of the winegrowers in the south in 1907 and in Champagne in 1911 (when
70,000 bottles were destroyed in a wholesaler's cellars by an
angry mob)[2] were not socialist at all.

The force of tradition was important. The leader of the
socialists in Vaucluse said it was not surprising that 'advanced
opinions' were to be found there: 'We are a department of the
south, a department which had the honour to rise against the
coup d'état of 2 December.'[3] Where such traditions were strongest,
Marxism was often weakest, and personal rivalries vigorous. In
Vaucluse, by his own admission, the struggle for socialism was
closely bound up with the desire to evict 'the petty tyrants of
the communes'. Neither economic nor sociological explanations
of the socialist vote are adequate.[4] One can see the importance
of personal factors if one looks at the way a few individuals
were actually converted. Paul Faure was the son of a republican
councillor general of Dordogne and grew up with 'advanced
ideas' but it was a Périgueux journalist who gave him Guesde's
and Lafargue's writings to read, which made him a socialist. At
twenty-five he was elected mayor of his commune—but not
because he was a socialist. When he said he was a socialist, his
supporters replied: 'That is of no importance.' They simply
wanted a new mayor. Arthur Groussier, an engineer, the son
of a left-wing grocer, got involved through trade unionism. He
discussed politics with the workers in his factory who invited
him to join their mechanics' union even though he was not a
worker. They then asked him to act as their delegate to the
Federation of Socialist Workers. He replied he was not a
socialist: they said it did not matter. But in this federation he

[1] Simone Derruan-Boniol, 'Le socialisme dans l'Allier de 1848 à 1914' in *Cahiers
d'histoire*, 2 (Grenoble, 1957), 115–61.
[2] P. Koukharski, 'Le Mouvement paysan en France en 1911' in *Questions
d'histoire* (1952), 160–77; P. Monette, 'L'éveil des paysans: La révolte des vignerons
champenois' in *La Vie ouvrière* (Feb.–Apr. 1911), 4 articles.
[3] Alexandre Blanc, *Le Parti radical et le parti socialiste dans Vaucluse* (Cavaillon,
1904), 11–12.
[4] H. Primbault, *Le Socialisme dans les campagnes* (Arras, 1902).

got to know one of the leaders who persuaded him to join the party. It was purely an interest in the practical improvement of the lot of the members of his union, not any doctrinal conviction, that determined his actions. J. B. Severac, the son of the republican deputy mayor of Montpellier, was converted at eighteen while a student at the university there by reading Malon's *Integral Socialism* and Zola's *Germinal* and by talking to his two socialist professors of philosophy there, Gaston Milhaud and Célestin Bouglé. Rather paradoxically for him socialism was never 'a game of ideas; it is a working-class thing. That is why I have never liked canvassing among the bourgeoisie.' Being a bourgeois and an intellectual himself, his conversion to socialism meant breaking with his class and keeping himself free of the contamination of capitalism and the state. 'What is seductive in socialism for me is that it creates true equality between men, it will end personal servitudes.' Vincent Auriol was likewise first introduced to socialism by his philosophy schoolteacher. Among industrial workers socialism was sometimes inherited: J. B. Lebas at fourteen was taken to hear Guesde speak by his father, a textile worker who was a member of the first socialist group of Roubaix; he joined the party at eighteen. At that same age, he wrote to ask Lafargue his opinion of Stuart Mill's book on positivism, which he had just read: Lafargue replied in a letter of four pages, excusing himself for not giving a complete criticism. Unlike Groussier, Lebas's study of Marx was serious, and he used to attend earnest discussions of it at a factory club.[1] These individual instances stress the rich variety of socialism in France, which was both more and less than what it claimed to be.

It might well be asked whether the differences between the socialists and their opponents were greater than the differences within the socialist party itself. It depends on what one stresses. If one is primarily studying institutions, the unification and growth of the party is a clear enough theme. But this traditional perspective has led to the neglect of the values which the socialists shared with other parties, and of the irrational elements in their lives, which were never expressed in official programmes. There is room for a re-classification of politicians on lines other than those which they themselves adopted. I make

[1] Louis Lévy, *Comment ils sont devenus socialistes* (1932).

suggestions on this subject in another volume.

The conclusion that seems to emerge from the studies in this volume is that the ambitions and frustrations it has revealed cannot be explained without investigating at least three further aspects of the lives of Frenchmen. A constant theme in these pages has been the wide regional variations which complicated and sometimes transformed every movement and every change. The limits of national unity, provincialism, the relations of town and country, and the attitudes of Frenchmen to foreigners need to be understood in order to appreciate the forces with which central politics had to contend. The extent to which, and the way in which, Britanny, Alsace, Provence and Paris were parts of the same country is a question which has too often been avoided in national histories. A second theme of this book has been the clash of innovation and prejudice. Two elements behind this can be disentangled: on the one hand the survival of superstition and traditional modes of thought, and on the other the changes introduced principally through the medium of the schools. To what extent and in what way did the advocates of modernisation alter the approach and mentality of the people they sought to influence? This raises the third problem, of the crucial role played, both in subduing disunity and in attacking traditionalism, by the intellectuals, the flower of this age of education. Their history deserves to be written, not just in terms of the theoretical interest of their work, nor of its literary merit, but also from the point of view of their relations with their public. These three problems represent three levels of national or popular consciousness, which the sequel to this volume attempts to penetrate.

EPILOGUE

ONE of the principles on which this book is based is that chronology should not dominate the study of the past. Once one has discovered what happened—and it is useful to establish the order of events precisely—the historian's task is to ask questions about the events, to reflect on their significance and implications. This means investigating not only the factors which seem to be directly connected with those events—and the study of economic history is the favourite way of pursuing this line—but also aspects of life which apparently were unconnected with political events, e.g. laughter, cooking, music. My aim is to look at man from every possible side, without preconceptions about what supposedly dominated his behaviour. Instead of offering the reader a single thread—ideological or economic—on which to hang all his explanations, I take each activity in turn, studying it for its own sake. In the process I hope I can disengage it from the interpretations that have been imposed upon it.

The reader determined to read only about politics will find the direct continuation of my analysis in three chapters, entitled Gerontocracy, Technocracy and Hypocrisy, which use the events of 1914–45 as the raw material for reflecting on longer term problems of political behaviour: these are in volume 2 of my *France: Intellect, Taste and Anxiety* (1977), pp. 1040–1154. My views on the 'class struggle' are in volume 1, under the title of Ambition; on women in politics in volume 1 also, chapter 13; on nationalism, in volume 2, part I; on foreign relations in volume 2, chapter 3; on the political press, volume 2, chapter 11; on the army and colonies, volume 2, chapter 18; on religion and anticlericalism, volume 2, chapter 19. But I would argue that everything is relevant to everything else, even if my conclusion is that each aspect of behaviour was capable of more independence than it is customary to allow it. The systematisers have tried to eliminate the contradictions from life: I see them as an essential part of it.

GUIDE TO FURTHER READING

BIBLIOGRAPHIES, by custom, list books in alphabetical order, or by subject matter. I shall not do this because what I offer here is neither a catalogue nor a guide to research on particular topics: readers with specialist interests can pursue them through the references in my footnotes. I aim rather to advise the amateur or general reader who simply wants to know more about French history and about the behaviour of the French people, who is uncertain as to how or where to begin, because he is a little intimidated by the enormous mass of publications, but who hopes that there might be enjoyment as well as instruction to be derived from further reading.

I do not believe that for this kind of person the best way of proceeding is that used by students, i.e. starting with an elementary textbook, covering each branch of the subject in turn, and going over the same ground at a slightly more advanced level each time. I should like to suggest that he should turn straight to the really good books, which can provide an exhilarating experience: it does not matter if occasionally he feels a little out of his depth, any more than it matters, when one goes to a picture gallery, if the masterpieces are not all entirely clear. History does have quite a lot of superior books of this kind to offer. Some may be out-of-date, from the point of view of modern scholarship, some may be biased, but, if they have character, such defects should not be allowed to let them be forgotten. The appetite for history should not be spoilt by indulging in too much *hors d'œuvre* in the form of textbooks, introductions and summaries. The absolute beginner will find that a couple of these, at most, will suffice, e.g. Gordon Wright, *France in Modern Times* (1962), which is a survey of general trends, and Paul A. Gagnon, *France since 1789* (New York 1964), which is a political narrative. There are collective histories of this period, e.g. the *Nouvelle Histoire de la France contemporaine* published by Le Seuil, covering the years 1787 to the present in 18 paperback volumes, written by different authors, which reflects modern research and methods; but it should perhaps be turned to at a later stage. If you are interested in politics you will find only 72 short pages in it, for example, on the politics of Napoleon III. For details of what actually happened in parliament and in cabinet meetings, you must go back to E. Lavisse, *Histoire de France contemporaine* (1921,

9 vols.): here the politics of Napoleon III is given at least ten times more space. But these works, despite their merits, are still summaries and commentaries. If you want to meet the politicians face to face, read Pierre de la Gorce, *Histoire du Second Empire* (1894–1904, 7 vols.) or better still, Emile Ollivier, *L'Empire Libéral* (1895–1916, 18 vols.). They are impressive books, full of documents, conversations, letters: they are triumphs of the art of narrative history. Anyone who wants to understand what political life was like must read lengthy works of this kind. For the earlier part of the nineteenth century, there is P. Duverger de Hauranne, *Histoire du gouvernement parlementaire en France* (1857–72, 10 vols.), Paul Thureau-Dangin, *Histoire de la monarchie de juillet* (1884–92, 7 vols.), and, less good, L. A. Garnier-Pagès, *Histoire de la Révolution de 1848* (1861–72). For the Third Republic, it is customary to read Denis Brogan's *The Development of Modern France* (1940), which is indeed both witty and well-informed, but beginners may also find it confusing, a whirlwind of constantly changing ministries. Better perhaps to go for the more leisurely Jacques Chastenet's *Histoire de la Troisième République* (1952–63, 7 vols.), brought up to date with two further volumes as *Cent ans de République* (1970, 9 vols.). The basis of political history must always be political narrative, and there is no way of getting through that quickly: the logical conclusion is to read the newspapers of the time, the parliamentary debates, day by day, to re-experience the uncertainty as to what is going to happen next; only in these long books does one come near to that.

The other way to get the feel of the past is to read the massive theses which French scholars write, usually after about ten years of hard labour. These may appear to be rather specialised and too academic, but they are illuminating precisely because they are so detailed. Among them may be mentioned: A. Tudesq, *Les Grands Notables en France 1840–9* (1964, 2 vols.); A. Daumard, *La Bourgeoisie parisienne 1815–48* (1970), not strictly about politics, but it tells you how the ruling class lived and what it did with its money; M. Agulhon, *La République au Village* (1970); P. Vigier, *La Seconde République dans la région alpine* (1963, 2 vols.); J. Maurain, *La Politique ecclésiastique du second empire* (1936); L. Girard, *La Politique des travaux publics sous le second empire* (1952); A. Corbin, *Archaisme et modernité en Limousin 1845–80* (1975, 2 vols.); Michelle Perrot, *Les Ouvriers en grève 1871–90* (1974); Claude Willard, *Le Mouvement socialiste en France 1893–1905: les Guesdistes* (1965); J. Maitron, *Histoire du mouvement anarchiste en France 1880–1914* (1951); Annie Kriegel, *Aux origines du communisme français* (1964, 2 vols.); Antoine Prost, *Les Anciens Combattants 1914–39* (1977, 3 vols.); J. J. Becker, *1914: Comment les Français sont entrés dans la guerre* (1977); P. Sorlin,

Waldeck-Rousseau (1968); J. Gadile, *La Pensée et l'action politique des évêques français 1870–83* (1967, 2 vols.); A. Siegfried, *Tableau politique de la France de l'Ouest sous la troisième république* (1913); J. N. Jeanneney, *Français de Wendel* (1977).

The third category of books I would recommend are biographies, though there are fewer available for France than for either Britain or the U.S.A. Here is a selection of which some are more readable than others. F. A. Simpson, *The Rise of Louis Napoleon* (1909); and *Louis Napoleon and the Second Empire* (1923); T. Zeldin, *Emile Ollivier and the Liberal Empire* (1963); J. P. T. Bury, *Gambetta* (in progress); H. Kurtz, *The Empress Eugénie* (1970); Leo Loubère, *Louis Blanc* (Evanston, Illinois, 1961); G. Woodcock, *Proudhon* (1956); D. R. Watson, *Georges Clemenceau* (1974); Edgar Holt, *The Tiger: the life of G. Clemenceau* (1976); Harvey Goldberg, *Jean Jaurès* (Madison, Wisconsin, 1962); Jacques Julliard, *Fernand Pelloutier et les origines du syndicalisme* (1971); Léon Roudiez, *Maurras jusqu'à l'Action Française* (1957); P. Miquel, *Poincaré* (1961); Geoffrey Warner, *Pierre Laval* (1968; J. Colton, *Léon Blum* (New York, 1966); R. Humphreys, *Georges Sorel* (Cambridge, Massachusetts, 1951); and though it is not a biography, I would add H. G. Kedward, *Resistance in Vichy France* (1978), which shows how less famous people made their individual decisions in a period of crisis.

There is no substitute for reading the politicians themselves. Among their works are: A. de Lamartine, *La Politique de Lamartine* (1878); A. de Tocqueville, *Recollections* (English translation, 1948); A. Ledru-Rollin, *Discours politiques* (1879); P. J. Proudhon, *Carnets* (1960, 2 vols.); Martin Nadaud, *Mémoires de Léonard, ancien garçon maçon* (new ed., 1976); Napoleon III, *Des Idées Napoléoniennes* (1830); Duc de Persigny, *Mémoires* (1896); Comte de Falloux, *Mémoires d'un royaliste* (1888, 2 vols.); L. Gambetta, *Lettres* (1938) or better still his *Discours et plaidoyers politiques*, (1881–5, 11 vols.); Bernard Lavergne, *Les Deux Présidences de Jules Grévy 1879–87* (1966); C. de Freycinet, *Souvenirs* (1913, 2 vols.); J. Caillaux, *Mes Mémoires* (1942, 3 vols.); E. Combes, *Mon Ministère* (1956); E. Herriot, *Jadis* (1948, 2 vols.); L. Blum, *Souvenirs sur l'Affaire* (1935) or his *Oeuvre* (1954 ff., 8 vols.); A. Tardieu, *La Révolution à refaire* (1937, 2 vols.); M. Thorez, *Fils du peuple* (1937) and his *Oeuvres* (1950 ff.); P. Reynaud, *Mémoires* (1960–3, 2 vols.); A. Lebrun, *Temoignage* (1945); C. de Chambrun, *Traditions et Souvenirs* (1952); C. de Gaulle, *Mémoires de guerre* (1954–9, 3 vols., also translated into English).

GLOSSARY

A.I.T. Association Internationale du Travail. The First International, founded on 28 September 1864 in London by Karl Marx, lasted to 1876. The Second was founded in Paris in 1889: the French Socialist Party was known as the Section Française de l'Internationale Ouvrière (S.F.I.O.). The Third International, founded by Lenin in March 1919, was distinguished as the 'Komintern'.

Action Française. A review (1899) and daily newspaper (1908–44) edited by Charles Maurras; also the short title of the political movement, the Ligue d'Action Française, advocating the 'integral nationalism' of Maurras, anti-democratic, anti-liberal, for a hereditary, anti-parliamentary and decentralised monarchy, pro-Catholic. But its violence and independence led to its being condemned by the Pope (1926) and by the Pretender (1937). Its links with the Vichy Regime led to its disappearance at the Liberation. The paper was continued by the weekly *Aspects de la France.*

Additional Act. Constitution added to that of Napoleon I's empire, on his return from Elba, drawn up by Benjamin Constant and proclaimed on 1 June 1815. It established a parliament of two chambers, with peers appointed by the Emperor and representatives elected by universal suffrage on a two-tier system. A liberal gesture which was regarded as insincere in 1815, but which was later admired as a model constitution.

Baccalauréat. State secondary school leaving certificate, a necessary qualification for university entry and for many state jobs. Originally awarded after only an oral examination, it was based on a written test after 1830, and after 1874 on two examinations, taken during the two final years of schooling. See Zeldin, *France*, vol. 2, chapter on secondary education, esp. pp. 269–74.

Bachelier. Holder of Baccalauréat, q.v.

Bottin Mondain. Social register of aristocratic and notable families of France, giving titles, names of children, addresses of residences, and also containing advertisements and information of interest to 'high society'.

Burgraves. Nickname given to the Committee of Twelve who presided over the conservative and monarchist groups in the Legislative Assembly, 1849–51: Thiers, Montalembert, Molé, Berryer, etc.

Cahiers de doléances. Documents formulating the demands of the electorate for the Estates General in 1789.

· *Capitation.* Established 1695, tax originally paid by everybody, though people were divided into 22 different classes, each of which paid differently. Later the clergy bought themselves freedom from it, and eventually it became a mere annex to the *Taille* (q.v.).

Centimes additionnels. A method of increasing direct taxation by demanding additional payments in the form of so many centimes. Imposed by and payable to the state, or to local authorities.

Commune. Independent revolutionary government established in Paris 18 March–28 May 1871.

Constituent Assembly. The one referred to in this book is that of the Second Republic, which sat from April 1848 to March 1849.

Convention. Assembly, founded by the First Republic, which governed France from 21 September 1792 to 26 October 1795. It had 749 members. It was supposed to be elected by almost universal suffrage, but in fact only about one tenth of those eligible voted, and a minority of revolutionaries was able to dominate it.

Corporatism. Doctrine placing particular emphasis on professional corporations as the most important units in economic and political organisation. A reaction at once against liberalism, capitalism and socialism. Favoured by the legitimists and social catholics before 1914, several different versions became popular after the war, under the influence of the economist François Perroux, of Marcel Déat ('neo-socialism'), Marcel Bucard ('francisme'), etc. After the defeat of France in 1940, the Vichy government adopted it in its Charte du Travail and especially in its Peasants' Corporation. There were several varieties of corporatism, each envisaging slightly different relations between the state and the workers.

Corvée. Free collective service, by serfs, peasants or tenants, given in the *ancien régime* to their lord, to help him maintain and farm his land. The state added a *corvée royale*, free labour for a certain number of days, on building and maintenance of roads: it affected only rural residents and the rich could buy substitutes to do the work for them. Abolished 1789.

Dreyfus Affair. In 1894 Alfred Dreyfus, a Jewish captain, was wrongly convicted of passing military secrets to the Germans. A campaign was started, by Clemenceau, Zola and others, to vindicate him, particularly when the evidence came to point to Major Esterhazy as the culprit. But the army refused to change its verdict. In 1898 one of the documents used to convict Dreyfus was revealed to be a forgery, and an officer in the Intelligence Service, Col. Henry, admitting to having fabricated it, committed suicide. In a new trial in 1899, Dreyfus was nevertheless again found guilty. He was pardoned ten days later by the President of the Republic, and his name was finally cleared in 1906.

Ecole Normale Supérieure. One of the *grandes écoles*, offering higher education to a small élite, recruited by rigorous competition. Nominally a training college for secondary teachers, it produced many leading politicians and writers. See Zeldin, *France* vol. 2, pp. 334-9.

Familistère. Industrial Cooperative, originally applied to a factory; more recently used for cheap retail cooperatives.

Fourth Republic. Regime of parliamentary government 1944-58.

Fifth Republic. Presidential regime established by General de Gaulle in 1958, and still in existence.

Garde mobile. Part of the National Guard, raised in 1848 to maintain internal order. An attempt to revive it as a reserve military force in 1868 came to nothing.

Institut de France. Consists of five Academies: Académie Française (composed of 40 members, about half of whom are men of letters and the rest statesmen, aristocrats, marshals of France, lawyers, etc.); Académie des Inscriptions et belles lettres (40 archaeologists, mediaevalists and literary historians); Académie des Sciences (68 scientists); Académie des Beaux Arts (50 members, of whom 14 are painters, 8 sculptors, 8 architects, 4 engravers, 6 musicians and 10 critics or friends of the arts); Académie des Sciences morales et politiques (40 members).

Instituteur. Primary school teacher (fem. *institutrice*). A public official, under government control, with official qualifications, though of an elementary kind. A title which began to be used in 1792 to replace maître d'école.

Interpellations. The right of members of parliament to question ministers, first used, informally, under Louis Philippe, was abolished by the second empire in its authoritarian phase, and then formally instituted in 1867. In 1869 a vote on the minister's reply was allowed and ministerial responsibility to parliament thus established. This right existed throughout the Third and Fourth Republics, but in 1958 interpellations were forbidden: ministers could henceforth be attacked only by a vote of confidence or censure.

Jacquerie. Peasant revolt.

July Monarchy, (*1830 48*). So called because it was established during the Revolution of July 1830, which overthrew King Charles X and established Louis Philippe as King. It was based on an electorate of (originally) 168,000 taxpayers.

Legitimists. Partisans of the elder branch of the Bourbons, in their claim to the throne of France, following the overthrow of Charles X in 1830. The latter died in 1837 and their allegiance then went to the pretender, the Comte de Chambord. See chapter 2.

Lettres de cachet. Used in the *ancien régime* by the royal government to imprison or exile, overriding the usual process of law; abolished 1790.

Licence. University degree conferred by faculties, roughly equivalent of British B.A. *Licencié*, holder of this degree. See Zeldin, *France*, vol. 2, chapter 7, on Universities.

Livret ouvrier. The workers' 'cards'. Originally the card the worker received on leaving his employment, certifying that he had fulfilled his obligations to his employer. A law of 1749 forbade employers to take on workers without one. Workers who did not carry it could be prosecuted as vagabonds. Abolished 1890.

Lycée. State Secondary School. See Zeldin, *France*, vol. 2, chapter 6.

M.R.P. Mouvement Républicain Populaire. Christian Democratic Party formed in 1944.

Ministries:

Bourbon Restoration. 9 July 1815, Prince de Talleyrand; 26 September 1815, Duc de Richelieu; 29 December 1818, General Dessolle; 19 November 1819, Comte de Decazes; 20 February 1820, Duc, de Richelieu; 14 December 1821, Comte de Villèle; 4 January 1828, Vicomte de Martignac; 8 August 1829, Prince de Polignac, overthrown 29 July 1830.

July Monarchy of Louis Philippe. 11 August 1830, J. Dupont de l'Eure; 2 November 1830, Jacques Laffitte; 13 March 1831, Casimir Perier; 11 October 1832, Marshal Soult; 18 July 1834, Marshal Gérard; 10 November 1834, Duc de Bassano; 18 November 1834, Marshal Mortier; 12 March 1835, Duc de Broglie; 22 February 1836, Adolphe Thiers; 6 September 1836, Comte de Mole; 1 March 1839, Adolphe Thiers; 29 October 1840, Marshal Soult (with Guizot as leading influence); 19 September 1847, François Guizot, to 23 February 1848.

Second Republic. Provisional Government of the Republic, 24 February 1848 (Dupont, Lamartine, Arago, Ledru-Rollin, Marie, Crémieux, Garnier-Pagès, Albert, Louis Blanc, Marrast, Flocon). May 1848 Executive Commission of the Constituent Assembly (Arago president, Garnier-Pagès, Marie, Lamartine, Ledru-Rollin); 28 June 1848, General Louis Cavaignac, head of the executive; 20 December 1848, Odilon Barrot, prime minister to President Louis Napoleon Bonaparte; prime ministership abolished 31 October 1849.

Second Empire. No prime minister till 2 January 1870, when Emile Ollivier virtually had that status, resigned 9 August 1870. Ministerial influences during the period 1850–70 include: Duc de Persigny (minister of interior 1852–4 and 1860–3); Achille Fould (minister of state 1852–60, of finance 1851–2 and 1861–7); Jules Baroche (president of council of state 1853–60,

1861-3, minister of justice 1863-9); Eugène Rouher (minister of justice 1850-1, 1851-2, minister of agriculture, commerce and public works 1855-63, minister of state 1863-9). Main foreign ministers: E. Drouyn de Lhuys, 1852-5 and 1862-6; Comte Walewski, 1855-9; E. Thouvenel 1859-62; Marquis de Moustier 1866-8.

Third Republic. 19 February 1871, J. Dufaure; 25 May 1873, Duc de Broglie; 22 May 1874, General de Cissey; 10 March 1875, Louis Buffet; 23 February 1876, Jules Simon; 17 May 1877, Duc de Broglie; 23 November 1877, General de Rochebouet; 13 December 1877, J. Dufaure; 4 February 1879, William Waddington; 28 December 1879, Louis de Freycinet; 23 September 1880, Jules Ferry; 14 November 1881, Léon Gambetta; 30 January 1882, L. de Freycinet; 7 August 1882, Eugène Duclerc; 29 January 1883, Armand Fallières; 21 February 1883, J. Ferry; 6 April 1885, Henri Brisson; 7 January 1886, L. de Freycinet; 11 December 1886, René Goblet; 30 May 1887, Maurice Rouvier; 12 December 1887, Pierre Tirard; 3 April 1888, Charles Floquet; 22 February 1889, P. Tirard; 17 March 1890, L. de Freycinet; 27 February 1892, Emile Loubet; 6 December 1892, Alexandre Ribot; 4 April 1893, Charles Dupuy; 3 December 1893, J. Casimir-Perier; 30 May 1894, Ch. Dupuy; 26 January 1895, A. Ribot; 1 November 1895, Léon Bourgeois; 29 April 1896, Jules Méline; 28 June 1898, Henri Brisson; 1 November 1898, Ch. Dupuy; 22 June 1899, R. Waldeck-Rousseau; 7 June 1902, Emile Combes; 24 January 1905, M. Rouvier; 14 March 1906, Jean Sarrien; 25 October 1906, Georges Clemenceau; 24 July 1909, Aristide Briand; 2 March 1911, Ernest Monis; 27 July 1911, Joseph Caillaux; 14 January 1912, Raymond Poincaré; 21 January 1913 A. Briand; 22 March 1913, Louis Barthou: 9 December, Gaston Doumergue; 9 June 1914, A. Ribot; 13 June 1914, René Viviani; 29 October 1915, A. Briand; 20 March 1917, A. Ribot; 12 September 1917, Paul Painlevé; 16 November 1917, G. Clemenceau; 20 January 1920, Alexandre Millerand; 24 September 1920, Georges Leygues; 16 January 1921, A. Briand; 15 January 1922, R. Poincaré; 9 June 1924, François Marsal; 14 June 1924, Edouard Herriot; 17 April 1925, P. Painlevé; 28 November 1925, A. Briand; 19 July 1926, E. Herriot; 23 July 1926, R. Poincaré; 29 July 1929, A. Briand; 2 November 1929, André Tradieu; 21 February 1930, Camille Chautemps; 2 March 1930, A. Tardieu; 13 December 1930, Théodore Steeg; 27 January 1931, Pierre Laval; 20 February 1932, A. Tardieu; 3 June 1932, E. Herriot; 18 December 1932,

Paul Boncour; 31 January 1933, Edouard Daladier; 26 October 1933, Albert Sarraut; 26 November 1933, Camille Chautemps; 30 January 1934, E. Daladier; 9 February 1934, G. Doumergue; 8 November 1934, P. E. Flandin; 1 July 1935, Fernand Bouisson; 7 June 1935, P. Laval; 24 January 1936, A. Sarraut; 4 July 1936, Léon Blum; 22 July 1937, C. Chautemps; 13 March 1938, L. Blum; 10 April 1938, E. Daladier; 21 March 1940, Paul Reynaud; 16 June 1940, Marshal Philippe Pétain.

Vichy Regime. 11 July 1940, P. Pétain Head of state (and prime minister to 17 April 1942), 13 December 1940, P. Flandin, General C.L. Hutzinger and Admiral F. Darlan, ministers; 9 February 1941, Admiral Darlan, vice-premier; 18 April 1942, P. Laval, premier; 25 August 1944, Liberation.

Provisional Government of the Republic. 3 June 1944, General Charles de Gaulle, President; resigned 19 January 1946; National Assembly of the Fourth Republic elected 10 November 1946.

Moniteur Universel. Newspaper started in 1789 to report parliamentary debates; in 1799 it became the official newspaper for the publication of government laws and decrees. Renamed in 1848 the *Journal Officiel de la République Française* and in 1852 the *Journal Officiel de l'Empire.* It was originally founded by Panckoucke, and continued to be owned by his family (allied with Dalloz) until 1869, when the government took full control of it. The *Moniteur Universel* (as distinct from the *Journal Officiel*) was the title of a private conservative newspaper from that date to 1901.

The Mountain. Extreme left politicians. A term originally used in the Convention (1793), it was revived in 1848, to refer to Barbès, Delescluze, Ledru-Rollin, Félix Pyat and about 56 deputies in all; in 1849 about 180 deputies belonging to this group were elected to the Legislative Assembly. Repressed by the laws on clubs and the press, and then by arrests and expulsion under orders from Louis Napoleon.

National Assembly. Elected 8 February 1871 with 768 members, and Jules Grévy as its first president. It appointed Adolphe Thiers Chief of the Executive Power, drew up the constitution of the Third Republic and then dissolved itself on 30 December 1875, to be succeeded by a Senate and a Chamber of Deputies.

National Guard. Para-military, partly political force, recruited under Louis Philippe from citizens aged 20 to 60, who were taxpayers and so supposedly partisans of order and of the Orléanist regime. The Second Republic abolished the tax qualification and increased its nominal strength from 56,000 to 190,000. In 1852 the Government ended its independence by appointing the officers, who were formerly elected.

Parlement. Court of Justice in the *ancien régime*.

Patente. Tax payable by tradesmen and some professional men. Composed of two parts: each trade had its own fixed rate, but in addition each tradesman paid a varying sum proportionate to the value of the property in which he exercised his trade.

Pays d'élection. Regions of France, under the *ancien régime*, which had not succeeded in maintaining their ancient Estates; their administration was in the hands of 'elections' or officials. (Paris, Alençon, Amiens, Soissons, Orléans, Bourges, Moulins, Riom, Grenoble, Poitiers, La Rochelle, Limoges, Bordeaux, Tours, Bayonne, Auch, Chalons, Rouen, Caen.)

Pays d'Etat. Regions which, by virtue of treaties with the French crown, had a right to administer themselves under the *ancien régime* and had assemblies which shared power with royal officials. They were mainly on the borders of the kingdom, e.g. Artois, Brittany, Béarn, Basse-Navarre, Languedoc, Provence, Dauphiné, Bourgogne, Flanders, etc.

Pays d'impositions. Recently annexed territories of France governed directly by the King, e.g. Alsace and Lorraine, Roussillon, Franch-Comté.

Phalanstère. Word invented by Charles Fourier to designate his ideal commune, of 1,800 people.

Philosophes. Political theorists and moralists of the late eighteenth century. Many of them contributed to the *Encyclopedia* (1751–80, 35 vols.), edited by Diderot and D'Alembert, which reflected the new curiosity and iconoclasm preceding the Revolution of 1789.

Planification. Economic planning. France claims to be the first non-socialist country to have developed indicative (as opposed to author-itarian) planning.

Polytechnic. École Polytechnique founded 1795 to give a scientific training both for the military and civil branches of government. See Zeldin, *France*, vol. 2, pp. 339–41, and for its political influence, 1068–72.

Ponts et Chaussées. Public service in charge of building and mainten-ance of roads. Used also as abbreviation for École des P. et C., the school where its officials were trained.

Ralliement. Movement by which Catholics accepted or rallied to the Third Republic, despite its anticlericalism, hoping to change it by legal means. Led by Cardinal Lavigerie, archbishop of Algiers, and Pope Leo XIII (1892). Formed into a political party by Jacques Piou and Albert de Mun, but disapproved of by most royalists, and the republicans long remained suspicious of it.

Rapporteur. Member of parliament who writes the conclusions of the parliamentary commissions which discuss legislative bills.

Regimes :

Ancien Régime. Period of monarchy ending with Louis XVI (King of France 1774–92, executed 1793).

First Republic. Proclaimed 20 September 1792 (Convention 1792–5, Directory 1795–9, Consulate 1799–1804).

First Empire. Napoleon I, 1804–1815. (Abdicated 11 April 1814, returned from Elba for Hundred Days, 1 March–22 June 1815).

The Restoration. Louis XVIII 1814–24, Charles X 1824–30.

Monarchy of July. Louis Philippe, 1830–48.

Second Republic. 1848–52. Constitutent Assembly, elected 23 April 1848, produced a new constitution and gave way to a legislative Assembly, which first met on 28 May 1849 and was dissolved on 2 December 1851. Louis Napoleon Bonaparte elected President of the Republic December 1848, assumed dictatorial powers 2 December 1851, proclaimed himself Emperor December 1852.

Second Empire. 1852–70. Napoleon III. Abdicated 4 September 1870 after his defeat at Sedan.

Third Republic. 1870–1940.

Vichy Regime. 1940–44.

Fourth Republic. 1944–58.

Fifth Republic. 1958– .

Rentier. Man living on his *rentes*, i.e. on income derived from investment. *Rentes sur l'Etat* are state bonds, long considered the safest investments.

Second Empire. Period of Napoleon III's rule, 1852–70.

Second Republic. Established after the overthrow of the monarchy in February 1848. It nominally survived to December 1852, although Louis Napoleon seized dictatorial power on 2 December 1851.

Taille. Main property-income tax of the *ancien régime*, paid by parishes, who assessed the contribution of individuals according to various criteria of wealth. With time its burden increased, but those who paid it decreased in number and the poorest were hardest hit by it.

Third Republic. Republic of France from 1870 to 1940.

Union conservatrice. Tactical and temporary alliance of conservatives and monarchists in 1885 election, aimed, unsuccessfully, at defeating the republicans.

White Terror. Royalist counter-revolutionary movement, involving assassination of their republican enemies, 1795–6, and more violently still after Waterloo, 1815–16.

INDEX